THE WORKS OF SRI CHINMOY

QUESTIONS & ANSWERS

VOLUME II

THE WORKS OF SRI CHINMOY

QUESTIONS & ANSWERS

VOLUME II

★

FLAME-WAVES

LYON · OXFORD

GANAPATI PRESS

LXXXVII

ISBN 978-0-9933080-2-4

See appendix for notice regarding this edition.

FIRST EDITION WENT TO PRESS ON 13 JUNE 2016.
2ND PRINTING, WITH REVISIONS, 27 DECEMBER 2017.

QUESTIONS & ANSWERS

VOLUME II

FLAME-WAVES

FLAME-WAVES

BOOK 1

FW I. *How do we know if it is the proper time for us to enter into the spiritual life? Can the spiritual life help us to overcome frustration?*

Sri Chinmoy: We can begin the spiritual life only when we feel the need. When we feel hunger we eat. Similarly, when we have the inner hunger we have to feed ourselves with Peace, Light and Bliss.

Now human beings are full of frustration. Every day begins with a new frustration, disappointment and sense of total failure. How can we conquer frustration, despair and other unaspiring and negative forces? We can do so only when we consciously feel that there is something beyond, far beyond these frustrations and so-called failures. Our human life cannot and does not end with failure precisely because the divine in us will never accept failure. The divine in us will eventually manifest the soul's Light and Truth on earth if we have the conscious cry, or conscious hunger for the Light that can transform our frustrations into radiant achievements.

He who does not aspire is a total failure in God's Eyes. But his aspiration is only a matter of time. God Himself will aspire in him and through him when the hour strikes. But if we consciously fight on the side of the inner Truth and inner Reality, if we listen to the dictates of the inner voice, then we hasten the progress of our own life and the progress of all mankind.

Frustration exists just because we do not see anything beyond frustration or do not consciously want to go beyond frustration. Let us take frustration as a thing that can be captured and offered at the feet of God or offered at the feet of any happiness or good experience we have had — even if it was ten or twenty years ago. The power of the happy experience will destroy the power of frustration or transform frustration into glowing inspiration at the feet of inner awakening and outer realisation.

FW 2. *How can we bring enough perfection into our own lives and into the world to be truly satisfied?*

Sri Chinmoy: If we want to accept only the limited insignificant perfection that we notice in the world, then we can never be satisfied. Hunger for perfection is like any other hunger. If you have an immense hunger, a very little portion of food will not satisfy you. We have the hunger now for infinite Peace, Light and Bliss. Our outer being will not be satisfied when it receives only an iota of Peace, Light and Bliss. It will be satisfied only when it has Peace, Light and Bliss in infinite measure.

The more we achieve inwardly, the clearer will be our conception of perfection. If we are satisfied with only a little inner attainment, like the mystics and mediums, we will say we have perfection according to our satisfaction. But the perfection that satisfies them need not and cannot satisfy the inner hunger of someone who cries for absolute perfection in his nature and the earth-consciousness. The higher we go, the more we receive and achieve and become aware of the possibility of integral perfection in our nature and elsewhere.

Complete and total perfection will come about only when we feel that our perfection is no perfection when the rest of humanity remains imperfect. If we call ourselves children of God, then others are also children of God. If we do not share with them what little we have, then what right have we to call them our brothers? They may be travelling a few miles behind us, or they may be fast asleep. But they must reach the Goal before perfect Perfection can dawn on earth.

Each individual has to make a decision. Each seeker has to discover within himself at what point he wants to stop his inner quest for Truth and Light. If he is ready to continue, to march on, to dive deeper within, and if he feels that there is no end to his achievement, only then will he be ready to offer the message of ever-fulfilling and ever-transcending Perfection. What you call perfection today, you may call imperfection itself tomorrow. A child's perfection is the ability to scream and shout and strike others. But when he grows up, his idea of perfection may be just the opposite. And if he enters into the spiritual life then his sense of perfection will be something else. He will try to conquer his fear, his doubt, his jealousy and other negative forces. But when he goes deep within after he has achieved what he wanted for himself, he will feel that only his limited self has been satisfied. His larger self, which is humanity entire, is far, far from perfection. So he will try to remove fear, doubt, anxiety, worries and other undivine forces from humanity.

In our path we feel that perfection has to be total and integral. We know that we have imperfection in our nature, and at the same time we have limited perfection. If the imperfection right now looms large, we have to brave that imperfection and transform it into perfection. Through our conscious prayer, meditation, concentration and contemplation the imperfection of the past can be perfected, and the darkness can be transformed into Light.

The perfection of the body lies in its conscious awareness of the ever-progressive dynamic Truth. The perfection of the vital lies in its acceptance of the Truth in a dynamic form. The perfection of the mind lies in its acceptance of the vast, the infinite, as its very own. The perfection of the heart lies in its acceptance of earth's cry and Heaven's compassion as its very own.

This is how we can see, feel and manifest perfection in our everyday life. The seekers of the infinite Truth can manifest perfection in the body, in the vital, in the mind and in the heart only through conscious awareness and acceptance of the ever-increasing, ever-transcending Reality.

FW 3. *Will the process of striving for perfection ever come to an end?*

Sri Chinmoy: It will never come to an end, because God Himself does not want to end His Cosmic Game. Today what we feel is the ultimate perfection, tomorrow will be just the starting point of our journey. This is because our consciousness is evolving. When the consciousness evolves to a higher level, our sense of perfection simultaneously goes higher. Let us take perfection as an achievement. When we are a kindergarten student, our achievement in perfection may be very good for that stage. But from kindergarten we go to primary school, high school, college and university. When we get our Master's degree in perfection our achievement is much greater than what it was when we were in kindergarten. But even then we may feel that there are many things more that we have to learn. Then we will study further and enlarge our consciousness still more. If the child thinks that the Master's degree will always remain unattainable then he is mistaken. The spiritual ladder has quite a few rungs. If we do not step onto the first rung then how can we climb up to the ultimate rung of the ladder? We start with inspiration, and from there we begin to concentrate, meditate and contemplate. And these three words — concentration, meditation, contemplation — are included in one word: aspiration. We start with inspiration and continue with aspiration. There is no end to aspiration, and there is no end to our achievement of perfection.

FW 4. I always felt it was selfish to look for salvation. I thought that this would come of itself if one did the right thing.

Sri Chinmoy: You are absolutely right. Salvation will come in its own way, at the chosen hour, if you do the right thing. And what is the right thing? The right thing is to pray, to concentrate, to meditate. If you climb up a tree then you get the fruit. But if you don't climb up, then the fruit will always remain out of reach. In the spiritual life, when we climb up, God's Grace descends.

Getting salvation is like getting a salary. You work at the United Nations. At a specified time your salary is bound to come. But that is because you also play your part — you come and work here. Similarly, if you do something for God, for mankind, salvation will come. Instead of living in desire, if you live in aspiration, salvation will come. What you are supposed to do is pray, concentrate and meditate, and if you do, naturally you will get salvation. It is not by saying, "Give me salvation, give me salvation," that you will get it. Salvation doesn't come that way. But if you do the right thing, which is to live a spiritual life, a life of dedication and devotion, automatically you will get salvation.

FW 5. What age were you when you commenced meditation?

Sri Chinmoy: I started consciously meditating at the age of eleven, but at four or five I used to say a daily prayer, as children do. When I was eleven I became fully conscious of divinity, that is to say, of concentration and meditation, and I started to take it very seriously. Before that I spent one, two, three minutes in prayer. By the age of thirteen I was meditating eight hours daily. I have to say that I began meditation seriously at the age of eleven.

FW 6. *You say we should meditate in the heart, but I find it easier to meditate in the mind.*

Sri Chinmoy: If you find it easier in the mind, then meditate in the mind. But if you do so, you will be able to meditate for perhaps five minutes, and out of that five minutes, for one minute you may meditate very powerfully. After that you will feel your whole head getting tense. First you get joy, satisfaction, but then you may feel a barren desert. For five minutes you will get something, but if you want to go on beyond that, you may feel nothing. If you meditate here *[in the heart]* a day will come when you start getting satisfaction. If you meditate in the heart, you are meditating where the soul is. True, the soul is everywhere — in the mind, in the body, everywhere. But it is like my situation now. I am here at the United Nations. If someone asks, "Where is Chinmoy?" you can say that I am at the United Nations, or you can say that I am in Conference Room 10. My presence is spiritually pervading the entire United Nations, but my living consciousness is right here in this room. If you come here, I will be able to do more for you than for others who are elsewhere in the building. Similarly, when you focus your concentration in the heart, you get much more inner satisfaction than when you meditate in the mind, because the heart is the seat of the soul. But it is difficult for some people to meditate in the heart because they are not used to doing it.

You have to be wise. There is a vast difference between what you can get from the mind and what you can get from the heart. The mind is limited; the heart is unlimited. Deep within us is infinite Peace, Light and Bliss. To get a limited quantity is an easy task. Meditation in the mind can give it to you. But you can get more if you meditate in the heart. Suppose you have the opportunity to work at two places. At one place you will earn $200, and at the other place $500. If you are wise, you will not waste your time at the first place. But you have to know that the Source and the Reality is in the heart. Reality is everywhere, but the actual manifestation of the Reality has to be in a particular place. Inside the heart is the soul, and if you meditate in the heart the result is infinitely more fulfilling.

Let us not be satisfied with the things that we get very easily. Let us cry for something which is more difficult to get, but which is infinite and everlasting. If you get something from the mind, tomorrow doubt may come and tell you that it is not real. But once you get something from the heart you will never be able to doubt it or forget it. An experience on the psychic plane can never be erased from the heart.

FW 7. *In meditation sometimes the mind stops functioning and there seems to be little information coming.*

Sri Chinmoy: In meditation we should not give importance to the mind. If there is no information coming it is good. Real meditation is not information; it is identification. The mind tries to create oneness by grabbing and capturing you and this may easily make you revolt. But the heart creates oneness through identification. The mind tries to possess. The heart just expands and, while expanding, it embraces. With the mind we only divide ourselves. The mind may try to do something and immediately the body or the vital may try to prevent it. But if the heart wants to do something, no matter how difficult, it will be done. This is because when the mind gets no satisfaction when it tries something, it just says that there is no reality there and gives up. But when the heart does not get satisfaction, it feels that it has not done the thing properly. So it tries again, and continues trying until satisfaction dawns at last.

FW 8. *What do you mean when you speak of unconditional surrender to God's Will, and how can we develop this quality?*

Sri Chinmoy: When we do something unconditionally, we do something really great, and for that we need much preparation. Ordinarily we do everything conditionally. We go to a shop and give the shopkeeper money and the shopkeeper gives us what we need. In this world it is always give and take. We are exchanging things of equal value. But God has everything in infinite measure. If we do something for God, then what we will get from Him will be far beyond our expectation. We will get much more than we give. If we give God an iota of prayer, one minute of prayer, the things that God will give us will be most fulfilling. But there comes a time when we pray to God with the feeling that this is what He wishes us to do. At that time we become the chosen instruments of God and the representatives of God on earth, and then we feel that we are really fulfilling God in His own Way.

As long as we are on earth we are fulfilling God according to our own limited, very limited capacity. Everybody is fulfilling God in this way. But when we do something with the conscious feeling that what we do is being done by God in us and through us, then even if we just give a smile, in that smile there is infinite potentiality, infinite capacity.

There comes a time in our life of aspiration when, if somebody says "God" we will feel that he is referring to us, and not to somebody else. Now God is a third person. I am somebody. You are somebody. And God is a third person. We are completely separate, each with a personality of his own. But a day will come when we make unconditional surrender to God's Will. At that time, when somebody speaks to us, we will feel that God is speaking to God. But it is all done gradually. It takes a few months of constant exercise to develop very powerful muscles.

Unconditional surrender is much more difficult to develop. It takes continual daily exercise, and that exercise is our prayer, our meditation.

FW 9. *While I am in the office how can I control my emotions? There is so much injustice and nothing we can do to help ourselves.*

Sri Chinmoy: You say that there is nothing you can do, but I am giving you a way to protect yourself. We have been meditating here for five or ten minutes. This meditation has real power. In your office there is much injustice. Injustice itself is a kind of negative power, a destructive power. Injustice is an undivine power and justice is divine power. Now injustice is creating suffering in your life. But there is something called God's Light. You can be well protected by God's Light and be unaffected by injustice. True, you cannot change the minds of the people who are causing this injustice, but you can protect yourself. They are striking you inwardly and because of your fear or your incapacity you don't strike them back. But if you become very strong, very powerful inwardly, your strength will take you to some other place or will give them some illumination. God's Compassion will save you from this kind of injustice if you enter into the spiritual life seriously.

Another way of saving yourself, which is quicker, is to have peace of mind. At our Tuesday meditation we bring down Peace, which is very solid. It is not something imaginary. You can feel Peace; you can swim in the sea of Peace when you meditate with us on Tuesdays. Here, too, on Fridays, we shall meditate and you will feel Peace if you join us. Injustice is undivine power, but Peace is an infinitely more powerful divine weapon. It is solid power. When you are in Peace, no human power can upset you.

When you have to defend yourself or protect yourself, try to use a higher weapon. If people say something and you retaliate on the same level, there will be no end to it. Again, if you simply swallow your anger they will continue to take advantage of you. But when they see and feel tremendous inner Peace in you, they will see something in you which can never be conquered. They will see a change in you, and this change will not only puzzle them but also threaten and frighten them. They will feel that their weapons are useless.

Peace is the most effective weapon with which to conquer injustice. When you pray and meditate your whole being becomes flooded with Peace. Then no matter what other people do, you will just feel that they are your own children playing in front of you. You will say, "These are all children. What more can I expect from them?" But right now, because they are grown up in terms of years, you become angry and upset instead. If you pray and meditate regularly, you will soon feel that your peace is infinitely stronger, more fulfilling and more energising than the unfortunate situation that they create.

FW 10. *It seems to me that the Will of God for us is not only to be silent but also to be active.*

Sri Chinmoy: Please excuse me. You have misunderstood me. By outer silence I do not mean not speaking. I mean the outer expression of one's inner silence. One silence is dynamic; another silence is static. Static silence is found in deep meditation, which is preparation. Dynamic silence is found in action, which is manifestation. The inner silence guides and illumines us. The outer silence reveals and manifests us.

FW 11. *So outer silence or dynamic silence is really divine action — doing the Will of God by serving man?*

Sri Chinmoy: Right. The role of dynamic silence is to fulfil the Will of God in humanity. But what God's Will is, we learn only from inner silence, static silence. Once we know the Will of God then it is our divine duty to dedicate ourselves to the service of mankind.

Some people only want to meditate. They do not want to give anything to the world. This is selfishness. Again there are some who want to give but do not want to meditate. This is foolishness. If we do not meditate, if we do not possess something, then how are we going to give? There are many people on earth who are ready to give, but what do they have? There are some people who have acquired something and do not want to give it. They are acting like misers. They are afraid that the moment they try to give their wealth to the ignorant world, the world will misunderstand them or misuse them. But we have to play our part. First we have to achieve, then we have to offer. In this way we can please God and fulfil mankind.

FW 12. *Inner silence is equated with prayer and meditation?*

Sri Chinmoy: Prayer, meditation, concentration, and contemplation are the inner silence. Outer silence is dedication, service, action. Dedicate yourself, fulfil the Will of God, but only after knowing the Will of God. We can know the Will of God only by practising inner silence. Otherwise, if we try to help mankind in our own way, we think that we are serving God but really we are just aggrandising our own ego. We say, "I have done this, I have done that." But the important thing is, "Was I inspired by God? Was I commissioned by God?" If our actions are not inspired by God, they are inspired by our ego. Then the service that we offer to the world will be full of darkness and imperfections.

FW 13. *You say that if fear is our problem we should feel that we are God's chosen children. Do you mean that we are chosen by God to experience fear?*

Sri Chinmoy: Fear is a negative force, a destructive force, and we are the soldiers of God who will fight against it. Fear comes from darkness, from ignorance. If we enter into a room which is pitch dark, we will be frightened. But as soon as we turn on the light, our fear vanishes. The darkness is illumined, and we see that there was nothing to fear in the darkness and that there is nothing to fear in the light either.

FW 14. *In your talk you said that if we see the problem and if we face the problem, then we have greater force than the problem. Do you mean, then, that a problem is not a problem if we know how to look at it?*

Sri Chinmoy: If we know how to look at a problem, half the strength of the problem goes away. But usually we try to avoid the problem; we try to run away from it. A problem is not an indication of any fault or crime of ours, so why should we be afraid to face it? Our difficulty is that when something unfortunate happens in our life, we immediately feel that we are at fault, that we have done something wrong. We must know that there are also wrong forces, undivine forces, hostile forces around us. We believe in the law of karma — that if we do something wrong, we suffer later. But even if we do not do anything wrong, the ignorance of the world may come and torture us. Think of Christ. He was a great spiritual Master. He did not have any bad karma. He did not do anything wrong. But the ignorance of the world crucified him. Of course, we cannot compare ourselves with Christ, but at our own level we have to feel that we are not necessarily at fault.

By blaming ourselves and then trying to hide, we do not solve the problem. We have to face the problem and see whether we really are to blame. If our own ignorance has made the problem then it may be difficult to deal with. But if somebody else is creating the problem then we have to stand like a solid wall and not allow the problem to enter into us. If it is my house, my wall, I will not allow anybody to break through. But if I am the problem itself then how am I going to prevent it from entering? This problem is infinitely more difficult to solve than the problem coming from without. In order to solve the problem of myself, I have to feel that I am not the problem maker but the problem solver. Then I have to practise the spiritual life and develop inner strength, aspiration and inner detachment. Slowly, gradually, I will become inwardly strong, and then I will be able to solve the problems caused by myself, by my own inner weaknesses.

FW 15. *I always wanted to ask you what is the spiritual significance of insanity and how it develops.*

Sri Chinmoy: Insanity is an imperfection in our nature. It is a result of our inner imperfection. In our outer life we have no need for Light. We have need for everything else but we are afraid of Light. When we think of Light, instead of feeling that we will be illumined we feel that we will be exposed, and we try to hide ourselves.

Insanity can start in any plane of consciousness, but when it develops in the mental plane we notice it. Before it develops in the mental plane it can develop in the inner plane, the psychic plane. When insanity starts it does not start all at once in the physical. It descends like rain, as a downward flow into our system. And only when it enters and captures the mind do we lose our mental balance. Insanity starts when we do not keep everything in our mind in the proper place. Thoughts, inner actions, inner ideas, ideals, facts — everything has a place of its own in the mind. When we misplace these things or when we do not give them their proper importance, then we develop insanity.

FW 16. *What do you mean when you say that the unaspiring man's eternity is uncertain?*

Sri Chinmoy: An unaspiring man is not sure of anything. He is at the mercy of all his whims. At this moment something may make him feel that he is absolutely useless and hopeless. At the next moment his ego will come forward and he will feel that he is everything, that he is the Lord of the Universe. Nothing is certain for the unaspiring man, even his own life. He lives in constant fear. He may feel that while he is sleeping somebody will come and kill him. An unaspiring man will never feel certain that there is a tomorrow, since he does not feel the flow. For him, tomorrow does not exist, not to speak of eternity.

But for an aspiring man, eternity is certain because he knows and feels that he is in the flow of eternity. He is the river which is entering into the ocean. For an aspiring man nothing is uncertain. He knows that inside him he has everything. Right now he is like a child. His Father cannot give him millions of dollars because, since he is only a child, he will misuse it. He knows that he can use at this time only a dime or a quarter. But he is certain that when he grows up his Father will give him all His wealth: infinite Peace, Light and Bliss. He is certain he will get all of this.

FW 17. *How can one accept and love one's fellow man?*

Sri Chinmoy: First of all you must feel that your fellow man is part and parcel of your own existence. I have two eyes. Now if my left eye does not function as well as my right eye, what do I do? Do I become angry with my left eye? Do I take it out of my body? Do I keep my left eye closed or cover it with my hand and say, "I won't let you see"? No. At that time I have the feeling of oneness. I simply accept my left eye as less capable then my right eye, but still as a part of me. If my left eye does not see well I use my right eye also. Whenever I have to use my eyes I use both eyes, and the eye that is more powerful naturally does more work.

You must regard the persons around you as limbs of your own body. Without them you are incomplete. You may feel they are less developed, but they also have their role to play. Your thumb is much more powerful than your little finger. But the little finger also has its job. God has created five fingers. Although some are shorter and weaker than others, you know that only when you have five fingers are you perfect. Now your middle finger is the tallest. If you feel that for this reason you don't need your shorter fingers, then you are sadly mistaken. If you want to play the piano or if you want to type, then you need all five fingers.

You can love the people around you only when you feel the necessity of real perfection. If you remain isolated as an individual, then your achievement will be limited. Your very sense of perfection will be limited, very limited. But when you think in terms of unlimited perfection, then you have to love humanity. For it is only by accepting humanity as part and parcel of your own life, and by perfecting humanity with your own illumination, that you can fulfil yourself.

FW 18. *What actually is illumination?*

Sri Chinmoy: Illumination is the conscious awareness of the soul. Illumination is the conscious vision of the Reality that is going to be manifested. Illumination is possibility transformed into practicality. Illumination is like God's divine magic wand. An ordinary magician in this world uses his wand to make one thing turn into another. When God uses illumination in the world, immediately the finite consciousness of earth enters into the Infinite and becomes the Infinite.

Illumination is humanity's first realisation of God's omnipotent Power, boundless Compassion, infinite Light and perfect Perfection. It is our illumination that makes us feel what God really is. Before illumination, God is theoretical; after illumination God becomes practical. So illumination is the divine magic power that makes us see the Reality which was once upon a time imagination. When illumination dawns in a human being, God is no longer just a promise but an actual achievement.

I spoke to you about illumination on your birthday. Illumination is in the mind and in the heart. When the mind is illumined we become God's Choice. When the heart is illumined we become God's Voice. Here in the physical world the mind has evolved considerably. Because man has developed his intellectual mind, he has become superior to the animals, for the standard of the mind is higher than the standard of the physical or the vital. Man has cultivated the capacity of the mind, but he has not cultivated the capacity of the heart. When we cultivate the heart, we will see that its capacity is far greater than we had imagined. When we cultivate the unique sense in our heart that we are of God's highest Vision and we are for God's perfect Manifestation, then illumination will take place.

FW 19. *How can we develop patience?*

Sri Chinmoy: How to develop patience? In order to develop patience, we have to feel that we have launched into a spiritual journey, an inner journey, which has a Goal, and that this Goal wants us and needs us as much as we want and need it. This Goal is ready to accept us, to give us what it has, but it will do this in its own way at the choice hour of God. We must know that God will give us His wealth in time. Patience will never tell us that it is a hopeless task. Patience will only tell us either that we are not ready or that the time is not ripe. We may have the feeling that we are ready, but we have to know that our integral being, our whole being, is not ready. Our soul may be ready, our heart may be ready, our mind may be ready, but our vital and physical may not be ready to reach the Goal, which is Light and Truth. When our whole being is ready, the Goal itself will dawn within our aspiring consciousness. When the hour strikes, the Goal will draw us towards itself like a magnet.

When we are in the spiritual life we have to feel that patience is not something passive. On the contrary, it is something dynamic. In patience we develop our inner strength, our inner willpower. It is true that if we have willpower we can easily acquire patience. But it is equally true that when we have patience, our inner willpower develops itself in a special way.

FW 20. *During a meditation, if something external to the meditation occurs — such as noise or something unforeseen — is it better to include it in the meditation or to try to shut it out and pursue the meditation?*

Sri Chinmoy: Each seeker has to know his own standard of meditation. If we are a beginner, we should feel that anything that is not part of the meditation is like an intruder. We should not allow an intruder, a foreigner, to enter into us and disturb us. But if we are very advanced, and there is a disturbing sound or a noise during our meditation, we can go deep into the sound itself and try to assimilate it. If we have the capacity, then in our own consciousness we can transform the attack of a most powerful, most challenging foreign element into an inner music, a thrilling or haunting music, which will really add to our meditation. But we have to develop this capacity to transform a disturbing, annoying noise into soothing, thrilling and soul-stirring music. When we have this capacity we shall include the disturbance in our meditation. As long as we don't have the capacity, we shall always exclude it.

If you have strength, inner strength, to transform someone, when he is transformed he becomes totally yours. Before you entered into the spiritual life you had darkness, ignorance. Now you have started transforming your own darkness and ignorance. When they are finally transformed and illumined, they will still be your own possession. But where they previously stood in your way, now, on the contrary, they shall help you. The darkness has been transformed into light, and it has become an added help.

FW 21. *I have an experience here at the Dag Hammarskjold lectures which I never am aware of at your other talks or at the Tuesday meditation. I know you are bringing down tremendous Peace which I feel in both places, but here at these lectures I have a feeling that I am falling asleep. Yet I hear what you are saying. I try very hard to keep awake but it almost seems an impossibility. Could you explain whether I am doing something wrong?*

Sri Chinmoy: You are not doing anything wrong. When I give talks I bring down Peace, and this Peace is something tangible for the seekers. When the seeker is eager to swim in the sea of Peace, he or she is allowed by the Supreme to do so. During this experience, the mind does not operate; only the heart operates. The activity of the mind is totally silenced, and the heart has started functioning in its place. The function of the heart is to identify with anything that is around it or before it or inside it. Your heart is identifying with Peace and this Peace is silencing the mind. It is not inertia; it is not an experience of useless futility or something bad. No, in this Peace you cultivate the inner truth and grow into the Light which illumines the darkness that you faced or the ignorance that you cherished before you entered into meditation.

I bring down Peace, Light and Bliss in boundless measure, and according to his receptivity each seeker receives this Peace, Light and Bliss. This Peace is not an unconscious way of putting you to sleep. No, this Peace silences the outgoing energy of the mind and, at the same time, illumines the inflow of the heart. And when you are in the heart, the aspiring heart, you become one with the Peace that sustains the divine Reality in you.

FW 22. *I once read that if you choose evil, you are not really free. I thought it was an interesting idea. Would you enlighten me?*

Sri Chinmoy: First of all we have to know what evil is. Anything that limits us, anything that binds us, is evil. Evil will come to us in the form of pleasure, and when we surrender, when we yield to the pleasure that evil brings, we are caught. The evil that wants to make us its instrument for its own purpose makes us feel that we are helpless and ignorant, and that is the reason we accept it.

Sometimes we may have no freedom in our outer life, but in our inner life we have freedom, a considerable amount of freedom. We can pray, we can concentrate, we can meditate even in a prison cell. But when evil possesses us, at that time our inner freedom goes away, and our outer freedom also deserts us.

At that time we are bound to seek the fulfilment of our desires or evil impulses.

Everything has a nature of its own. The very nature of evil is to bind; the very nature of divinity is to liberate. The nature of scorpions is to sting. We cannot expect them to behave differently. Therefore, we must not give them the opportunity to sting us. We have to stay away from them at all times. If we stand in front of a scorpion to exert our own freedom, it is foolishness.

We have to feel the necessity of staying only with something which constantly liberates and illumines us, and that is Light.

FW 23. *When we come to meditate with you, you give us Light. But we have to keep coming back to get refilled. How much of the Light which you give us remains permanently in us?*

Sri Chinmoy: It entirely depends on how long you maintain the consciousness that you feel here. When you go back to your office, you can totally forget about what you have done here for one hour. Or you can remain conscious of the Peace, Light and Joy that you felt here even while you are typing or taking dictation. In this way you can keep the entire amount if you want to.

We sometimes say that a person is doing something, but his mind is somewhere else. Now, instead of the mind, let us say that the aspiring heart is not there. Your mind will take dictation from your boss, but your aspiring heart will keep its oneness with this room where it received Peace, Light and Bliss.

If you can maintain your inner connection with this divine consciousness until your early morning meditation tomorrow, then you will keep the full amount of Light that you have received from me. That doesn't mean that you can't talk to friends, or can't eat, or can't do any ordinary things. You *can* do these things, but you have to be careful not to lose your precious inner wealth. Once you have assimilated the Peace and Light that you have received into your inner system, it is safe. Before assimilation it can be lost. Even the full amount can be lost. If you go to your office now and enter into a quarrel or some unpleasant situation, not even an iota will remain. If you can keep it safe until your next serious meditation, then you are totally free from the possibility of robbery, because your whole spiritual system will have assimilated it. But assimilation takes quite a few hours, so the Light that you receive has to be maintained through inspiration or through your conscious inner awareness until your next meditation. It depends on your inner awareness and your care in dealing with the outside world.

FW 24. *In practical terms, how can we give the world love and concern?*

Sri Chinmoy: A practical thing is something that comes spontaneously from within and not from without. When you get up in the morning, if the thought comes to your mind to show love or concern for the world, that is a practical idea. Now how can you transform this practical idea into fruitful reality? In the morning or in the evening, during your regular prayer, you can add to your prayer this: "O Lord, I wish this world to be better, more illumining and more fulfilling by Your infinite Grace." God is the Creator and Sustainer of the world. If your prayer reaches the Creator, which it will certainly do if it is sincere and intense, He can easily carry your concern and love for the world into the field of manifestation.

As an individual you are here. You cannot be somewhere else at the same time. But your prayer, your aspiration, can approach Someone who is Omnipresent. All of us have been praying and meditating here in this room, but spiritually we have been spreading Peace and Love into the world. Physically we are bound in this tiny room, but spiritually we are flying like birds; our wings are widespread with Peace, Joy and Love.

When you feel something, when you see something, you may call it a practical experience. Here we have been meditating for fifteen or twenty minutes. During that time our experience of inner Peace and Love was absolutely practical. To us these things were most tangible. While you are praying or meditating here next week look at yourself. Is it not a reality — the Peace, the Joy, the Love that you are getting?

What we get we can easily give to others. But the process is an inner process. And the best way to carry out this inner process is to approach the Source. We know that we cannot go everywhere and we cannot approach everyone during our prayer. But there is Someone who can do this on our behalf, and that is God. During our prayer, if we ask Him to offer Peace, Concern and Love to the world at large He can do it. If He is pleased with our request, naturally He will do it. So our daily communion with God is the best way for us to offer the world our love and concern.

FW 25. *How can an individual truly know what God's Will is for him?*

Sri Chinmoy: God's Will in an individual is progressive, like a muscle developing — strong, stronger, strongest. God's Will is to make an individual feel that there is something abiding, lasting, everlasting. When an individual reaches that stage, he will know God's Ultimate Will. God's Will we can know from the sense of abiding satisfaction it gives us. Anything that is eternal, anything that is immortal, anything that is divine, is God's Will. Even though God deals with Eternity, He is not indifferent even for one second. For it is from one second, two seconds, three seconds that we enter into Infinity and Eternity. Let us try to feel God's Will in us at every second.

There is a very simple way to know what God's Will is for us as individuals. Every day when we start our day we build our own world. We make decisions. We feel that things have to be done in a certain way. I have to deal with this man in this way. I have to say this; I have to do this; I have to give this. Everything is I, I, I. We all do this. If, instead of all this planning, we can make our minds absolutely calm and silent, we can know God's Will. This silence is not the silence of a dead body; it is the dynamic, progressive silence of receptivity. Through total silence and the ever-increasing receptivity of the mind, God's Will can be known. When the human mind works powerfully, the Divine Will cannot work. God's Will works only when the human mind does not work. When the mind becomes a pure vessel, the Supreme can pour into it His infinite Peace, Light and Bliss.

We are constantly building and breaking our mental house. But instead of making and breaking the house at our sweet will, if we can empty our mind, make it calm and quiet, then God can build His Temple or His Palace in us in His own Way. And when He has built His Abode within us, He will say, "I have built this for you and Me to reside in together. I have built it, but it is not Mine alone. It is also yours. Come in."

So the easiest way for us to know God's Will is to become the instrument and not the doer. If we become only the instrument for carrying out God's plans, God's Will will act in and through us. God does the acting and He is the action. He is everything. We only observe.

FW 26. *How can we attain lasting inner peace?*

Sri Chinmoy: We can attain lasting inner peace, only when we feel that the Supreme Pilot, our Supreme Pilot is in the many as One and in the One as many. When we consciously feel this truth in our life, we get lasting peace in whatever we say, whatever we do, whatever we offer and whatever we receive. We do not get everlasting peace when our mind tells us that if the One is One, He cannot be many, and that the many cannot be One.

The day I feel my existence, my illumining heart in everyone, is the day I immediately become one in many. When I receive or bring down Peace from Above, immediately I feel that I am many, not one. Then when I assimilate the Peace in myself, I see the Peace has been assimilated in all of us. Then I have a conscious feeling of oneness, of the oneness in the many and the many as one.

Peace comes in and we lose it because we feel that we are not responsible for humanity, or that we are not part and parcel of humanity. We have to feel that God and humanity are like a great tree. God is the tree, and the branches are His Manifestation. We are branches, and there are many other branches. All these branches are part of the tree and are one with each other and with the tree. If we can feel that we have the same relationship with God and with humanity as the branch has with its fellow branches and with the tree as a whole, we are bound to get everlasting peace.

FW 27. Every time I act, I am not certain if I am doing the right thing, and I was wondering if perhaps the best way to find real peace would be to withdraw from the world and not act at all.

Sri Chinmoy: If you think that you must withdraw from life in order to achieve peace then you are making a serious mistake. In withdrawal our satisfaction will never dawn. It is in activity that we progress and achieve. It is in action, in fulfilment, in creation, in manifestation, that we can be satisfied.

But we have to know that if we expect something from our action, peace will never come in our lives. If we expect some particular result from our action we will be frustrated when the result does not meet with our expectations. We will feel that we have failed. When this happens, naturally there can be no peace.

We have to feel that action itself is a great blessing, but the result of action we have to take as an experience. According to our own limited understanding, we see it as either failure or success. But in God's Eye, failure and success are both just experiences which help to develop our consciousness. When acting we have to expect only the fulfilment of God's Will.

Whatever happens we should see as the experience that God wanted to give us. Today He may give us the experience of failure. Tomorrow He may give us another experience which will satisfy us outwardly. But if we live a spiritual life, no matter what result comes to us from our action, we shall be satisfied.

Let us look at a river. The river flows constantly towards the sea. It carries all kinds of rubbish — dirt, stones, leaves, sand — that it picks up as it moves towards its goal, but it always continues flowing towards the sea. We should also think of our lives as a river running to the sea. This sea is the sea of fulfilment. If we are afraid to act because we don't want to get involved with the imperfections of the world, if we become still and inactive, then we will never reach the goal.

You may say that you do not know where the goal is right now. No harm. Just move. If you go in the wrong direction, soon you will realise it and go in another direction. Eventually you will reach your goal. But if you do not move at all, there is absolutely no hope that you will go in the right direction. If you cannot do disinterested work, selfless work, then work with a motive first. If ego and vanity come in while you are helping someone, let them come. A day will dawn when you will feel that the satisfaction that you are getting is not enough. You will realise it does not last more than a few seconds. Then you will try to work in a more divine way.

Activity is always far better than inertia. Even if you run around like a mad elephant at first, eventually you will start acting like a deer and run straight towards your goal. You may start your movement with the crude and destructive strength of an elephant but you will complete it with the grace and speed of a deer.

We have to act. If we withdraw from life then we are consciously and deliberately telling God that we do not want to be players in His Game. God will allow us to withdraw for a few days or a few months or a few years. But then God will compel us to participate again, so He can fulfil Himself in us and through us. The world has to be accepted and faced. If you don't accept it, the world will remain as it is and then you will feel miserable that you have done nothing for the world.

FW 28. *I have recently felt quite distinctly a force that people throw around themselves for protection, or even when they don't want to speak to someone. I have felt it like a solid object, like a wall. I would like to know how it is built. Is it built consciously or unconsciously?*

Sri Chinmoy: Usually it is built consciously. Some seekers feel that when they are around unaspiring people they need protection to maintain their high consciousness. They are afraid they will be attacked by unaspiring people who will enter into them like arrows and destroy their aspiration, so they consciously build a wall around themselves. Sometimes ordinary people who are not aspiring have a tremendous insecurity. They are afraid that others will take away whatever little wealth they have. And spiritual Masters may build this wall to protect themselves from the attacks of the consciousness of the world around them. Some people come into the presence of a spiritual Master and feel that once they have come that is more than enough. They do not want to accept anything. The moment the Master wants to give them Peace or Light, they attack him inwardly. Or people come to a Master without knowing what they want, and when Peace is offered, they feel that it is something strange. When Light is offered or Bliss is offered, they feel it is something strange. They feel that they are not being given what they want, so they come and attack. Or they come and bother the Master, saying, "Give me, give me, give me!" Then when it is given they don't take it. At that time the Master creates an aura for self-protection.

Each individual has a special aura, of which he is not conscious. That aura, the most important aura, goes around the person from head to foot. It consciously protects the person. When you meditate you may see that there is an aura constantly revolving around you. Other auras you may also see, behind pictures of the Buddha or Christ, for example, but usually these do not revolve or move. But this aura that we all have is constantly moving around us. But we have to know that this aura is not all-powerful. It is only a strong protection on the physical, vital and mental level. It does not protect the whole being. This aura becomes all-powerful only through our prayer and meditation. Each day when we pray and meditate this aura is strengthened. It moves faster, very, very fast. And when the movement becomes extremely fast, the aura acquires tremendous strength, enough to protect the entire being.

FW 29. *In the Meditation Group's bulletin you spoke about the importance of meditating on the heart instead of in the mind. Could you speak more about this?*

Sri Chinmoy: Our philosophy gives more importance to the heart than to the mind. We feel we can get more fulfilment from the heart. We are not saying that the mind is bad. Far from it. But the mind is limited while the heart, which is very close to the soul, is unlimited. At most, what we can get from the mind is inspiration. But inspiration itself is limited. When we meditate on the heart, inspiration turns into aspiration. And not only do we get aspiration, but we also get the fulfilment of that aspiration: the soul's infinite Peace, Light and Bliss.

FW 30. *Can you tell if something comes from the mind or the heart, or does something always go from the heart to the mind?*

Sri Chinmoy: One cannot always tell absolutely if something is coming from the mind or the heart. We should always listen to the heart, for the heart is childlike and pure. But the mind thinks that the heart is childish and does not want to listen to the heart. It cares only for its own knowledge, and not for the heart's wisdom. Needless to say, we should always see the world through the heart.

Now, something from the heart does not have to go to the mind. That is, the heart need not communicate through the mind or through anything else. The heart is very eloquent in its own right. If I enter into a room and just see someone, I can immediately know all about him. The other person does not have to say a word to me outwardly; his heart tells me everything in a fleeting second. My heart is speaking to him and his heart is speaking to me. In this case the heart is not using the mind at all to communicate. It is speaking in its own language.

FW 31. *Some people are very absent-minded and they seem to be in another world. Are they meditating all the time?*

Sri Chinmoy: No. Absent-mindedness has nothing to do with the spiritual life. It is a Himalayan mistake to think that absent-mindedness is due to aspiration. Many absent-minded people, of course, are not even aspiring. And those absent-minded people who are aspiring are not absent-minded because of their meditation. They may seem to be in another world because they neglect their duties, but they are not actually staying in a higher consciousness. In the spiritual life it is very important that we live in the outer world and do our best in the outer world. We should look upon the world and humanity as our very own. To allow ourselves to he absent-minded is to be rude and inconsiderate of others.

There are some spiritual Masters and very advanced seekers who appear to be absent-minded and forgetful at times. But with them, it is a different story. At that time their consciousness is not in the physical. They are on a very high plane. Again, a few — very few — Masters can remain on this high plane and still function normally in the world.

But in the case of a beginner, a spiritual seeker, absent-mindedness is not aiding him in his spiritual journey. It is not a positive expression of his aspiration; it is a hindrance, an obstruction. He is running towards his Goal with a heavy load on his shoulders. After a few years, when he has made more progress, the seeker will realise that he is carrying this burden. He will feel that he cannot go any farther while carrying it, and his progress will come to a standstill. At that time the seeker makes every effort to transform his weakness, and finally sheds his heavy load so that he can continue towards his destination.

FW 32. *Sri Chinmoy, how can we become childlike in spirit?*

Sri Chinmoy: In the outer life we see that when the grandfather talks to his grandchildren, if he is wise he becomes actually another child. He knows that only by acting like a child will he be able to give the children satisfaction and get satisfaction from them. We have to feel that God Himself is a Divine Child who is always playing with us. A child is ready to play twenty-four hours a day. And we have to become like a child in order to play with God.

If a boy of nineteen does not have the capacity to draw something from the world or offer something to the world, if he remains aloof, if he does not care for the world and feels that he does not need anything from the world, then he is ninety-nine years old in spirit. On the other hand, if somebody of ninety-nine wants to learn the inner language, the language of divine love, the language of divine peace, the language of inner wisdom, the language of inner Light, then he is a child in spirit. But if he wants to get only information from the world, this will not help him spiritually at all. For this kind of information is given by the mind and received through the mind. And if a person lives in the mind he will never be able to act like a child. Who cannot act like a child? He who cares more for the intellect than for the heart. He who cares more for outer achievement than for inner achievement. He who cares more for society around him than for God within him.

If you really want to become a child, then you have to feel that there is someone who is thinking of you constantly. You have to feel that there is somebody who is not only thinking of you and meditating on you, but who is also taking responsibility for you. A child always feels that his mother or his father will take care of him. All the time he feels that there is protection, there is guidance, there is assistance. So naturally he has confidence in his life. A child can rely totally upon his parents because of his child's heart. Because he is always in the heart, he feels that there is no need which his parents will not fulfil. If he lived in the mind he would immediately think, "Oh, perhaps my father will not be able to do this. Perhaps my mother will not be there to help me." Then he would become fearful. He would become doubtful and anxious. In the spiritual life, no matter how old you are, you have to feel that there is someone with infinitely more wisdom-light who is constantly thinking of you, loving you, guiding you and protecting you, and that this person is God. And you have to rely upon God with a child's heart. We can have Peace, Light, Love and Bliss in infinite measure only when we feel that we are children.

When a student goes to his spiritual Master he must feel that his Master has infinitely more wisdom than he has. He must maintain his feeling of humility. Whenever we deal with somebody who is superior to us and who has more capacity in the inner world, then we become a child. If we think that our Master is either of our standard or of a lower standard, how can we act like a child? How can we have faith or confidence in him? Immediately our superiority will come to the fore. Our mind will make us feel that we know better. And the moment we feel that we know everything and can do everything, we lose our childlike qualities.

A student is always a child in the presence of his teacher no matter how old or sophisticated he may be. Always we have to feel that we are learning. In the spiritual life, we learn everything every day, every hour, every minute, every second from our Father, God. If we constantly have the feeling that we are learning in the inner worlds, there is no end to our receiving and achieving God's Divinity. We can become childlike when we know that there is something to learn and that God is there to teach.

FW 33. *It seems to me that it is easy to have this feeling if one has a spiritual Master, is living in a spiritual community and has all his needs provided for. But what about someone who is a separate individual living in the world?*

Sri Chinmoy: Why do people enter into a spiritual community? Because it is easier. And why do people mix with other spiritual people? Because it is easier. There are always opportunities and ways which present us with fewer difficulties, fewer problems. What you are saying is absolutely true. Sri Ramakrishna used to say that we are all children. Before realising God we play with ignorance. After realising God we play with Wisdom. If we are wise, we will go where the things we want are easier to achieve. No matter how much wealth we get, how much appreciation we get, how much admiration we get in the outer life, we will not get much satisfaction. But if we get an iota of Love, Peace, Light, Bliss, Concern from the inner life, we get everything. An iota of inner Truth is infinitely more powerful, more convincing and more fulfilling than the boundless wealth of the outer life. If the seeker realises this, then naturally he will find a spiritual Master and associate with spiritual people. In a spiritual community it is much easier to be childlike. There you will have a Master whose concern you can feel constantly. Then it becomes easier, infinitely easier.

But even a person who is living in the world can have a childlike attitude towards God. To be childlike does not mean to be childish. We can be simple, sincere and spontaneous in our dealings with the sophisticated world without being stupid or foolish. We can have implicit faith in God's protection and guidance even while living and working in the ordinary world. For this we must feel that whatever job we are doing, it is God who has given us this job out of His infinite Compassion, it is He who is giving us the necessary capacity to do the work satisfactorily and keep the job, and it is He who will enable us to find another job if we lose the one we have. This kind of childlike faith is not foolishness. Far from it. It is the spontaneous trust of a child in his father or mother. This kind of feeling will never stand as a hindrance in our life in the outer world.

If one does not take a childlike attitude his speed will be hampered. It is a child who can constantly be moulded. A child is like a lump of divine clay. He can easily be shaped into something divinely beautiful. But if one follows the spiritual life and at the same time tries to maintain his independence, he will not make much progress. There is only One who is truly independent, and that is God. The more we can be dependent on that One, the faster will be our progress. There is no human individuality; there is only divine individuality. What we call human individuality does not last. No matter how hard we try to maintain it, we must eventually give it up if we sincerely want to become close to God, one with God. If we try to expand our human personality, very soon it bursts like a balloon. But the divine Individuality which is the Highest, supreme Individuality is already infinitely vast. It can embrace all our human individualities. When we surrender our human individuality it does not mean that we are becoming a slave. We are only allowing ourselves to be shaped the way the Highest wants us. The individuality of the Master does not enter into the student. The Master has long ago given up his individuality to the Highest Supreme. Now it is the Will of the Supreme which he is executing when he guides and moulds his disciples.

FW 34. *How can a person detach himself emotionally from irritating people and situations?*

Sri Chinmoy: First, you have to identify yourself with the standards of the person who is creating the irritation. Suppose you are in your office and somebody is creating unnecessary problems. If you get angry with him, that will not solve the problem. Instead, you will be tortured inwardly by your anger and outwardly by the person. If you allow yourself to become angry, you will only lose your own inner strength. But if you come down to the standard of that person and identify with him, you will see that he himself is very unhappy and therefore wishes consciously or unconsciously to make others unhappy as well. The moment you identify with the person who is creating the situation, you will see that there is nothing to be gained by irritation. Half of your irritation will go away. It will feel that half of its domain is now captured by something: identification. When you identify yourself with the lowest standard of the person who is creating this undivine disturbance in you, your presence inside that person's ignorance will take away half the strength of his attack.

Another way to avoid becoming involved in irritating situations is to invoke Peace. For the spiritual person, for the sincere seeker it is always advisable to bring down Peace from Above.

While invoking peace you will feel enormous strength inside you and around you. The power of inner peace is infinitely greater, more solid and concrete, than any outer situation created by anybody on earth. Your inner peace can easily devour the irritation caused by somebody else. If you are in the office, it is difficult to invoke peace. If you pray before others, they will mock at you. They will misunderstand you. But if there is a quiet corner where you can meditate undisturbed by others and bring down peace, then you can do it even in your office. Otherwise, the best thing to do is to invoke peace during your morning and evening meditations, and keep that peace locked inside your heart to be used during the day whenever you need it most.

FW 35. *I read something in one of your books about the control of breath in meditation. Could you elaborate on that?*

Sri Chinmoy: In Yoga, there is a systematic way of breathing called *pranayama*. This is a Sanskrit word. But this is dangerous if you do not have a teacher to guide you at every step. Without the proper guidance of a real Master of pranayama, many people have developed tuberculosis and died. But if you want to learn a very simple way of controlled breathing which will help you in your meditation, and at the same time will not create any danger, then I can teach you what to do. When you breathe in, try to breathe in as slowly and as quietly as possible. The highest type of spiritual breathing, which is not at all dangerous, is to breathe in so slowly and quietly that if somebody placed a tiny thread in front of your nose it would not move at all.

When you breathe in as slowly as possible, feel that you are breathing in not just air, but cosmic energy. Feel that tremendous energy is entering into you, and that you are going to use it to purify yourself: your body, vital, mind and heart. Feel that there is not a single place in your body that has not been occupied by the flow of cosmic energy. It is flowing like a river inside you. When you feel that your whole being has been washed or purified by the cosmic energy, then feel that you are breathing out all the rubbish inside you, all the undivine thoughts, impure actions, obscure ideas. Anything inside your system that you call undivine, anything that you do not want to claim as your own, feel that you are exhaling it.

This is not the traditional yogic pranayama, which is more complicated and systematised. Pranayama is a traditional yogic discipline. But what I have just told you is the most effective spiritual method of breathing. If you practise this method of breathing, you will soon see that it is not imagination; it is reality. In the beginning you have to use your imagination, but after a while you will see and feel that it is not imagination at all, but reality. You are consciously breathing in the energy which is flowing all around you in the cosmos, purifying yourself, and emptying yourself of everything undivine. But this breathing has to be done in a very conscious way, not in a mechanical way. If you can breathe this way for five minutes every day, you will be able to make very fast progress.

When you reach a more advanced stage, when you breathe do not feel that your breath is coming and going only through your nose. Feel that you are breathing in through your heart, through your eyes, through your nose, through your pores. Now you are limited to breathing only through the nose or the mouth, but a time will come when you will know that any part of the body can breathe. Spiritual Masters can breathe even with their nose and mouth closed. When you have perfected this spiritual breathing, you will feel that all your impurity and ignorance is gone. What has come to replace your ignorance and your imperfection is God's Light, God's Peace and God's Power.

FLAME-WAVES

BOOK 2

FW 36. *How can we know whether we are meditating well or not?*

Sri Chinmoy: How can we know whether we are meditating well or not? We can easily know whether we are meditating well or not just by the way we feel and see and think. Right after our meditation, if we have a good feeling for the world, then we know our meditation was good. If we see the world in a loving way in spite of its imperfections, if we can love the world even while seeing its teeming imperfections, then we know that our meditation was good. And if we have a dynamic feeling right after meditation, if we feel that we came into the world to do something, to become something, this indicates that we have done a good meditation. This feeling that we have to do something does not mean that we are feeding our human ambition. No! The moment we try to feed our ambition, it will entangle us like a serpent. What we have come into the world to do is what God wants us to do. What we have come into the world to become is what God wants us to become. What God wants us to do is to grow into His very image. What God wants us to be is His dedicated instrument. During our meditation if we get the feeling that God wants us to grow into His very image, wants us to be His dedicated instrument, and if this feeling is translated into action after our meditation, then we can be sure that we were meditating well.

But the easiest way to know if we have had a good meditation is to feel whether Peace, Light, Love and Delight are coming to the fore from within. Each time Light comes forward, or Love comes forward, or Peace or Delight comes forward, the whole body will be surcharged with that divine quality. When we have this experience, we know that we have done a very good meditation. Each time they come to the fore, we are bound to feel that we are remembering a forgotten story. It is only through meditation that we can remember our forgotten story.

43

This story was written by the seeker himself, by the seeker in us. The story was not written by somebody else. It is our own creation, but we have forgotten it, and it is meditation that brings it back. When we remember this story we are overjoyed that we have created such a beautiful story and that this is our life story.

FW 37. *How can we learn to meditate? I believe in God, but it is very hard for me to meditate.*

Sri Chinmoy: The best way to begin to learn how to meditate is to associate with people who have been meditating for some time. These people are not in a position to teach you. Far from it. But they are in a position to inspire you. If you have some friends who know how to meditate, just sit beside them while they are meditating. Unconsciously your inner being will be able to derive some meditative power from them. You are not stealing anything from them, but your inner being is taking help from them without your outer knowledge.

If you want to be under the guidance of a spiritual Master, the Master's silent gaze will teach you how to meditate. The Master does not have to explain outwardly how to meditate or give you a specific form of meditation or a *mantra.* He will simply meditate on you and inwardly teach you how to meditate. Your soul will enter into the Master's soul and bring the message, the knowledge of how you should meditate, from his soul.

Outwardly, I have given very few disciples a specific way of meditation. But I have a few hundred disciples and most of them know how to meditate. How do they learn? When I meditate at the Centres or at public meetings they see something and feel something in me. And what actually sees this? It is their souls. Their souls enter into my soul and learn from my soul, and then with this wisdom they teach the disciples how to meditate.

All real spiritual Masters teach meditation to the disciples and admirers in silence. When a genuine spiritual Master meditates, Peace, Light and Bliss descend from Above and enter into the sincere seeker. Then automatically he learns how to meditate from within.

If you have a Master it is easier to learn how to meditate, because you get additional help from the Master's conscious concern. But if you do not want to follow a specific path, or if you do not want to be under the guidance of a spiritual Master, if you just want to learn how to meditate a little and not go on to God-realisation, then the best thing is to associate with spiritual people in whom you have faith. Unconsciously they will help you. But this process will not take you to your Goal. You will learn to walk, but you will not be able to walk fast. You will not be able to run fast, faster, fastest towards your Goal. For that you will need higher lessons, inner and deeper lessons, from some spiritual Master.

FW 38. *I do not know what is going to happen to me in the future, and I worry a lot about my destiny. Is this right?*

Sri Chinmoy: No, we should not worry. We should have implicit faith in God, in our Inner Pilot or in our spiritual Master. We have to feel that not only does God know what is best for us, but He will do what is best for us. We worry because we do not know what is going to happen to us tomorrow, or even the next minute. But if we can feel that there is Someone who thinks of us infinitely more than we think of ourselves, and if we can consciously offer our responsibility to Him, saying, "You be responsible. Eternal Father, Eternal Mother, You be responsible for what I do and say and grow into," then our past, our present and our future become His problem. As long as we try to be responsible for our own life we will be miserable. We will not be able to properly utilise even two minutes out of every twenty-four hours we have.

Let us consciously offer our very existence — what we have and what we are — to God. What we have is aspiration to grow into the very image of God, into infinite Peace, Light and Bliss. And what we are right now is just ignorance, the ignorance-sea. If we can offer our aspiration-cry and our ignorance-sea to God, then our problem is solved. We should not and we need not ever worry about destiny. On the strength of his surrender a spiritual person becomes inseparably one with God's Cosmic Will. Right now we do not surrender to God's Will, and that is why we suffer. We feel that if we do not do something for ourselves then who is going to do it? But this is not true. There is Someone who will do everything for us and that is our Inner Pilot. But what is expected from us? Only conscious surrender to His Will. He will act in and through us only when we become His conscious instruments. When we can feel that we are the instruments and He is the Doer then we will not worry about our destiny, we will not be afraid of our destiny. For we will know and feel that it is in the all-loving hands of God, who will do everything in us, through us and for us.

FW 39. *Why should you concentrate on the heart instead of concentrating on the mind?*

Sri Chinmoy: Before you concentrate on the heart or anything, just think about the mind for a few minutes instead of allowing the mind to think of something else. Separate yourself from the mind and observe the mind. Observe what it has done for you and see whether you are really satisfied with its capacity. The mind has given you many things, but are these things worth having in the spiritual life or not? In the ordinary human life, the mind is of paramount importance. Without it we would not be able to function properly. But if you enter into the spiritual life you will see that most of what the mind has given you is information and not illumination. There is a great difference between the two. You read books and talk to people and there you get much information. But where is illumination? You can read hundreds of pages or talk to hundreds of people but you will not get illumination. So when you think of what the mind has given you, think at the same time of the thing that you really need most and you will see that the mind has not fulfilled this need. Since your mind has disappointed you, why should you concentrate there?

Once you are totally dissatisfied with the limited capacity of the mind, it will be possible for you to concentrate on the heart. As long as you have tremendous faith in your mind, the mind that complicates and confuses everything, you will be doomed to disappointment in your meditation. Ordinary people think that complication is wisdom. But spiritual people know that complication is dangerous. God is very simple; Light is very simple. It is in our simplicity and sincerity, not in complexity, that the real Truth abides. Complexity cannot give us anything. Complexity itself is destruction.

You know that there is something called the soul. Now where is the soul? The light, the consciousness of the soul permeates the whole body, but there is a specific place where the soul resides most of the time, and that is in the heart. If you want illumination, if your ultimate goal is illumination, you will get that illumination from the soul, which is inside the heart. When you know what you want and where to find it, the sensible thing is to go to that place. Otherwise it will be like going to the hardware store to get groceries. If you concentrate on the mind you will be disappointed and disheartened and you will not get what you want because you have gone to the wrong place. Your inner aspiration does not come from your mind. No! It comes directly from your heart. The heart can give you everything. Aspiration is the harbinger of realisation or illumination. In aspiration is the seed of realisation. Aspiration comes from the heart because the illumination of the soul is always there. Since you want illumination, and since the heart can give it and the mind cannot, you should always concentrate on the heart.

FW 40. *I have read in the writings of modern Western philosophers that the soul and the body are inseparable. Can you please tell us your own philosophy on this matter?*

Sri Chinmoy: Body and soul are like a house and its owner. The soul is the owner and the body is the house. They are to some extent inseparable for a period of time. We may call the body a temple. Inside the temple is the shrine, the heart. On the shrine is the deity, the soul.

Now let us speak only of the soul and the body, since that is your question. We have to know what the soul can offer us and what the body can offer us. The soul can offer us realisation. The body can offer us manifestation. When we enter into our soul through meditation, we realise Peace, Light and Bliss. Then, through the physical, we offer these gifts to the world. When we look at someone or say something or do something, the physical is manifesting what the soul has experienced or realised. We have meditated here for about twenty minutes. All of us have entered into the realm of soul according to our capacity. Some have greater aspiration, so naturally they have entered deeper into their souls; others have less aspiration and they have not gone very deep. But whatever they have felt in the inner region will now be manifested by the body. About an hour ago when you came in here you did not bring Peace or Light in with you. After you came in you invoked Peace, Light and Bliss. Now this Peace, Light and Bliss have entered into you through the soul, and from the soul they have now entered into your physical consciousness. If you go and stand in front of a mirror you will see the difference between what you were an hour ago and what you are now. This obvious physical difference you will see is due to the fact that the physical consciousness is manifesting the Light that the soul has invoked.

The soul and the body are complementary. Without the soul, without the owner, the house is useless. As long as the soul is inside the body we can hope to realise something, we can hope to manifest something, because the owner is there. But when the owner leaves the body permanently, the body is of no more use. When the owner is there and the body is in perfect condition, then the message of the soul can be revealed and fulfilled. The owner of a store does not work in the street. He works inside the store itself. Similarly, the soul works inside the body, as well as with the body, through the body and for the body-consciousness. The body will manifest what the soul realises. For its manifestation the soul needs the body; for its realisation the body needs the soul. The body offers its capacity in service, and the soul offers its capacity in meditation. In this way they go together perfectly.

But you must know that this is the aspiring and illumining soul. If the soul does not try to inspire and illumine the body, the body will remain blind, ignorant, obscure and impure. And without the body's co-operation the soul will remain unmanifested, almost useless. Often we see that the soul is crying for realisation and manifestation through the body, but the body is not responding to it. More often we see that the body is physically strong, but it is not aspiring for the inner light and truth which the soul can offer it.

This is our philosophy on the relationship between the body and the soul. Body and soul are not inseparable, but complementary. The soul can exist without the body, although it cannot

49

manifest itself. The body cannot exist for more than a few hours without the soul. For their total mutual fulfilment, body and soul need each other.

FW 41. *What do you think about transcendental meditation which is meditating with the use of a* mantra?

Sri Chinmoy: I cannot speak specifically on transcendental meditation as the Maharishi Mahesh uses the term, because I know next to nothing about his path. But about the use of a *mantra* I can easily tell you.

A mantra is an incantation. It can be a syllable or one word or a few words or a sentence. When you repeat a mantra many times it is called *japa*.

What benefit do we get from repeating a mantra? The first benefit we get is purity. Purity is of utmost importance in our spiritual life. If there is no purity, there is no certainty in the spiritual life. Today we may make progress and tomorrow we may drop back to where we started. But when we repeat a mantra which has been given by a spiritual Master, not by anybody else, we are bound to get purity. And from purity we get energy, pure energy. When we have pure energy we get something else: the feeling of universal oneness. And in our oneness with God's universe, we attain oneness with God Himself.

The moment we have the feeling of universal oneness, we will know who the Owner of the universe is. God is the Owner and Creator of the universe, and the Creator and His creation are inseparable. In the case of ordinary people, the creator or owner of a thing can pick it up or put it down; he can keep it or give it away. But in the case of God and the universe it is not like that. Look at God; you will see the universe inside Him. Look at the universe. If you see with your spiritual eye, your third eye, immediately you will see God inside the universe.

Human possession comes and goes. Today you have millions of dollars; tomorrow you may be an absolute beggar. But in God's case the possession and the Possessor cannot be separated.

The best way to repeat a mantra to attain purity quickly is to ascend by steps. Today repeat the mantra 500 times; tomorrow, 600; the day after tomorrow, 700; and so on, until you reach 1,200 in one week's time. Then begin descending each day until you reach 500 again. In this way you can climb up the tree and climb down the tree. When you climb down please feel that you are trying to distribute this fruit through your heart to the aspiring people around you.

There are two ways to do japa. One is audible, the other is inaudible. If you repeat the mantra out loud, you will get physical purity. If you repeat the mantra in silence, you will get purity in your inner existence. Physical purity is necessary in the spiritual life, but if inner purity is lacking the seeker will make no progress. A person may be physically clean, physically pure, but in his mind he may be thinking of undivine, impure things. Inner purity is lacking at that time. So it is better to practise japa in silence and feel that there is somebody inside you, your inner being, who is repeating the word on your behalf. From this use of the mantra you will get inner purity; your heart will be pure, your mind will be pure. Just by repeating your mantra devotedly and soulfully you can have everything, the Highest, the Supreme.

FW 42. *In your talk yesterday you said that if we do less thinking and planning we will be happier. Could you elaborate on this, please?*

Sri Chinmoy: Yes, yesterday I said think less and meditate more, and plan less and act more. This is absolutely necessary. We see that cultured men, educated men, think in one way and ordinary men, uncultured and undeveloped men, think in another way.

But both the mentally developed and the mentally undeveloped constantly suffer from one thing: confusion. They go on thinking and thinking, and the moment they think they have arrived at the Truth, they discover that it is not Truth at all, but just more confusion. The difficulty is this: when we think of someone or something, we form a positive conception which we think is absolutely true. But the next moment doubt comes and changes our mind. And a few minutes later, we ask ourselves, "Who am I to judge this person?" This moment you will think that I am a nice man. The next moment you will think that I am a bad man. Then after that you will think something else. Eventually you will see that there is no end to your questions and there is no solution.

Each time we think we are lost. But each time we meditate we are illumined. Thinking is done in the mind, but the mind is not yet liberated. Only the soul is liberated. Our problem is that we want to be liberated by thinking. But the mind itself is still in the prison cell of darkness, confusion and bondage, so how can we expect liberation from the mind? No matter how highly developed a person is mentally, he is still extremely limited.

When we plan we very often are frustrated because we do not see the truth right from the beginning. We plan to do something because we feel that if we do it we will achieve a certain goal. But in between planning and executing, different ideas, different ideals enter into us and create confusion for us. Then our planning goes on and on forever and we never enter into the world of action because our plans are never complete or certain. There is a yawning gap between our mental plan and the action itself.

But if we have an inner will, the soul's will, which has come to us from meditation, then the action is no sooner conceived of than it is done. At that time there is no difference between our inner will and our outer action. But if we plan something with our ordinary will, with our human mind, it may take five years to execute that plan, or it may all come to nothing after all. When we enter into the totally dark, obscure, unlit room of action with our mental plan it is like carrying a candle. But when we enter the room with our soul's light the room is flooded with illumination.

The mind is in the prison cell of thoughts, ideas and habits, whereas the soul is a free bird. It has accepted the cage like a fort, but at any moment the bird can fly away. And although the bird stays inside the body, when we pray and meditate it constantly brings us the message of the Infinite. In the soul's world, realisation is spontaneously followed by action. But in the ordinary life thinking is the realisation, and one person's thought-power is contradicted by another person's thought-power. But will-power cannot be contradicted by will-power, because will-power comes directly from the soul. Will-power is flooded with infinite Peace, Light and Bliss, and it always brings oneness. But in thought-power there is no oneness. In the mental world my thought-power will not be the same as yours, and your thought-power will not be the same as mine. We will always be confused and at variance. But when I use my will-power, immediately you will feel your oneness with my will-power, because it has come directly from the soul, and in the soul's world we are all one.

FW 43. *When you speak of a nation, you speak of it as if it were one person, but a nation is composed of thousands and millions of people with different levels of consciousness. Also, when you speak of a nation as an individual, it implies that there is such a thing as a karmic past. How can you reconcile the idea of karma for a nation with the fact that you have within the nation millions of people with their own individual karmic pasts, unless being born in one particular nation is part of an individual's karma?*

Sri Chinmoy: Each individual can raise or lower the standard of his nation. If one person in a nation aspires, the consciousness of that particular nation is elevated. We must feel that a nation is like a body which is made up of millions of cells. If one cell achieves something great, it is the achievement of the entire body. If one cell attains a higher consciousness, the consciousness of the entire body improves. On the other hand, if one cell becomes weak, sick, diseased, then the entire body is weakened. The consciousness of a nation is a collective phenomenon. The achievement of each individual person adds to the achievement of the nation as a whole. Likewise, each nation should feel that it is a branch of the cosmic tree. The attainment of one particular branch is the attainment of the entire tree.

If we, as a nation, try to transcend our limitations or even our achievements, only then can we be perfect. As we are transcending our limitations and surpassing our achievements, we feel that consciously or unconsciously we are inspiring other nations. If they live in the vital they will be jealous of us. But if they live in the heart they will see that they, too, have the capacity to do as we are doing. A sincere nation will see and feel that another nation is rising or has risen to a high standard through its personal effort, through its aspiration to improve itself. A sincere nation will then ask itself what has prevented it from coming up to that standard, and it will see that it is just from lack of enthusiasm, lack of effort.

Some people say that opportunity is not given to some nations. I wish to say that this is not true. What is opportunity? Opportunity is the conscious acceptance of the presence of divinity within. A nation may say it has fallen or failed because it did not have equal capacity or equal opportunity. But I will say no! Opportunity came from Above; capacity came from within. However, the nation did not seize the opportunity, it did not exercise its capacity. In this world no nation can remain unsatisfied or unfulfilled if it sincerely aspires — that is, if its citizens sincerely aspire.

We have to know what God wants from each nation. God wants my hand to work, my eyes to see, my ears to hear, my nose to breathe. If a nation goes deep within, it will see what God wants it to be. If I can become what God wants me to become, then God will be more than satisfied. If God wants me to be an ant, then He will be pleased with me only if I become an ant, and not if I become an elephant. The role and goal of each individual nation has to come directly from within, from God. If I as a nation really want to do something for the world, then let me go deep within and do what God wants me to do, instead of competing with another nation which is doing something entirely different. As a nation, if I can become what God wants me to become, then I shall feel that I have fulfilled my own existence and I have fulfilled God's Divinity and God's Reality. If I want to compete, I should try to compete with my own ignorance, with my own limitations and bondage. I should try to surpass myself — my own achievements — instead of the achievements of other nations. If I have weaknesses as a nation, I should try to become strong by transforming and perfecting them. If I am sick I should try to cure myself, and not depend on another nation to cure me. Right now each nation is far from perfection. But each nation has the capacity to be absolutely perfect because the message of perfection dwells within each nation, the seed of perfection is sown inside each nation. Like any seed, it takes time to germinate.

A nation does have a karmic past, and when a person is born into a nation or lives in a nation, he participates or shares in that karmic past. He also helps to build the karmic future of that nation. So you have to know that if a nation is undeveloped, it is not because of lack of opportunity, but because of lack of aspiration or lack of development in its inhabitants. If a nation has certain good qualities or good fortune, or certain bad qualities or bad fortune, it is because of the consciousness of the people of that nation.

FW 44. *When I first began meditating at 3:00 in the morning, I used to have very good meditations and I was very inspired. But when I continued, I didn't have the same inspiration and it became very difficult.*

Sri Chinmoy: When we start something for the first time, we get inspiration. Anything that is new gives us tremendous inspiration, just because it is something new. But if we continue doing it we do not have the same enthusiasm, the same impetus, the same inspiration. We want to get something very deep, very high, very sublime, something most illumining from our early morning meditation. We are like a long distance runner. When the starter fires the gun, at the very beginning he is so inspired and he starts running very fast. But after about two or three miles, he becomes very tired. Running becomes tedious and difficult. Now if he gives up running just because he is tired and because his inspiration is gone, he does not reach the goal. But if he continues running he will finally reach the goal. Then he will definitely feel that it was worth the struggle and suffering of the body.

It is like that in the spiritual life also. When you start your journey at three o'clock in the morning, feel that tomorrow is the continuation of that journey. Do not take it as a new beginning. And the third day, feel that you have travelled another mile. Every day you feel that you have travelled another mile. The day you start your spiritual journey is actually the most important. You will have the most inspiration at that time. But if you can feel that each morning during your meditation you are travelling a little farther, you will know that you will one day reach your Goal. Even if your speed decreases, you have to continue running and not give up on the way. When you reach the Goal you will see that it was worth the struggle. So every day when you meditate, it will help you if you think that it is a continuation of your previous day's meditation. One step at a time you reach the Goal.

FW 45. *I was wondering about the relationship between the heart and the mind. How can we integrate the two?*

Sri Chinmoy: There are two ways. One way is for the heart to enter into the mind. The other way is for the mind to enter into the heart. Let us take the heart as the mother and the mind as the child. Either the child has to go to the mother, who is calm, quiet and full of love, or the mother has to go to the child, who right now is uncertain, doubtful and restless.

Now when the mother comes to the child, the child has to feel that the mother has come with good intentions: to calm the mind, free the mind, to fulfil the mind in a divine way. If the doubting and restless mind feels that the mother has come to bother him, and that his restlessness is something very good which he wants to keep, then he is lost. If the child is restless, doubtful, suspicious and if he cherishes all these undivine qualities and feels that they are his best qualities, then what can the poor mother do? The heart will have the good intention of transforming his doubt into faith, and his other undivine qualities into divine qualities. But the mind has to be prepared, has to feel that the heart has come with the very idea of changing him for the better.

The other way, when the child has gone through everything negative and destructive — fear, doubt, suspicion, jealousy, impurity — he comes to a point where he feels that it is high time for him to go to someone who can give him something better. Who is this someone? The mother, the heart. The mother is more than eager to illumine her own child. If the mind is aspiring, it will immediately feel that the heart is the mother, the real mother. And the heart will always feel that the mind is a child who needs instruction.

Both ways are effective. If the mind is ready to learn from the heart, the heart is always eager to teach it. The mother is ready to help the child, to serve the child twenty-four hours a day. It is the child who sometimes becomes irritated, disobedient or obstinate, who feels that he knows everything and has nothing to learn from anybody else. But the mind must learn from someone else. Even the mother, the heart, gets knowledge from someone else — from the soul, which is all Light. Let us call the soul the grandmother. From the grandmother the mother learns and from the mother the child learns. The soul teaches the heart, and the heart teaches the mind. If we can see the relationship between the heart and the mind as a relationship of mother to child, that is the best way to integrate the two.

FW 46. *Yesterday when I was meditating, I got a message from the silence which said, "Love one another. If you love one another, then you will be known as my disciples." When we get this kind of message in our meditation, should we meditate on it and take it into ourselves?*

Sri Chinmoy: When we get a message in our mind during meditation, we have to know whether it is in the lower mind, the physical mind — the restless, aggressive, destructive and doubtful mind — or in the calm mind, the vacant mind, the silent mind. When we receive a message in the silent mind, we should accept it and feel that it is the foundation stone on which we can build the Palace of Truth, Love, Divinity and Reality. This message actually originates in the soul or in the heart, and then enters into the mind. When the mind is absolutely still, calm and peaceful we can hear that message.

Suppose you are meditating and after a few minutes a thought or idea comes into your mind. Let us say that it is about sacrifice, that you will sacrifice something for a friend or relative or someone you know. This is not just an idea at that time; it is an ideal. When you accept an idea as your own, the idea does not remain an idea but becomes an ideal.

Whenever a divine thought enters into your mind, try to expand it. When an undivine thought comes into your mind, either reject it or, if you have enough inner strength, transform it. It is like this. Somebody has knocked at your door. If you know that you have enough strength to compel him to behave properly once he enters, then you can open the door and allow him to come in. But if you do not have the power to compel him to behave, then it would be wise to keep your door closed. Let it remain closed for a day or for a month or for a year. When you gain more strength, then accept the challenge and open the door. For if these wrong thoughts are not conquered, they will come back to bother you again and again. First you reject, then you accept and transform, then finally you totally transcend.

We have to be a divine potter with the dirty clay of our thoughts. If the potter is afraid to touch the clay, if he refuses to touch it, then the clay will remain clay and the potter will not be able to offer anything to the world. But the potter is not afraid. He touches the clay and shapes it in his own way into something beautiful and useful. It is our bounden duty to transform undivine thoughts. But when? When we are in a position to do it safely. If I am not a potter, what can I do with a lump of clay? If I touch it, I will only make myself dirty.

In the spiritual life a beginner should not allow any thought to enter his mind. He would like to allow his friends to enter, but he does not know who his friends are. And even if he does know who his friends are, when he opens the door for them he may find that his enemies are standing right in front of them, and before his friends can cross the threshold, his enemies are deep inside the room. Once the enemies enter, it is very difficult to chase them out. For that we need the strength of solid spiritual discipline.

There will come a time, as in your case, when you can build on your divine ideas. Build your life of love on this thought that came to you. Love is absolutely necessary in the spiritual life. This is the love which permits us to see that all human beings are God. If we truly love God we love all mankind as well. We cannot separate Divine Love from man and God. Man and God are like a tree. If you go to man, the foot of the tree, with your Divine Love, from there it is very easy to go up to God, the top of the tree.

FW 47. *Do you feel that parents should give young children religious instruction, or should children be free to choose their own form of worship when they are old enough?*

Sri Chinmoy: When a child is young, he does not know which food is nourishing and which food is bad, so as a mother or father it is your responsibility to give him what you feel is good for him, and you do it. This is not an imposition; it is an offering. You have discovered that something is true, that something is good or bad. Is it wrong for you to then offer your discoveries to your child? When the child is old enough to make his own discoveries, let him discover his own path. When he is thirteen or fourteen and his mind has developed, at that time he can make his own choice.

At the beginning a child is absolutely innocent and ignorant. If we do not feed the child because we do not know what he will like, then he will simply starve to death. In the spiritual life also, if we do not feed a child right from the beginning by teaching him to have faith in God and pray to God or repeat God's name, to be generous, kind and so forth, then how will he learn these things? It is the bounden duty of the parents to teach their children. When the children grow up, if they do not stay with their parents' path, if they feel that they know everything better, then that is their business. But the parents should at least give them some foundation upon which to build good lives.

When a child is born, the parents do not say, "We do not know whether he will like our home or not, so the best thing is to leave him in the street, and when he grows up he can decide whether he would like to live with us or with somebody else." The idea of doing such a thing would strike them as ridiculous. But if parents do not give their child any religious instruction when he is young, they are doing essentially the very same thing to their child's inner life. So parents are making a terrible mistake when they say that children should be left alone to discover their own path when they grow up. If children are not offered any path when they are young, when they grow up they will have no path at all.

People say that America is the land of freedom and that when children grow up they will do what they feel is best. Right from the beginning they give their children endless freedom to do anything they want, and when the children grow up to be ignorant and undisciplined, the parents say, "Oh, I never expected my children to be like that." But this is a mistake. When children are being brought up, the parents cannot simply lead their own lives and ignore their children. They must give boundless love, affection and concern to their children. If they give love to their children and one day the children do not respond, the next day they must be ready to give more. Parents have to know the meaning of patience. They have to give unreservedly today and, even if they do not get any response, tomorrow they have to do it again. Parents' business is to give, give, give, and not to expect. When the time comes, children will be grateful.

FW 48. *What is the best way to get peace of mind?*

Sri Chinmoy: We do not have peace of mind because we feel that we are the most important people on earth. We feel that if we do not do this, if we do not say that, then the world will collapse or everything will go wrong immediately. We can get peace of mind if we can consciously feel that we are not important, we are not indispensable. The moment we can sincerely feel that we are not indispensable, we will not have to go anywhere to get peace, for peace will immediately come to us. If we feel that it is our duty to serve the world, that is good. But if we feel that it is our duty to illumine the world, and that if we do not illumine the world the world will remain full of darkness, that is wrong. I am not indispensable. You are not indispensable. Only God is indispensable.

Another easy way to have peace of mind is to feel that nothing is unduly important. If we have lost something, we must feel that that thing is unimportant in our life, that our life will not be ruined just because we have lost it. Everything on earth can desert us as long as we do not desert God and God does not desert us. God will never desert us because He is all Compassion, and even if we try our hardest, we will not be able to desert God because He is omnipresent. So we need not worry about anything on earth. We need not become upset or agitated about anything on earth.

We have to know and feel that, except for God and our inner cry for Truth, nothing on earth is indispensable. If we have the inner cry, then we get God. And once we consciously get God as our very own, we have everything. Ordinary people do not pray, do not meditate. God is only a vague idea to them. They know that God exists, but where is He, who is He, what is He doing? They cannot answer these questions. Only spiritual people know that God is inside the heart, that He is all Love, and that He is playing His divine Game in and through us. For spiritual people, God is a Reality, a constant Reality.

FW 49. *When you are meditating on us and I am looking at you, I think perhaps I should try to be as humble, pure and receptive as possible. Is that right or should I just forget about all this and keep my mind open?*

Sri Chinmoy: This is a most significant question. It depends on the individual. If the individual is a student of mine, or a disciple of mine — that is to say, someone who has consciously given the responsibility for his spiritual life to me — if he becomes humble to me, if he becomes polite and very devoted, then he will get the utmost from me. If he is arrogant, stubborn and haughty, however, naturally he will not be able to receive anything from me.

Right now you are coming to the New York Centre, so you can consider yourself a student of mine. In your case, when you offer your humility, please feel that this humility is not touching my human personality. Feel that this humility is entering into the Supreme in me who deserves everything from you. I am not anybody's Guru. Your Guru, your Master, is God. Your real Master is inside me. My Master, my real Master, is inside you. Just because I have the inner light and inner wisdom, when you enter into me, I try to bring your aspiring soul to the fore. When there is a devoted feeling to me, devoted love, divine love, then when you become one with me, you get what I have. I lived a life of spiritual discipline for twenty years in an ashram, and the inner peace, the inner light, the inner wisdom that I have gained, I offer to you.

In the beginning, when you are a student, it is better always to enter into the teacher's heart consciously and with humility. This humility is not humiliation. When somebody is humiliated, he is crushed; but humility is a feeling of total oneness. You feel that you are absolutely one with me because God is the Lord of everything, the Cause of All. When you show humility, it is your own divine quality which enables you to become totally one with me. I am not superior and you are not inferior. But with your humility you can establish your oneness with me with the utmost sweetness. Try with your humility, softness, sweetness, divine love, to enter into me and feel your existence inside me. Once you enter into me, then it is my problem, my duty, my responsibility, to give you what you need by the Grace of the Supreme.

But some individuals come here just to get inner peace or inner joy. They are not my students; they have not given me the responsibility for their lives, and I have not taken the responsibility. In their case, what they should do when they look at me is forget about everything and make their mind absolutely calm, quiet and vacant — like an empty vessel — and not allow anything to enter into it during meditation. If they keep in their mind-vessel fears, worries, doubts and so forth, the vessel will be full. Then what can I do? The vessel has to be emptied so that I can fill it with divine Peace, divine Love, divine Joy, divine Harmony.

When the vessel is empty, the divine thought can enter into the individual aspirant and grow. As ordinary thoughts, undivine thoughts, grow in us, so also divine thoughts grow in us. When the undivine thoughts grow in us, ultimately they destroy us. Doubt enters into us, then anxieties, worries, despondencies and destructive qualities. But the same vessel can hold divine Truth, divine Peace and divine Light instead. When the vessel is full to the brim with divine thoughts, ultimately it will open the door to divine Peace, divine Light. If the vessel is not filled with divine thoughts, all the visitors that come will be undivine. They will act like thieves, robbers and murderers. But when the vessel is filled with divine thoughts, one receives all the divine gifts which God has to offer.

This is to be done by those who are not my students, who just come here once a week and who want to have a little peace and nothing else. But those who want to realise God in this life, who want to have infinite Peace, infinite Light and infinite Bliss, who really want to realise the highest on earth, have to follow a spiritual path. I have a path; so do other spiritual Masters. Each Master has a path of his own, and ultimately, each path leads to the same goal. All roads lead to Rome but one has to follow one road. Those meditating here who are not my students eventually will feel the necessity for a spiritual Master. Here I am giving them inspiration. Then, when they are inspired, when they want to go to the end of the road, to the ultimate Goal, they will try to get a teacher of their own. At that time, the teacher, the spiritual Master, will tell them what they should and should not do.

FW 50. *It is said that if one can sit on the floor with his legs crossed for an hour or so without any thought or any feeling, just completely quiet and peaceful, some kind of inner energy or inner force would arise from underneath the navel, and that force would circulate within the body. I never have had that kind of experience. When I practise concentration sometimes one foot will become warm, sometimes both feet will become warm, but I never have that experience of the navel energy awakening from inside. Some people call it Kundalini.*

Sri Chinmoy: People say many things, books tell us many things, but the individual experience is of paramount importance. I am not saying that the books are telling you lies or that the people who have had this experience of energy are mistaken. No, they are right in their own assertion, in their own experiences. And what you are experiencing is also right for you. But unfortunately you are making one mistake. If you feel that just by sitting cross-legged for fifteen minutes or half an hour you are going to develop inner energy or get higher experiences, then you are mistaken. There are many people in the Indian villages who can sit for hours cross-legged. But ask them if they have had any spiritual experiences and, if they are sincere enough, they will say no. There are many who have been practising *asanas,* physical postures, for many years without ever having had even one solitary experience. Why? It is not just the actual posture. It is not the pose or how you sit. It is the aspiration. If you have the capacity, you can even lie down and meditate. You can run and meditate. Meditation has to come from deep within like the cry of a child hungry for food. When the child is hungry, he cries desperately, and the mother comes running, whether she is in the kitchen or in the living room, to feed the child, because she feels that the cry comes from the child's heart. If you feel the inner cry for God or if you feel that you need to develop this divine energy within you, then you are bound to develop it. This energy is bound to climb up.

But you are making a mistake when you concentrate on your navel centre. At this point in your spiritual development the navel centre is not a safe centre. It is the centre of dynamism, strength, power and so forth. You should meditate on your heart centre to get peace and love and joy. When you have peace, love and joy, you will feel that peace itself is power, love itself is power, joy itself is dynamic power. If you open the navel centre, where there is dynamism, and if you misuse this dynamism, it becomes brutal aggression. The navel centre is also the emotional centre. With this emotion you can expand yourself and become the Infinite. But again, when you start receiving the emotion of the navel centre, you may become a victim to pleasure, earthly pleasure and human weakness. So God is not allowing you to open this centre. He is protecting you.

God does not want you to misuse your dynamic qualities which you have inside and around your navel centre. What He wants from you is the inner cry for Him, and this inner cry is not here *[navel]* or here *[throat]* or here *[third eye]* or here *[crown of head]*. It is only here *[heart]*. The one place to cry for God is here. If you really cry for God, no matter where you are or in which position you are, you are bound to feel God's Presence. And when you feel God's Presence, you can feel that the divine energy, the Kundalini, is already awakened and is rising towards the highest. From one centre to another, it is going up, up, up. If you can feel God's living Presence inside you, this energy that you are speaking of will be yours in boundless measure in a very short span of time. Please cry for God's living Presence. You cannot live without God; I cannot live without God. Everybody has to live with God, but to feel His living Presence is something else. Those who have realised God feel God's living Presence twenty-four hours a day. If you cry for that living Presence, your whole being, your inner existence and outer existence, will be flooded with divine dynamism and boundless energy.

So please do not worry about sitting in the strict lotus posture, *padmasana.* Just sit straight but relaxed. When you meditate, do not stiffen your body. Sometimes people do padmasana, this cross-legged lotus posture, but they bend forward or make their whole body very stiff. And when the body is stiff, naturally the divine qualities, the fulfilling qualities, which are flowing and streaming, will not be received. So when you sit cross-legged, if your body is rigid, then please immediately forget about your posture. Only try to sit straight but relaxed. In your case, unfortunately, I can clearly see that your position is correct, but the thing that is actually needed in the lotus posture is missing. When you are sitting cross-legged and are breathing in, the whole body should consciously feel a stream of divine love flowing in and through it. Without love there is no God, and there is no human existence either. You love yourself, you love God, you love your dearest and nearest ones and you love humanity as a whole. So first please try to bring to the fore God's love aspect, and once you have established within yourself the love aspect, then you will see all other aspects are bound to come. Love is the pioneer of all divine qualities. So when you cry for God, feel love — immediate, spontaneous, unreserved, soulful love. All the divine qualities of God are bound to follow this divine love.

FW 51. *Sir, do you feel it is necessary to assume a particular posture when you meditate, to sit in the lotus position, for example?*

Sri Chinmoy: It depends on the individual. If you can breathe in properly, you can have a proper meditation even while you are lying down. The main thing is to keep the spine erect and straight, and to keep the body relaxed. There are many people who meditate very well while they are seated in a chair. And there are many who sit in the lotus posture only to show off, while their mind is roaming elsewhere. You have to know how much control you have over the mind. If you have control over your mind, you can meditate while running, while talking to people; but if you do not have control over your mind, then it is better to sit in a particular corner of the room and keep your body, especially your back, erect. Usually when a beginner enters into a spiritual path, he becomes a victim to laziness. Meditation is something new to him and he may not get a satisfactory result all at once, or he may not have the necessary patience. So it is necessary for him to discipline himself as quickly as possible. But for one who has already tasted some inner food — inner Light, Peace or Bliss — it is not necessary to go through this rigorous discipline because meditation has become spontaneous. While he is walking, while he is doing office work, his mind is on God, he is meditating on God. While he is talking to a person, only his mouth is functioning but his mind is somewhere else! In your case you are the best judge. When you start to meditate, what happens? If your mind roams, then you have to be very careful. If your mind does not roam, if you know that you can hold the reins, then it is not at all obligatory to sit in the lotus posture while you meditate.

FW 52. *In a recent talk you spoke about Light. Now, I am not afraid of seeing Light. My question is, how can I see Light, that is, divine Light? Of course, I know about concentration and meditation but aside from concentration and meditation what concrete or practical things can I do to see the divine Light? Also, during concentration and meditation, what kind of practical things can I do to see the Light?*

Sri Chinmoy: You are using the word "practical". Here I wish to say that concentration *is* practical; meditation *is* practical. We have to know that God, who is all Light, is natural. Only what is natural can be practical plus practicable. So from now on please feel that concentration is something natural in your life. Meditation is also something natural in your life. Feel that when you do not meditate, you are doing something unnatural, abnormal, unusual, because inside you is God and the effulgence of divine Light.

You are trying either to enter into the vastness of this Light or you are trying to bring to the fore the Light that you already have. This Light that you are referring to comes when the aspirant is ready. You want to see the Light. You say you are not afraid of Light. Wonderful! But there are many people who *are* afraid of Light. You have relatives, friends, neighbours, who say, "Yes, we want Light." But the moment Light comes to them, they feel that they are going to be exposed. People feel that if they can hide themselves in a dark room, from inside they will be able to see the whole world, appreciate or criticise or do anything. They think that they will be in a position to see the world and pass judgement, but that nobody will be able to see them. This is their hope. So their darkness, they feel, is a kind of safety, security. When Light comes and is ready to enter into them, they feel that all their weaknesses and limitations, all their negative ideas and negative thoughts, will be exposed. But the very function of Light is to illumine, not to expose; to transform our negative and destructive thoughts into positive and affirmative thoughts.

You want to know how you can receive Light or how you can bring Light to the fore. For that you need preparation, and what is that preparation? The preparation is your pure concentration, your pure meditation. When you start your meditation or concentration, try to feel that you have come from Light and you are inside Light. This is not your imagination; this is not your mental hallucination. Far from it! When you start meditating, just feel what you are. It is a real, solid, concrete truth that you embody Light and that you are Light itself. You will see that there is a spontaneous flow of Light from within. First you will feel it inside your heart. Then you will feel it in your forehead, in the third eye; and finally you will feel it all over.

There is another way of seeing Light. While breathing, when you draw in the breath, please feel that you are breathing in something that is purifying all that has to be purified inside you and, at the same time, energising all that is unfed. In the beginning, there are quite a few things inside you that have to be purified. There are quite a few things which are hungry. So when you feel that you are feeding, energising and at the same time purifying, then you will see that Light becomes absolutely natural.

There is another way of seeing Light. Since you have accepted our path, please look at my forehead in my transcendental picture. Then you will be able to see your Light inside me, or my Light. You will see Light and that Light you will feel inside you also, because there is only one Light, and that is God. He is operating inside me, inside you, inside everyone. But in my case I can consciously see it and make others feel it. So if you concentrate on my transcendental picture and soulfully repeat the word "Light" fifty, sixty, one hundred times, then I assure you that you are bound to see Light — either blue or white or gold or red or green — because from my transcendental consciousness I am ready to offer Light to anybody who sincerely wants it. This is the secret that I am telling you.

On Thursday at the New York Centre, when you sit in front of me, you can concentrate on my forehead when I am in deep meditation. Take your time and say the word "Light" silently, and while you are saying it, try to feel that you have formed a bridge between yourself and me. Then you will feel continually that you are entering into me and that I am entering into you. You don't have to meditate for four hours or ten hours. No! In a matter of a few minutes, if you have a soulful feeling of oneness with me, you are bound to see Light. This I will be able to do for you, and for other sincere seekers who are my students and disciples. But for others I will not be able to do this, because they have not accepted me as their own.

It is not at all a difficult thing for a sincere seeker to see Light. But those who want to see Light out of curiosity may be denied by God, because they only want to see, and not to grow into, Light. However, if God wants me to show them Light, in spite of their unwillingness, in spite of their disbelief in God, I can show them. But that is God's way of acting. I cannot interfere in God's operation. It is God who knows what is best for us. In your case, today you will see the Light and tomorrow you will aspire to grow into it. This is what a seeker does: today he sees the Goal, tomorrow he reaches the Goal, and the day after tomorrow he grows into the Goal. So you try; I shall help you.

FW 53. *Could you please tell us the difference between concentration, meditation and contemplation?*

Sri Chinmoy: When we concentrate we do not allow any thought to enter into our mind, whether it is divine or undivine, earthly or Heavenly, good or bad. The mind, the entire mind, has to be focused on a particular object or subject. If you are concentrating on the petal of a flower, try to feel that only you and the petal exist, that nothing else exists in the entire world but you and the petal. You will look neither forward nor backward, upward nor inward. You will just try to pierce the object that you are focusing on with your one-pointed concentration. But this concentration is not an aggressive way of looking into a thing or entering into an object. Far from it! This concentration comes directly from the heart, or more precisely, from the soul. We call it the soul's indomitable will, or will-power.

Very often I hear aspirants say that they cannot concentrate for more than five minutes. After five minutes they get a headache or feel that their head is on fire. Why? It is because the power of their concentration is coming from the intellectual mind or, you can say, the disciplined mind. The mind knows that it must not wander; that much knowledge the mind has. But if the mind is to be utilised properly, in an illumined way, then the light of the soul has to come into it. When the light of the soul has entered the mind, it is extremely easy to concentrate on something for two or three hours or as long as you want. During this time there can be no thoughts or doubts or fears. No negative forces can enter into your mind if it is surcharged with the soul's light.

So when you concentrate, try to feel that the power of concentration comes from here, the heart centre, and then goes up to the third eye. The heart centre is where the soul is located. The physical heart is tiny, but the spiritual heart — your true

73

home — is vaster than the universe. When you think of your soul at this time, please do not form any specific idea of it or try to think what it looks like. Just think of it as God's representative, as boundless Light and Delight, which is in your heart. The Light comes from your heart and passes through your third eye, and then you enter into the object of your concentration and have your identification with it. The final stage of concentration is to discover the hidden ultimate truth in the object of concentration.

What concentration can do in our day-to-day life is unimaginable. Concentration is the surest way to reach our goal, whether the goal be God-realisation or merely the fulfilment of human desires. It is concentration that acts like an arrow and enters into the target. He who is wanting in the power of concentration is no better than a monkey. A real aspirant sooner or later acquires the power of concentration either through the Grace of God, through constant practice or through his aspiration. Each seeker can declare that he has a divine hero, a divine warrior, within himself. And what is that divine warrior? It is his concentration.

When we concentrate, we have to concentrate on one particular thing. If I am concentrating on a certain disciple, then he will be the only thing in my mind, nothing else. He becomes, at that time, the sole object of my attention. But when we meditate, we feel that we have the capacity deep within us to see many, deal with many, welcome many — all at the same time. When we meditate, we have to try to expand our consciousness to encompass the vast sea or the vast, blue sky. We have to expand ourselves like a bird spreading its wings. We have to expand our finite consciousness and enter into the Universal Consciousness where there is no fear, no jealousy, no doubt, but all Joy, Peace and divine Power.

When we meditate, what we actually do is enter into a vacant, calm, still, silent mind. We go deep within and approach our true existence, which is our soul. When we live in the soul, we feel that we are actually meditating spontaneously. On the surface of the sea are multitudes of waves, but the sea is not affected below. In the deepest depths, at the bottom of the sea, it is all tranquillity. So when you start meditating, try to feel your own inner existence first. That is to say, the bottom of the sea: calm and quiet. Feel that your whole being is surcharged with peace and tranquillity.

Then let the waves come from the outside world. Fear, doubt, worry — the earthly turmoils — will all be washed away, because inside is solid peace. You cannot be afraid of anything when you are in your highest meditation. Your mind is all peace, all silence, all oneness. If thoughts or ideas want to come in, you control them with your inner peace, for they will not be able to affect you. Like fish in the sea, they jump and swim but leave no mark on the water. Like birds flying in the sky, they leave no trace behind them. So when you meditate, feel that you are the sea, and all the animals in the sea do not affect you. Feel that you are the sky, and all the birds flying past do not affect you. Feel that your mind is the sky and your heart is the infinite ocean. That is meditation.

When we are in meditation, we want only to commune with God. Now I am speaking in English and you are able to understand me because you know English well. Similarly, when you know how to meditate well, you will be able to commune with God, for meditation is the language we use to speak to God.

Through concentration we become one-pointed and through meditation we expand our consciousness into the Vast. But in contemplation we grow into the Vast itself. We have seen the Truth. We have felt the Truth. But the most important thing is to grow into the Truth and become totally one with the Truth. If we are concentrating on God, we may feel God right in front of us or beside us. When we are meditating, we are bound to feel Infinity, Eternity, Immortality within us. But when we are contemplating, we will see that we ourselves are God, that we ourselves are Infinity, Eternity, Immortality. Contemplation means our conscious oneness with the Infinite, Eternal, Absolute. In contemplation we discover ourselves. When we contemplate, Creator and creation become one. We become one with the Creator and see the whole universe at our feet, the whole universe inside us. At that time, when we look at our own existence, we don't see a human being. We see something like a dynamo of Light, Peace and Bliss.

One should concentrate for a few minutes each day before entering into meditation. You are like a runner who has to clear the track — see if there are any obstacles and then remove them. Then when you begin meditating, feel that you are running very fast, with all obstacles out of your way. You are like an express train, an inner train, that only stops at the final destination. Then, when you reach the Goal, you have to become the Goal. This is the last stage, contemplation. Seekers who are just entering onto the spiritual path should start with concentration, for a few months at least, and then enter into meditation. Then they must meditate for a few years and finally enter into contemplation.

FLAME-WAVES

BOOK 3

FW 54. *I used to feel and see a golden light around my heart, but now I no longer do. How can I regain this wonderful presence?*

Sri Chinmoy: Let me start with the words "golden light". Each light has its significance. Golden light actually comes from a level of consciousness which we term the supermind. The supermind is infinitely higher than the physical mind. Above the physical mind is the abode of intuition, the overmind, and above the overmind is the supermind. The golden light descends from the supermind.

This golden light has a special significance. Golden light is divine manifestation. When this light of divine manifestation comes down and touches the earth consciousness, it becomes red. Sometimes the light recedes if it feels that it is unable to stay in the heart due to lack of purity. When the heart is not pure it is impossible for the light to stay indefinitely. When the heart is pure, this light first functions most properly and satisfactorily in the heart region, and then it moves into the vital and the physical.

If you do not see this light, do not be depressed. It is functioning on another level of consciousness. When a beginner sees light, he feels that he is making extraordinary progress. To some extent, it is true. God gives you light, naturally you will try to dive deep into the sea of spirituality. But if God feels that light is not required and that what you need is peace, then He will act through you in a different way. In you, because of your abundant purity, the light still abides. Now it is working inside your vital and sometimes it comes into the physical. To regain the visible presence of light is not necessary. If you want to follow the spiritual path, it is not the light that you want — it is God's constant Concern for you, God's real Love and God's Blessing. When you have God's Concern it can take the form of Light or Peace or Power. The most important thing is to please God in God's own Way. You can ask, on the strength of your surrender, "God, make me anything You want so I can be Your instrument." You are trying to regain the wonderful presence of this light. But you will not get utmost satisfaction from seeing this light because you are not fulfilling God in His own Way. If you want the Grace of God, I can pray to God on your behalf and I assure you you will get back the golden light. But it will not please you because you know that the highest aim is to please God in His own Way. When God gives us an experience, we should be most grateful to Him. And when He does not give us one, we have to be equally grateful, because He knows what is best for us. It is your business to meditate faithfully, wholeheartedly and soulfully, and God's business is to give you Light or Blessings or Peace or Power. God will give you what He has and what He is if you give Him what you have and what you are. What you have is ignorance and what you are is aspiration. So my request to you is to please God in His own Way and not to care for the thing that you once had and which now you are missing.

FW 55. *How can you tell the difference between true intuition and imagination?*

Sri Chinmoy: If you soulfully follow a spiritual path for a few months, if your prayer, concentration and meditation are intense, and if you know how to contemplate intensely also, then you will be able to feel inner guidance within you. When you meditate early in the morning, your inner being will tell you what is going to happen, what others are going to think of you. But in order to develop proper intuition, or the intuitive faculty, aspiration has to be very, very sincere and intense. Otherwise, it will be all imagination or mental hallucination.

Try to feel that there is a burning flame inside you which is mounting all the time. In the process of mounting high, higher, highest you will see that it is spreading its divine Light all around. And in this Light you are bound to develop a direct vision of Truth. You will see that the length and breadth of the world — your inner world — has been illumined. In darkness, we do not see anything. Even if you place the most valuable treasure right in front of me, I will not see it, because there is no light. But if the flame of aspiration within me is rising towards the highest and spreading its Light, then I will get an immediate flash of intuition. For in Light there is reality. In Light there is constant divinity. So when you have the flame of aspiration within you, divinity and reality are at your disposal. In this way, you will always feel these flashes of intuition and you will not remain in the world of imagination.

But again, if you imagine something nice about God, do not worry at all. If you imagine that God is all Compassion for you, but you have not yet felt God's compassionate aspect, or if you imagine that God is all Concern and Love for you, but you have not felt God's divine Love and Concern, no harm. Today it may be imagination but tomorrow you will feel it as the truth, because these are all realities. You have not yet felt it, but many spiritual seekers and all spiritual Masters have felt it and realised it.

FW 56. *How can one tell the difference between the Will of God and wishful thinking?*

Sri Chinmoy: In order to know God's Will, one need not be a great spiritual Master or a highly advanced spiritual soul. There are very few of these on earth, very few. But one has to be at least a seeker in order to know God's Will. And how can one be a real seeker? One can be a true seeker, an aspirant, if he feels that he is not only helpless, but also hopeless, meaningless and useless in every way without God. Without God he is nothing but with God he is everything. He is aspiration. He is Realisation. He is Revelation. He is Manifestation. If one has that kind of inner feeling about oneself, then one can be a true seeker overnight.

How can a seeker know whether something is God's Will or just his own fanciful or wishful thinking? A real aspirant, a sincere seeker, tries to meditate devotedly each day. And one who meditates devotedly each day will soon have a free access to God's inner realm and be able to hear the message of God.

Of course, it is easy to say that you have to meditate devotedly, but actually to meditate devotedly may seem like climbing up Mount Everest. When you start meditating you have to feel that your very life, your very existence, your very breath, is an offering to the Inner Pilot within you. Each time you breathe in, try to offer your life-breath consciously to the Inner Pilot within you. Only in this way can you meditate devotedly and have a devoted feeling towards God.

Now, how to feel God's Will. During your meditation there comes a time when your mind is totally blank, absolutely calm and quiet. There is only purity, serenity and profundity in your mind. All this purity, serenity and profundity have one common face, which is called tranquillity. When tranquillity is with them, they are perfect. When the mind has become calm, quiet, tranquil and vacant, here inside your heart you will feel a twinge, or you will feel something very tiny, like a soft bubble. It is a tiny thing, but there in golden letters is written a message. Even if you keep your eyes closed, no harm. Sometimes the message is transferred from the heart to the head, and with your mind you can see that the message has come. But if you have the capacity to go deep within, you will see that the message has already been inscribed in the heart. Just because you cannot see the message there, it has to come to the physical mind to convince you.

Inside the heart's inmost recesses, where everything is flooded with purity, a message cannot be written by anybody other than God. There no hostile force, no undivine force, can enter. But this is not true about the mind. In the mind there can always be a mental hallucination, a fabrication, or some self-imposed truth that we have created. But in the very inmost recesses of our heart, no disturbing thought, no struggling thought, no strangling thought will ever dare to enter. For there it is well protected, well shielded by God Himself, because God's own wealth and treasure is there. He Himself is there as a soldier, a gatekeeper, guarding His treasure. If you get a message from the head, it does not mean that the message will be wrong. No! Sometimes you may get a genuine message which has come directly up from the heart, and sometimes you may get a message from elsewhere. It enters into your mind and you feel that it has come from God, but this is not the case.

When you meditate, please try to feel the necessity of opening your heart fully and closing your mind fully. What mind? The physical mind, which thinks of your near and dear ones, your friends, the rest of the world. When you bolt the door of your physical mind and open the door of your heart, at that time the mind becomes calm and quiet and the heart becomes all receptivity. When your concentration and meditation are focused on the heart and the heart is receptive, then naturally what the heart treasures — the message from God — will come to the fore and you will be able to read it and utilise it in your day-to-day life.

Now, it is one thing to hear the message of God correctly and another thing to listen to it and fulfil it. There are quite a few who hear God's message, but in their outer life they cannot execute it. For that, you need faith in yourself — faith that you are not just a child of God but a chosen child of God. Everybody is God's child, but everybody cannot be God's chosen child because everybody is not consciously aspiring. The chosen are those who really want God here and now, those who feel that they do not exist, cannot exist, without God. Just because you aspire sincerely, you can claim yourself as a chosen child of God. But please try to feel that it is not your own capacity, but God's capacity, God's Grace, that has enabled you to become His chosen child. There are millions of people on earth who are not aspiring. Why are you aspiring? It is because God wants you to aspire. When we say that God is most pleased with those who consciously aspire, it is true. But, at the same time, we have to know that this aspiration which they have has come and is coming from God. From the beginning to the end we have to feel the necessity of expressing our deepest gratitude to God, for He is our aspiration, He is our realisation. He is the aspiration in us and He is the realisation for us.

The soul's will is God's Will. The soul, which is the representative of God, is inside the heart. God's Concern is offered to the heart, and the heart offers it to the entire being. When we are aware of God's constant Concern, we will not make any mistake. When God's Concern becomes ours, we feel that God is the doer, God is the player, and we are the instrument. And God, being the Supreme Musician, will naturally play most divinely and supremely on us.

FW 57. *Did you see any basic differences in the quality of aspiration or the quality of the souls in different countries of the world? And do you feel that your trip was successful?*

Sri Chinmoy: Aspiration I noticed in all the places I visited, although some places naturally had more than others. On the inner plane each country, each city is aspiring according to its capacity, but on the outer plane we can observe slight differences. For example, in one city I saw tremendous determination even in the people who were not spiritually conscious or aspiring. There was tremendous determination on the physical plane and the vital plane. In another city, even though there was aspiration on the inner plane, on the outer plane there was tremendous chaos, confusion, uneasiness, uncertainty. Aspiration was there — each place has aspiration — but when it is a matter of manifestation on the outer plane, at one place the inner message is properly carried, and at another place it is not.

Also, the inhabitants of different cities tend to invoke spiritual Light in different ways. In one city I visited they invoke spiritual Light more through the mind than through the heart. They are invoking Light, praying and meditating, but through the mind. And there are places where the people invoke Light through the aspiring and dynamic vital and the physical. I also saw some fortunate cities where the majority of the people invoke Light through the psychic, the inner heart.

The first time I went to Europe, I entered into an unknown world. I knew nothing about Europe, and Europe knew nothing about me. The second time I went, the European countries saw something in me. This time, they saw something more in me. The atmosphere, the vibration, was more respectful and devoted than on my previous visits. I wish to say that I am the same man, with the same consciousness and the same boundless love, as I was two years ago. But when there are friends, admirers and devotees around, then the rest of the world gives more attention. So fortunately or unfortunately, now that I am a little well-known, people see more in me. In my case, however, my disciples and other seekers do not have to become well-known in order for me to see what they are. To me they are all instruments of God, divine instruments. From the very outset, the first time I see someone I see him as a divine instrument who will definitely work for God either with my dedicated assistance or under the guidance of some other spiritual Master.

Another thing I noticed is that the world is aspiring more and more. On the outer plane we see quarrelling, fighting and war, so we misunderstand. But on the inner plane, I see that these places have more aspiration and more determination than they did during my previous visits. Just because they are becoming more spiritual, more divine, they are seeing more in our path.

Sometimes we are inspired to run towards the goal because there are many others who are running, and this makes us feel that the goal has something to offer. And sometimes we go to the goal, not because others are running, but because we ourselves have the intense inner cry. Our inner cry has increased, our need for Love and Truth and Light has increased, and so we run towards the goal. So this time people have been attracted to our path for two reasons. One reason is that people have come to know about me through radio, television and newspaper articles, through Mahavishnu and Devadip, and through my writings. And the second reason is that the aspiration of all the disciples who follow my path devotedly and faithfully has definitely entered into the world atmosphere, and this helps the rest of the world to see something more in me. This is why we can say that my visit to Europe has been a tremendous success.

FW 58. *Your philosophy states that the soul is always making progress, but how do you reconcile that with the fact that when someone commits suicide his soul falls?*

Sri Chinmoy: When one commits suicide the soul of that person actually does not fall. But it remains at a particular place and is covered by infinitely more veils of ignorance. It is absolutely covered by ignorance — layer upon layer of ignorance. It is the consciousness of the individual that falls. It goes backwards right to the starting point, almost to the mineral consciousness where there is no evolution. The soul is eclipsed by teeming ignorance, that is to say by infinite layers of ignorance. Before, the soul had perhaps ten layers, but now it has countless layers of ignorance. The soul has to begin again removing them one by one. Of course, it becomes infinitely more difficult for the soul to carry the individual to perfect perfection, liberation or salvation. The consciousness descends so far that it goes back absolutely to the starting point. That starting point, you can say, is the mineral life, where there is no consciousness, no sense of evolution.

But if the Supreme wants to operate in a particular human being who has committed suicide, on very, very rare occasions, the Supreme asks the spiritual Masters, who have the capacity, to take care of that soul and not to allow it to be enveloped by teeming ignorance. In these cases, whatever the soul already has, is enough to bring the Grace and Compassion of the Supreme, and He will not allow a veil to cover the soul more than usual. But this is done only on very rare occasions. Otherwise, if a person commits suicide, evolution stops for that individual indefinitely — for one hundred, two hundred, five hundred, six hundred years or even more. He cannot go forward, and the heaviest possible load is placed on his shoulders. The process of his evolution stops. Because he has violated the laws of the cosmic game, he has to undergo the cosmic punishment. This punishment can never be imagined by any human being on earth. The worst possible earthly torture is simply nothing in comparison to the cosmic punishment the individual gets when he commits suicide. You cannot say to the cosmic forces, "I have done something wrong and it is none of your business. I shall reach my goal when I feel like reaching it." You have jumped out of the cosmic game intentionally, without God's permission and against His intention. He has not allowed you to leave the game, but you have actively and openly defied Him and tried to ruin the game. For this wrong action the punishment is most severe. This punishment is so intense that with our human heart we cannot feel it, with our human mind we cannot imagine it.

FW 59. *Different organisations like the United Nations or the government of a country have souls. I know that you feel that these different souls have different qualities. But is there something inherent in all of them that is unchangeable and the same?*

Sri Chinmoy: One thing that every soul has is consciousness. It is in this consciousness that we see the role of Peace, Light, Bliss and Power. There is no soul that does not have consciousness. But we have to see the consciousness within us. We have to see how it wants to manifest itself: with the help of Power or with the help of Light or Bliss or Peace. There will be some souls who would like to manifest themselves through Light, others through Bliss and still others through Power. But if you want to know the common characteristics that each soul has, then I wish to say that there is no soul that totally lacks consciousness. This consciousness is like a house. A man has to live in his house. He may fulfil himself by becoming an artist or an engineer or something else, but still he dwells inside the house. Likewise, the soul becomes all Light, all Power, all Bliss or all Peace just as a man adopts any profession he wants to adopt.

There are souls that do not want to function at all through Power. Again there are souls that do not want to function through Bliss. These souls prefer to function through Light or Peace or some other divine qualities. But all of them have consciousness. The unchanging, or unchangeable quality within every soul is consciousness. But at the same time, this consciousness can be expanded. It cannot be annihilated, but it can be expanded. In each individual consciousness it can be expanded. But if we enter into the Universal Consciousness then it becomes infinitely easier for us to transform the limited human consciousness. We are constantly dwelling in the human consciousness. Ordinarily it is impossible for us to enter into the Universal Consciousness. But if we meditate on the Universal Consciousness it can illumine and perfect our individual consciousness.

FW 60. *Many years ago, when people got certain diseases they would have died quite quickly. But medical science has developed medicines that allow people who have these diseases now to stay alive, although they are usually unable to function normally and have to remain in a hospital bed. If a person's life is prolonged by medicines in spite of the agony of the body, when it would have been given up at an earlier period of history, is there any spiritual benefit from it?*

Sri Chinmoy: From the spiritual point of view it is not a matter of how many years you stay on earth, but of how you utilise your time. Every second, every moment has to be considered of paramount importance. You can go to India and to other parts of the world and find people who have been enjoying sound health for, say, two hundred years. They are two hundred years old but have no aspiration at all. Last year when I went to India I saw a man who was, according to some people, three hundred years old, and according to others only two hundred. But when I entered into him I saw that he had no aspiration. Now, in the spiritual world, people who do not aspire are dead soldiers. Whether they stay on earth or leave is of no importance in the Eyes of God. This old man was just wasting his time on earth.

But if you are aspiring and in spite of your aspiration you are caught by ignorance-forces and have contracted some disease, if the medical science can be of help to you by prolonging your stay on earth, and at the same time if you can continue to invoke

Light from Above in order to continue your spiritual march, that is a great opportunity for you. If one is aspiring and making progress in the spiritual life, then if that person can stay even one second more on earth, it is a great blessing for him and also a great Joy for God. But if one is not aspiring, only wallowing in the pleasures of ignorance, and medical science enables that person to stay on earth for a number of years, then in God's Eye it is of no value. Only he who makes inner progress is of importance to God. If one stays on earth for two hundred or three hundred years, only killing time and not inspiring anybody else on earth, then he is a disgrace to God's cosmic evolution. But if a person is aspiring and hostile forces have attacked him, or if nature's law is causing him to suffer, and he has tremendous eagerness to do the right thing and to become the right thing, to please God and to fulfil mankind, then in his life on earth every second is of greatest value, not only for himself but also for God, and for humanity's life.

We have to know if the individual is aspiring or not. If he is a seeker, every second on earth is of paramount importance in God's Eye. If he is not, then he is a failure in God's Eye and he is a disgrace to aspiring humanity. If a person feels that just to stay on earth is enough for him, God may say, "All right. If that is your goal, you stay." But if somebody has a higher goal, if he has a real goal, God will give him the opportunity in every possible way to stay on earth and reach his goal. Otherwise, he has to come back again. Human life is like a constant battle. If you have been fighting for a long time and if you become too tired to continue, naturally you will go and take rest, and then enter into the battlefield again later. But if you do not become tired and if you do not have to go and take rest, then you will continue to fight against ignorance, against imperfection, for a long, long time, and perhaps you will win the battle once and for all. And once you conquer the undivine forces which are constantly attacking you, once you are successful, at that time you manifest God, the inner Divinity within you.

FW 61. *Guru, you said if we wish to serve the world we must have the proper attitude. Could you explain please what that attitude is.*

Sri Chinmoy: If we wish to work in the world and for the world, our attitude should be one of dedicated service. We have to feel that the rest of the world is ours, that everyone is a member of the same family. When the attitude of help comes into the picture, we become proud. When we help others, immediately we feel that we are superior to them. But if we take the attitude of service, if we remain in the ordinary consciousness we may feel that we are inferior to others; but if we remain in the divine consciousness, we feel that we have been given a golden opportunity to serve the vast world. Now this opportunity is given to us by the Inner Pilot, the Supreme who is within us and within everyone. So when we are working for others, we have to feel the Inner Pilot has given us the golden opportunity to serve Him in others.

If we are sincere and have the idea only of serving, and if we feel that somebody else could have been given this golden opportunity, then we become humble. Humility is not humiliation but rather the expansion of our consciousness. It is like this. The conscious Light that feels everything as one is in our heart. Now this Light comes and takes my hand as the instrument and says, "Touch your head." I touch it, and then the Light says, "Now touch your feet." But now I am unwilling, because I feel that this time I am becoming a slave whereas before, when I touched my head, I was the master. But when I know that my feet, my heart, my head are all one, I don't feel that it is beneath my dignity to touch my feet. Our attitude here should be the one of surrender, surrender to the command. So if we serve the world with the idea that the world is ours and we are part and parcel of the world, the question of superiority and inferiority can never arise.

We are asked to do something. Why is it that God has asked us and not somebody else? Because He feels that we have the inner surrender, the inner willingness, and we want to do it in a divine way. Now two persons can do something and their outer success will be the same; but their attitudes may totally differ. In God's Eye, the attitude is most important, not the so-called success. If we do something devotedly and unconditionally, then God feels that is a real success. If we achieve something by hook or by crook, by deceiving the world, we may get the success on the surface. But our conscience will torture us and then a day will come when everything will be exposed and we will become victim to both our own inner conscience and the outer public.

When we serve the world, we have to feel that we are not the doer, but that Somebody else is. We may not know Him, we may not see Him, but we can feel Him. God is nearer than our nose, nearer than our eyes, much nearer, but we don't have to see Him in order to know it. We have been sitting here meditating for half an hour; we may not have seen the golden Face of God, but we have felt something guiding and inspiring us. Hundreds of people are working at the United Nations, but why have just you people come here to meditate? It is because Someone has inspired you to do the right thing and to become the right person. And that Someone is God. If Somebody from within had not inspired you, then by this time you would have gone for your lunch break or left to mix with your friends.

Now others who are not paying attention to the spiritual life may be much greater than we are. In the eyes of the world greatness is determined by who has the authority, who has the power of autocracy; it depends on how much physical power or vital power or mental power one can wield. But in God's Eye, whoever wants to expand his heart's capacity, whoever has the heart's magnanimity, is really great. In God's Eye, greatness means goodness. Whoever is good becomes God's chosen son or chosen daughter.

In order to serve God in man and man in God, the first thing we have to do is pray and meditate. When we meditate, inside our meditation we will find the divine message or command, and we will also see how this order can be executed. If we discard prayer and meditation and become world-lovers, philanthropists, we are making a mistake. We will be like a human body without a backbone. No! First we have to become a God-lover, and then see humanity inside God. If through our meditation we see God and feel His Presence, then naturally we shall care for mankind. God is like the root of the cosmic tree. If we want to water the branches or the leaves and fruit, it is impossible; we have to water the base of the tree, the root. That is to say, we have to please God first and only in this way shall we be able to serve and fulfil mankind.

FW 62. *When one enters into the spiritual life, does the kundalini automatically arise, or does this only happen in certain people?*

Sri Chinmoy: There are various paths that lead to the Goal. Kundalini is one path that offers special power, but there are other paths which also offer similar powers. Let us say there are three roads leading towards the same destination. One road has quite a few trees and flowers, the second has a few trees and flowers and the third one does not have any at all. While walking the kundalini path, you see some power, but this power is definitely not the ultimate power. For those who have no spiritual or occult power, kundalini power seems very vast. But in comparison to the power that the Goal has, this power is nothing. Now on some other path, this kind of power is not there. The road is clear, and you just go and reach the Goal. Then once you reach the Goal, you get the omnipotent Power, whereas the follower of kundalini often just stays with his limited power. On very rare occasions have seekers fallen from the spiritual path because they have achieved spiritual power, but kundalini power, occult power, has taken many, many sincere seekers away from the Truth. Most of the time, kundalini power is a curse and not a blessing. If you misuse kundalini power, then you are ruined. You destroy all your possibilities to realise the Highest, and God knows how many incarnations it will take you to come back to the right path again. Now ninety-nine per cent of the time the kundalini power is misused. But if you properly use it, then you get inspiration to do something good for the world.

There are many spiritual Masters of the highest order who do not have kundalini power because they have not followed that path, but they have spiritual power which is much stronger. The real power, spiritual power, comes to the seeker in the process of his inner growth. Again, if God is pleased with a seeker who is following a different path, He can give the seeker a little bit of kundalini power. If He feels that the seeker may need kundalini power in the future in order to manifest Him in a specific way, then God sends some messenger who is working in kundalini to give that person power. All the different spiritual qualities are in God's room. If you enter into God's room, here you will see a box marked Peace, and others marked Light and Love and Delight and Power. Now you are only caring for Peace, but God feels that you may also need a little bit of Power. The world is such that if you don't show a little bit of power, people don't believe. So if God feels the necessity for Power in your life, even though you don't want kundalini power, God will give it. But if God does not feel any necessity, then even if you cry for kundalini power, He will not give it to you.

People start their spiritual journey with a good attitude; they care only for God, Truth, Light. But after walking for two or three or six months, they find that the path is very dry. They see that they are not getting name and fame or that they are not getting the miraculous power; so they give up and follow another path like kundalini. That path is easy because as soon as you get something, you can show all your miraculous power to the world and feel that you are something. But this power will never give you even an iota of peace of mind. First of all, you will be misunderstood by many because the use of occult power in no way elevates anybody's consciousness. Like a magician, you are showing something and it creates a kind of excitement that lasts for a few minutes or an hour. But then you and those who have become excited feel miserable because you know that this is not going to last forever, that there are higher truths and higher realities. You say, "We came into the world for peace, for love, for joy, for happiness, for satisfaction. Now is this the satisfaction that we want?" So you enter into the real spiritual life, where kundalini is not required. Here what is required is only an inner cry for Truth, Light and Bliss. Once you get Truth, Light and Bliss you won't care for kundalini power. It is just like a child who has five cents. He knows that he will be able to distribute those five cents to five children of his age. But when the child knows that his father has thousands of dollars, then he will not be interested in the five cents. So here, the thousands of dollars is the real spiritual power.

If you want to be satisfied with a little bit of kundalini power, meditate for a few hours daily, for six or seven years, which is nothing. In order to realise God it takes quite a few incarnations, unless you have a good spiritual Master. If you *only* concentrate on the *chakras* and meditate for kundalini, then as you complete your school course in fourteen or fifteen years, so also you will easily get kundalini power. And, if you are a very good student, you can skip a few grades and get kundalini power in just four or five or six years.

FW 63. *Can you give us some suggestions on how we might use in our jobs the Light, Joy, Bliss and other things that we receive in our meditation here?*

Sri Chinmoy: When you meditate here you do get something — either Peace or Light or Bliss, or some other divine qualities. These divine qualities are your treasure. When you want to buy something in the outer world you need money to buy it. You keep your money in your wallet and you use it whenever you want to. With your inner treasure, please try to feel that your wallet is your heart. When you meditate you earn money in the form of Peace, Light and Power — and you keep it in your heart. Do not feel that when you are here you get things and later, just because you are not meditating consciously, you no longer have any wealth. No! You work for eight hours a day for five days, and you get paid. This money you can use any time you want to. It is absolutely yours. Because you have prayed and meditated, you have earned this divine wealth. Now with ordinary money-power you buy things that you want. But with Light-power or Peace-power you try to conquer something instead of buying it. You conquer ignorance by inundating it with your inner Light and Peace. When you go to your office you have to associate with many people who are not aspiring at all. They have their own world, their own life. Now with your Peace, Light and Bliss you keep a solid, adamantine wall between yourself and these unaspiring people. On the outer plane you may be quite cordial, friendly and sympathetic, but on the inner plane you have to be very strong always. You have to remember that right now you are a tiny, fragile plant which can be easily destroyed. But you do have the power within you to create a protective barrier between yourself and your associates, a power to fight ignorance. This power, which is in the form of Peace, Light or Bliss, you get from your meditation here.

Now you must be constantly aware that you do have this inner power. If you do not feel it, then in spite of having it you will not be able to use it to solve your problems. You have money in your pocket, but if you forget that it is there, then naturally when you see something you want you will not be able to buy it. This very often happens. Even now we are all inseparably one with God, but we have forgotten. Only by practising meditation for years and years do we come to realise what it means to be inseparably one with God. People who have realised God say that God was always there within them but they had totally forgotten. All of us have divinity within us, but a spiritual Master has become conscious of it. We are praying and meditating in order to become conscious of the fact that inside us God exists. When you pray and meditate here, try to keep the experience that you get constantly alive inside you. You have something, but it is up to you to utilise it. If you do not use it, then after some time it loses its power. So when you meditate here you *do* get Power, Peace, Light and Bliss. Peace is power, Light is power, all divine qualities are power, power to stand against the ignorance of the outer world. So always try to remind yourself of the divine qualities that you achieve during your meditation and then you will see that it is quite easy to stand against ignorance. If you just remember the qualities that you have achieved, these very qualities will fight on your behalf against ignorance.

FW 64. *Can an individual have a feeling of insecurity because of a feeling of separation from God?*

Sri Chinmoy: We feel insecure in our outer life because we are not one with the rest of the world. When we feel our oneness with the rest of the world then we never feel insecure. Now what after all is this feeling of universal oneness, oneness with the rest of the world? It is the Consciousness of God, who is all-pervading and all-embracing.

An ordinary person may not think of God, but he immediately thinks of his brother, sister, friend, neighbour. Each human being appears to him as a stranger, someone alien and therefore unreal. He feels that only he exists. Others do not exist for him. The rest of the world is for someone else or for something else. But if he feels that the rest of the world is also for him and that there is no difference between his existence and the existence of others then his consciousness will immediately expand. There is only one existence. This One has become many, like a tree with many branches and many leaves, many flowers and many fruits. In the ordinary life, we immediately think of ourselves as individual entities. But if we can think of everyone as our very own, as part and parcel of our existence like the limbs of our body, then this problem of insecurity can be solved.

We feel insecure, we are bound to feel insecure as long as we do not feel the living Presence of God, as long as we feel that we are separated from our source, which is God. We feel insecure because we feel that our source is ignorance and that our ultimate destination is also ignorance. But if we can feel that we are not separated from God, but that God has sent us here to earth to be His instruments, then we shall not feel insecure. If we can feel that our source is Light and Delight, and that at the end of our soul's journey we shall return to that source, then we will not feel insecure.

We can feel that our source is God only when we aspire, pray and meditate. When we do not aspire, when we do not pray and meditate, we are bound to feel that our source is something unknown and unknowable. And this unknown and unknowable to us is ignorance. But the seeker who has launched into the spiritual path will feel that what is unknown today will become known tomorrow. Today his God is unknown but knowable. Tomorrow his God will be something known. The day after tomorrow his God will be at once the Knower and the Known.

When we know who the source is and who is piloting us all the time, we cannot be insecure. When we feel that we are responsible, that we are doing and must do everything, then we are insecure. But if we feel that there is a higher force guiding our destiny, and we are mere instruments, then we shall not feel insecure. When we feel that it is God's Will that we are cheerfully, soulfully and unconditionally executing, then how can there be any sense of insecurity?

FW 65. *What is our duty to our close ones living on earth and also to the ones in the other world? I think it is probably good to pray for them, but sometimes I feel close to someone and sometimes I feel a long distance away. Also, I have a feeling sometimes that people may be reincarnated.*

Sri Chinmoy: Here we are dealing with the feeling of oneness. Somebody may stay beside you for twenty-four hours, but you may not feel any sense of oneness. Here at the United Nations you have quite a few friends and colleagues. Every day you spend seven or eight hours with them, but when you go home they are totally forgotten, obliterated from your memory. On the other hand, while you are in the office with all these people, some sweet memory of your mother, who is in France, may be constantly knocking at your heart's door. Then you become like a boat, constantly plying between the shores of America and France. Why? It is because of your oneness: your constant inseparable oneness with your mother, which is making you feel her presence.

Similarly, the departed ones are on another shore. You are on this shore of life and they are on the other shore of life. If you are very advanced in the spiritual life, or if you are realised, you will always have a boat in which to go to the other shore at your sweet will and enjoy the company of your departed friends and relatives. And if they have come back to this shore, reincarnated in a different body, that also you will always be able to know. This entirely depends on your inner growth and inner achievement.

Now sometimes you feel that your departed dear ones are not close to you, and sometimes you feel that they are very close. Why? When the inner bond is not strong, you are bound to feel that there is something missing, something lacking, something imperfect in your connection with these loved ones. But if it is God's Will that you should keep a close connection with your dear ones who are on the other shore of the life-river, then you are bound to feel their living presence in your day-to-day life. If it is not His Will, then you have to feel that this connection is not at all necessary. Only the ones who are your brothers and sisters in the spiritual realm, here on earth, are really yours. The departed and dear ones were once also yours. God gave you the responsibility to think of some people, to help some people once, and now He has given you the responsibility to think of other people and to be of help and service to them. This does not mean that those departed souls do not exist in your life. They *do* exist, but the responsibility for them God has taken away from you. God has now given you a new responsibility, for new friends, for other souls who are on earth.

Again, you have every right, and it is a divine accomplishment if, during your meditation, you offer your goodwill to the departed ones. You may not know whether they are in Heaven or on earth. But if you offer your heart's goodwill and your soul's light, no matter where they are, whether in Heaven or on earth, they are bound to feel some light from somewhere. Their outer mind, if they have taken human incarnation, may not know that it is coming from you. But it is not at all necessary that they should know from whom it is coming. The only important thing is that something is coming. Who gives it is of no importance. Whether I bring down Peace and Light from Above, or whether your soul brings it down, or whether it descends of its own accord is of no importance. But whether Light enters into you from Above, and whether your inner being is surcharged with Light, is of paramount importance.

So offer your soul's light to your departed dear ones if you want to, but also feel that God has given you the supreme task of serving Him in those who are on earth, and that you should fulfil that task.

FW 66. *Now, I would very much like to learn something about what the spiritual heart is like, and what connection it has with the other* chakras *and with the Kundalini power. Also, how does the* ajna chakra, *the centre between the eyebrows, affect the spiritual heart?*

Sri Chinmoy: First of all, let us know the difference between the ordinary human heart and the spiritual heart.

The human heart is in the chest, a small muscle which the doctors can show us. The spiritual heart is something which a seeker sees, feels and grows into. The spiritual heart is vaster than the vastest. Right now Infinity is an imaginary concept for us. But when we discover our inner heart, our spiritual heart, Infinity is no longer imagination; it is reality.

The universe, the Universal Consciousness, the Eternal Consciousness, the Infinite Consciousness, Immortality, Divinity and so forth — where are they? They are all inside the spiritual heart. On the one hand this spiritual heart houses Divinity, Immortality, Eternity, Infinity; on the other hand it transcends everything. We use the term Transcendental Consciousness. Again, we speak of the ever-transcending Transcendental Consciousness. The Transcendental Consciousness, *turiya,* is the highest, but this Transcendental Consciousness is not static. It is also constantly being transcended. God is infinite, eternal and immortal. But all spiritual Masters know that God is also ever-progressing. God Himself is in the process of evolution. He is making progress, constant progress, in and through everyone, in order to establish perfect Perfection on earth.

When we think of the *chakras,* we think of them as being inside something — that is, inside the subtle body. *Sthula sharira* is the gross physical body. Inside this body is the *sukshma sharira,* the subtle body. And inside the subtle body is *karana sharira,* the causal body. These bodies are totally different, but they are all members of the same family. The subtle body at times operates through the physical. At times the causal body, which is in seed form, can operate in and through the subtle body and the physical body. Although the causal body is like a tiny seed, from this seed a banyan tree can grow. It takes a few years, but then the banyan tree bears thousands of fruits. The potentiality of the seed is infinite.

Mentally we will never know what Infinity is. It is all imagination. But there comes a time when imagination is transformed into reality. If somebody had once told me that there is somebody by the name of Sri Krishna Ganesan, until I had seen that person, he would have remained all imagination. But now I have seen you. Now you are a reality to me. According to the physical reality, you are perhaps 5'6" in height, but inside the physical reality is the inner reality — your teeming inner experiences. Some of these experiences are very high, very deep, and some are not. Again, some of these experiences are from this incarnation, and some are not. When I see the experiences only of this incarnation I see that you have had thousands of experiences. Now, who is holding these experiences? The soul or what we call the psychic being. In Sanskrit we call it *chaitya purusha*. This psychic being has gathered and kept the experiences of previous incarnations as well as of this one. The quintessence of all your previous incarnations has been preserved by the psychic being. Deep inside our existence, inside the soul, inside the psychic being, inside the mind, inside the vital, inside the gross physical, all these experiences are there. But when the doctors operate, or when they examine you, they cannot discover it, this inner wealth of yours. Why not? Just because this infinite inner wealth that you have can be seen only by something which is also infinite. Only Infinity can measure Infinity; only Light can measure Light. We may see something right in front of us, but in order to evaluate it we have to have something which is equally powerful or equally illumined.

Here the third eye comes into the picture. Let us say that the heart is Consciousness and the third eye is Light, although there is no actual difference between the two. The third eye or *ajna chakra* can annul or destroy the previous karma, it can expedite the present evolution, and it can bring to the fore the future wealth. The third eye has infinite Light, and at the same time *is* infinite Light; and the heart or *anahata chakra* possesses infinite Consciousness, and at the same time *is* infinite Consciousness. These two are eternal friends. Let us say that the infinite Light is a building, and inside it is the heart, which is the resident. But the next moment, the infinite Consciousness, which I am now calling the heart, can become the building, and the infinite Light, which I am now calling the third eye, will become the resident.

Like this they constantly change. Now, if the third eye is not fully open, the spiritual heart cannot function properly. That is why we try to open the third eye. Now, in order to open the third eye, this physical body must undergo some transformation. Purity must descend. We have to control the senses. We have to have infinite patience. We want to reach the Highest sooner than at once, but we cannot reach it by hook or by crook. We are crying for Infinity and Eternity, as a child cries for candy or milk. The Eternal Child in us is also crying, but we have to have infinite patience. Sri Ramakrishna used to cry every day to the Supreme Goddess, Kali: "O Mother, come! Come and stand in front of me." When the day had passed and the Mother had not come to him, he felt that the following day he would have to pray and meditate with more inner intensity. On the one hand, we must try our hardest to see our Beloved Supreme right in front of us; on the other hand, we have to feel that we are in the process of eternal time, and that we must have infinite patience. If we have infinite patience then the finite earthbound time expands itself into the infinite, or the infinite time enters into the finite.

God is omnipotent, not because He is larger than the largest but because this moment He can be the tiniest and most insignificant ant and the next moment He can be infinitely vaster than the ocean. Him we call God precisely because He can be whatever He wants to be: vaster than the vastest or tinier than the tiniest. *Anoraniyan mahato mahiyan....* The spiritual heart also has the same capacity. Although it is infinite, eternal and immortal, it can easily reside inside the gross physical heart. Again, it has the capacity to take the physical heart into its Vastness, into its Infinity, into its Eternity. At one moment the Infinite will separate itself from the finite; at the next moment it will welcome the finite into itself and become totally one with the finite. In the spiritual life, not only can the drop of water enter the ocean, but the ocean also has the capacity to enter into the tiny drop.

The spiritual heart is here *[in the chest]*, here *[in the forehead]*, everywhere. Because it is infinite, it pervades the entire universe. But although Consciousness and Light are inseparable, some spiritual Masters have seen Light before Consciousness, or Consciousness before Light. And the one which they see first, they feel is the Source of the other. It is like this. These two fingers are on the same hand. Suppose the name of this finger is Light and the name of this finger is Consciousness. If you see this one first then immediately you will say, "The Source is Light." And you will see that Consciousness itself is inside this Light. But if you have seen the Consciousness finger first, then you will say, "The Source is Consciousness." And you will see that Light is inside this Consciousness. Some spiritual Masters of the highest order see Consciousness first, while others see Light first. And depending on which they see first, they feel that the Source of everything is either Light or Consciousness. But a time comes when they see that both Light and Consciousness are inseparable. They go together, like the obverse and reverse of a coin. When I am buying something from you, if I give you a quarter, it does not matter which side is turned towards you. You accept it because you are sure that the other side is there, too. Whatever is required is there. So Light and Consciousness always go together.

Yes, we can separate them when we use our human knowledge, human wisdom. But when we use our divine wisdom, divine light, divine consciousness, we cannot separate the heart from the ajna chakra. They are complements, like husband and wife. We can say the third eye is the husband and the heart is the wife, since the heart usually is all sweetness and love, and the third eye is power and illumination-light. The wife's main quality is softness, kindness, while the husband's main quality is knowledge, wisdom and other mental things. But again, those who are very wise feel that the third eye is also the heart, for what else is the heart except that which gives us satisfaction? And what can give us satisfaction? Only Light! Only Light can give satisfaction. So if Light from the third eye gives us satisfaction, naturally we are dealing with the heart quality. What can give us a constant sense of wisdom? Wisdom comes only when we are deep inside the inmost recesses of our breath, inside our heart where Infinity, Eternity and Immortality play. To possess Infinity as our very own, to possess infinite Light and Bliss eternally as our very own — this is wisdom. So we can say that wisdom also comes from the heart. When we have the feeling of eternal wisdom, we feel that it comes from the heart. Like this the heart and third eye, the anahata chakra and the ajna chakra, go together. Like purusha and prakriti, God as the Father and God as the Mother, the heart and the third eye go together.

Now, about the connection of the heart with the chakras and the Kundalini power. There are six chakras. Starting at the base of the spine, they are: *muladhara, svadhisthana, manipura, anahata, vishuddha, ajna*. A seventh chakra, *sahasrara*, at the crown of the head, is not counted along with the other six, because it is not directly connected with them.

Kundalini power, you can say, is on the surface, absolutely on the surface of the spiritual heart. It is this way. On the surface of the sea are waves and all kinds of movement. When a child sees the waves of the ocean he is so fascinated. But an adult will try to go deep within the ocean to where there is quiet and calm, absolute tranquillity, for there he will get the greatest joy. The adult cares for the silent and eternal depths.

All the miracles that you may have heard of or may see are like the play of children in a garden. A child has the capacity to pick a flower or to pinch someone or to show how much strength he has by throwing a brick and doing all kinds of mischief. The

Cosmic Mother observes the games of her children. Like an ordinary mother, she enjoys having her children playing around her. "My children can jump, they can run, they can throw," she says. "Let us enjoy the game, this Cosmic Game." But the Father feels that the children cannot go on playing all the time. They have to study sometimes, or they will remain fools.

When a child is playing he is getting joy, physical joy. But when he studies he gets another kind of joy, a joy which is deeper and more fulfilling. On the physical plane when somebody achieves something we appreciate him. If somebody does something great on the mental plane, we appreciate that person more. When somebody achieves something on the psychic plane, those who are in a position to appreciate him appreciate him even more. And when somebody achieves something on the soul's plane, God's plane, those who know of it appreciate him most of all. Maharshi Ramana did not care for study; Sri Ramakrishna did not care for study. There are many spiritual Masters who did not care for study. But all the scholars of the Western world should go and touch the feet of these illiterate men of infinite Wisdom. The higher, the deeper we go, the more convincing, the more illumining, the more worthwhile is the wisdom we get. In the spiritual realm, Kundalini power is like the achievement on the physical plane.

A mother feels that even if her son is sixty years old, he is still her young child, her baby. But when a father sees that his son is thirteen or fourteen years old, he immediately tries to give the son all his wisdom. He says, "You cannot call yourself a child any more. Tomorrow I may die and you will have to replace me and take full responsibility for all my jobs." But the mother says, "No! No! No! I want my children to remain here with me." Now I am not saying a word against the Mother. Only it is the Mother's nature to regard Her sons as Her eternal children. The Father says, "Yes, you are eternal children, true, but you have to work for Me. You have to take the responsibility of the entire universe. Showing off and doing all these things is good for five years, ten years, twenty years, but it cannot last forever."

The son of God, Jesus Christ, was on earth for thirty-three years, and only during the last three years of his life did he perform miracles. But do you think the world still adores and worships him because he could walk on water or cure people or resurrect a dead man? No, it is not because of his miracles that he is still worshipped, but because he brought down the Eternal Consciousness, the Infinite Consciousness within him. Ramakrishna performed practically no miracles, and there were many, many spiritual Masters who did not do miracles. They felt that performing miracles on the physical plane would be like acting in the capacity of a child in comparison to what they were capable of doing on the spiritual plane, in the heart's region where infinite Peace, Light and Bliss abide.

The Father tells the child to go beyond the Cosmic Game. For it is only when one goes beyond the Cosmic Game that one will attain infinite Peace, Light and Bliss. The Father says, "You have to go beyond the Kundalini into a higher state of consciousness. First enter into the *sushupti,* the state of deep sleep. Then go into *swapna,* the dreaming state; then into *jagriti,* the waking state; and finally enter into *turiya,* the Transcendental Consciousness. And, My children, you can even go beyond that and remain in *sahaja samadhi,* a constant, spontaneous and dynamic oneness with Me on all planes of reality."

The same Mother, the same cosmic Divine Mother who holds all the Kundalini power, who is the Kundalini power, is far, far beyond it. With Her aspect of the ever-transcending Beyond, She is mixing with Her consort, Purusha, Shiva, or the Absolute. With Her ever-transcending Consciousness, She is one with the Absolute. Again, with Her playful consciousness, She is playing with Her children in Her Cosmic Game. Kundalini power, and all the miraculous powers on earth, are fleeting, for Kundalini power is an earthbound power. But the Power of the Self is infinite, the Power of the Transcendental Self is infinite and immortal. The most important thing on earth for a spiritual seeker is the realisation of the Self, the awakening of the consciousness, for this is eternal. If somebody comes here and performs some miracle, we will be fascinated. But the moment we go home there will be nothing to sustain our faith in it. It seems to be all magic and trickery. And how long can we cherish the magician inside us or before us? But when somebody lifts up our consciousness even for a second or we ourselves do it on the strength of our intense aspiration, our faith in that experience lasts, because it is our own experience, our inner experience. Anything that lasts forever we need. It is Immortality, inner Immortality that we need, and this comes through the awakening and elevation of our consciousness.

FW 67. *I would like to know the difference between prayer and meditation.*

Sri Chinmoy: The difference between prayer and meditation is this: prayer is something absolutely intense and upward-soaring, while meditation is wide and vast, expanding itself ultimately into the Infinite. When we pray, we feel a vibration from the sole of our feet to the crown of our head. Our whole being is praying, invoking, calling upwards. Where meditation is concerned, we throw ourselves into a vast expanse, into a sea of Peace, a sea of Delight, into Infinity; or we welcome the Infinite Vast into us.

In prayer, we feel a one-pointed flame rising and soaring upward. The very nature of prayer is to reach God by going up. Our entire existence is going up like a flame. Even if we pray to God for humanity, for the entire world, we will see that by the very nature of prayer, we are going up. Prayer is intense and ardent. It does not usually spread. But meditation does spread; in fact, it is immediate expansion. Meditation, like the wings of a bird, is always spreading, widening into Peace, Light and Delight. The entire universe of Light and Delight we see, feel and grow into when we meditate.

Whenever we pray there is a subtle desire or aspiration for something. We pray to become good, or to have something divine which we do not now have, or to be free from fear, danger, doubt and so on. There is the feeling of being — let us use the term — a divine beggar. We are praying because we need something. Even when we pray for Peace, Light and Bliss, there is still a certain feeling of demand. Sometimes there is a personal feeling of give-and-take and the prayer takes this form: "I am bringing my prayer to You, Lord. I am giving, Lord. So You please do something for me. You please save me, help me, fulfil me."

But in meditation we do not do that. We just allow ourselves consciously to enter into the effulgence of Light, or we invoke the Universal Light to transform our ignorance into wisdom. The aspirant who has become successful in his meditation, and has been able to enter into the deeper regions of Infinity or Eternity, does not pray the way we pray in churches or synagogues or temples. In his meditation, he enters into the divine consciousness and leaves everything in God's Hands. Here we see the true surrendering attitude. The seeker feels it is not necessary to ask God for anything, since his divine Father knows exactly what he needs and when to give it to him. He lets God do what is best for him, what will allow him to manifest God in God's own Way. In the deepest meditation, the seeker just enters into his own infinite aspect. He dives deep into what he already has: an inseparable oneness with his Eternal Father. Then it is his Father's business to do what is best for him or give him what is best for him.

Now I wish to say something which you Westerners may not like. According to strict Indian philosophy and Yoga, prayer is not on the same level as meditation. It is a lesser form of aspiration than meditation. Some yogis have stated that prayer is just a beginning for sincere seekers who aspire to later enter into deeper meditation.

For the real seeker, I must say that meditation is more important than prayer. But prayer is also of great importance. I will never say that prayer is not needed at all. Prayer *is* needed, but if one meditates, then it is easier to attain the universal Consciousness or the unlimited Consciousness. When one prays, he most often has a definite objective in mind. But when one meditates, he is encompassing and embracing the entire universe. One has to know what one wants from life. If one wants Infinity, Eternity and Immortality — infinite Peace, Light and Bliss — then meditation will be of greater and more immediate help.

FLAME-WAVES

BOOK 4

FW 68. *How would you define ultimate Truth?*

Sri Chinmoy: In the world of the mind, we feel if we can get our Ph.D. we will have the ultimate Truth in terms of outer knowledge. But when we actually get our Ph.D., if we are sincere, we feel it is just the beginning, a starting point for a vaster, more profound knowledge. If a person is sincere, even when he gets his degree he will feel that there are millions of things which he does not know even in the outer plane, not to speak of the inner plane.

Ultimate Truth we do not define, we cannot define. The ultimate Truth, like the ultimate Goal, is constantly going beyond its own height. As there is no end to our progress, no end to our achievement, so also there is no end to the ultimate Truth. What we achieve in our eternal Godward journey is the experience of the ever-transcending Truth.

The ultimate Truth is like God-realisation. The realisation of a Master who has been perfecting his realisation for several lifetimes on earth will be infinitely higher than that of a Master who has just attained his realisation yesterday.

In the spiritual life, the ultimate Truth or the ultimate Goal is only the farthest horizon of today's vision. As far as we can see, from where we stand, is the ultimate Truth for us, so we try to go there. But the closer we get to that Goal, the farther we can see beyond it. At first we think the ultimate Truth is to become inseparably one with God. But when we do become inseparably one with God, we see that we can go much farther if we want to. We have to become conscious and spiritual instruments, divine instruments of God. God-realisation is just the starting point for God-revelation, which takes us to a higher level. Then comes God-manifestation, which again can be infinitely expanded.

Today's ultimate Truth for a seeker can be the attainment of divine Peace, Light and Bliss. But when he gets these qualities in abundant measure he wants them in infinite measure. In infinity there is no boundary, only constant transcendence. In the spiritual life, the Ultimate is never a finality, a fixed place, because the inner urge is always to surpass and go beyond, beyond, beyond. The ultimate Truth of today is the starting point for another, higher ultimate Truth tomorrow. And the day after tomorrow that new Truth becomes a starting point for the realisation of a Truth still higher. This process is what is happening to God in His own Life. God created the world, and He Himself is evolving ever higher in and through us. In the process of evolution we cannot say what the end will be.

FW 69. *How can I acquire lasting inner joy?*

Sri Chinmoy: By constant, unconditional self-giving. Each time we give something of ourselves unconditionally, God immediately gives us in return something of His own. If we give to humanity what we have — just a little concern, just a little love — immediately something divine will spontaneously enter into us.

Suppose you give five dollars to a human being. Naturally you expect something in return, if only a smile or a "thank you" or some recognition. Give and take is the law of life on earth. In divine giving, you have to feel that your task is to give the person five dollars because you have received an inner command from within. As soon as you have given you feel that the transaction is complete, and then your role is over. That is the divine way of giving.

Now, inside that particular person there is someone, and that someone is God. In some way God will immediately give you joy by expanding your heart, your consciousness, your aspiration. But if you expect to get something from the other person, you are the real loser. God simply says, "All right, since you want to settle your own account, I don't want to be involved. You give him five dollars and he will give you something in return. The shopkeeper and the customer are there; it is a business deal. They don't need Me in their business." If you behave in this way you will never get real, abiding joy. Even if, after you do someone a favour, that person gives you back something in boundless measure, far beyond your imagination, still you will not get abiding joy. But if you just give what you feel from within, whether it is money or love or concern or anything that is yours, then a third person, God, will give you what He has. He will give you immediately His Love, His Pride, His boundless Peace, Light and Bliss.

Unfortunately, in today's world we do not do anything un-conditionally. We do not even meditate unconditionally for a minute. When we sit to meditate, we expect a little Light or a little joy. But are we beggars? We are related to the Supreme as a child is related to his father or mother. He is our Father, He is our Mother, He is everything to us. Now if He asks us inwardly to think of Him, to meditate on Him, we shall do it out of our boundless love for Him. The rest entirely depends on Him.

The moment we pray, we have to know that this capacity has come from God. The moment we meditate, we have to feel that this capacity has come directly from Him. If He has given us the capacity to pray and meditate, will He not also give us the capacity to receive His Light and Bliss? Giving is a form of capacity and receiving is also a form of capacity. He will automatically give us this capacity if we do not expect or demand anything from Him.

We make our lives miserable because of our expectations, either from relatives, from friends or from associates. Even when we expect something from ourselves, which we think we can legitimately expect, we are disappointed. Also, expectation ruins the divine nature of a selfless action. The moment we expect something from someone, we unconsciously or consciously push or pull ourselves beyond our capacity. Then we enter into terrible confusion. But if we love the reality and divinity in ourselves and in others, then the Supreme in that reality and divinity will give us much more than we expect.

No human being on earth can give us lasting joy; it is only the Supreme within us who can inundate us with lasting Peace and Bliss. No matter how many times I smile at you, no matter how popular you are with others, you will not get satisfactory joy. But if you play your role divinely, you will get gifts from the Supreme. And any gift from the Supreme's Light is bound to give you abiding joy.

The Supreme gives either from deep within us or through another individual. He does not have to appear in front of us in a most luminous form. No, He can give us this abiding joy in many ways. He may reward us in a personal way or in an impersonal way. We have simply to play our role, and the Supreme will offer us abiding joy in His own Way. We do not know what His Way is. So let us leave it up to Him to do as He pleases with us and for us.

FW 70. *I have had the experience that, when we try to help others, sometimes a kind of barrier builds up in ourselves and also in those we try to help. Could you speak about this.*

Sri Chinmoy: Our world still is not the ideal world. At times unconsciously, if not consciously, the world takes away some divine qualities from us. It is not that we do not want to share our divine qualities; but it is just that the world exploits and misuses them. So I feel that there are times when we have to be careful. We are generous. We have come into the world to aspire and, at the same time, to illumine the world. But we have to know who is worthy and who is unworthy. Just because we are all God's children it is very easy for us to feel that everybody in the world is worthy. But let us take it in this way: who is ready and who is not ready? Many times we have observed that there are some people who are not ready. When we try to awaken their consciousness, when we try to help them or serve the divine in them, their vital immediately feels a great resentment. And this resentment takes the form of a wall between them and, let us say, our searching mind or struggling, striving vital. Our searching mind has found some truth inside the heart, and it wants to offer this truth to others. Our vital is striving, divinely striving, to give them the light that we are entrusted with. But just because most people are not ready to receive, we feel that there is a strong, solid barrier between our realisation and our self-giving.

When we see a partition in ourselves, it means that we are not always one hundred per cent consciously one with our Source. We are of the divine and for the divine; we are of the Supreme and for the Supreme. But it happens many times that, even though we are very sincere and devoted, when we give we expect something in return: either recognition or progress in the persons we have served. Even if they do not recognise or acknowledge our self-giving, we immediately expect some success, or let us say, some kind of gradual progress or growth in their life of inner aspiration. We are giving, giving, giving; but if we do not notice the world receiving, then at times we are frustrated. We feel that earth does not deserve us. We may wonder if we are doing the right thing, since these people are not making any progress. We may even doubt our own sincerity.

But these thoughts are wrong. We are doing absolutely the right thing because we are inspired and commissioned from within. Earth will eventually receive our light, but right now earth is not ready. If the Supreme tells us that someone needs more sleep, that we shouldn't awaken him, then we shall not approach that particular person. But if the Supreme within us tells us that we have to serve the Supreme in someone even though that person is sleeping, even though he is unwilling and reluctant to receive our light, then we shall do that too, because we are His instruments. Every day we have to think of ourselves as a little child of five or six years old. If we are asked by our Eternal Father to offer something, then He Himself will tell us whom to offer it to.

The human heart sometimes makes us feel that it is so big that it is ready to help everyone. But this is absurd. There is something called God's Hour. God's Hour need not and cannot be the same for each and every person. Today it is my Hour, tomorrow it is yours, the day after it is time for somebody else. It is not that some people are bad, or that God does not like them. No! He loves all equally, but for some the hour has not yet dawned.

God is progressing in and through us. On the one hand He is Transcendental; He is all Divine and absolutely Supreme. On the other hand, at every moment He is progressing in and through that particular moment and through each individual life during that moment. In the finite, He is singing the song of Infinity, His own Infinity. Now, in the process of evolution, He is trying to perfect everybody. But He knows His own development best; He knows how much He wants to achieve in and through you today and how much He wants to achieve in and through me. We cannot expect the same kind of treatment or same kind of light for each individual, because God Himself has not created the same capacity and receptivity for everyone.

God is trying to divinely and supremely enjoy Himself. But if we try to increase somebody's capacity or receptivity by virtue of our own will, we are doing the wrong thing. Let us become God's Will; let His Will flow through us. And then He Himself will tell us who is the right person to help. In this way we shall go to the right person today and go tomorrow to someone else who will be the right person then. If we approach the right person timely, then we will see that there can be no barrier or partition, because the right person is always ready to receive us and welcome us. But if we go to the wrong person, he will not welcome us and there will be confusion; and in this confusion frustration will loom large. So, let us try to approach the right person at God's choice Hour, and then we will see that God is fulfilled, we are fulfilled and the world of aspiration is fulfilled in and through us.

Again, sometimes we feel a barrier or a wall in ourselves because at one moment we are identified with the soul and the next moment we are identified with the mind and vital. It is like this. The soul and the heart are one side, and the mind, vital and physical are the other side. Between them there is all the time a barrier. At this moment we call the mind the sole reality, the next moment we call the vital the only reality, and the following moment we regard the heart as the only reality. These are all realities, but the only real reality is God, and the direct representative of God's Reality is the soul.

Now, just as the soul is the representative of God, the heart is the representative of the soul. The heart and the soul are trying to perfect the mind so that it can represent the psychic being, the soul and the heart. Then, when the mind becomes illumined, the mind will have the vital as its representative. Similarly, the vital will have the body as its representative, and when the body becomes pure and the physical consciousness is aspiring, then the body also will become a perfect instrument.

Reality is a most complicated experience in ordinary earth life, but in the higher planes it is most simple and most fulfilling. When we enter into the lower plane, or the physical plane, there the reality is very uncertain. There the reality is just what we see with our own eyes. Let us say that we are seeing a flower, and that this flower is the reality for us. But as soon as we go a little deeper within, or come into a higher level of consciousness, we do not see the flower as such. The reality is no longer the flower, but the fragrance of the flower or the beauty of the flower. Here on the physical plane, the flower is the reality and the fragrance, which is the inner reality, we can't appreciate. And the beauty, which is still higher, we do not notice at all. So the thing that is reality on the physical plane need not and cannot be the same kind of reality on the inner plane.

Again, there are many things which we see on the physical plane as real which are absolutely unreal. When a thought comes from the mental world, in our everyday life it is absolutely real and concrete for us. But when we go deep within, immediately the thought vanishes; like a drop, it melts into the ocean of the Will. So what is a reality on the physical plane, such as a thought, is not at all a reality on the inner plane. On the inner plane, the reality is Divinity, Immortality and Perfection. On the outer plane, things that are real to us may not or need not be eternal. But on the inner plane, only what is eternal and fulfilling is real. So there is a great difference between reality on the physical plane and reality on the inner plane.

The outer world has a very mighty weapon, doubt; and the inner world has a most powerful weapon, faith. If we remain in the outer world more than the inner world, its doubt-weapon attacks us. Even though our own existence and our own powerful faith-weapon are inseparable, when we live in the outer world doubt fights against our faith and weakens us.

Now when we feel a barrier between one reality and another reality, between our mind-reality and our heart-reality or be-tween what we have to offer and what we try to give, our spiritual life becomes a barren desert. Not only seekers, but almost all spiritual Masters have gone through this barren desert. Even spiritual Masters of a very high order, like Vivekananda and others, used to confess that they went through periods when they could not meditate at all. They entered into the world arena and offered their Peace, Love, Light and everything they could. But then they felt a kind of frustration because their Light was not accepted and the progress they expected from humanity was not achieved.

Here we are all seekers. If we find ourselves in a barren desert, if we find that multifarious thoughts or ideas are entering into us and making it impossible for us to meditate, we can do one thing. We can offer our gratitude to the Supreme, to the Inner Pilot. We can offer one minute of soulful gratitude that the Supreme has given us the divine aspiration to be of service to mankind, to the Supreme in mankind. If, even for a fleeting minute, we can offer Him our soulful gratitude, then immediately the barrier that exists between the mind and the heart in our inner being disappears. For the power of our gratitude immediately makes us one with God's Reality. And there is no power either on earth or in our inner existence which can ever be as powerful as our soulful gratitude.

When we look for the word "gratitude" in the mind, it is something dry, silly and unnecessary. When we look for the word "gratitude" in the vital, immediately we see that the word does not even exist. And in the physical, gratitude is all the time dormant. But if we live in the aspiring heart and can become one with the Supreme on the strength of our gratitude, then there can be no dry periods; there can be no wall, no barrier, no undivine forces that delay our progress. When we have gratitude, we are like a flower that petal by petal is blossoming in the Heart of the Supreme. This flower is full of fragrance, and its fragrance constantly illumines, energises and fulfils the human in us, the divine in us and the Supreme in us.

When our gratitude-flower blossoms, the dormant, sleeping humanity also begins to blossom, because our gratitude will have entered into God's choice Hour. When we enter into God's Heart with our gratitude, He expedites His own Hour for His children, for He feels that some of His children are more than ready to serve and please Him in His other children who are still sleeping.

Everybody cannot be a chosen instrument. Everybody cannot play the role of a king, true. But everybody can serve God according to his own capacity. When God has given someone the capacity to illumine others, to serve Him in others in abundant measure, it is that person's duty to clear the way if there is any obstruction, if there is any thorn on the road. And we can easily free the rose from the thorn when we see gratitude growing inside our heart.

The Supreme has made you the chosen instrument to illumine and increase the aspiration of hundreds and thousands of people. If you play your role as a conscious instrument, then in your conscious awareness you become a river that is flowing with all its light, love and dynamic energy towards the sea of Enlightenment. When you and the rest of humanity have become one, and when you enjoy this oneness divinely, there can be no partition, no barrier, no desert. It is all ever-increasing Bliss and ever-transcending Freedom.

FW 71. *How can we remain unaffected by other people's undivine consciousness without cutting ourselves off from them?*

Sri Chinmoy: In order to be unaffected by the undivine consciousness of others you have to surcharge your body, vital, mind and heart with peace and purity. Peace and purity go together. The more peace you have within you, the more purity you will have, and the more purity you have, the more peace you will have.

When you have peace and purity, at that time you will not be affected by others.

Now, you don't want to be affected by other persons' undivine consciousness and, at the same time, you don't want to cut off all connection with them, you would like to be of some help to them. What you have to do is try to feel that you are standing on the bank of a river. The others are drowning in the river, and you are offering them your hand to catch hold of. But in order to be of help, you yourself have to remain all the time safe. If you jump into the river to save them, then you also will drown.

So first you have to concern yourself with your own salvation, your own protection. First you have to make yourself very strong, very powerful inwardly, and only then can you try to help others. If you have a big heart and want to help others and give them some inner light, but if you are not strong enough, then you are making a deplorable mistake. Not only will you fail to help them, but you will also lose what little inner light you have and end up in the same position they are in. In a school, if a teacher knows a little more than a student, he can teach. If someone has finished high school, he can easily teach the kindergarten class, because his knowledge is much greater than that of his students. But the spiritual life unfortunately is not like that. In the spiritual life, if one is only an inch higher than somebody else in terms of inner awakening, or if one has only a few drops more of inner Peace, Light and Bliss, then that person should not try to help the other person. If he does so, the other person's ignorance will literally devour him. Suppose you have five drops of spiritual consciousness, or fifty drops or five hundred or five thousand drops, and the other person does not have a single drop. Still, you have to know that he has something else; he has five million drops of poison. So you have to be very careful. If the other person has many undivine qualities, then your little drop of love or joy or peace or bliss will be of no help to him at all. And worse, you will be devoured by his sea of poison and of ignorance. So the best thing is to make yourself as powerful and strong as possible. Then, no matter who is around you or wherever you are, you will be in a position to offer your light without being affected. That is the right way.

FW 72. *If our fulfilment lies in our utter consecration to the life divine, could you say something about consecration.*

Sri Chinmoy: In the divine life, consecration is fulfilment; but this fulfilment is not the fulfilment of the vital. Let us say you have achieved something or you are successful in a particular field of life. This is a kind of fulfilment. But this fulfilment we regard as success and not as progress. Consecration means an upward journey, or inward journey or forward journey. Each time we consecrate our body, mind, heart and soul to a higher or inner cause, we are proceeding forward; we are climbing upward and diving inward. And this movement is continuous progress.

Consecration is self-giving. To whom? To the divine in us, to the divine in others. It is through self-giving that we eventually become God-like. So let us consecrate our existence, our divinity, our inner cry, our good qualities to the divine in others. Each human being houses a few good qualities and a few bad qualities. If we offer our own good qualities to the good qualities of others, they become most powerful. Then it is like two persons in a tug-of-war against ignorance; in this case, naturally the divine shall win. This is the correct and safe way to transform ignorance and change the face of the world. But if we consecrate ourselves to the undivine, to our undivine vital or mind or to somebody else's, then our own divinity enters into the undivine and increases the power of the undivine.

If, out of pity or compassion, we say, "Oh, what is the use of dealing with the divine, for it is always divine. Let us deal with the undivine, for it is the undivine that needs change," then we have to be very careful. When we consecrate our existence to ignorance with a view to transforming it, we have to know whether or not our power is sufficient. Our power is like an army, a divine army fighting an undivine army. Now, if our power is not strong enough, the divine army will lose and become the slave of the undivine army. When we lose to ignorance, ignorance utilises us for its own purpose to destroy the whole world. So if we consecrate our spiritual life to transforming the undivine, if we lose in the battlefield of life, then we will become true soldiers of the undivine forces. So if we are not powerful enough alone to transform someone else's ignorance, then let us side with the divine of that individual and together conquer ignorance. But if we are very powerful, very strong, then we can accept the challenge of the undivine forces, for we know we can defeat them. And once we conquer ignorance, we try to change its existence and essence so that it, too, can become a perfect instrument of the divine.

FW 73. *Is there any way that we can meditate specifically to help the United Nations?*

Sri Chinmoy: Inside your heart there is the soul, the direct representative of God. You feel that when the soul comes to the fore, you will have abiding satisfaction from life; that is why you pray and meditate every day. So when you meditate here at the United Nations, please feel that inside the body of the United Nations, this building, there is a soul — most powerful, most illumining and most fulfilling — which has to come forward. If you can feel the presence of the soul of the United Nations, then your meditation will be most helpful.

There are many, many who are not present here today to meditate with us. But when they work for the United Nations most devotedly and selflessly, they are doing their meditation in their own way. The soul of the United Nations blesses these people and offers them its gratitude.

All those who are working at the United Nations are unconsciously being illumined by the soul of the United Nations. And all those who are aspiring in their own way are deriving special blessings from the soul of the United Nations.

The soul of the United Nations embodies the dream of the United Nations: peace, brotherhood and oneness founded upon self-giving and the recognition of universality in the heart of each individual. If you can cultivate these sublime ideas or ideals during your meditation, you will most effectively and most fruitfully help the soul of the United Nations. In this way, the soul of the United Nations, and eventually the body which houses the soul, will find their true significance.

The United Nations is a world-wide organisation. During your meditation, if you can concentrate on the seed, which is the soul, then in the course of time this seed will grow into a plant and eventually into a huge tree which will serve and shelter the entire world. The soul embodies, in essence, the infinite capacity of the Supreme. If we can bring to the fore the capacities of the soul, on the strength of our sincere, dedicated, devoted and soulful meditation, we will serve the United Nations most fruitfully in the way the Supreme wants us to serve and fulfil it.

FW 74. *How do you eradicate negativities and imperfections in the soul?*

Sri Chinmoy: There is no negativity in the soul. The soul is all divinity and perfection. The soul is our divine, immortal existence on earth; its source is Light. The soul carries the message of perfection within us.

We feel that whatever is inside our heart is the soul, but this is not true. Inside our heart is the vital as well, and inside the vital is a lower vital, an aggressive vital, a destructive vital. Since we are not aware of the presence of the soul, whatever we feel inside our body, vital and mind we take as the soul. There are many wrong, undivine tendencies and movements within us, but these have nothing to do with the soul. What we should actually feel is that these are enemies that have entered into our living room. We wanted to have only our friends, but in an unguarded moment we opened the door and at that time our enemies entered. These enemies we have to either transform or throw out. We cannot stay with them unless we can transform them into our true friends.

How can we do this? We do it through conscious and continuous effort. When we want to learn something, we practise or study for hours and hours. Similarly, if we want to be perfect in our life of aspiration, then we have to pray and meditate. When our prayer goes up, it reaches the highest Height. And when we meditate most soulfully, Peace, Light and Bliss descend into us in abundant measure. If we want to know how we can perfect our nature, then we have to bring to the fore the presence of the soul. Then these wrong forces within us are automatically illumined and perfected.

FW 75. *About two weeks ago, a Hatha Yoga Master came to the United Nations and said that first you must conquer and overcome the body and only then can the Supreme be manifested. What are your feelings about this?*

Sri Chinmoy: It is true that the body has to be a perfect instrument of the spirit. But we have to know that for the body to be a perfect instrument, it need not be a perfect body. The world's best athletes, the world's strongest men, are not necessarily manifesting the divine Will unless they are conscious instruments. God only knows when these people will accept the spiritual life. So physical perfection does not indicate receptivity to the spiritual message or the light of the spirit. The message of the spirit, the message of the soul, our heart's inner cry for God, for Truth, for Light — these things are not connected at all with bodily strength. We become aware of our inner, spiritual life only through prayer and meditation.

If you compare the physical strength of any of the world's greatest spiritual Masters with the physical strength of the world's great boxers or wrestlers, the spiritual Masters are nowhere. But if any of these Masters were to challenge a fighter with his spiritual strength, inner strength, soul's strength, then that fighter would be compelled to surrender. If the Master used his occult power or spiritual power, he could immediately take away the life-energy of the fighter. This has happened in India many times. If somebody mocked at a spiritual Master's occult and spiritual power, in the twinkling of an eye the Master would make that person so weak and lifeless that he could not even lift up a pencil. In India many years ago, a great wrestler was swimming in the Ganges alongside a spiritual Master. The wrestler was tormenting the Master, pushing him under the water and in every way trying to drown him. Finally, the spiritual Master said, "Now you have played your role. Let me see you lift up your arms." Then he used his occult power and the wrestler who had been bothering him for about twenty minutes could not even move his arms. He would have drowned if the spiritual Master had not released him. So physical strength in comparison to spiritual strength is nothing, absolutely nothing.

If our body is strong enough and healthy enough to perform its natural functions, and if it is capable of sitting quietly for two hours or three hours without any difficulty or unusual discomfort, that is more than enough. The body has to be a fit instrument, but that does not mean we have to become the strongest or most powerful of men. It is sufficient to have the amount of strength that our body requires in order to stay on earth and play our God-ordained role efficiently. The body needs strength so that it can receive and manifest the message of the spirit. If matter is not strong or receptive, then how can the message of the spirit be manifested in the physical?

Suppose we want to meditate in the morning. If we are physically weak, if we have a stomach ache or headache or some other ailment, then how will we meditate well? That is why we have to give due importance to the body. But due importance does not mean extravagant concern. Early every morning if we exercise for fifteen minutes or so, and if we have a proper diet, that is sufficient. Western exercises are all right, but if we do Indian exercises, *asanas,* we get a kind of relaxation that helps in meditation. But one can become expert in the Indian system of exercises without attaining any spiritual advantage. There are hundreds of Indian villagers who can do these exercises, but how many incarnations will it take before they even begin to accept the spiritual life?

I do not deny the role of the body. But you have to know how much you can expect from the body. If this body is five-feet-eight, then it will remain five-feet-eight no matter how hard I try to make it taller. A runner may reduce his time if he practises, but eventually he will reach his maximum speed. The body's capacity is always limited. Its height, its strength, its speed all have a point beyond which they cannot develop. And, after many years, these capacities will gradually decrease. But as long as we continue to pray and meditate, our inner capacities will go on increasing until we grow into something infinite and boundless. Our inner power, inner light, inner wealth have no limit. There is no boundary for the soul within us. Peace, Light and Bliss can be increased in infinite measure. So eternal progress, infinite Peace, Light and Bliss are what we can expect from the spiritual life, whereas temporary fitness is all we can expect from Hatha Yoga or any other form of physical culture, no matter how faithfully and devotedly it is pursued.

FW 76. *Last week you mentioned something about wrestlers and people who are engaged in physical activities, saying that competition on the physical level is not what we are after. Do you feel that people who are professional wrestlers and boxers do not have a place in society?*

Sri Chinmoy: They do have a place in society, according to their own development. In God's creation everything is necessary. A boxer is necessary, a wrestler is necessary. If you are attacked by an undivine person and if a boxer happens to be nearby, the boxer can easily come to your rescue. There is a special time and place for the use of physical strength. But if somebody says that tremendous physical strength will help you to aspire more, that is not true. In fact, those who are deeply involved in training the physical body are usually too preoccupied with the physical to pay proper attention to the spiritual.

Physical strength as such is not bad, but it is very often misused. If someone has more physical strength than somebody else, the stronger person will usually try to dominate the weaker one. This tendency is not at all spiritual. Boxers and wrestlers may be very kind-hearted and most devoted to their friends and to the members of their families. But if they want to use their physical strength undivinely, they can destroy the whole family in a minute. Our highest aim is to become spiritually great, inwardly great, to embody Peace, Light and Truth in infinite measure. For this we do not have to be the strongest person on earth. We only have to know how to aspire. While aspiring we have to keep this physical body in good condition so that we can meditate well.

In the spiritual life we do not dislike anybody. But we have to be very careful about the bad qualities which people embody. So we do not dislike the person; we dislike his undivine qualities. Somebody may have many good qualities and many bad qualities. If we hate or dislike a person, because of a few undivine qualities, then we are not allowing him to increase his divine qualities. But if we love him, all his good qualities will come to the fore, and these good qualities can be utilised for a divine purpose.

FW 77. *What role does the vital being play in our spiritual progress?*

Sri Chinmoy: First, there is not just one vital being. Each person can have four, five, six or more. When I speak of the vital being, I am generally speaking of the main vital being in a person. If the vital being does not aspire, then it tries to devour the good qualities of others. Also, at times it becomes very jealous of the achievement of the mental being. There is also more than one mental being in each person. But there is one principal mental being, as there is one main vital being. But if the vital is aspiring, if there is an integral sincerity in one's aspiration, then the vital being helps the mental and physical beings.

The mental being cares for light. The vital being cares for power. The physical being cares for manifestation. And the heart, the psychic being, cares for total perfection. If the entire existence of the seeker wants God, then the vital, instead of trying to devour or suppress the mental brilliance and good mental qualities, will use its strength to try to help the mental being. The process is something like this: when the mental being is doing something, the vital being comes and says, "Can I be of any use?" The other being immediately says, "Yes, I need this or that to enter into higher illumination." Then immediately the vital being plays its role. In the same way, the mental being will use its capacities to try to help the psychic being. But this only happens when the seeker aspires in an integral way.

The vital being is like a knife. A knife can be of immense help to us when we want to cut something. But the same knife can be used to stab somebody, too. So if the vital being cares for light, it can be of great help. But if it does not care for light, then it will always act like a hungry wolf. If it wants to, the vital being can spread its wings and shelter the physical being. But also it can simply destroy one's physical and mental possibilities. But if there is aspiration in the physical being, in the vital being and in the mental being, these beings will never try to destroy each other or be jealous of one another's achievements. On the contrary, they will act like a most harmonious family. A seeker will never be able to realise the highest Truth unless and until he has achieved harmony among his physical, vital, mental and psychic beings. These beings have to establish a divine harmony before the seeker can realise the Ultimate Truth.

FW 78. *How can we more fully surrender to the Supreme?*

Sri Chinmoy: The easiest and most effective way to make our full surrender to the Will of the Supreme is to increase our necessity for Him. In this world, when we feel the necessity of something, immediately we surrender to that necessity. If you feel the necessity of money or material power, what do you do? You surrender to the necessities involved in getting and keeping a good job; you surrender to your boss. If you want to be a good singer, you surrender to the wisdom and capacity of your teacher because you feel that he is superior to you and will be able to show you how to attain your goal. By surrendering to a real authority, we can learn how to achieve our necessities.

Now, the higher authority within us is the Supreme. How do we surrender to Him? First, we must feel the necessity of oneness. When we feel the necessity of inseparable oneness with the Supreme, immediately we offer our will to His Will. Next, we must ask ourselves if we want this oneness to be constant. If it is not constant, at one moment we are inseparable, and the next moment we will be totally separated from Him. This moment if the Supreme says, "Go and sit down," we will go and sit down. But the next moment we may refuse. We will go and mix with our friends who do not care for the spiritual life at all. At that time, something else becomes our necessity. Our necessity will be to go to the movies or to a party or a dance. When we become one with this undivine necessity, we will see how far we go from the spiritual life. Only if our necessity for oneness with the Supreme becomes unconditional and constant will we be with Him, in Him, of Him and for Him twenty-four hours of every day.

Right now you want to be spiritual. You want to be totally dedicated to the Will of the Supreme, so you have come here to meditate. But you may not be able to meditate as deeply and soulfully all day as you have just done here. However, if you can remember what happened here, how devotedly you prayed to the Supreme, this memory will help you. Here we have been doing dynamic, soulful meditation. But while you are working in the office or talking to your boss or your colleagues, if you can remember what you have done here for an hour, that will give you tremendous inner strength and confidence.

The difficulty is that at the time of our meditation we become totally sincere and cry to become one with the Will of the Supreme, but the moment we come out of meditation we are a totally different person. When we come out of meditation, we identify ourselves with the outer activities of life, and we feel that from them we will get satisfaction. But we will get satisfaction from our outer activities only when we can place our spirituality inside our heart.

When you go back to the office, you have to think of office activities, because if you think all the time of what is happening with your friends and family, your work will not be satisfactory and the boss will fire you. But these thoughts are all on the mental plane. On the inner plane, on the psychic plane, you can think of God to your heart's content. If you have a large amount of money inside your pocket, nobody is going to see that it is there. Similarly, if you keep the presence, the Light, the Peace which you felt during your meditation inside your heart, nobody will know what wealth you are hiding there. And although it is quite possible for someone to snatch away your money from your pocket, from the heart-pocket no thief can steal away anything.

So when you meditate, please feel that you have stored up a divine treasure trove inside your heart. This treasure is Light, Peace, Bliss and the presence of God which you have felt. If you can establish a permanent feeling of God's presence inside your heart, then it is not at all difficult to listen to the dictates of the Supreme, to become one with the Will of the Supreme all the time. Even when you talk and mix with people and enter into all kinds of activities, you will not lose your oneness with the Supreme. It is not only possible and practicable to do this, but it is inevitable for each seeker, in the course of time.

FW 79. *When we meditate, to what extent do we represent and are we responsible for humanity and the world?*

Sri Chinmoy: We are all seekers here, but unfortunately our level of consciousness is not the same. Each one has his own level of consciousness. If someone's consciousness is large and illumined, then he feels that he is representing a large section of humanity. If someone has a very vast and fully illumined consciousness, he feels that he alone represents the whole of humanity, and not only earth-consciousness, but also Heaven-Blessing. He feels that he is the supremely chosen instrument of God and has to be fully responsible for earth-transformation and earth-perfection. The higher one goes, the more responsible he is, or feels he is, for the upliftment of human consciousness. God is responsible for everything and we are just His instruments. But if we become conscious and chosen instruments, then He can act in and through us most perfectly.

Each seeker has to feel how high he has gone, how deep he has gone and how illumined or how fulfilling his consciousness is. If he feels that he has already achieved an all-embracing consciousness, then he feels that he is entirely responsible for the total change and transformation of human consciousness. He is like a mother; when her child does something wrong, the mother sincerely feels that she is responsible for the child's misdeeds. And when the child does something good, the mother feels in the inmost recesses of her heart that the child was able to achieve this success because he is her own creation.

If we can claim the length and the breadth of the world as our very own — not with our vital ego, but with our heart's feeling of oneness — if we have accepted the world with a feeling of inseparable oneness, then we are absolute representatives of earth and, at the same time, absolute representatives of God as well. In our oneness with earth we feel that we are embodying earth's aspiration and in our oneness with Heaven we feel that we are embodying God's Compassion and God's Light. We ascend with our aspiration and we descend with God's Compassion and Light. So, we are not only representatives of both Heaven and earth, but also we are the connecting link between Heaven's Light and earth's aspiration. When do we become the connecting link? We become the connecting link when we feel that we are working unconditionally for both earth and Heaven — when we feel that it is our bounden duty to please Heaven, but do not expect anything from Heaven in return, and when we feel it is our bounden duty to please earth, but do not expect anything in return from earth.

It is we who have to unify both earth and Heaven; this is our task. We have seen something in Heaven and we feel that this very thing is what earth needs; therefore, we have to offer that thing to earth. Again, we have seen something on earth which we feel is precisely what Heaven needs. So earth's achievement we offer to Heaven and Heaven's achievement we offer to earth. How do we do it? On the strength of our inseparable oneness with the one from whom we are receiving and with the one to whom we are offering the wealth. So, according to the extent of our oneness, we are representing humanity and divinity.

The moment we identify ourselves with something or some-one, we become that particular thing or person. If we identify ourselves with the universal Consciousness or the Absolute Supreme, we will feel inside them both earth and Heaven. When Christ said, "I and my Father are one," he became totally one with his Father. As an individual, I say, "I and my body are one." The necessity of the body, the consciousness of the body, the physical consciousness, I feel as my own. I identify myself with my hunger, with my earthly need, with earthly name and fame. But when I am illumined I do not say, "I and my body are one." I say, "I and my Inner Pilot are one." I am the instrument and my Inner Pilot is directing and guiding me. I and my Pilot are one; I am His vehicle and channel. It is through me, out of His infinite Bounty, that He is fulfilling His own Dream.

FW 80. *I have just started coming to your meetings and I would like to know how to meditate. I really don't know exactly what you mean by meditating.*

Sri Chinmoy: Some spiritual teachers give specific lessons on meditation. In my case, I tell my students to first read spiritual books written by spiritual Masters to gain a little general information. The books will tell you to keep the mind calm and quiet and lead a pure life in the mental, vital and physical plane. In our pure life automatically we feel an inner meditation. And if we remain calm and quiet, it is also a form of real meditation. We are constantly being attacked by ideas, by forces, by thoughts. But we should try not to allow these thoughts to enter into our minds in our day-to-day lives. Some people may think that if they do not have any thoughts, they will be like fools. But fools are not without thought; they have thoughts, but thoughts that we cannot appreciate or admire. These thoughts lead them to do silly things. But if we do not have normal, ordinary thoughts, but instead have inner will and determination, then we will do the right thing and we will grow into divine instruments. That is a form of meditation.

When my students meditate with me, I tell them to forget the mind and try to feel the presence of the heart. Inside the heart they try to feel a vessel. This vessel is full to the brim with ignorance, imperfection and undivine things. I ask my students to try to empty the vessel with God's help and their own aspiration. This action of emptying oneself has to be done with devotion and a feeling of surrender to God's Will. It also has to be done with love — love for God and for humanity. Once the vessel is emptied, then the God inside them will fill it with divine Light.

FW 81. *Could you speak about the need for individuals to defend themselves?*

Sri Chinmoy: Before you defend yourself you have to know whether you have done the right thing or not. If you have done something wrong, it will be a mistake to try to defend and justify yourself. If you have done something wrong, you have to pray for forgiveness to the Supreme in the individual who has been the victim of your wrong action. But if you are doing something right and if you are misunderstood or criticised or attacked, then you will try to defend yourself. If you are attacked, you should always try to be calm, quiet and tranquil within. Peace is the greatest strength; if you have inner peace, then you have a lion's strength.

Since you follow the spiritual life and are devoted to Love, Truth and God, you will not exploit anybody. But if somebody wants to exploit you or harm you in any way, you have to protect yourself. Spirituality is not the same thing as stupidity. You have to be wise. There is no wisdom in surrendering to circumstances and saying, "I am helpless, what can I do?" There is no wisdom in remaining silent and waiting for the person who is harming you to reap the karma of his action if you yourself have the power to take action. How do you know that God wants you to give that person an opportunity to continue committing wrong acts? That person has deceived you or done something harmful to you, and God has awakened you so that you are aware of it. So it is your bounden duty to defend yourself.

This is called a sincere approach to reality. If you remain silent, the other person will go on exploiting you. His ignorance will increase and he will never open to the Light, and he will not give you a chance to open to the Light either. You will be continually at his mercy, and your own sense of justice will disappear.

To be sincere is to defend one's inner cause. To be sincere is to breathe in divine qualities and breathe out undivine qualities. To be sincere is to see the truth as it is, on its own level, and to utilise the truth in its own way. When a new divine thought dawns, you try to execute it, and use it to build a castle of truth.

But ignorance cleverly comes into our mind and tells us to wait, since Eternity is at our disposal. If we listen to ignorance, we are not defending truth. Truth needs immediate recognition and acceptance. We accept the truth and we try to manifest the truth. Let us live the divine truth. In living the truth we will be justifying our own existence. By living the truth, we will be accepting our own inner Immortality, which is our birthright.

FW 82. *How can we remember to forgive the world for its defects and to forgive ourselves for our own defects?*

Sri Chinmoy: On rare occasions we see imperfection in ourselves, but we always see imperfections in others. Now, when we discover that we are imperfect or have done something wrong, what do we do? We forgive ourselves immediately, or we ignore the fact that we have done something wrong, or we decide to turn over a new leaf and never do it again. We do all these in order to get satisfaction.

If others do something wrong, if we don't forgive them, if we harbour undivine thoughts against them or want to punish them, we will never find true satisfaction. In order to satisfy ourselves, our reality, we must forgive others, too. Forgiveness is illumination. We have to feel that by forgiving others we are illumining ourselves, our own enlarged, expanded Self.

If we do not forgive, what happens? We place a heavy load on our shoulders. If I have done something wrong and I don't try to forgive myself or illumine myself, I will harbour the idea that I have made a mistake. And each time I think of my wrong action I will only add to my heavy load of guilt. Similarly, if others have done me an act of injustice, the more I think of this the heavier becomes my load of anger and resentment. Now, I have to run towards my goal. If I place something heavy on my shoulders, how am I going to run? I will see that others are all running very fast, while I can hardly walk.

It is always advisable to forgive others and to forgive oneself. Again, we have to know who is forgiving whom? I as an individual have no right to forgive others or even to forgive myself. It is the Divine within me that is inspiring me to raise my consciousness to Light, to higher Light, to highest Light. An act of forgiveness means a movement to a higher reality. And when we reach the highest Reality, we become one with the omnipresent Reality.

We are all integral parts of a living organism. If I have only two arms, I am incomplete; I need two legs, too. I need everything in order to be complete, perfect and whole. So I have to accept others as my very own. First I accept them and then I transform them. And whom am I transforming if not my own expanding, enlarged reality?

FW 83. *How can we avoid falling asleep during meditation?*

Sri Chinmoy: We need sleep because the nerves need rest. But when we have dynamic energy, we can conquer sleep. When we have a free access to the infinite inner energy, we do not need sleep at all. Right now, for a few years, or for this incarnation, the body needs six or seven hours of sleep a night. But gradually we can decrease this need from seven hours to six, five, four, even three or two.

When we have enjoyed deep meditation — enjoyed in the sense of having drunk divine nectar — sometimes we feel drowsiness. We feel we are not totally awake and not fully conscious of what is happening within us. But this is not actual sleep. Deep within us there is constant, continuous, eternal silence, peace and poise. When we are absolutely calm and quiet in our inner life, we see that the inner life offers us its own energy. Our human mind cannot understand this energy, because it never gets it or even sees it. Only our heart receives this energy from the soul. If we can feel this inner energy during our meditation, then for hours and hours we can meditate without any interruption.

In our inner life of realisation we are well-established. We know that we are of God and for God. We know that we belong to God and God belongs to us, and that God-realisation is our birthright. But this inner realisation is static. It is the static way of holding the truth. But in our outer life of manifestation we have to prove that we are of and for God. We do this through our manifestation of the Divine within us. The divine manifestation needs constant movement. We have to feel inside ourselves a flowing river, a river of dynamic energy and dynamic light. Then we have to feel that we have become that river. Now, the river is not the goal; the goal is the sea. So we have to feel that we are in the process of continuous movement. We are running forward, climbing upward, diving inward towards our goal.

Silence-life we embody, but sound-life, unfortunately, we do not manifest in a divine way. We manifest it in a destructive way. When we fall asleep during our meditation, it is a kind of unconscious destruction of our own inner divinity. But when we feel that we are a river of dynamic energy and light flowing towards our goal, then we cannot be attacked by lethargy or sleep.

Some seekers feel that just because they have entered into the meditation room, their role is over. They feel that they have already reached their destination and now they can relax. That is why they fall asleep. But our role will be over only when we have meditated well and, at the end of our meditation, when we have offered our gratitude, or whatever we have achieved, at the Feet of the Supreme. If we are going on a long journey, we have to know that when we come to the airport, that is only our first destination. The final destination is not the airport, it is some distant city or country.

If we are supposed to meditate for an hour, we may sleep for forty-five minutes and do nothing but feel miserable for the remaining fifteen minutes. But let us feel that coming to the meditation room is only our first goal, that there is another goal which will take us an hour to reach. Once we reach this goal, then we can relax and enter into the earthly life, which is necessary for manifestation.

FW 84. *What is the subconscious?*

Sri Chinmoy: The subconscious is something of the past that usually remains inside the unconscious part of our life or the ignorant part of our life. It is the part which consciously or unconsciously does not want to be illumined. The subconscious plane is one step higher than the inconscient plane. The inconscient plane is the lowest, but the subconscious plane is only a few inches higher, let us say.

In the inconscient plane there is no light at all; but the subconscious plane also does not care for light. In the subconscious plane the undivine realities or qualities that do not want to progress come forward whenever they get an opportunity and try to fight against the qualities that are trying to invoke Light from Above. But it is not as difficult to bring light into the subconscious plane as it is to bring light into the inconscient plane. The subconscious plane is better than the inconscient plane, but eventually both these planes have to be conquered and perfected.

Light has to enter into all planes of our being, for only then can we be totally perfect. But it is not advisable for the seeker to enter into either plane in the beginning or middle of his journey, for there he will encounter powerful forces of darkness. Only when one is on the verge of illumination or when one has actually received some illumination is it advisable for him to enter into the subconscious plane to try to illumine it.

FW 85. *When I feel that my spiritual progress is not fast enough and that my meditation is not deep enough, sometimes I feel the Supreme is not happy with me. Then feelings of depression and frustration enter. How can I deal with this?*

Sri Chinmoy: First of all, when you are not making progress the way you want to make progress, that is to say, when you are not making the fastest progress, it is because you are making some mistake. But if you become depressed, then you are making your problem worse; you are making another mistake. Depression is not the answer. In the spiritual life you have to try to be as cheerful as possible. Cheerfulness will never help to bring out the undivine in you. If you can be cheerful, then automatically half of your spiritual fever is gone, and you can walk faster.

But why are you not running fast? This is the important question. Sometimes it happens that a runner, knowing well that the goal is very far, slows down. Since the goal is very far away, he says, "I can go slowly and, without fail, I will reach the destination. Why try to run the fastest and become totally exhausted?" But the runner has to know that there is not one but three goals. When he reaches his first goal and realises the highest Truth, he cannot stop and relax. He has gone only part of the way. There are two more goals: the revelation of the Truth and the manifestation of the Truth. If he loses his enthusiasm and relaxes before he reaches even the first goal, then he will reach the ultimate Goal at a very late date.

All those who are sincere seekers must know that the realisation of Truth is still a far cry. Once they have realised the Truth, the game is not over. If you have three things to study, you won't relax as you would if you had only one thing to study. If you know that there are three things you have to learn, one after the other, you will be more alert, more conscious, more devoted, more aspiring. So please feel that in order to make the Supreme happy in your spiritual progress, you have to study three subjects one after the other. Do not feel that you have Eternity at your disposal. No! You have to be alert and feel that every moment is either helping you to reach your Goal or preventing you from reaching your Goal. So let each moment be utilised to dive deeper, run farther, fly higher. Then you can easily make the Supreme happy.

FW 86. *Is there something that we can consciously do or practise to cultivate humility?*

Sri Chinmoy: You can meditate on a tree. A tree that does not have fruits, that has nothing to offer, stands proudly erect. But a tree that has hundreds of fruits always bends down with utmost humility and offers its fruits to mankind. When it bends down to offer its countless fruits, it is not looked down upon by others. On the contrary, the tree is appreciated, admired and adored. Why? Because it is offering most delicious, nourishing fruits to us. The tree with fruit has humility. The tree that possesses some light and truth is humble while the tree that does not have light is not humble. So when you see something that has achieved some truth — like the tree with fruits — and when you see how humble it is and how it is appreciated by others, this helps you develop your own humility. When you have some fruits, some achievements, you are of greater necessity to mankind. And when you offer your fruits with humility, the world needs you and loves you infinitely more than it would do otherwise.

The mother is very tall, but when she wants to offer food to the child, she bends down. The child's love for the mother is not less just because she bends down. On the contrary, it increases considerably. The child sees that the mother is tall and could easily stay at her own height while the child struggles to grow up. But out of her kindness she does not do that. When we have something and want to give it to the world, if we do so with humility, then we get appreciation and admiration from the world in boundless measure. When we realise the after-effects of humility, then we can easily cultivate humility.

FW 87. *How can I have deeper meditation?*

Sri Chinmoy: You can have deeper meditation through constant remembrance of your goal. Always think of your goal as something high, higher, highest. If your goal is not the highest, if your goal is not boundless Peace, boundless Light, boundless Bliss, then your meditation cannot be very deep. Only when you pitch your aim to the highest, do you go high, higher, highest. If you want to be satisfied with only an iota of Peace, Light and Bliss, then you cannot go deeper; you cannot go higher. Always when you meditate, try to bring into your being boundless Peace, Light and Bliss or throw yourself into something infinite, something vast. These qualities will act like a springboard. If you press hard on the springboard, then you jump higher.

In order to have good meditation you should also try to dedicate your life to the right cause. The right cause is to see the divine in others and the divine in yourself all the time. If you can see yourself only as divine, then you are bound to have a deeper meditation. The moment you think of yourself as a bundle of ignorance, as a sea of ignorance, you are taking the wrong way of approaching the truth. Try to see the divine in yourself as often as you can; then automatically your meditation becomes deeper, more illumining and more fulfilling.

FLAME-WAVES

BOOK 5

Sri Chinmoy: In the ordinary life, power means supremacy. If you have power, consciously or unconsciously you will try to be one step ahead of me or one inch above me. Human power tries to make you lord it over others. It does not allow you to be one with someone else.

But spiritual power, divine power, is the power of expansion, identification and oneness. With spiritual power you try to identify yourself with the rest of the world. The sufferings, the joys of all human beings will become yours for a while. When you first achieve spiritual power, it takes the form of identification. But then you will go higher and deeper to oneness. Human power tries to make you lord it over others.

Identification lasts for a short time — for an hour, a half-hour, a minute. When you see a person suffering, you will momentarily identify with his suffering. And if you see someone in a very cheerful frame of mind, you will identify yourself with his happiness for an hour or so. Then it becomes, "out of sight, out of mind". The particular person is not in front of you any longer, so you do not know whether he is suffering or in a happy mood. But when you have established oneness, no matter where the person is, in some way or other the suffering or the joy of that person will become part and parcel of your life. When you have oneness, it is for twenty-four hours a day.

After achieving oneness, you have to reveal and manifest your oneness. One thing is to embody oneness; another is to reveal it; still another is to manifest it. The difference is this. Say that you have any kind of power, the capacity to write a poem, for example. This is also a form of power. This capacity or power you embody. When you actually write the poem you reveal the power. Anybody can see it if they come and ask you. Then, if the poem is published and people are getting benefit out of it in any way, that is called manifestation, which is a third kind of power.

In the spiritual life, power will enable you to identify and help make you one with the rest of the world. Then it will help you to reveal your capacity, and finally it will help you to manifest your capacity — all without any sense of supremacy.

FW 89. *In the message for the New Year for 1974 you mention diving deep within. Could you please speak about that?*

Sri Chinmoy: When we dive deep within two things usually happen: we see all our good qualities and we see all our bad qualities. Normally when we see our bad qualities, we become frustrated. We feel that we are full of imperfection, and that in every field we are weak, insecure and useless. But when we go deep within and see these imperfections looming large, we are not disappointed or disheartened. Why? Because we see our perfections as well at the same time. We see our love for God, our love for mankind, our cry for Beauty, Peace, Light, Harmony, Bliss. Then it is up to us to choose either imperfection or perfection. When we choose perfection, we feel tremendous strength in ourselves. We feel that we can easily overcome the imperfections that we see within and around us.

But there is no end to our inner journey, and we can go still deeper within. When we go deep — very, very deep — at that time we do not see any imperfection either in ourselves or in anybody else. What we actually see is that we are having an experience and that they are having an experience. This experience is neither good nor bad. What you call bad I may call good, and somebody else may say it is neither bad nor good. These distinctions of good and bad are all in the mind, which is very limited. If we go a little within, we see good and bad as two different things. But if we go to the deepest, there is nothing bad. All creation and all experience is good.

If you accept a path, when you go deep within you feel that that path is everything. If you have a Master, when you remain deep within, you feel that that Master is everything. Otherwise, you will feel that that path is very bad, the Master is very bad, your friends are very bad, everybody is very bad, even God. And you will feel also that you yourself are very bad. But when you go deep within, even your so-called enemies will seem good because you will feel at that time that God is having an experience in and through them in a different way. You will say: "What right have I to criticise my enemies? After all, they are also God's children." Because you are spiritual, you will try to feel your oneness with the whole world. As an ordinary human being you may find it difficult to accept your enemy as your own. But the moment you accept the spiritual life, the life of God, how can you have an enemy? You will only have friends whose views are different from yours.

If I want to play an instrument and my right hand plays well, then my right hand becomes my friend. But if my left hand cannot play at all well, shall I call my left hand my enemy? No! The right hand has the capacity, so it plays. That is why I am very happy with my right hand. My left hand does not give me the same result as my right hand. It is not in a position to do the same thing for me that I expect from my loving and devoted friends.

In the inner life, if I see that somebody cannot do something, I immediately become one with that person's incapacity. If somebody is helpless, hopeless and useless in the outer life, I become one with that person in his incapacity, weakness and imperfection. I know I am quite safe in the inner world. There I have capacity, there I have perfection, there I have everything. The other person does not have it, but just because I have established my oneness with that person, I can go deep within and bring from there Peace, Light, Bliss in abundant measure to pour into him. And when I pour these into him, I see and feel that the person receiving my inner wealth is none other than myself.

Right now we feel that the outer world is one thing and the inner world is something else. In the inner world we feel safety, purpose and a sense of perfection. In the outer world we feel that everything is chaotic, everything is meaningless, everything is useless, everything is hopeless. The more we can stay in the inner world, which is the deeper world, the easier it becomes for us to control our outer life. We see the outer world as an extension of our inner life. Once we accept Peace or Light as our very own, we feel that Peace is enough, Light is enough to carry us to our destined Goal.

To dive deep within means to cry for the perfection without. I go deep within for the perfection, harmony, peace and bliss of my outer life. The outer life is mine and the inner life is also mine. But if I do not have the seed, how am I going to get the plant and the tree? The seed and the tree must go together. The seed is the inner life and the tree is the outer life. If I sow the seed today, in a few months I will get the plant, which will gradually grow into a giant banyan tree. Without the seed, the tree cannot come into existence. And again, when there is only the seed and no tree, how will the world appreciate the capacity of the seed or get any benefit in the form of fruit? The ultimate capacity of the seed is the fruit, and it is with the fruit that we fulfil our daily need and hunger. But the first thing is the seed. So let us go deep within, to the life of the seed, and let us then grow into the life of the tree and the fruit. When the seed of the inner life has grown into the strong and sturdy tree of the outer life, the outer world and the inner world will perfectly harmonise.

FW 90. *Which is better: morning meditation or evening meditation?*

Sri Chinmoy: They can be equally beneficial, equally fruitful. But in the evening, meditation becomes a little more difficult because for eight or ten hours during the day you have been in the hustle and bustle of the world. You have met with many unaspiring people, and unconsciously their undivine thoughts and impure ideas have entered into you. Unless you are very powerful spiritually, you will have assimilated many unaspiring and uninspiring forces from the world. So it becomes very difficult in the evening to meditate with the same hope, with the same freshness. If you take a shower it will help. If you associate with spiritual people, it will also help you. But usually it will not be the same.

But the following morning, everything will be out of your memory, at least for a while. During the time that you slept, the distractions of the outer world were washed away. All the impurities that had come into you from others were washed away. During the eight hours that you are asleep your soul, like a divine thief, is observing. An ordinary thief will steal something from you. But this divine thief will only give and give. If you need peace at one spot, your soul will put peace there. It is like a mother. A mother comes into the child's room secretly, early in the morning. So as soon as the child gets up, he will be able to get the things he needs and go to school. At night the soul gets the opportunity to do what is necessary for you while you are sleeping. But during the day, when you are absorbed in the activities of the outer world, it becomes extremely difficult for the soul to give and for you to receive. For these reasons, morning meditation is usually the best.

Now, when you sit down to meditate, if you are ninety-nine per cent in the world of sleep and one per cent in this world, then how can you have a fruitful meditation? In the morning if you can conquer your lethargy, take a shower and sit down fresh and alert for meditation, then it becomes one hundred per cent good. Otherwise, your meditation will be useless.

Early in the morning there is no hustle and bustle, there is no commotion. You have taken several hours of rest, and you feel the strength of a lion. Next to early morning, the evening is the best time for meditation, because in the evening the atmosphere is calm and peaceful. You feel a kind of soothing sensation. In the evening you are tired, and you feel that the whole world is also tired. But there is a slight difference between the world's approach to the truth, and your approach, when both of you are tired. When the world is tired, it will not aspire. It wants to rest. But you feel that your tiredness or lethargy can be overcome only by bringing more Light, more energy into your system. An ordinary person will not pray or meditate. If he is tired he will go to sleep. He will feel that there is nothing else to do. But you will say, "No! I am tired, but there is a specific way for me to energise my life, and that is to bring down Peace, Light and Bliss." When you pray and meditate, at that time new life, new energy enters into you and refreshes you.

If you want to meditate in the evening, then meditate a half-hour or forty minutes before you eat. If you are really pinched with hunger, you can drink a glass of water or juice or milk. But if you meditate after you have eaten a heavy meal, the thousands of subtle nerves in your body will be very heavy and you will not be able to meditate well. The body will be heavy, the consciousness will be heavy, the nerves will be heavy, and your meditation will be useless. When you meditate properly, your consciousness flies like a bird. If you meditate well, you feel that your whole existence, like a bird, is flying high, higher, highest. But when you become heavy, immediately you sink, and your consciousness will not rise. So if you are unable to meditate in the morning, evening meditation is the next best thing, not noon or 11 a.m. or 2 p.m. At these times, meditation is not good. But once you become very advanced in the spiritual life, any time is good for you. The best thing, however, is to meditate both morning and evening. If you meditate well in the morning, you get one million spiritual dollars. And if you meditate well in the evening, you get ten thousand spiritual dollars. But if you can get even one dollar more towards the spiritual sum that you need for your realisation, then if you are wise you will take it.

FW 91. *Can you tell us exactly what the psychic being is? Also, if it is useful for the aspirant to try to establish some kind of relationship with his psychic being, how can he do it?*

Sri Chinmoy: Just as the soul is the representative of God for us, the psychic being, to some extent, is the representative of the soul. Everything on earth, whether animate or inanimate, has a soul. You, as a human being, have a soul; this glass tumbler has a soul; animals have a soul; flowers have a soul. But the psychic being is found only in those human beings who have started to aspire consciously.

Animals do not have psychic beings. Not even all men have psychic beings, because there are many human beings on earth who do not aspire. When you walk along the street you can easily see that some people have had only a few human incarnations. Some have just come from the animal kingdom, and are in their first incarnation. They are half animal. Now these people do not have a psychic being yet. Only spiritual people who are sincerely and devotedly aspiring have psychic beings. Now the soul is not born on earth; the soul is born in the soul's region. But even though there is a world that we call the psychic world, the psychic being only takes birth on earth when the seeker begins to aspire. The psychic being, this most beautiful child, is born on earth and also develops here on earth. The psychic being grows like a seed. It germinates into a small plant that grows into a huge banyan tree.

The psychic being is most beautiful. When one develops the psychic being, purity incarnate and divinity incarnate grow within his heart. When the psychic being is first formed, one may feel a very sweet, delicate sensation in the spine.

The psychic being is like the youngest child in the family, like a baby. In the physical world, the parents feel that it is their constant, bounden duty to please their young child. The baby cries and the parents give the baby what it wants. Constantly the psychic being is making fervent requests to the Eternal Father, the Supreme, or to the eldest brother, the soul, to make the whole body, the entire being, divine and perfect.

When the psychic being is six or seven years old in terms of human age, then it takes a little responsibility. But when there is something very urgent, very important, to be done, or when power is needed, the psychic being cries, and the soul within us takes the responsibility.

In the spiritual life, there are quite a few ways one can know if danger or success is imminent even if one has not developed occult vision or spiritual power. If the psychic being is developed, it will immediately bring the news that something serious is going to happen — something dangerous or some catastrophe. The psychic will be like a messenger boy. Also, if something most encouraging and inspiring is going to happen, the psychic being will bring this news too. The psychic knows and sees everything, but the psychic does not have the necessary power to change what will happen; it can just inform us. Only with the help of the soul or with the guidance and blessing of the Supreme can the psychic being change something. However, it does have the power to transform our human nature with purity. But the psychic being does not have the same amount of power that the soul has. And the soul does not and cannot have the same amount of power as God.

In our path we see the necessity of always consciously feeling the Presence of God. The psychic being helps us to feel the Presence of God all the time. There are many divine gifts that we get from God through the aspiration of the psychic being. For instance, we get constant joy, a constant sense of security and a constant feeling of our own progress from the psychic being. Right now we *are* making progress, but we do not feel sure about it. But if the psychic being comes to the fore and remains to the fore, then our progress is noticeable to all.

If you pay attention to the psychic being, you can bring it to the fore without fail. When you develop real surrender to the Supreme, giving your whole life over to the path of love, devotion and surrender to God's Will, automatically the psychic being appears. To make your surrender beautiful, soulful and unconditional, you have to meditate every day. When you make complete surrender, immediately the psychic being comes to the fore. Before that, if you have love for God, the psychic may come to the fore. If you have devotion for God or do devoted service, the psychic may come, but that is not the rule.

If we can feel the presence of the psychic being, and if the psychic being prays and invokes the presence of God in our outer being, then we will make fast progress. But if we do not want to adopt that method, the most important thing we can do and the only thing that is necessary is to offer our conscious gratitude to the Supreme. The moment we offer our gratitude to the Supreme, our progress becomes the fastest.

The psychic being is like a messenger or a beautiful child. We do not actually need a messenger boy, or a little beautiful child. We do not absolutely need this little brother in the family to cry and speak to the Father on our behalf. We need only God. So if you do not want to have any connection with the psychic being, or if you feel that the psychic being is unnecessary, then you can do without its help.

Some of you sometimes see your psychic being, but if the Master does not tell you, then you may not know what it is. You may feel that you dreamt that you saw a most beautiful child. Or you may feel that you had a vision. In your case, also, once you saw it, but you did not know that it was your psychic being. A seeker can see the psychic being on rare occasions. Only someone who is realised or most advanced can see the psychic being at any time.

One can also see the psychic being of another. As a child, I saw the psychic being of my sister, Ahana, before I saw my own. I did not recognise it as her psychic being at the time. But one year later, when I started regaining all the spiritual and occult vision of my previous incarnations at the age of fourteen, I knew that it was her psychic being which I had seen.

The psychic being cannot come to the fore and grow most powerfully when the mind is still roaming in worldly information, worldly thoughts and worldly ideas. The psychic being comes to the fore only when we have the sweet, pure, innocent feeling of our oneness with the rest of the world, even with those we now consider our enemies. The psychic being has no enemies.

The psychic being finds it extremely difficult to deal with the developed mind. By the developed mind I mean the sophisticated mind, the dry and intellectual mind where there is no sweetness, but only a barren desert. The psychic being is a child. A child tries to play in the eternal garden of God, the Eternal Child. So the mind, which some people consider the greatest or the most developed part of our existence, is not and cannot be the real friend of the psychic being. The heart and the psychic being always go together. The heart, the psychic being and the soul forever go together.

A man will see his psychic being as a beautiful boy, and a woman will see hers as a beautiful girl. A man has a masculine psychic being and a woman has a feminine one. The soul, however is neither masculine nor feminine, but when it incarnates it takes on a masculine or a feminine body. If it takes a masculine form in the first human incarnation, then it goes on taking this form in all future incarnations, and the same if it takes a feminine form. Only three times since the creation has a soul changed from the masculine to feminine once it began incarnating in a human body. There are some spiritual Masters who tell people that in their past incarnations they were men and in this incarnation they are women, but this is not true. I have to say that, in the inner world, I know that the soul has changed this way only three times.

Now, the psychic being does not age like a human being. After forty or fifty years, the human body decays and we lose our strength, capacity and energy. As one matures spiritually, the psychic being comes to the psychic age of between eighteen and twenty-two. After that, it gains strength and capacity, but it does not age. It not only retains its beauty, strength, power, light and divinity of that time, but it actually continues to increase these. It may be two hundred years old in terms of human age, but the form that you will see will always be that of a youth. I am now forty-two, but my psychic being looks like a youth of twenty. My psychic being is now like a most powerful soldier or warrior.

When the seeker dies, the physical body is dissolved into the five principal elements. The vital enters into the vital world, and the psychic being goes to take rest in the psychic world. The soul will remember, however, which psychic being it had. Then, before the soul comes into the world for its next incarnation, it will go to its psychic being and say, "Now I am going down. You come also." First the soul goes to the Supreme for His blessings and to make a promise about how much it will accomplish for the Supreme in its next incarnation. Then the soul goes down. On the way down it asks the psychic being to join it. The psychic being is very happy to come back at that time. After the psychic being, the soul takes a spiritual heart from the heart's world. Next, if the mind is developed, the soul goes to the mental plane for subtle intelligence. Then it goes to the vital plane for the dynamic vital, and finally to the gross physical.

FW 92. *For the past year I have been practising concentration and meditation with my attention focused on my navel chakra. But I don't seem to be making as much progress as I would like in controlling my thoughts. Have you got any suggestions?*

Sri Chinmoy: What you are doing is extremely good. We have six spiritual centres in the body. You are concentrating on the centre which is called *manipura*. This is the centre that they usually give importance to in Zen practice. From this centre, according to our Indian spiritual teachings, you get dynamic energy. If you use this divine energy for a divine purpose, then you create. If you use it for an aggressive purpose, then you destroy.

Now if you want to control your thoughts, you should concentrate on the centre between the eyebrows. If you become very stiff and your concentration is intense, then you should not concentrate here for more than two minutes. Otherwise, you will become exhausted in the beginning. Now if you concentrate on the heart centre, you will get peace, love and joy. Try to hear the cosmic sound, the soundless sound, when you enter into the heart. If you bring love, joy, peace and bliss up from the heart to the centre between the eyebrows, then you will see that there will be no thoughts.

The heart is the safest place for you to concentrate and meditate on. If you do this, automatically you will get purification, because inside the heart is the soul, and the soul is one with the Infinite. It is from here that you will get everything.

FW 93. *Could you speak a little about the significance of dreams?*

Sri Chinmoy: When we have a dream, we have to know which plane of consciousness the dream comes from. There are seven higher worlds and seven lower worlds. When we have dreams coming from the lower worlds, the subconscious worlds — or you can say, inconscient worlds — we have to feel that these dreams have no value. They cannot change our nature. They cannot inspire us. They cannot give us any hope for our future fulfilment. When we get a dream from the vital plane, we will see that the dream will be constant movement. It is like a battlefield; everything is breaking and smashing, people are being killed. These dreams cannot help us at all in our spiritual life. The best thing we can do is forget them. If the dream comes from the mental plane, there will be some poise — not full poise, but a little poise, a little calm and quiet there. If it comes from the psychic plane, we will feel affection, sweetness, compassion and concern for the things or persons we are seeing. And if it comes from the soul's plane, it will be all Light and Delight, all Peace.

When we have a dream from the lower worlds, we do not want to identify ourselves with it, for we are badly frightened by it. The dream comes to us as a threat. But a dream that comes from the higher worlds comes as an invitation. We get inner joy and inner satisfaction, and immediately feel our identity there. We enter into it; we grow into it. A dream that comes from the subconscious world, where we are quarrelling and fighting and doing many undivine things, will not necessarily materialise. But a dream that comes from the higher worlds is bound to materialise. Today's dream is tomorrow's reality. Why? Because the dream is coming from a world which is living and palpable. With our limited consciousness we do not know this. But when we meditate we consciously enter into many higher worlds, and the reality of these worlds enters into us in our dream.

If you want to have sweet dreams, inspiring dreams, then you should meditate most soulfully early in the morning — say 3:30 or 4:00 or 5:00 a.m. — and then go to sleep for about half an hour or forty minutes. If your meditation is sound and genuine, if it comes from the very depths of your heart, any dreams you have afterwards will be divine, significant dreams. They will be about angels and gods, or about your dear ones; or you will see some encouraging, inspiring things. If you want to have good dreams before 3:00 a.m., please try to meditate on your navel for about ten minutes at night before you go to bed. The navel is where emotion starts. Emotion itself is not bad; it is a question of how we use it. When we have human emotion, we only bind and bind. But when we have divine emotion, we extend; we extend our consciousness. So if you concentrate on your navel centre for ten minutes, you can bring the human emotion under control and allow the divine emotion to go up from the heart, upward to the highest.

If you read books for the interpretation of dreams, each book will give a different answer. Perhaps each book is right in its own way. But you have to get your own interpretation from your dreams. When you have a dream, try to feel your own existence in the dream; try to feel that you are inside the dream itself. Those who meditate daily will not find it difficult to do. But others may find it difficult. An ordinary man sees a dream as something totally separate from the rest of his life. He feels that he is living in the reality and the dream has nothing to do with reality. It is something sweet, something precious, something encouraging, something inspiring, and so forth; but he does not feel that it is more than that. But when a spiritual man has a dream, he immediately feels that this dream is the precursor of reality. Something more, he will see that this dream is tomorrow's reality. How does he do that? He does it on the strength of his meditation. When he meditates for ten or fifteen minutes in the morning or in the evening, he widens his consciousness. Right now our consciousness is separated into three parts. At this moment we are in the waking consciousness. But when we sleep, we will have another consciousness: sound sleep, deep sleep. Then we have a third, dream consciousness, in the dream state. But one who meditates widens his consciousness into all three planes.

How can we derive benefit from our dreams? We can derive benefit from dreams if we feel that each dream is a step or stepping stone towards our divine Goal. There are some people who say they do not have any dreams at all, but they are mistaken. They do dream, but when they come out of the dreamland, they totally forget. Some people have the capacity to retain their dream consciousness while they are fully awake, early in the morning. If you feel that you had a dream at night but cannot remember it, then early in the morning, try to concentrate on this particular point, at the back of the head, just at the top of the neck. When you have dreams, either they will manifest through your physical mind or, for some time, for a few hours or even for a day or two, they will be registered there. So if you want to recollect any dream, try to concentrate there. If you can concentrate there for ten or fifteen minutes, you will be able to feel that you are knocking at a particular door. And when the door opens, you will be able to remember your dreams completely. Everything will come back to you.

When you have a frightening dream, please pay no attention to it. Suppose you dream that something bad is going to happen in your life. If you are frightened, you are already dead. But if you are not frightened, then during the few hours or the few days that lie between your dream and the actual occurrence you can fight against it. And the divine Grace is bound to come and help you at that time. Suppose you have a dream that a friend or relative of yours will pass away, and your dream is absolutely correct. Tomorrow he will surely die; but if you are frightened now, then today he is already dead for you. If you surrender to the dream, you will suffer unnecessarily before the actual hour. Also, your fear will immediately enter into the future victim and create an additional burden for that particular person. What you should do at that time is try to fight against the possibility of his death through prayer and meditation. Pray to God, "I have seen it. O God, save him, save him." Instead of being frightened, try to offer your prayer to God. Perhaps you think that prayer is something feminine or delicate. No! Your prayer is your greatest strength. God's strength is His Compassion and man's strength is his prayer. Or you can meditate. That will be an even mightier strength. If you fight and God's Grace descends, I assure you that you can delay the possibility of this person's death. Many times it has happened that spiritual seekers have dreamt that their relatives are going to die and immediately they have started meditating and praying to God. Then, God's Grace has descended. But God does not nullify the possibility. No, He may just delay the actual event.

Now, why does God help the aspirant in cases like this? God helps because God is not bound by cosmic law. Cosmic law is created by God, and at any time He can break His own law. That is why He is omnipotent. If He cannot break His own law, then He is not omnipotent. And you can make God break His law through your soulful prayer. God says, "This is to be done." He has recorded this, but when human prayer enters into His Heart, He may cancel His own decree.

When you have hopeful dreams, illumining dreams, encouraging dreams, when you see that something significant is going to take place in a friend's life — what you should do is consciously try to identify your soul with his soul. How will you do this? Through your meditation. He will eventually get joy from the event because it belongs to him. But this joy, by God's Grace, you have received before he actually has. So if you are wise, you will go deep within and assimilate the joy that you have received and then try to offer it to him inwardly before he gets it directly from God. Otherwise, if you tell him, "You know, I had a wonderful dream about you," he will be happy for a second, and then he will doubt you. He will say, "Oh, it is all mental hallucination." Despite your best intention, his doubtful mind will throw cold water on your encouraging message. So instead of telling the person verbally, try to offer him the joy of the dream consciously through your meditation. At that time, he will get additional strength. Before he gets the experience of your dream, which will come to him in the form of reality, he will start getting inner peace, inner joy, which he cannot account for, because you have started injecting him, preparing him to receive something very high, very meaningful and fulfilling. And when you have dreams about yourself, go deep within and prepare yourself to be ready, to be a fit instrument for the reality, to receive the reality as it should be received.

One thing more I wish to say. It is not bad for an ordinary seeker to pray to God for dreams. Dreams are necessary, as experiences are necessary. But again, if you do not have dreams, if you do not have experiences, that does not mean that you are not fit for the spiritual life or that you are not fit for God-realisation. There are people who do not have any experiences. They curse themselves and think that God is displeased with them. Far from it! God is most pleased with them. Suppose I want to reach a door. Now there are two ways of going. One way is to go there consciously. My calculating mind says that I have to take four or five steps to get there: one, two, three, four, five. Each step is an experience for me. If my physical mind wants to be convinced at every moment while I am walking towards my goal — towards the door — then I can say that step one is an experience, step two is an experience, and so on. But again, if I know that my destination is there, it may not be necessary for me to have constant experiences each step of the way. What is necessary, in my case, is only my destination. So I just go there and God is ready for me.

If you want to have dreams or experiences, they can serve as preparatory steps — one, two, three — or they may not be necessary at all. The human mind always wants to be convinced and wants to get joy at every step when it does something. But if we live in the soul, in the heart, then we need not give that kind of importance to experiences and dreams. They are not necessary because God is preparing us in His own Way. If He does not want to give us convincing experiences, no harm. But again, if we pray to God for convincing experiences or sweet dreams, there is no harm in our prayer either. Eventually a day will come when we shall offer to God the highest prayer: "O God, if You want, give me dreams. If You want, give me experiences. If You don't want to give me dreams or experiences, it is all up to You. Only make me worthy of Your Compassion. And if You don't want to make me worthy of Your Compassion, it is also up to You. Only do with me as You will. Let Thy Will be done in and through me. I care for nothing except Your own fulfilment in and through me." When we have that kind of prayer within us, then God comes to us and says, "Do not be a beggar. Do not cry for dreams; do not cry for experiences. Take Me, the Reality itself."

FW 94. *What is the best way of obtaining peace in our inner life and in our outer life?*

Sri Chinmoy: In the outer life you cannot have peace unless and until you have first established peace in your inner life. Early in the morning, if you treasure a few divine thoughts before coming out of your home, then these thoughts will enter into the outer life as energising, fulfilling realities. But they perform their task only according to their capacity. The peace you get from the inner world you offer to the world at large. But the outer world does not want it; the outer world does not care for it. The world says it needs peace, but when you give the world the peace-fruit, it just throws the fruit aside.

In the morning you pray to God for peace, and then you come to the United Nations. There your colleagues, who have not prayed or meditated, are quarrelling and fighting. They are in another world. Now you may say, "I prayed for peace. How is it that my colleagues today are still quarrelling over minor things?" But I wish to tell you that if you had not prayed for peace, it could have been infinitely worse. Your prayer has definitely made the situation better than it might have been. Again, if your prayer had been more intense, more soulful, then I wish to say that the turmoil in your particular department could have been less. And if you had had a most powerful meditation early in the morning, I assure you the power of your own prayer and meditation in the inner world could have easily averted the wrong forces, the misunderstanding, among your colleagues.

It is in the inner world that everything starts. The inner world is where we sow the seed. If we sow the seed of peace and love, naturally it will produce a tree of peace and love when it germinates. But if we don't sow the seed, then how are we going to have the plant or the tree? It is impossible! Unfortunately we do not all pray for peace. We pray for joy or for our personal satisfactions. Of course, it is true that we need these things. Today we may need joy, tomorrow we may need love, the day after tomorrow we may need the fulfilment of a particular desire. But again, there is a desire, an aspiration which everybody has, and that is the desire for peace.

The peace we try to bring forward from the outer world is not peace: it is only temporary compromise. You see the political situation. For a few months or years, two parties remain at peace. They feel that while keeping an outer compromise they will secretly strengthen their capacity. Then, when they get the opportunity or when the vital urge compels them, they fight. I wait for the opportunity when I can more powerfully, most powerfully, attack you. But the inner peace is a different matter. The peace we bring to the fore from the inner world through our prayer and meditation is very strong, very powerful, and it lasts. So when we have that peace in our inner life, the outer life is bound to be transformed. It is only a matter of time.

FW 95. *Does the peace that you bring down during the meditations in the conference rooms have any effect on the delegates who do not attend these meetings?*

Sri Chinmoy: All those who are at the United Nations have definitely come to bring about peace. But some people consciously run towards the goal, while others unconsciously run. If somebody consciously runs, naturally his progress will be swifter and more convincing. If someone wants to consciously partake of the fruit that we bring down with our soulful aspiration, then that person gets more nourishment and more confidence and he feels the all-fulfilling love, which is peace. On Fridays when we pray and meditate here for peace, it *does* help the United Nations' aspiration. Sometimes I do feel that it affects the delegates who do not come here. But, forgive me, I have to say that for those who do not come here and do not consciously aspire for peace as we do, the effect cannot be the same. Here, all those who are coming to bring down peace from Above undoubtedly get infinitely more than those who do not attend these meetings. But we have to know that when we pray and meditate here, it is not only for the seekers who are here, but it is for everyone. We are like a father. The father works and then he shares his money with his family. So here, also, we are limited members of the world family. Whatever we earn, we try to share with others.

FW 96. *All around us we hear of wars and conflicts. I want to know if these conflicts are all part of the divine order?*

Sri Chinmoy: Very nice. It is true that sometimes it is a Divine Game. The good, the bad in everybody has to come to the fore, and then finally the good is victorious. Then again, there is something called the attack of the undivine forces within or around us. After you leave here, somebody may come and snatch away your wallet. Now is it your karma or some wrong action on your part that has caused you to be robbed? Far from it! You have prayed, you have meditated, you have done everything right here. But there are many undivine forces around us, and no matter how spiritual, how divine we are, they attack us. So we have to pray for constant protection from God.

Now, regarding the present-day political situation, it is not the intention of the Divine to let the forces fight it out so that, out of evil, good will come. At times we say that the Divine Game is being played; that the good, bad, Divine and undivine play and finally the Divine dawns. But right now, it is not like that. The present day wars are not God's intention; they are the product of human weaknesses: "*I* want to prove to the world at large that my views are correct and that your views are all wrong. I want to prove that I am something, I have the capacity to lord it over you; you have to be under my feet." This is the thing. It is the expansion of our authority, our blind authority, that we want.

What happens is that the wrong forces within us come to the fore and make friends with the undivine forces that are already around us. These forces around us are like mad elephants, ready to crush us at any moment. So the elephant inside us and the elephant outside come together, and wars begin. But again, inside us is also a deer that wants to run the fastest towards its divine Goal. Our aspiration or the aspirant within us is like the deer, and the vital within us is like a blind elephant. So the outer elephant and the inner elephant meet together and try to crush the deer within us, before it reaches its Goal. There is every possibility that the two elephants will destroy the deer. But once the deer reaches the Goal, then we are safe. The Goal is all Light, all Beauty, all Joy, all Power: and no elephant, no matter how powerful, can destroy this Goal. This Goal is our inner peace.

FW 97. *Sometimes when I meditate, I feel that I am about to go through some experience, but nothing happens. What is the cause of that?*

Sri Chinmoy: The reason nothing happens is that you have not reached the height, the ultimate. You are just on the verge of it, but you do not quite reach it. It is like lighting a stove. When you turn on the gas, you have to turn it to a certain point before the flame comes. You may come almost to that point, but you stop too soon. If you had turned just a fraction of an inch farther, you would have succeeded.

It is the same with your meditation. If you had gone just a bit higher or deeper, you would have had your experience. But your attention was diverted or something made you pull back instead of going on. Something inside you failed to maintain the same type of aspiration that you had before and then your consciousness fell. It is as if you were climbing up to the highest branch of a mango tree, but all of a sudden somebody called you from below and you forgot about the delicious mango at the top of the tree and you climbed down. This is what it is like when consciousness falls. But if you can maintain your height and not respond to any call from below, then you will reach the Highest, and here you will get the experience.

While you are praying and meditating, imagine that you have a bicycle inside you. When you ride on a bicycle, you have to pedal it all the time. If you don't pedal, you cannot make any progress and you will fall down. While you are meditating you have to aspire all the time; otherwise you will fall. You cannot balance motionless at one point. In the spiritual life movement has to be constant. Either you move forward or you move backward. If you try to remain motionless, the ignorance of the world will pull you right back to your starting point.

While we are aspiring we have to make ourselves conscious at every moment that what we need is not success, but progress, progress, progress. Progress itself is the active form of success. When we start meditating early in the morning, if we think, "Today I have to get the highest experience or I will feel miserable," then we are making a mistake. Right now we are full of ignorance, imperfection, limitation and bondage. But if we remain imperfect, how are we going to be the chosen instruments of God? And if we cannot become instruments of God, then God remains unmanifested. In the morning when we pray, if we cry for our progress, then automatically God will make us His chosen instruments. But if we cry for success, then God may give us the experience which we call success, but He will not utilise us as His instruments because we are already trying to get something from Him. We are demanding that He give us the highest experience of Peace, Light and Bliss, whereas we should be asking only for the opportunity and privilege of being His instrument to serve Him in His own Way.

So I wish to say that if experience is your aim, until you actually reach the height from which you can get the experience, please continue to aspire intensely. But if your aim is only to become an instrument of the Supreme, no matter how high or how deep you go, then you are bound to get all the experiences which God has in store for you, even without climbing up to the top of the tree. Right now it is you who are trying to climb up to a great height in order to get an experience. But it is very easy for God to bring the fruit down and give it to you. He is an expert climber: He can climb up and climb down. So if you can please God, even if you remain at the foot of the tree, God will climb up on your behalf and bring the experience down, if it is His Will that you have it.

FW 98. *What is the difference between going high and going deep in meditation?*

Sri Chinmoy: There is a great difference in the methods of meditation, although ultimately height and depth become one. When we want to go deep in meditation, we start our journey from the heart. The spiritual heart is the beginning point. From there, deep is not downward or backward, but inward. We should feel that we are digging or travelling deep, deep, very deep into our heart. But it is not like digging downward, somewhere far below our feet. No! Below the knees, the plane of inconscience starts. If we go downward, then it is not actually spiritual depth that we are getting, but only the low, lower, lowest planes of consciousness. The spiritual heart is infinitely vast; therefore there is no limit to how deep we can go. We can never go too deep; we can never touch the boundaries of the spiritual heart, because it embodies this vast universe that we see and, at the same time, is larger and vaster than the universe.

When we want to go high in meditation, then our direction is upward. Our aspiration goes upward; we are climbing, climbing fearlessly towards the Highest. We must pass through the mind, through the thousand-petalled lotus at the top of the head. Again, the distance is infinitely vast. There is no end to our upward journey because we are travelling in Infinity. We are climbing towards the ever-transcending Beyond. In terms of distance, if you want to measure, upward and inward are both infinite journeys towards one Goal, the Supreme.

We cannot go high by using only the mind, however. We must go through the mind, beyond the mind, and into the realm of the spiritual heart once more. The domain of the spiritual heart is infinitely higher and vaster than that of the very highest mind. Far beyond the mind is still the domain of the heart. The heart is boundless in every direction, so inside the heart is height as well as depth.

The higher you can go, the deeper you can go. And again, the deeper you can go, the higher you can go. It works simultaneously. If we can meditate very powerfully, then we are bound to feel that we are going both very high and very deep. The highest height and the deepest depth both are inside the spiritual heart. Height and depth go together, but they work in two different dimensions, as it were. But if a person can go very high in his meditation, then he has the capacity to go very deep also. It is a matter of choice.

FW 99. *Does the psychic being have certain fixed characteristics, like age, or does it grow and change along with the person?*

Sri Chinmoy: The psychic being is constantly in the process of evolution. But if you are interested in its so-called physical characteristics, then I wish to say that in a human being you will see it growing from a young child into a youth of about twenty-two years. But this is psychic age, not human age. When we see a young man of say twenty or twenty-two, he is fully mature. A person usually does not gain physical strength after that age. But the psychic being constantly acquires strength, strength, strength. The psychic being is not like a human being, who deteriorates and becomes old after forty, fifty, sixty years. The strength of the psychic being will always increase and increase. But its basic characteristics it sometimes retains and sometimes does not. It depends on how the psychic being wants to please the Supreme, the Inner Pilot. Some psychic beings feel that by keeping their characteristics they will be able to know their own way of operating. But some psychic beings do not care for this individuality. They say, "We won't have any characteristics of our own. At every moment we shall be moulded by the divine Light. The divine Light will do everything for us." The psychic being and the soul do not have infinite Power. Infinite Power, infinite Light, infinite Bliss only the Supreme has. So when abundant Light, infinite Light from Above descends into the psychic being, the psychic being automatically loses its own characteristics and personality, even though that personality is divine. The psychic being is very, very beautiful, extremely beautiful. You cannot express it in words or imagine it. Some psychic beings prefer to express themselves through Beauty, some through Love, some through Power, some through Bliss and some through the many other divine qualities. If you see that someone is very kind to people, always loving, always affectionate, then the psychic being is probably trying to express its Light through him in the form of divine Love. If someone shows the power aspect all the time — not the power that destroys but the power that energises and helps others — then his psychic being wants to express itself through Power. Like the soul, each psychic being wants to offer or manifest the ultimate Truth in a specific way. Also, as some souls want to manifest the Supreme in two ways, psychic beings may also do the same.

FW 100. *Is it right for spiritual Masters to take the suffering of their disciples? If the disciples do something bad and they do not suffer themselves, how will they learn the lesson?*

Sri Chinmoy: It is often true that if one does not have the firsthand experience, then one will not understand or learn properly. One will not understand the seriousness of his actions if he does not suffer the consequences. If I see that somebody has put his finger in fire and burnt himself, I know that that person is feeling pain but I will not suffer to the same extent that he does. But if God has given me a heart, I will feel the suffering that he is going through. It is not that these people are making mistakes for the first time, and it is not that they have never seen others make these mistakes. They have seen others make these mistakes, and they have seen how much suffering the others have gone through. But out of temptation, or because they have allowed some undivine forces to enter into them, they make the same mistakes and earn the punishment. But the spiritual Master has the heart of a real mother. If the mother knows that her child has done something wrong and will be punished, the mother says, "O God, let me suffer on my child's behalf. Let him be protected." This is a mother's heart. And if the child is divine, if he is loving, if he is sincere, when he sees his mother suffering he says, "I deserved this suffering, but my mother is suffering on my behalf. She has all love for me. Let me not cause her more suffering. Let me not do this again." When the son sees and feels that the mother is suffering for his misdeeds, if he has real love for his mother, he does not want to repeat them. His mother has shown her real love by accepting his suffering as her own. And the son also can show his real love by doing the right thing from then on. In the case of the spiritual children and the Master, the same truth is applied. The spiritual children do not want their spiritual Master to suffer again and again on their behalf.

You may say that if one does not suffer himself, he will not learn. This is true in most cases. But if a person is sincere, if he is aspiring, if he has love for his Guru, he will feel a kind of inner obligation not to do the same thing again. And what is more important, if he truly loves his Guru, he will suffer badly when he sees that his Guru is suffering, especially when his sincerity makes him feel that it is because of him that his Guru is suffering. The Guru takes on the physical suffering of his dear disciples, and when he does so it is much milder and briefer than it would have been in the disciples themselves, because the Guru has the capacity to throw this suffering into the Universal Consciousness. But when the disciple sees the suffering of his beloved Master, his divine heart of oneness simply breaks. In this way he does suffer and he does learn his lesson, although the direct karmic results of his actions go to the Master and not to him.

There are two ways to make progress. One way is to reap the results of what you sow. The other way is to be swept along by the Guru's Grace. The Master sees that some of his disciples have a good heart, that they have sincerely accepted the spiritual life and are determined to reach the Goal. He sees that they are not ordinary people. They are praying and meditating, but while following the spiritual life sometimes they enter into the world of temptation and are captured by it. Then naturally they will suffer. But at the same time the compassion of the Master says, "Since you are serving God, or you are trying to please God in various ways through your daily prayer and meditation, let me help you so that you do not have to suffer." This is sheer divine compassion. The Master hopes that when they see his suffering, eventually they will realise that it was they who were going to suffer.

But before he takes anyone's bad karma or before he cures a person, a real spiritual Master will always ask God if it is His Will. I have to ask God if I should help someone even to cure a headache. You can tell the person to take an aspirin and his headache will go away, but I have to speak to God about it. Now God can say yes or no. If He says yes, that means He wants to allow a sense of gratitude to grow inside that particular disciple. He wants that disciple to feel that there is somebody who loves him and has taken his suffering upon himself. If God says no, it means that He wants that person to go through the normal process of suffering and learn the lesson by himself.

God has two ways of operating, either through Compassion or through Justice. This moment He can show all His Compassion and the next moment He can show all His Justice. If He wants to show His Compassion, which He quite often does, then He will tell the Master, who is His instrument, to take all the suffering of the disciple. If He wants to show His Justice, then He will tell the Master to allow that person to meet with the consequences of his wrong deed.

FW 101. *Does Christmas, the way it is celebrated, elevate the consciousness in any way?*

Sri Chinmoy: If it is a matter of spiritual consciousness, it does not elevate the consciousness. But if it is a matter of enthusiastic consciousness, vital consciousness, exuberant consciousness, it does help. Only at rare places, in some private homes where people are really devoted to Christ, there in those few places, the consciousness is elevated. On the whole, the decorations that you see in stores and on streets and so many other places do not at all elevate the consciousness. It is only a game, just like children playing. It helps to some extent in this respect, that when you have Christmas or some other special occasion, it takes away tension from the mind and strengthens the possibilities of the vital — not in a bad sense, in a good sense. In the vital some hope dawns and the tension of the mind goes away; that is in a good sense and it is a great blessing.

FW 102. *You have written an aphorism which says: "God is at once finite and infinite. He is space. He is beyond space. He is measured. He can be measured. He must needs be measured. He is measureless. He is boundless. He is infinite." Could you please explain this?*

Sri Chinmoy: God is finite and God is infinite. You have stressed the word "finite". It means that you cannot agree with the idea that God can be finite. Omnipotent — this is our feeling about God. God is omnipotent, God is omniscient, God is omnipresent. Now, let us take this divine quality which we call omnipotence. If God can be only as vast as the universe, but not as tiny as the tiniest atom, then where is His omnipotence? When we think of omnipotence, our human mind has a feeling of a power very vast, measureless. But the term "omnipotent" simply means having unlimited power. This means that the Supreme has the power to be immeasurably vast or inconceivably small, at His sweet Will. At our sweet will we can do nothing, but just because God is omnipotent, at His sweet Will He can do anything He wants to. God is infinite because He is omnipotent. Again, God is finite precisely because He is omnipotent. For He who is omnipotent can do and be anything He wants to.

As human beings, we are evolving towards our transcendental Perfection. God is infinite, but He entered into this finite body of ours which lasts for fifty, sixty or seventy years, then dies. God is infinite, but He houses Himself in each tiny child. Here in the finite, He wants to enjoy Himself and play the tune of the Infinite. Only then does He get the greatest joy. It is in the finite that we are aspiring towards the Infinite, aspiring to achieve the Infinite. Again, the Infinite gets the greatest joy by making itself as tiny as possible. Finite and infinite: to our outer eyes they seem opposite to each other, but in God's Eyes they are one. The finite and the Infinite always want to go together; the one complements the other. The finite wants to reach the absolute Highest, which is the Infinite. The Infinite wants to manifest itself in and through the finite. Then the game is complete. Otherwise it will be only a one-sided game. There will be no joy, no achievement, no fulfilment. In and through the Infinite, the finite is singing its song of realisation. And in and through the finite, the Infinite is singing its song of manifestation.

FW 103. *Could you please tell us the best way to conquer the ego?*

Sri Chinmoy: The easiest, best and most effective way of conquering the ego is to feel constantly not only that we are *in* God, *with* God and, at times, *for* God, but also that we are *of* God. *In* God and *with* God: this is very easy for us to feel. Also, we can easily say that we are *for* God. God is good, so we are for God. But the moment we can say wholeheartedly that we are of God, that we are made of God as something is made of paper or wood or some other material, then immediately our consciousness is changed. If we are of God, we are not helplessly or hopelessly bound by earthly human limitations. We feel that naturally we will have Peace, Bliss, Power and all divine qualities at our disposal. And when we feel that these divine qualities are within us and we are of them, then our immediate feeling is one of expansion. Light cannot remain without expanding. Peace cannot last without expanding. The very nature of divine Peace, Light, Bliss, Power and other divine qualities is to expand, expand, expand. So if we have the conscious feeling of our oneness with God, the feeling that we are of God, immediately we will feel the automatic expansion of our limited selves into unbounded Peace, Light and Bliss. Then we can go beyond the earth-consciousness and transcend our limited ego-bound selves. We go beyond the creativity, beyond the manifestation of the earth-plane.

We have to feel every day, if not every second, that our body, vital, mind, heart, soul and everything is of God, and that God is not something vague, but something real. To a seeker, God is the *only* Reality — not *a* reality, but *The* Reality. So, when we are crying for The Reality, we shall see that this Reality is all-pervading, all-fulfilling and at the same time, all-transcending. This Reality is God and if we feel that we are a part of it, if we can have our conscious place in the lap of the all-pervading, all-transcending and all-fulfilling Reality, then we can easily conquer our limited earth-bound ego. At that time we will feel that God is not only here on earth, but everywhere. He is the vast universe and again, He is beyond, far beyond the universe.

Ego is our earth-bound consciousness. This earth-bound consciousness tries to limit us. My and mine, it says. *My* family, *my* house, *my* friends, *my* children — everything my and mine. When we think of earth, immediately we think of possession.

Earth has all our friends and relatives; earth has its own joy, suffering and so forth. The very function of ego is to bind us and also to make us want to bind others. We are bound by the earth-atmosphere and, at the same time, we are binding earth because we are unwilling to aspire. We are constantly in desire, but not in aspiration. When we desire, we try to possess and be possessed.

But the consciousness of our aspiring soul makes us want to transcend, expand. When we expand, we transcend; and when we transcend, we expand. When we aspire, at that time we consciously enter into our own infinitude, divinity and plenitude. We came from Infinity, Eternity and Immortality. When we aspire, we enter into them consciously, but not with a sense of possession. We cannot possess anything — certainly not Infinity, Eternity and Immortality. But we can consciously, on the strength of our aspiration, re-enter our Homeland whence we came. We have every right to go back home with our conscious aspiration. To make a journey back home on the physical plane, we need money. In the spiritual life, our constant inner aspiration buys our return ticket to our eternal Home. Desire is pulling and pushing. Aspiration is just letting ourselves be carried back to our eternal Home.

If we live in the world of aspiration, ego is bound to be conquered because the fire of aspiration will purify the ego. It will not kill the ego, but it will purify it; and when purification takes place, realisation is bound to dawn. At the end of the road of purification is realisation. The more our outer nature is purified, the closer we are to God. And the quicker we are purified within, the faster is our realisation of the Ultimate Goal. Ego can be conquered, must be conquered and will be conquered only through constant aspiration.

Aspiration is the inner flame that is glowing all the time and spreading its flames all around, within, without. Aspiration is bound to carry us to the land of our origin. Here there is no ego, but only all-pervading Oneness — all-embracing, all-fulfilling, all-illumining Oneness. In this Oneness there is a constant sense of divine fulfilment, boundless fulfilment. In boundless fulfilment, there can be no limited ego, no limited bondage. Nothing limited, nothing imperfect, nothing obscure, nothing destructive, nothing binding can last there. It is all Infinity, all Reality. There Reality grows in the soul of Infinity, and Infinity grows in the soul of Reality.

FLAME-WAVES

BOOK 6

Sri Chinmoy: I wish to invite a few questions on patriotism. I shall answer the questions from the spiritual point of view.

FW 104. *What is patriotism?*

Sri Chinmoy: Patriotism is love of one's country, the country that has given one shelter, the country that claims one as her very own son or daughter. Patriotism is a golden opportunity for an individual to work together with his dearest motherland. When mother and son work together, they see their need of each other. The son needs the mother's sacrifice, sympathy, love and concern; the mother needs the son's heroism, dynamism and will-power. When all these divine qualities meet together, the country becomes a perfect instrument of God. Some countries are regarded as the fatherland. In these cases, the father's wisdom, height, light, peace and bliss can meet with the dynamic qualities and boundless will-power of the son. At that time perfection dawns in the particular country. Both the country and the child become perfect instruments, supreme instruments for God-manifestation on earth.

FW 105. *How can we be patriotic without separating ourselves from other countries?*

Sri Chinmoy: I shall live in my own country, in my own home, and you will live in your own home. I will keep my house clean, and if you want to come, I shall welcome you as a divine guest and invite you to stay as long as you want to. I also will expect you to keep your house clean and welcome me when I want to come and visit you.

According to my experience and my capacity, I have built a house. According to your capacity, your talent, your aspiration and your determination, you have also built a house. Now our aspiration, capacity and ability have become one. We will come together, but your home will remain your home and my home will remain my home. While staying in my own home and loving my own home, I shall not criticise or belittle yours. I won't say that my home is far superior to yours. I will feel that mine is good for me and yours is good for you. When the time comes, you will visit my house and see what it looks like and I will visit yours. This means we shall accept each other and derive benefit from each other's experience.

When I love my country first, then my real power of love never becomes stagnant; it always runs, runs towards the Source, which is all-pervading. It is like a river flowing towards the sea. If I really love my country, then I will be able to love other countries, because by loving my own country I will learn to know what a country is to its children.

If I really love one thing, then I have the capacity to love something else. If I really love my body, I will some day have the capacity to love my soul or to love my vital or to love some other part of my being. But if I do not have love for myself, then I won't be able to love anybody. I won't even love God. Patriotism is a kind of expanding capacity. Today I love my mother, tomorrow I love my father, the day after tomorrow I love my brothers and sisters. Then, when I go to school, I love my teachers. Gradually I learn to love my town, then my province, then my country, then the whole world. But I start by loving one thing which is very close to me. From there my vision increases. From my mother I go to my father, then to my brothers and sisters and so on. But if I don't love my own country, how will I be able to love somebody else's country? If

I really love my country, then gradually, gradually I will be able to expand my consciousness until finally I love the whole world.

Divine love, true love expands and expands. It has the power of constant expansion. If I really love my country divinely, then I will have a cosmopolitan view; I will love other countries as well. But if I constantly and deliberately try to find fault with my country, then gradually I will try to find fault with my city and with the members of my family, with myself and everything I have. I will find that my nose is not beautiful, my eyes are not beautiful, my hands are not beautiful and so on.

We start by loving something small and gradually we learn to love the whole universe. For a child his mother is the whole universe. Then, as he grows older, gradually his vision expands. That doesn't mean that he loves his mother less, but inside his mother he learns to see the whole world, little by little. Similarly, inside your country you can see the existence of all other countries. Then, if you love your country, naturally you will also love all the other countries that exist inside the heart of your own country. Inside the divine qualities of your own country you are bound to see the existence of other countries; for anything that is good is vast, anything that is divine is all-pervasive. And since patriotism is good and divine, it is vast, it is infinite, it is all-pervasive.

FW 106. *If we love our country but live elsewhere, how can we serve our country?*

Sri Chinmoy: If geography separates you from your country, you can offer your goodwill to the soul of your country. You are from South Africa. Do you think that your goodwill, your love, your concern in the inner world will not enter into the soul of South Africa? When a mother is in India and her son is in America working in an office, the moment he gets a letter from his mother his whole face changes, his whole consciousness changes. He swims in the sea of his mother's affection and love. Then immediately gratitude grows inside his heart; he becomes gratitude itself. And even if he has not received a letter, how many times his mother's consciousness enters into the son when she thinks of him with her boundless love and concern. The mother may be far away and busy with many projects, but she constantly feels the existence of her son inside her.

If you really love your country as a son loves his mother, geographically you may remain far away, but spiritually your mother-country can be inside you and you can be inside your mother-country. This feeling is not an illusion or a product of the imagination. Far from it. From the inner world you have come to the outer world. When you cherish a divine thought, the world is divine. When you cherish an undivine thought, the world is undivine. The moment you cherish a divine thought you are bound to feel your existence inside that world. The moment you think of your mother's love and concern for you, immediately you create a divine world of your own. And inside that world you feel the existence of your dearest mother. And when your mother thinks of you with all her affection, love, concern and blessings, she immediately creates a world of her own for you to exist inside her heart.

It is not the outer location but the inner feeling that is important. Where real concern exists, where real love exists, there the bond of oneness, inseparable oneness, reigns supreme. The son can stay in any part of the world and the mother can stay in any part of the world, but the bond of oneness which is inside their hearts can be felt and utilised at every moment. The mother will see the fulfilment of her existence inside the son no matter where he is. And the son will feel his success, his progress and the meaning and purpose of his life inside his mother.

FW 107. *Is not patriotism restrictive even at its highest level?*

Sri Chinmoy: If the patriotism is based upon the physical consciousness or the vital consciousness or the mental consciousness, then it restricts, because that patriotism does not want to go beyond the boundary of the physical, the vital or the mind. But if the patriotism comes from the soul's oneness with the universe or from the feeling that the soul is a divine instrument, a perfect instrument of the Supreme and for the Supreme on earth, then it will not restrict. Then the physical in us, the vital in us, the mind in us will want to become part and parcel of the soul's light and the soul's acceptance of light here on earth. That kind of patriotism is not a hindrance at all. It is a real benefit.

Some people have tremendous feeling for their country, but it is all on the physical level or on the vital level or on the mental level; it is not on the psychic level. In the psychic there is always oneness, constant oneness, and it is the nature of oneness to expand, if I love my country, I have become one with my country. Then, if I feel the inner urge to expand my oneness, to embrace other countries, I will find no inner restriction in my patriotism. But if I keep my love and oneness only for *my* country, naturally I will be restricted. This kind of patriotism will not allow me to go to the Highest, the Absolute, the Universal.

We have to know that oneness is not enough. From oneness we have to grow into vastness, I can have oneness with one finger, but I want to have oneness with all my fingers. If I love my eyes, I can establish oneness only with my eyes. But my poor nose, my poor ears — what will they do? I have to establish my oneness with them too. The moment I establish oneness with everything within me and around me, I enter into universality. There God is omnipresent. While I am for all, I am also in all. At that time I am in God, I am with God and I am for God. The real reality in me is the omnipresence of God — inside me, inside you, inside everything. If I consider the omnipresence of God as the only reality, then patriotism is a true blessing.

So our patriotism has to be based in our psychic consciousness. If it is in our psychic consciousness, it is constantly expanding its oneness and entering into the Infinite. This kind of patriotism will never limit our God-realisation. On the contrary, it will teach us the process of growing from the one to the many. As I expand my consciousness, gradually, gradually the whole world becomes mine. If we accept our country for the fulfilment of the real reality in us, and not for the pleasure of our physical or the fulfilment of our vital or mind, then patriotism is a gift, a real gift, the highest gift from Above which will illumine and liberate the human in us.

Otherwise, patriotism can become a curse. When it becomes narrow-minded, then I am only for my village or my country, and against yours. Narrowness comes when patriotism is in the physical, the vital or the mind, which are limited. But in the psychic, in the soul, there is no boundary. The soul's feelings are based on oneness inside vastness. That kind of patriotism is all God-embodiment, God-revelation and God-perfection on earth. This is what God wants from patriotism.

FW 108. *When a person who doesn't belong to the chosen few is faced with a decision in life, how does he or she know what is God's Will in matters like marriage, studies, professions and things like that?*

Sri Chinmoy: If one is among the chosen few, then naturally one has a free access to one's inner world, and from there one gets the direct message from the Inner Pilot. But if he is not one of the chosen few, what should he do? Since he feels that he is not in a position to decide what is best for himself, he should go to someone in whom he has all faith. Then his problem can easily be solved. Suppose you are sick. If you cannot cure yourself, you go to the doctor because you have faith in him and you feel that he will be able to cure you. You already have this faith in him; it is not something you have to acquire. In the spiritual life also, when you want to make a major decision regarding your earthly life — marriage and so forth — go to a spiritual person in whom you have faith. He will be able to enter into your soul and bring to the fore the real message from your soul. He will be able to tell you whether the marriage is a good idea or not.

But if one is not among the chosen few, this doesn't mean that he will never be. Today he is not among them, but tomorrow he has every possibility of becoming one of them. In the spiritual life a time will come when the seeker will have more aspiration, abundant aspiration, boundless, infinite aspiration. When he has constant, burning aspiration, naturally he will become one of the chosen few. At that time, he can solve his own problems. But right now, if one feels he does not have the necessary capacity to solve his earthly problems, then it is advisable for him to go to a spiritual Master, who is bound to give him the correct message.

FW 109. *How does spirituality help one decide between what is right and what is wrong?*

Sri Chinmoy: Even a child knows what is right and what is wrong. He has something in his inner being which we call conscience, and this has been there from his very birth. Seekers of the infinite Truth, who walk along the path of spirituality, will especially be able to know what is right and what is wrong, because at every moment they try to listen to their inner voice or, you can say, conscience. The further we go along the path of reality, the deeper within we go, the clearer it becomes to us what is right and what is wrong. When we live on the surface, it is next to impossible for us to distinguish what is right from what is wrong. But when we follow the inner life and have the capacity to bring forward the inner message, then at every moment we are safe. From within we get the inner urge to do only the right thing.

The very purpose of spirituality is to enable us to have conscious oneness with the ultimate Truth. If somebody has this conscious oneness, naturally he will be able to distinguish right from wrong. Whoever practises the spiritual life has a special advantage as well. When he gets an inner message, he also gets the inspiration to obey the message. He gets additional inspiration or, let us say, aspiration, to do the right thing. But an ordinary person very often does the wrong thing in spite of knowing that he is doing something wrong. Why does he do it? Because his inner urge is not strong enough to compel him to do the right thing. In the case of a spiritual seeker it is otherwise. When a seeker feels the right thing, he gets abundant capacity from within to do it.

FW 110. *Could you please explain why you give your followers spiritual names?*

Sri Chinmoy: Everyone has all the divine qualities, but one quality is often pre-eminent. One divine quality is usually more manifest in a certain person than the other divine qualities, and the soul has a way of manifesting the highest Truth through that particular quality. One soul will manifest through light, another through beauty, a third through power, a fourth through compassion, a fifth through peace, a sixth through joy. Each Sanskrit name I offer has a spiritual significance, and each aspirant has the capacity to realise and manifest the Highest through a particular quality which his name reveals and embodies. If the soul wants to realise and manifest the Highest on earth, then if the aspirant knows that particular quality, it becomes infinitely easier. When the disciples have spiritual names and they meditate on their names, at that time their divine qualities come to the fore most powerfully and make them feel what they are here for and why they have come into the world. That is why we give these names.

FW 111. *Why should spiritual people accept life around them?*

Sri Chinmoy: If you say that those who enter into the Himalayan caves and neglect society will find less difficulty in realising God, I may agree with you. But if they do not accept humanity, what do they ultimately gain? If I love God, my Father, and if I see that my brothers and sisters cannot yet approach Him, if I am a really fine person, what will I do? I will offer my light and my achievement to my brothers and sisters. I have received realisation from my Father, but if I do not give it to my brothers and sisters, then is it not shameful on my part?

You may say that other paths are easier than mine because there the seeker escapes from the world. But in the ordinary world only a culprit wants to escape. If one has done something wrong, he tries to escape. Some spiritual Masters do want to escape even though they are not thieves. They are sick of the world and sick of the world's ingratitude. Constantly they try to help humanity, but humanity ignores them, misunderstands them, criticises them, abuses them. They become disgusted and feel that the thing to do is to escape from the world. Again, there are some who are real heroes. They say, "Let humanity insult us, speak ill of us; still we shall give humanity what we have to offer."

Our path is the path of acceptance. If we do not accept something, how are we going to transform it? If the potter does not touch clay, how is he going to shape and mould the pot? If his ultimate aim is to make a pot or pitcher, he has to touch the clay. This clay is the world. A spiritual Master enters into the inconscience and ignorance of the seekers and throws light into them. Then he moulds, shapes and gives strength to their inner being. Our path is undoubtedly the heroic path. Those who follow our path are playing the role of divine warriors. Divine warriors are those who fight against doubt, worry, fear, obstruction, limitation, imperfection, bondage and death. Our path is a path for the brave.

At the same time, the results one gets from following our path come in infinite measure, because our path has accepted humanity. If you have a large plot of ground and if you have the capacity to cultivate it, then you are bound to get a bumper crop of realisation for humanity. But if your plot of land is very tiny, then what are you going to get? Our path is difficult because it has accepted the outer life. If you don't love God, everything is difficult. But nothing is really difficult when you have true love for God. If you really love God, our path does not seem difficult at all; it seems very safe, secure, easy.

Our path is the path of acceptance. We accept our brothers and sisters as they are; then we give them what we have and what we are. Only then is God pleased with us and will He be eternally pleased with us, because we have consciously made our life a life of self-dedication. This is the easiest path for the sincere, the most fulfilling path for those who are totally dedicated and the best path for the brave souls who want to walk, march and run along the road of Eternity.

FW 112. *How can I be more soulful and devoted in my work at the United Nations?*

Sri Chinmoy: You can be more soulful and more devoted in your work if you feel that you are working here not just to earn money, but to serve God inside the soul of the United Nations and inside the body of the United Nations. The moment you think of the United Nations, you have to feel that it is a world organisation that sincerely wants to bring about peace and harmony on earth. To work here and serve the soul of the United Nations is a great honour, a great privilege, no matter in which capacity you are working. If you think of the soul of the United Nations and of your own soul's commitment to the United Nations, your soul will work very hard in and through you. The United Nations has a very high, sublime goal. If you think of this, automatically you will become soulful and devoted because the goal itself will try to bring from the depth of your being your devoted heart qualities.

FW 113. *How can we have more feeling of oneness with our fellow workers?*

Sri Chinmoy: If your fellow workers are not spiritual or spiritually inclined, then you have to exercise more compassion and sacrifice. If somebody needs more kindness and affection, then you should be ready to give to that person — not according to what he deserves, but according to your own heart's magnanimity. If somebody is nasty to you, or is not helping you in your work, you have to feel that this is another challenge to become extra nice, extra kind, extra sweet so you can bring forward the good qualities in that person. Some people are good, some are bad. Bad ones we try to conquer through patience, concern and love. If we treat them the way they treat us, we will enter into the animal world. So we have to work in a divine way.

FW 114. *How can I illumine my mind?*

Sri Chinmoy: Just by allowing your soul's light to come to the mind through the heart. It is as if you have three rooms — mind, heart and soul — and the only way to reach the third room is to go through the second one. The soul has to come to the mind-room through the heart-room. First concentrate on the soul and feel its presence in the soul-room. Then try to bring the soul into the heart-room. Once the soul is well established in the heart-room, illumining the heart, the time has come to enter into the mind-room. So you bring the soul into the mind-room and the mind becomes illumined. The only way to illumine the mind is to bring the presence of the soul into the mind. First you bring the soul into the heart and let the heart be illumined. Then, when the heart is illumined, you let the soul come and serve the Supreme in the mind. There is no other way.

FW 115. *If we find that certain situations disturb us, should we avoid the situations or try to face them and cope with them?*

Sri Chinmoy: Avoiding a situation is not the right answer. We have to face the situation with our soul's light. Today you will avoid a circumstance and, just because you have avoided it, the wrong forces of this circumstance will get more strength. Either they will think that you are avoiding them because you are weak, or they will think that you are avoiding them because it is beneath your dignity to deal with them. And in that case, they will come against you with more power.

If you try to escape you may escape *here,* but *there* you will be caught. So it is best to face a problem when it arises, and not try to escape. But you should not face the situation in a military way: somebody is challenging you, so you will strike him. No, that is silly. Try instead to bring the divinity of the circumstance forward. If some undivine quality is inside an individual, it is not by striking or hitting him that you will overcome it, but by becoming more friendly. With more confidence in your approach to God you have to bring forward the divine qualities in the human being or the incident that is causing the problem. Accept the situation with compassion and love, and eventually these unpleasant circumstances are bound to become pleasant, soulful and fruitful.

FW 116. *How can I develop and maintain a feeling of worthiness and self-respect?*

Sri Chinmoy: You have to feel that you need God and that you have God. You are not aware of the fact that the thing that you want and need in order to discover your worth is already there. God is already there, but you don't see Him. You are an instrument of God; His Capacity, His Vision, His Reality are there and He wants to manifest through you. But how can you be conscious of it? You can become conscious through your dedicated, soulful aspiration and service. If you pray and meditate you will become aware of God's presence in your life, and you will see that you are really worthy of God's Love. Because of your prayer and meditation, the Inner Pilot will make you conscious of His activities; and you will see that He is manifesting His Divinity in and through you. When you are conscious of this, who else but you can be worthy? So if you become more soulful, devoted and sincere in your approach to the Inner Pilot, you can easily become conscious of your own divine qualities. For you will realise that everything that God has, you are going to have as your own.

You have to feel that divine confidence is most necessary. Divine confidence makes you feel that you are worthy of becoming God's instrument. And what is divine confidence? It is confidence in God and in yourself. Unless you have confidence in God and in yourself, you can never be worthy of anything. Your self-confidence tells you that you will do everything for God; and your God-confidence tells you that He will do everything in and through you, that He is more than eager to manifest through you. When you have confidence in yourself and confidence in God, you will be able to see your inner progress and inside that progress you will see that you are really worthy of God's Compassion, Joy and Pride.

FW 117. *How can I be more selfless?*

Sri Chinmoy: You can be more selfless by watching the world situation, by watching people who are not selfless and by watching people who are selfless. People who are not selfless are greedy. Greedy people can never be happy. You want to become selfless because you want to be happy. People who are not selfless, who are greedy and miserly, are not happy at all. Again, people who are selfless and sacrificing are happy.

It is like night and day, and you are in between. When you are in night you want to grab and bind the world, and when you are in day you want to dedicate yourself to the world and serve the world. So you can either go to your friend darkness or to your friend day. When you are entering into darkness you are only struggling and binding; but in day-consciousness you are loving, showing concern and becoming one. So you have to see what is happening to those in day and those in night, and then make the choice. Once you are in the room of light, it is all love, sacrifice and concern. Once you enter the room of darkness, it is all fighting and struggling. That door is also open to you. It is you who have to make the choice. Enter the room of selflessness and don't enter the other room.

FW 118. *If someone comes to me and speaks sharply in a negative way, is it undivine on my part to ask that person not to speak to me in that way or should I be more compassionate?*

Sri Chinmoy: It depends. Suppose you feel that it is a very important matter and that the person is talking in a rude, undivine manner. At that time say to the person, "Please be calm and quiet and talk politely. I am ready to hear you." But if the person is only coming to harass and bother you, at that time you have every right to tell him to leave. If it is only casual talk and the person becomes unnecessarily rude and unkind, at that time tell him to leave you.

FW 119. *How can we not bother about other people's opinions of us?*

Sri Chinmoy: When you realise God, He will not ask you, "What did *he* think of you?" or "What did *she* think of you?" God will immediately ask you, "What did you think of yourself?" or "What did you think of Me?" God will not ask you what others thought of you. As soon as you stand in front of God, He is not going to give you a pass-mark according to others' opinions of you. He is not going to look to see whether others appreciated or admired you. No, He is the boss; He doesn't need others' recommendation. When you go to the Supreme, at that time He will not ask what the world thought of you: He will ask if you paid attention to your spiritual life of aspiration and dedication. And you will have to prove that you have done this and you have done that for Him.

Suppose someone speaks highly of you. Do you think that person is lifting you up to the top of the Himalayas? Similarly, by depreciating you, by speaking ill of you, that person can't bring you down. No! His opinion has no value. You are to God what you actually are: what you think of yourself and what you think of God in yourself. Your assessment is your own value. Again, our assessment may not always be right. Sometimes we think we are pure, but we are impure; but no harm. When we make a wrong assessment, God is there to show us compassion and kindness. But God doesn't want us to waste a single minute worrying about what others think of us. Your life is God's Life. God's Life and your life are inseparable and God doesn't need the opinion of the world to assess what you are doing. If you are praying and meditating, you are an excellent seeker. Your action is your certificate; your action is everything in God's Eye.

FW 120. *How can we keep our awareness?*

Sri Chinmoy: When we don't keep our awareness, what happens? We become friends with inconscience and ignorance. And when we keep our awareness, when we remain alert, what happens? If we are alert we go much faster. Alertness is speed in life. If we have to cover twenty miles, if we are alert, nothing can distract us or prevent us from running the fastest towards the goal. If we have a goal, then we can discard unnecessary things. Suppose your goal is a Master's degree. If you go to movies and night clubs, how can you reach your goal? There is a goal and you want to run the fastest to the goal. So naturally you are going to do the thing that will automatically make you run the fastest. And that is to keep your awareness. If always you think of the goal, then there will be inspiration, aspiration and an inner urge to reach the goal as soon as possible.

FW 121. *How can we conquer the dark forces in us?*

Sri Chinmoy: You can conquer the dark forces provided you know who your boss, your supreme boss, is. You have to feel that the forces are like two little boys. One is divine and the other is undivine. The divine one is afraid of the undivine one because the undivine one wants to strike him and he feels he doesn't have enough strength to put up a brave fight. But if he sees that his father is standing beside him, he knows his father has more power than the other boy and will protect him. If you feel the presence of the Supreme inside you, the hostile forces can't attack you because there is someone to protect you. If they attack, immediately He will come and frighten them. Just as the little divine boy knows his eternal Father is inside him to protect him, save him and illumine him, you also have to feel that the Absolute Supreme is inside you to do the needful for you. Provided you have confidence in Him, He will do everything for you and He will not allow the undivine forces to come and attack you.

FW 122. *What is meditation?*

Sri Chinmoy: Meditation is conscious awareness of God. Here we are all seekers. When we are seekers, it is our duty to become aware of God twenty-four hours a day. If we are believers in God, then naturally we feel that God exists. But this feeling is not spontaneous; it does not last twenty-four hours a day. When we meditate, we come to feel and realise twenty-four hours a day that we are of God and we are for God. Constant and conscious awareness of God — His Truth, Light and Bliss — is called meditation.

FW 123. *How can one increase one's purity?*

Sri Chinmoy: One can increase one's purity by repeating a special word or mantra. There can be no better word than "God". One can repeat "God" while breathing in and out. While breathing in, you have to feel that at least seven breaths are coming inside each breath and offering you more life-energy. While breathing in, repeat "God", and inside the breath try to see God seven times. And then, after some time, try to see or feel God fourteen times. In this way, try to increase your purity by increasing your count.

There is also something else which I advise my students to do. Start repeating God's Name right from today. Today you try to repeat God's Name twenty times most soulfully, tomorrow thirty times, the next day forty times. In this way, you bring the number up to one hundred. Then you start descending: ninety, eighty, seventy, sixty, fifty, forty, thirty, twenty, until the circle is complete. When you try to increase the number, please use your imagination to feel that your purity is increasing. And when you decrease the number, at that time please feel that you are not decreasing the number; you are only assimilating the increased purity that you have felt. While going up, try to increase your purity, and while going down try to assimilate in your system the purity-force that you achieved by repeating God's Name.

FW 124. *What Is God? Where is He?*

Sri Chinmoy: God is everywhere. But if we do not see Him or feel Him inside our hearts, then we will not be able to see Him anywhere. First, we have to see Him within us and talk to Him inside our hearts. If we do this, then only will we be able to see God elsewhere also. If inside our heart God is missing, then we shall not be able to see God anywhere and we shall not be able to speak to God or mix with God.

Now, what is God? God is both formless and with form. He is pure energy and, at the same time, He is the most luminous form. He is endless energy and beginningless energy; and He is also the most luminous form. God is both water and ice. Some people like water, while others like ice. Again, some people at times like to drink water and at times like to have ice.

It depends on the seeker and what he wants. He may want to see God in a human form — but as absolutely divine, supreme, perfect. He feels that if there is a form, then it will be easier for him to recognise God or realise God. So he likes to see the personal God. But again, if one says that he wants to go beyond the personal God, beyond form, beyond duality and remain always in the infinite Peace, Light and Bliss, that also can be done. And the same seeker can in the morning ask for God with form-attributes and in the evening cry for God as formless, boundless energy.

FW 125. *How can one maintain inner tranquillity at work when he is in an atmosphere with a great deal of pressure?*

Sri Chinmoy: One can maintain inner tranquillity no matter what happens in his office or how many wrong forces from the office try to assail him. He can do this provided he feels that the forces which are attacking him are in no way a match for his love of Light.

Let us take an attack as a force of darkness. When you are in the office you are constantly attacked by the force of doubt, which is the representative of darkness. If you feel that you have nothing to break these forces, then you are totally lost. You have to feel that inside your heart there is something called Light — boundless Light — and that this boundless luminosity is definitely more powerful than the attacker. This Light that you have inside you can easily transform these forces. When darkness consciously or unconsciously enters into Light, it is bound to be transformed. You will be able to feel this just because you pray, just because you meditate, just because you want to increase your love of God every day, every hour, every minute, every second. Each second you are aware of God's Presence inside your heart, so you can rest assured that you definitely embody Light and that this Light is constantly increasing in you. And if you see a constant increase of divine Light inside your heart, that means there is something immortal inside you which will never surrender to the wrong forces.

The wrong forces are coming from outside; and inside, the strongest force, the mightiest force, is Light. When you can bring your mightiest force, Light, to the fore, then you will see to your great astonishment that the outer forces immediately will give way, because the inner force is in constant communication with the Source, the Almighty Absolute. So the more you can increase your inner Light, which is the divine force, the sooner you will see that the outer wrong forces which are attacking you will be transformed into Light. When darkness consciously or unconsciously enters into Light, it is bound to be transformed.

FW 126. *How can spiritual seekers working at the United Nations make other workers feel that prayer and meditation are a tangible way of dealing with world problems?*

Sri Chinmoy: You have colleagues in your own department, and they speak to you every day. The days you meditate they see something totally different in you from the days when you do not meditate. If you have achieved something in your meditation, they are bound to see something pleasing, soothing, beautiful, enlightening and illumining. So the higher and deeper your meditation, the more your face and outer being will radiate. When your being radiates, your friends and colleagues will see something totally new. At the same time, they will feel something familiar although they don't know what it is. Why familiar? Because we have all come from the same Source. They have not discovered this secret, whereas you have discovered it. You have tried, you have practised meditation. They have not yet practised it, but they will. Your own example — not only your example, but your very presence — will inspire them.

Here on earth oneness is not established. Oneness you cannot establish on the ordinary human level where there is anxiety, worry, fear and doubt — unless you aspire. If you aspire, then your inner being tries to act all the time like a magnet. It tries to see whether there is someone whom it can call its own. So, if somebody is sitting beside you with divine joy, divine love, divine peace, then naturally the magnet that you have inside you will draw these divine qualities from that person. Again, if an unaspiring person sits beside you, who is given to worldly life and worldly temptation, immediately you will find a kind of restlessness inside your own being.

Outwardly, you don't have to tell others hundreds of times how you have changed your life or what you can do for them. This you can tell them once in a blue moon, but it will be almost useless. But they will see you on two different days: one day when you have not meditated well and on another day after you have had a good meditation. The day you have meditated well, they will see a tremendous change in you. They will try to know what makes you on one day divine and what makes you on another day undivine. What is it that they want to have from you when you meditate, and what is it that they don't want from you when you do not meditate? What they do not want is darkness and ignorance. What they want is the inner divinity which comes to the fore and tries to illumine the persons and the things around you.

FW 127. *Is meditation for everybody regardless of whether a person is consciously seeking God?*

Sri Chinmoy: Yes, meditation is for everybody whether he is consciously seeking God or not. The only thing is that one has to know how far one wants to go. Somebody can study at the kindergarten. Again, somebody else can go on to high school, college and university and get a Master's degree or Ph.D. But this is outer knowledge. Meditation gives us inner wisdom.

You may be satisfied with an iota of inner wisdom. Again, you may find that you can satisfy yourself only with boundless Peace, Light and Bliss. So it depends on where the seeker wants to stop. Just as we go to school for outer knowledge we have to meditate in order to get inner wisdom. If the seeker wants to be satisfied only with a fraction of Peace, Light and Bliss, then he will get it. And if he wants to get boundless Peace, Light and Bliss, then he shall also get that provided he continues to meditate regularly, devotedly, soulfully, unreservedly and unconditionally.

FW 128. *Can you tell us the place of good character in the spiritual life?*

Sri Chinmoy: In the spiritual life good character is of paramount importance. Good character means that life-energy — soulful, boundless energy — is operating in and through the seeker. If the seeker does not see the boundless Energy, Peace, Light and Bliss, then how can he remain in his highest consciousness?

If one is a seeker, then he has to be a man of character; otherwise, his life will be contradictory. God is all purity. It is through purity that one realises God. If one wants to realise

God as fast as possible, then purity must come first. To make real, solid, tangible progress, purity is indispensable. Now, if one does not have a good character, then how can that person have purity? And if one does not have purity inside the heart and inside the physical then how can he make progress?

Purity and character come simultaneously. If someone has inner purity, then he also has good character. And if there is somebody with good character, then he is maintaining in his inner life tremendous purity. Purity is the ladder we climb up in order to reach God's Abode. If there is no ladder, then how can we climb up?

FW 129. *What does it mean to be a spiritual Master?*

Sri Chinmoy: A spiritual Master is a private tutor. He is the elder brother in the family. Either you can call him a private tutor or you can call him an elder brother. The school teacher examines the student and either fails or passes him according to merit. If he has done well, the teacher will pass him in the examination. If he has not done well, the teacher will dispense justice. But the private tutor will all the time teach the student at home so that he can pass the examination. The spiritual teacher privately teaches the student how to stand in front of ignorance and face ignorance so that when ignorance challenges him, he will be able to pass the examination.

Again, the teacher is the eldest member in the family. Just because he has a little more Peace, Light and Bliss than others, God has chosen him to give his little Peace, Light and Bliss to his younger brothers and sisters. He knows that he is not the father. And, also, his younger brothers and sisters know that he is not the father. The father is somebody else. But because he is the elder brother, he is supposed to know where the father is. The elder brother of the family tells the younger ones, "Come,

I will show you where our Father is." And once he can bring the younger ones to their common Father, his role is over. They will be on their own as soon as he shows them where the Father is.

FW 130. *How can we as individuals encourage a world-wide recognition of the basic unity of all major religions?*

Sri Chinmoy: If we practise spirituality, if we pray and meditate soulfully, our very illumination will encourage others. It is we who have to be illumined first before we can encourage others. The world will be inspired by us only when we grow into something and become something. Each individual's religion is, after all, his code of life. His code of life is his religion. When his life responds to some higher, deeper realities, then it is meaningful and fruitful and it can inspire others.

FW 131. *How can the different religions best respect and value each other?*

Sri Chinmoy: Each religion must feel that it is nothing but a branch. If there is a branch, then there has to be a tree; and the tree is love of Truth. Truth finds fulfilment only when it embraces the Vast as its very own. Each religion has to feel the necessity of embracing other religions for its own satisfaction, for its own perfection. Alone it can never be satisfied; alone it can never be perfect. Two hands are required to produce a sound. Similarly, two things or even more will be needed to create something beautiful, soulful and fruitful. But when you go deep within, you do not see two things or three things; you see only one thing that is operating in and through many forms, many ideas, many ideals and realisations.

FW 132. *I was brought up as a Roman Catholic, but when I grew up I stopped attending church. Now that I am again interested in the spiritual life, my mother cannot understand why I don't want to attend church again. How should I explain this to her?*

Sri Chinmoy: You can tell your mother that you studied in that particular school and you did not care for it. Now you are studying in a different school and you like the teacher, you like the students and you like what you are being taught. The Catholic Church teaches Truth, Light, Peace and Bliss. You are also trying to bring to the fore Truth, Light, Peace and Bliss in a different way. So if you take the Roman Catholic Church as a school and our spiritual organisation as another school, then you have every right to say that you like one particular school and not another, and that is why you are going to that school.

FW 133. *Can we transcend our religion for a more vast spirituality?*

Sri Chinmoy: There comes a time when we have to transcend our religion-barriers. Religion is good, but we have to go far beyond religion. Religion will tell us about God; sometimes it will create fear in us when we do something wrong. The religious approach to God is mostly through fear. But the spiritual approach to God is always through love. It is not out of fear that we approach God but out of love. We want to establish our inseparable oneness with God. I don't want to say that religion does not have love for God, because it has. But fear of God very often looms large in people who practise religion. People who practise Yoga do not have that kind of fear. They have only love of God. Oneness with God is what they want.

Religion feels that there is someone called God who is high above, in the sky or in Heaven or somewhere else, and that all Peace, Light and Bliss are with Him. But Yoga will say that where I am is Light, Peace and Bliss; where I move around is Truth. Truth and I are inseparable. Religion does not claim that oneness. Religion will say Truth is somewhere else; we can have a free access to it eventually. It says Truth is somewhere, Light is somewhere, and only if we pray and meditate will we one day see the face of Truth and Light. But Yoga will say, "No. Where I am, the very thing I am looking for is also there. I am the very thing that I am now looking for, searching for, striving for. Everything is already inside me, only I have forgotten it, I cannot recognise it or I have misplaced it." Yoga tells us to look for our inner wealth, to discover and bring to the fore what we eternally have. Spirituality is Yoga in a vast and broad sense.

FW 134. *Is it possible to reach the state of God-realisation by devotedly practising one's religion?*

Sri Chinmoy: Yes, by practising one's own religion one can realise God. But one has to feel that there is something else higher and deeper than religion and that is the constant inner cry. Religion as such will tell us there is a God. It will tell us that we have to be good, we have to be kind, we have to be simple, sincere and pure. This much religion will offer us. This is general religion. But there is also a spiritual religion which is higher and deeper. It will say that it is not enough just to know that God exists. We also have to see Him, we have to feel Him, we have to grow into Him. And this we do through prayer and meditation.

FW 135. *Why does reference to God or religion embarrass so many people?*

Sri Chinmoy: People have become very sophisticated; they now have a machine-like consciousness. Anything that does not give them satisfaction on the physical plane, vital plane or mental plane, or anything that does not exist right in front of their nose, that thing they feel is unreal, embarrassing. And anything that they do not or cannot know immediately, or anything that they do not have an immediate need for in their life, they do not value.

Also, many people who claim to follow a religion at times do not lead even an ordinary, simple human life. In the name of religious life, in the name of spiritual life, they do quite a few unthinkable, unbelievable, unimaginable things. So people who feel and think that they are normal, feel that this kind of life is all abnormality. But I wish to say that the strange behaviour of some so-called spiritual people is in no way an indication of their inner progress or illumination. Some people are fanatic; some people are not sincere in their approach or they approach religion in a very aggressive way. Some people are at times embarrassed when they happen to mix with those individuals.

But the really religious people never create embarrassment. Actually, who should be embarrassed? He who has seen the light, or he who is crying for the light? No! Only he who does not care for the light should be embarrassed. If I as an individual have seen the light, then why should I feel embarrassed to speak to you? And if you as an individual need light and are crying for light, then why should you be embarrassed? He who has and he who needs light will never be embarrassed. We should be embarrassed only when we do not have something that others need and have, and when we do not care for that very thing and do not appreciate the persons who have it. We should be embarrassed only then.

FW 136. *Please explain the difference between "religious fervour" and "Delight". Can the two complement each other?*

Sri Chinmoy: No. Religious fervour can be in the vital, in the mind or in some other part of our existence. It can satisfy us only on the vital or mental level. Religious fervour, religious joy we get mainly on the vital level. But when one experiences Delight, it permeates his entire being. Delight is something infinitely higher than religious fervour. It is on the strength of our oneness with the Absolute Supreme, or on the strength of our total dedication to His Will, that we get Delight. Delight deals with our own birthless and deathless inner existence, with the full manifestation of the divine within us. So these are two different things.

FW 137. *Is religion indispensable for our Self-realisation?*

Sri Chinmoy: Everything within us that is good is responsible for Self-realisation. But if you ask what is indispensable, then I will say that only one thing is indispensable and that is our inner cry, our constant, inmost cry.

FW 138. *How does religious discipline differ from spiritual discipline?*

Sri Chinmoy: Religious discipline is not asking you to pray and meditate every second of your life. Religious discipline may tell you to go to church once a week and pray to God. That is more than enough for religious discipline. But if it is spiritual discipline, then it will tell you to be conscious of God twenty-four hours a day and to pray and meditate at least twice a day —

in the morning and in the evening. Spiritual discipline is a conscious, constant process. It is infinitely more significant than religious discipline, for when one practises spiritual discipline, one tries to be a conscious and constant living instrument of God so that God can manifest in and through him in His own Way. If one follows spiritual discipline, then at the end of the road one feels that one is growing into the very Image of God; whereas if one follows religious discipline, at the end of the road one will say that one has come and seen the goal. Religious discipline at most can lead you to the goal, whereas spiritual discipline or yogic discipline will not only take you to the goal but also make you feel that you are nothing short of the goal itself.

FW 139. *How can self-offering be distinguished from other kinds of actions?*

Sri Chinmoy: Somebody may do something to fulfil his own purpose without a higher goal or even without a higher ideal. Each thing we do is not necessarily a self-offering. You may be working in an office — your physical is working, your vital is working, your mind is working — but your attitude need not be spiritual. Self-offering has to be done with a consecrated attitude inside the entire being. If the attitude is spiritual, only then is it self-offering. While working, you have to feel that this is what the divine within you, the Supreme within you is asking you to do. And then you have to go one step ahead. You have to feel that God Himself is acting in and through you for His own satisfaction. This is the divine attitude. Only when we embody this attitude is our work a self-giving and a self-offering.

It is the attitude inside the action that determines whether the action is selfless self-giving or whether it is something done in a subtle way for self-glory. If an action is motivated and inspired by a higher cause, then only can we say it is self-offering. Otherwise, here on earth we do thousands and millions of things just because we have to meet with earthly responsibilities and earthly obligations. Here there need not be any divine inspiration; there need not be any divine inner awakening. If there is no inner awakening, if there is no inner awareness of what we are doing, why we are doing it and how it should be done, then we cannot call it self-offering.

FW 140. *Sometimes when I am meditating I fall asleep, not because I am tired, but because I feel that I am somehow trapped in my mind. I try to get into my heart, but I do not succeed; thoughts keep racing through my mind, and then I fall asleep.*

Sri Chinmoy: You are having a terrible battle inside your mind and you are an unwitting victim. Your thought-world is attacking you and your life of aspiration is fighting with the thought-world, and finally aspiration gives way to the thought-world. Take thought as a soldier and aspiration as another soldier. Aspiration is trying to go up and thought is trying to put an end to aspiration. Now they fight and you are the battlefield. When soldiers fight in the battlefield and one side wins, they win the field itself. In your case, they fight inside you. When the thought-world wins the fight, it takes you. At this time you are tired from the battle and you fall asleep. When you fall asleep, there can be no aspiration and there cannot be any thought either.

How can you prevent yourself from sleeping? There are various ways. The simplest way is to repeat the name of the Supreme or any other word you like, as fast as possible. Imagine that you are an express train with only one destination. The driver of that train is constantly repeating God's name to derive energy, strength, stamina, encouragement, concern and all divine qualities. Now, an express train stops only at the end of its journey, the goal; on the way it does not stop at all. Your goal will be to reach or achieve a profound meditation. Always try to feel inside you a dynamic and progressive movement, but not an aggressive one. This movement undoubtedly will take you to your destination. If there is a dynamic and progressive movement, then you cannot fall asleep. Inside you, feel that the train is running, running towards the destination; feel that you yourself are this very train. Then you cannot fall asleep.

When you meditate you try to create inside yourself a dynamic peace, not a lethargic peace. Peace need not be lethargic. Sometimes people feel that they are enjoying peace when they are fast asleep, but this is a lethargic peace.

FLAME-WAVES

BOOK 7

FW I4I. *What is the relationship between the soul of the United Nations and the soul of the world?*

Sri Chinmoy: If you look at the body of the United Nations, then you can easily know what the soul of the United Nations is. The soul is the seed and the body is the tree. This is the relationship between the soul of the United Nations and the body of the United Nations. Now, if you think of the soul of the world and the body of the world, then you will also know what they actually are. The soul of the world is a vision in the higher plane, or in Heaven; and the body of the world is something that exists on the physical plane for manifestation.

The soul of the world embodies the soul of the United Nations. There are many nations which have not joined the United Nations. There are many places on earth which unfortunately do not have any connection with the United Nations. But the soul of the world must have some connection with everything that is in God's creation. There is nothing on earth that does not have a direct connection in the inner world with the soul of the world. But the soul of the United Nations unfortunately does not have or has not yet established that kind of connection with the entire world. You can call this connection oneness or awareness of the things that have been created here on earth.

When the soul of the United Nations grows into perfection, then it becomes the satisfaction-triumph of the soul of the world; it actually becomes the world soul. The soul of the United Nations must eventually grow into the world soul because it has to embody and embrace the length and breadth of the entire world. When we speak of the United Nations we have to speak of united creation. If it is united creation, then it becomes one world. When we use the word "nation", at that time we imagine a plot of land, a country, a few thousand or a few million people put together. But when we think of creation, at that time we don't think of human beings or countries or plots of land; we just think of God in His Manifestation. Right now when we think of the United Nations, that idea does not immediately come forward. But a day will come when the United Nations will expand its vision and encompass the whole horizon. At that time it will be another world soul, another form of world-reality, where God the Creator and God the creation can easily be found in every action.

FW 142. *Unless the peoples of the world as a whole aspire collectively, will there ever be abiding peace in the world?*

Sri Chinmoy: Collective aspiration need not or cannot take place all at once. If collective aspiration means twenty people all meditating and praying together for world peace, then I have to say that even among twenty people the standard or height need not to be the same. If they are praying together but are not of the same standard, not of the same sincerity, then I tell you the result cannot be of deep value. Suppose your aspiration is of the highest and somebody else's is not as high as yours and the third person's aspiration is even lower. True, this kind of collective aspiration is better than nothing, better than no aspiration at all. But it produces many problems. When you meditate together, if you are of different standards, there will be some inner conflict. It is like somebody studying in college and somebody studying in kindergarten. It is very difficult to study together in the same class.

Suppose in your family there are three brothers. You are the eldest member in the family, so you know more about the inner world, more about God, more about spirituality. You have to run according to your own speed, according to your own inner light and wisdom, and they will also run in their own way. When we use the term "collective", we have an idea of people sitting together or doing something together. But this is not the right approach. We will do it in our own way, according to our own capacity. You will begin to aspire when the hour has struck for you, and somebody else will begin to aspire two months or two years later when his own hour has struck. The result in this case will be far better than that achieved by putting everybody together to meditate. Aspiration has to be spontaneous. You reach a certain goal, so you go and stand there as a perfect human being. Tomorrow my time will come and I will start aspiring sincerely; then I will go and reach the destination that you have already reached. And the following day somebody else will go.

Each day if some human beings can achieve perfection in the inner world, then that means that these particular human beings are freed from imperfections. No longer are they quarrelling and fighting. Peace will come about in the world from the perfection of individuals. When ten individuals have achieved perfection, then it becomes a collective perfection. But in the beginning, while you are walking along the path, if you feel that the whole world will aspire together, it will not work. The whole world will aspire, but in its own way according to its receptivity. And if your aspiration is genuine, it has to be much more sincere, much deeper and more profound.

It is the ideal for the world to aspire collectively. But the world is not ready. So collective aspiration will come when you aspire individually and somebody else aspires individually. But if you put all human beings together and meditate for world peace, it won't work out. It is through individual readiness that world peace will come into existence. And when a number of individuals have established peace in themselves and are ready to bring down peace into the world atmosphere, then you can say that it is collective aspiration.

FW 143. *How can our imagination be used to help raise our conscious-ness or improve our meditation?*

Sri Chinmoy: First of all, we have to know that imagination is not mental hallucination. If we take imagination as something unproductive, as something that has nothing to do with reality, then imagination will never be reality. If we think that imagina-tion is the South Pole and reality is the North Pole, then it is all useless. We have to take imagination as a reality in another world, in an inner world or a higher world. And that world we have to bring into the world of reality that we are now living in. Imagination is a world of reality which is waiting for revelation and manifestation here in this outer world, which we know as reality.

Inside us are many worlds; imagination is one of these worlds. We have a free access to the world that is around us and before us, whereas we do not have a free access to the worlds that are inside us. So what we have to try to do is bring the world that is inside us into the world that is around us. It is like this: somebody is inside the house and somebody is outside the house. You are friendly with the person who is outside the house. You know him well because most of the time you stay outside. But when you come inside, you see that somebody else is there. You can also make friends with that person and ask him to come out with you and make friends with the person who is staying outside.

So, think of imagination as a reality in its own right which is on another plane of consciousness. That plane of consciousness you are trying to bring to the fore and make one with the plane of consciousness which we call reality. You are trying to establish friendship between the two: between the imagination-world, which is a reality-world in another plane of consciousness, and the reality-world which is the outer plane of consciousness. But this you can do only if you take imagination as a reality in another plane, in its own world.

Imagination plays a most significant role in the spiritual life. Suppose you are not having good meditations, but six months ago you had a very good, powerful, high meditation. What you can do is try to imagine that powerful meditation. Then your imagination will become reality. After fifteen minutes or half an hour, you will get a good meditation. Vivekananda was such a great spiritual figure, yet sometimes for six months at a time he did not have a good meditation. What did he do? He used to imagine a time when he did have a good meditation, and inside his imagination was aspiration. So imagination is very good.

FW 144. *How can the various world religions respond more co-operatively and effectively to humanity's aspiration?*

Sri Chinmoy: It is the followers of religion who have to come forward and offer the qualities of their respective religions to other religions. It is the followers of religion who can and must work effectively to create humanity's sincere aspiration. Religion as such cannot do anything, but the people who give life to religion and who breathe in the breath of religion must come forward and create a new aspiration in humanity's heart. If this is done, then all religions will be able to work together without losing anything of their own; on the contrary, they will gain everything for they will become one.

FW 145. *Is man growing away from organised religion and moving towards meditation?*

Sri Chinmoy: In some countries it is true that people are growing away from organised religion and running towards meditation. In other countries people are still fond of their religions and they feel religion is the only answer. On the whole, many people from various religions have resorted to meditation, but they feel that meditation is in no way an obstacle to their religious beliefs. On the contrary, meditation increases the power and the light in their own religious beliefs.

FW 146. *People are often afraid of practices like meditation which are not prescribed by their own religion. Why is this?*

Sri Chinmoy: People are afraid of practising meditation just because meditation is something new to them. Anything that is new to us often creates fear in us. Something more: in the West especially, prayer is given much more importance than meditation. People feel that if they meditate instead of praying, then they are being disloyal to their religious beliefs. This is one of the reasons why some people, especially in the West, are afraid of meditation. They have not been habituated to meditate whereas they have all along been praying. So anything that is new to our system, to our mind, to our understanding, creates a kind of conscious or unconscious fear in us.

FW 147. *Can one find the fulfilment of his life in religion?*

Sri Chinmoy: It depends entirely on the individual, on what kind of fulfilment he wants and needs from his own life and what kind of religion he is practising. If his religion is not broad, wide, all-embracing, then he is not going to get a fulfilment that is everlasting and complete. Partial fulfilment he will definitely get if he sticks to his own religion and does not want to come out of it. If he wants total fulfilment, however, then he has to enlarge his vision: he has to bring his religion into one world religion and he has to increase his heart's capacity. His capacity has to increase infinitely so that his own religion can function in and through all religions.

Again, if one really wants fulfilment, he has to know that real fulfilment will not come just from following a particular religion or even all religions. Real fulfilment can come and will come only from one's own sincere cry. Religion is like a house. Either in this house or in that house you can remain. But if you do not pray while you are inside the house, then there can be no real fulfilment. It is not following a religion but practising the principle that inwardly dictates the form of a religion which offers the way to real fulfilment. And this is what we call prayer and meditation.

FW 148. *Is your path a religion?*

Sri Chinmoy: No, mine is a path. A path cannot be a religion; a path only accepts — gladly accepts — the votaries or followers of all religions. It is a path, therefore, that anybody can follow. People from different countries, different cultures, different backgrounds can walk along the same path, but they perhaps will not be able to follow the same religion. One can walk along the spiritual path regardless of religion, regardless of culture, regardless of his inner and outer growth.

FW 149. *How can religion be made more spiritual?*

Sri Chinmoy: Religion can be made more spiritual just by bringing to it more widening beliefs, more illumining compassion and more fulfilling satisfaction, which are founded on one's consecration to God's Will. In order to make religion more spiritual, spirituality in its pristine purity must be brought into the heart of religion.

FW 150. *How can I lose my suspicion of the outer world?*

Sri Chinmoy: How can you lose your suspicion of the outer world? First you have to ask yourself whether your suspicion has helped you in any way. The answer will be no. It has not helped you at all. On the contrary, it has only lowered your consciousness, lowered your aspiration. Then you have to ask yourself one more question: are you wise or are you a fool? If you are a wise human being, then you will always act wisely. You are not a fool, so you are supposed to act like a wise individual. Anything that stands in the way of your God-discovery or Truth-discovery or life-manifestation has to be discarded.

Then you have to know where your suspicion is. Is it in the mind? Is it in the vital? Is it in the body? There can be suspicion in the physical and in the vital, but the suspicion that exists in these places is negligible. But the suspicion that is in the mind is like a mountain. So first you will enter into the place where suspicion is lurking all the time, which is the mind. Then you can tell suspicion, "Look, I have got nothing from you except misery, so why do I need you? You pretend to be my real friend, but you are not. A real friend does not create problems. It is only an enemy that creates problems. For a long time I did not know that you were an enemy; I considered you to be my friend. For this reason I allowed you to remain inside my mind. But now I know that you are not my friend. Just because you are my enemy, you have to leave. This is my house, absolutely mine. Here you have no place."

But again, you have to realise that nobody and nothing can remain an eternal enemy. You will invoke and create boundless Light inside the mind and then either you shall allow suspicion to come into your mind for its illumination, or your illumined mind will enter into the human suspicion which has been discarded from the mind. The mind will enter in order to transform and illumine suspicion.

Nothing negative, nothing undivine can always remain undivine, for God's Vision is eventually to make everything divine. But in the meantime certain things stand in our way inwardly and create problems for us. You have to tell them to remain far away and to let you reach your destination. Then, from the destination you can bring infinite Light to them. Or you can say, "Once I reach my destination, if you want to come and visit me, I shall allow you because at that time I shall have full authority and full capacity to transform you." At that time, either suspicion will come to you for transformation or you shall come to it with illumination. For once you are illumined, you are no longer afraid of your existence. So in this way you can conquer suspicion.

FW 151. *Is there one divine quality which encompasses all the rest or does a seeker have to meditate on each one?*

Sri Chinmoy: For a seeker, one quality is enough in his own life and that is gratitude. And in God's Life one quality is also enough, and that is God's Compassion. God's Compassion encompasses all His divine qualities, and the seeker's gratitude encompasses all his divine qualities. So if one wants to feel the presence of all his divine qualities, then he has to look in his gratitude. And if he wants to feel all the divine qualities of God, then he can easily find them in God's Compassion. If one wants to see all God's good qualities or all one's own good qualities individually, one can easily do that too. But if one wants to see one good quality which embodies all the good qualities, then in God's case it is His Compassion and in man's case it is his gratitude.

FW 152. *Is the reason for this that there is a feeling of oneness in human gratitude and God's Compassion? Is that why these two qualities are so all-encompassing?*

Sri Chinmoy: In oneness you get everything. A child has established oneness with his parents, so he knows he will get everything. If the parents have material power or any power, any capacity, then it is all his: the parents are going to give it to him. If you are one with someone, that means all his qualities are your very own, and vice versa. Your eyes are one with your legs and arms. Your arms want to perform something at a particular place. Your eyes show you how to get there and your legs take you. Just because oneness has been established in all your limbs, one complements and fulfils the other. So if you establish your oneness with God's Compassion on the strength of your gratitude for God's Compassion, then inside God's Compassion you will get everything.

But again, if you find it extremely difficult to think of God's Compassion all the time or your own gratitude, then try to bring to the fore individual aspects of God's Capacity. If God's Power is what you want, then concentrate on God's Power. If you want inner cry, which you need, then try to bring this to the fore. Or if you need sincerity, try to get this. Anything you need, you bring forward individually.

But if gratitude is there, then inside gratitude you will find power, sincerity, simplicity and all divine qualities, because gratitude means oneness. God has played His role by giving; you have played your role by expressing your gratitude. By giving, God has shown his oneness with you; and by offering your gratitude, you have become one with Him.

FW 153. *Is the way to get rid of anxiety to ignore it?*

Sri Chinmoy: You can get rid of anxiety for a short time by ignoring it, but if you want to get rid of it permanently, then you have to bring light into it. In the beginning, if you are weak, then ignore it. If you can convince your mind that anxiety does not exist, then you get temporary relief. If even for one day you are freed from anxiety, then you have accomplished something. By ignoring it you can keep it away for a few days, a few weeks or a few months, but you cannot indefinitely ignore it. The anxiety still exists and it will come back.

But in the meantime, while it is away, you may create or develop or acquire or achieve light. Then, if you have brought light into your system, when anxiety comes you can put light into it. At that time, anxiety is transformed and then it no longer exists. In this way it will not bother you again.

If you do not have enough light or illumining power inside you, then the next best thing is to ignore anxiety. But unless and until you have illumined anxiety, there can be no abiding satisfaction. In the beginning you ignore it and wait for God's capacity to develop in you, which is Light. Then, when the hour comes, you must enter into anxiety itself with your soul's light. But if you have this capacity right from the beginning, why do you have to ignore your anxiety? Everything in God's creation needs God's attention for its perfection. Anxiety is not a good quality; it has to be perfected. Since you have the capacity, pay attention to it and perfect it.

FW 154. *Should we advertise in our offices that we belong to the U.N. Meditation Group?*

Sri Chinmoy: No, we should not advertise, but we should not be timid either. Only we should try to inspire people. If someone is kind, sympathetic, thinking of leading a better life, a higher life, we can speak to that person. But we don't have to advertise or "missionise". That would make it something commercial, and people will misunderstand us. They will think we are trying to convert them. We shall not do that. Only we shall try to inspire people with our own spiritual light.

Let them see something in us. If they see something in us, which is joy and peace of mind, then they will ask where we got it. Then we can tell them that we go to a place to pray and meditate and if they are interested, they can come. But we should not go around advertising our views everywhere at the United Nations. That is the wrong approach.

FW 155. *How can our own spiritual efforts within the Meditation Group assist the work that you are performing in serving the soul of the U.N. and the family of nations?*

Sri Chinmoy: Each member of the Meditation Group must feel that his service is of paramount importance. Service can be of different types. Somebody may be able to come regularly to the meditations and somebody else may not be able to come to the meditations regularly because of the heavy pressure of his work, or because he cannot get a lunch break at the right time, or for some other reason. But if an individual comes to the meditation room, he should offer his prayers not only for his own soul but also on behalf of the ones who could not come to the meditation.

All the members of the Meditation Group must establish a soulful oneness. It is like a tree that is offering flowers. Each flower is of supreme importance. The Meditation Group is the tree: each individual is a flower, a flower of dedication. The seeker has aspired. That is why he has become a real flower. But now this flower has to dedicate itself. At every moment each member of the Meditation Group has to feel that the purpose of his life is dedication — dedication not only to one particular nation but to all nations.

We pray and meditate in this room. A few hundred members of the United Nations know about us, but most of them do not care for what we are doing. But still we have to care for them. We have to play the role of the mother. Very often children do not care for their mother. They take the mother for granted, knowing she will do everything for them, even if they do not do anything for her. In the inner world, I see that there are many, many who do not participate in our group or come to our meetings but who get a kind of inner strength unconsciously from us. The child won't come to the mother, won't listen to the mother, but he feels that if he has some need, the mother will be the first person to protect him and help him. Here also, those who do not come still feel our soulful assistance. When they dive deep within even for a few minutes, their inner beings tell them that there is a Meditation Group that prays and meditates for the U.N.

What we do for the United Nations as members of the United Nations Meditation Group or as members of a spiritual community — any community — is recorded in the soul of the United Nations. A day will come when we will be recognised as a true asset to the body and soul of the United Nations. And something more. Now we do not have even a proper place to meet in; from here to there we move. But one day there will be a permanent place at the United Nations for our Meditation Group. Now it is in its infancy, but a day will come when it will grow into a mature young man. It will shoulder inwardly and silently much spiritual responsibility. The politicians won't believe it; their minds won't believe it. But their souls will believe it, and their souls will make them believe it in their hearts' inmost sincerity. There will be many, many problems that will arise and there will be no outer way to solve these problems; but they will be solved. The human mind will say it was a stroke of fate that has solved the problem. But the heart will say, no, it was because there are some sincere seekers who are crying for world harmony and world peace. It is the accumulated prayer and meditation that we do regularly at home and, especially, twice a week here at the United Nations, that will solve these problems. So our prayer and meditation will be recorded in the gratitude-heart of all the U.N. members who really want a world of harmony and a world of peace.

Now, we are acting like farmers. A farmer cultivates the field, then he sows the seeds, and then he waters it. But all of a sudden, in the twinkling of an eye, the seed will not germinate. It takes time. We are all playing the role of farmers. In the depths of our hearts we have found fertile soil, and we have cultivated it. We have sown the seeds of peace, light and harmony. In the course of time, at God's choice Hour, those seeds will germinate. And when they grow into strong and healthy plants, the world will see them. Then a day will come when the plants will grow into trees, and the world will have more faith, abundant faith in our soulful attempt to establish world peace, world harmony and world oneness in an inner way. Finally, these little seeds of peace, light and harmony will grow into huge banyan trees. At that time, in number we may have two hundred or three hundred members or more, and the strength of our prayer, the strength of our sincere effort, will be acknowledged as the backbone, the supporting pillar of world peace. Something more, the world will feel that it is our prayer-dynamo, our meditation-dynamo, which is the source of world peace in the U.N. It will take time, but our Meditation Group is destined to play that sublime role. Everyone who is praying and meditating here is indispensable to bring about this transformation, illumination and perfection. We have all been given the golden opportunity by the Absolute Supreme to bring about this world harmony.

FW 156. *People at the United Nations, in our offices, think of the Meditation Group as a family. Is that a helpful attitude?*

Sri Chinmoy: Here at the United Nations we are trying to have a world family. If we can have a feeling of family, even with forty or fifty members, that is a great achievement. We do not have any dogmatic attitude. We do not say that if you do not accept our Meditation Group, then you will not be able to go to Heaven, or if you do not accept our Meditation Group, then there will be no perfection in your life. That we will never say. Only we pray and meditate and try to offer our dedicated service. Our family is not a religion; our family is only a conscious dedication to the Supreme in each individual. On the strength of our prayer and dedication we have formed a small family. We are not preaching or advocating any specific religion. But if others feel that we have a sweet, harmonious family, and that this family is not standing in their way at all, then they can also join us if they wish. Today our family is small, but tomorrow our family will become big, very big. This will happen not because we have converted people, but because we have inspired people to lead a better life, a more illumining and fulfilling life.

FW 157. *How can I make the staff members of the United Nations feel that the Meditation Group is available to them?*

Sri Chinmoy: You have friends, you have colleagues; you can speak to them. If once in a while you share with them your views on life, they will have no objection. If your colleagues don't accept your ideas, you need not discuss them any more. You can also give them some of our writings, and tell them about our various activities. You have every right to give some material to your friends, but not when you are supposed to be working. During office hours you are serving the U.N. and getting a salary, so you should not talk to your friends when you have work to do. But during lunch or after office hours you can do whatever you want. Another thing you can do is to inspire your colleagues by the way you act, and by your service and dedication.

You can be like a mother with her child. The mother knows that something is good for the child, so she gives it to him. But the child may say, "No, I don't like it," and reject it. Then what can the mother do? Here at the United Nations, the Meditation Group is like a mother. All her children, the workers at the United Nations, may not know that there is something that is good for them. But the mother will try to show them. She will offer them kindness, oneness, sympathy, peace, joy, light, satisfaction. So you give to your colleagues your peace, your joy and your concern for light and universal harmony. If they reject it, that means that their hour has not come. Then you can approach some other people.

It is your business to give, but not to say that what you give is the only thing worthwhile in God's creation, or that the Meditation Group is the only salvation. You can say, "We have something to offer. Do you care for it? If you care for it, we are more than willing to share it with you. If you don't care for it, then I am sorry." This should be your attitude.

FW 158. *Is it possible that the United Nations will one day be a nucleus of world-wide spirituality?*

Sri Chinmoy: That is not only a possibility. It is more than a possibility; it is an inevitability! The United Nations does not need to be in this building. This building need not be here at all. But the symbol, the truth, the light that the United Nations embodies is bound to cover the length and breadth of the world. The United Nations that we are seeing — the body and form — may not last. But the reality that is behind the United Nations, the dreams that each dedicated individual member has — not in his mind but in his soul — have to fulfil themselves. It may take fifty, two hundred, or four hundred years, but the dreams must eventually be fulfilled even if the outer form, the structure, does not remain the same. But the essential thing is the soul's full blossoming into perfection, the expansion of "United Nations" into "Oneness-World".

Previously there was the League of Nations, the dream of Woodrow Wilson. Now we see the United Nations. A few things are changed and modified and for the better. The League of

Nations was Woodrow Wilson's dream. It no longer exists. Instead, it has blossomed into another dream, a greater dream. The United Nations is also a dream. And this dream will eventually take a better and more fulfilling form also. At that time it will be Oneness-World.

A League of Nations is like a cluster of flowers. A United Nations arranges the flowers harmoniously. When we have a Oneness-World, at that time we will not see several individual flowers; we will see all as one whole. That also will take place.

This outer form may not last, but there will always be another way of approaching the reality. And that reality is bound to dawn. It will dawn and we will have Oneness-World. This is God's Dream, God's Vision of Perfection. The Kingdom of Heaven that we talk about, that we have heard about, is Oneness-World, nothing else. Oneness-World must dawn. And even Oneness-World is not the ultimate thing in God's Vision. In God's Vision, oneness need not and cannot be total perfection. In oneness there should be constant aspiration to transcend. There are twenty members of a family and they have become one. But if there is no aspiration to grow higher, to grow deeper, to grow better, then that is not perfection. Even when oneness is established, we can't say that that is the end of the game. No, inside oneness there should be a continuous aspiration to go beyond, beyond, beyond. God's Vision is always a Self-transcending Reality, so after oneness we still have the message of continuous transcendence, which is real perfection.

So, first there was the League of Nations. Now we see the United Nations. From the United Nations we shall see the Oneness-World, and inside the Oneness-World we shall see the song of self-transcendence, world-transcendence, universal transcendence. And inside that transcendence we shall see perfection, which is satisfaction.

FW 159. *What should be the attitude of those who work at the United Nations?*

Sri Chinmoy: Each individual connected with the United Nations in any capacity must be worthy of the word "united". At the United Nations we are trying to unite all the nations, to establish world peace and world harmony. If we can serve the United Nations, consciously knowing at every moment the meaning of the role of the United Nations — unity — we will succeed.

Some of the members of the United Nations Meditation Group are conscious of this, but in spite of being conscious they are not taking it seriously, while others are not even conscious of it. They feel that they happen to work here just as they might happen to be at any other job. But each member of the United Nations Meditation Group must feel that his job is a golden opportunity to serve the Vision of God's Oneness.

The United Nations is the song of oneness, and the song of oneness we are going to sing. We are going to sing it just because somebody has inspired us. Who has inspired us? The Absolute Supreme. Therefore, we have to be grateful to Him. If we are grateful to Him, then we will be able to sing our song. We will have a more soulful voice, and in our voice, in our action — which is dedicated service — there will be more spirituality, divinity and feeling of oneness.

If we want to serve anyone or anything in the best way possible, the best thing is to discover gratitude in our life. We are grateful because we are given the chance. God could have given the golden opportunity to somebody else, but He gave it to us. There should be no fear, no doubt, no anxiety, no worry — only gratitude. People who serve the United Nations in any capacity should feel some sense of gratitude inside their hearts. Here they are given the opportunity of serving humanity. There are many places where people are not even given that opportunity, but here at the United Nations they are.

The workers at the United Nations may quarrel, fight and do many undivine things, but they have a goal. There are many places on earth where there is no such thing as a goal. Here we know there is a goal. We may not walk along the right road to reach the goal, but we know about the goal, and one day perhaps we will feel miserable that we just talk about the goal but we don't do anything to reach it. So when talking will no longer satisfy us, then we shall try to be really sincere. When we become sincere, we feel that there is something to intensify our sincerity, to illumine our sincerity, to fulfil our sincerity, and that thing is gratitude. Gratitude is self-expansion, gratitude is God-expansion within us. Once we offer an iota of gratitude to the Supreme in us, to the Inner Pilot within us, our heart is immediately expanded. There is no better way to expand our heart than to offer gratitude.

FW 160. *How can we have purity in the mind?*

Sri Chinmoy: You can have purity in the mind by constantly remembering the Supreme. Think of the mind as a runner. The runner is running very fast; you cannot catch it. But the Supreme runs infinitely faster than the mind. If you can think of the Supreme, He will give you the capacity to run very fast and reach the destination before the mind. As long as the mind embodies impurity, it feels it will be able to affect the other runners around — the body, the vital and the heart. But when we run faster than the mind with the strength of the Supreme, the mind gives way. It feels it is a hopeless case and it gives up the race. Then the mind will give up its impure thoughts, limited thoughts.

FW 161. *Does it help our spiritual progress to understand things intellectually?*

Sri Chinmoy: It is not at all necessary to understand something intellectually. There have been many spiritual giants who don't use the mind; they use the heart instead. On the strength of their heart's oneness with God, they felt and realised everything. Understanding is a very tricky word. When today we understand something in a particular way, that very understanding may not satisfy us tomorrow. We may develop another kind of understanding and see that yesterday's understanding was absolutely useless. So, to use the intellect is not the right way.

Again, the intellect may surrender to the heart's oneness and say, "I don't get abiding satisfaction from understanding intellectually. So let me get joy by identifying myself with the highest Reality." The decisions of the mind are constantly changing, so we can never find real certainty and satisfaction on the path of the mind. But if we follow the path of the heart, we see that the heart immediately identifies with the Reality — no matter what the substance or the essence of the Reality is. If this is the substance, if this is the essence, then the heart will claim it as its very own. If we want to learn something soulfully and understand it fully, then the heart is the answer.

Sometimes the mind is ashamed of its conduct, ashamed of its cruelty. It is merciless not only to the other members of its family, but also to its own existence. But by becoming cruel to others or to itself, the mind cannot solve its problem. Only by looking for a higher reality can the mind become as happy as the heart. And this it eventually is bound to do. To say that the mind will never cry for Light, that the mind will never receive Light, would be a mistake. The mind will undoubtedly cry for Light and receive Light, and there will come a time on our earthly calendar when the mind will get the same joy as the heart. Otherwise, God's creation can never be perfect, and God will never allow us to remain imperfect.

FW 162. *Is the mind ever self-giving?*

Sri Chinmoy: The mind *can* be self-giving like the heart. But right now the mind that we use is the limited mind. When we live in the mind, we feel that we have only five cents and if we give it away, then we will have nothing. But there is also an unlimited mind. If we become one with the unlimited mind, then there is no question of becoming empty-handed in life. If the mind comes to feel that it is limitless, then no matter how much it gives of its own, it remains infinite.

FW 163. *How can we increase the mind's sincerity?*

Sri Chinmoy: We can increase the mind's sincerity by compelling the mind to remain inside the heart. This is the easiest and most effective way. The earth-bound mind is not sincere and cannot be sincere. But when the mind becomes calm, quiet and vacant, it automatically becomes sincere. If a great boxer does something wrong, undivine, he will not be afraid of a weakling who criticises him. If the other person is of his standard, however, the boxer may deny his deed. The greatest boxer may do many things that we may not approve of, but his life is an open book. He does not care what we think. So the superior who has the strength, the power, even if he does something wrong, does not have to tell a lie. By telling lies he is not gaining anything. But an ordinary person will try to hide.

Here we are speaking of mundane reality. On another level, if the heart identifies itself with infinite Reality, the infinite Power, and if the mind goes and takes shelter inside the heart, then the mind automatically becomes sincere. For the mind does not have to tell a lie and justify itself. It does not have to be afraid of anything. So the mind must take shelter inside the heart.

FW 164. *Does the mind have a will of its own?*

Sri Chinmoy: The mind has a will of its own; again, the mind can fall victim to hostile forces and it can also surrender to higher forces. Limited will everybody has. When we don't use our limited will, we can allow either God to conquer us or ignorance-force to conquer us. But if we use the mind properly, we will not surrender to undivine forces that assail us.

We have limited capacity. We don't have sufficient capacity to reach our destination. We are like helpless children. If the Goal sees that a little child is trying desperately to reach it, then the Goal comes to the little child. Either the divine Being who is at the Goal will come or the hostile forces will come. In the beginning, the mother stands at the destination and observes whether the child is making a sincere effort to come to her. If so, then the mother goes and stands in front of the child. With the limited mind we can walk towards the Goal, we can at least go one step forward. So if we use the limited capacity, the limited will, of the mind to aspire, a divine Being will come to us. Otherwise, an undivine being will come. So the mind, if it is sincere, can be inspired by the divine Will or, if it is not sincerely trying, it can be instigated by the undivine will.

FW 165. *What is the difference between the mind of a world-renowned statesman and the mind of a world-renowned scientist?*

Sri Chinmoy: Most statesmen or dictators live in the vital world. In the twinkling of an eye, they will try to make the whole world sit at their feet. As Julius Caesar said, "I came, I saw, I conquered." This is what a statesman or a dictator will feel. Quite often dictators will try to operate on the physical plane with vital strength. They don't use mental strength, although mental strength is superior to the vital strength. Psychic strength is superior to the mental strength, occult strength is superior to psychic strength and the soul's strength is superior to occult strength. Again, God's Strength is infinitely superior to the soul's strength. The more subtle the strength, the more effective it is.

A scientist uses another strength. His strength is the strength of imagination-reality. Imagination has a plane, a reality of its own. But we call it "imagination" until we see it with our ordinary, naked human eyes. Then we try to go to the intuitive world. The scientist often goes to the intuitive world, but on very, very rare occasions in world history will a statesman or dictator have that kind of mind.

Again, I must say that in the second World War, once or twice Churchill's utterances came from the psychic plane, intuitive plane. When he spoke, it was on a very high level. Kennedy and Nehru also spoke sometimes from the intuitive and psychic planes. But these are all very rare exceptions. Usually, dictators or statesmen try to dominate the physical world with their vital strength. But the scientist deals mostly with imagination-strength and, if he is successful, he goes one step ahead, to intuition. When the scientist discovers something, he enters into the subtle world and brings forward its capacity. His discovery has a physical shape, but its real essence comes from the imagination-world, intuitive world. He may think he has used the mind, but it is a reality in subtle form to which he is bringing physical form, in its own way.

So a world statesman will have access to vital or dynamic worlds, whereas the scientist will have access to the imaginative world or intuitive world. The worlds that the scientist explores are much higher than those explored by eminent political figures. But even the scientist surrenders to the spiritual person. Spirituality houses everything, including science. But, unfortunately, science does not give value to the spiritual life. The scientist wants constant proof on the physical plane, vital plane, mental plane. He wants to prove the reality he has seen. Spiritual people will say, "As the physical plane is real to you, even so, the spiritual plane is real to us. Why do I have to prove my existence by coming down to your level? If I am on the top of the tree, you climb up to the top of the tree to see whether I am enjoying the sweetest fruit or not."

The scientist right now has not climbed up as high as the spiritual Master. What the great spiritual giants have achieved in the march of evolution is right now far beyond the imagination of the scientist. So the discovery that the spiritual Masters have made is not yet possible for the scientist to accept, and he tries to deny the spiritual Master's discovery. Spirituality at that time tells the scientist, "No matter what you want to do with my existence, even if you deny it, I am not going to be the loser. I come from a very far-off land. This land is totally pure and this reality is absolutely authentic. If you want to taste my achievement, then come to the place where I can supply nectar. You have to come to my standard. If I want to prove my achievement to you on a mental level, then instead of giving you illumination, I will only add more confusion to your discovery. Your discovery will not and cannot give you abiding satisfaction, because it is mixed up with the mental and physical world."

Political figures, scientists and spiritual figures are all correct according to their own standards. Politics is trying to operate from a particular level. Science is trying to operate on a particular level. Each is trying to tell the world how creation has to be accepted, according to its own level of evolution. And spirituality also tries to offer its truth. It does not explain. It says, "Become one and then enjoy; I don't want to explain." In politics you have to prove, in science you have to prove. But in spirituality it is not necessary, because you become what you achieve. In politics, if you give a most wonderful speech to the nation, the speech may be one thing and you may be something else. Your life may be totally different from that; you don't remain in that consciousness. If you discover something, the atom bomb or hydrogen bomb, you don't become what you have created. You can claim whatever you have created in the political or scientific field as your own, but your possession has not become inseparably one with its possessor. In spirituality, however, whatever you realise on the spiritual plane, you become. The creator and creation become inseparably one because of their oneness-capacity.

FW 166. *You have started offering songs to the United Nations Meditation Group to sing and I was wondering if you would like to expound upon the purpose of this?*

Sri Chinmoy: Not only each song but each tune embodies aspiration. When we embody aspiration, we feel that we are serving the Divine in us. When we do not aspire, we feel that we are serving the undivine in us. Song is a universal language; it is the heart's easiest and most effective way to unite the inner world with the outer world, which is separate or has been fragmented into many pieces.

So this year I am executing an inner command to compose a good many songs. Like my paintings, each song is my dedication to aspiring mankind. Each song embodies my aspiration, my realisation and my dedicated oneness with you all.

It is my wish that the seekers of the ultimate Truth will learn these songs if they can sing well. While practising them, they are bound to get delight, and when they perform before the rest of the world, they should feel that they are offering their aspiration in the form of dedication.

Those who are listening to the songs will be meditating as much as those who are singing. Meditation does not mean to remain closeted, to keep your eyes and ears shut and not to know what is going on around you. Meditation is a form of self-dedication, and this dedication comes from our aspiration. Those who are singing can offer their dedicated service through their soulful music, and those who are listening to them soulfully and devotedly can also be doing their best meditation.

Suppose I sing fifty songs and it takes two hours. During these two hours, your mind can roam and think of millions of things, or you can feel that singing is not important, so you will feel drowsy and fall asleep. Or you can take it as an opportunity to do your best meditation because here the music is adding to your own aspiration. If you are trying to aspire, the soulful songs will add to your own aspiration.

Each song is a golden opportunity to increase our spirituality, to increase our aspiration. Each song is like an additional plant in our garden. Naturally the plant will offer us more beautiful flowers. Each song soulfully sung gives us tremendous inner joy, and this joy gives us the message of heart-expansion. Our heart expands when we are in joy. If we are wise, we shall adopt all means in order to expand our heart so that in our heart's joy and delight we can see the entire world.

A song is a seed. The seed will germinate and grow into a tree and the tree will mature and offer many flowers and fruits. The flowers will offer their fragrance and beauty to increase our aspiration, and the fruit will give us immortal joy. So these soulful songs will give us the message of Immortality by helping us to become one with the universal Light, the universal Delight, which they embody.

It is my wish to write at least fifty songs for the United Nations. We will have a book with fifty songs and it will be the possession of the United Nations Meditation Group. You will learn them and sing them at various places, and many things will be done with these songs. Very soon I shall be able to offer the Meditation Group quite a few songs, which will be most applicable to the United Nations ideas and ideals.

FW 167. *During our Sixth Anniversary celebration on 14 April, you spoke about serving the United Nations with gratitude. Could you please elaborate on this?*

Sri Chinmoy: We all serve the United Nations because we feel the United Nations offers us a unique opportunity to help bring about world peace, world harmony, and world oneness. We have tried in every way to serve the United Nations. "We" means each individual, not only as a member of the Meditation Group but also as a member of the United Nations staff. But people who are working at the United Nations and serving the United Nations are at times assailed with fears, doubts and anxieties that their services will be dispensed with. Misunderstanding, controversy and other unhealthy experiences they get quite often. So we have come to realise that there should be a new method of serving the United Nations, and that new method is with the heart's gratitude.

So far, in spite of our teeming ignorance, limitations and imperfections, we have achieved something for the world, we have done something for mankind by serving the United Nations. If we want to separate the United Nations from the world at large, we can say we have achieved something for the United Nations proper. If we want to separate the United Nations from our own existence, we can say we have achieved something for ourselves. Even if we take the United Nations as something other than the world or as something other than ourselves, still we can say we have achieved something.

Instead of saying there is one, we can say there are three complementary friends: the world, the United Nations and the individual Meditation Group member. If we can't take them as one, let us then take them as three intimate friends. These three intimate friends may at times find it difficult to see eye to eye with each other. The world is seeing something wrong with the United Nations and the individual is seeing something wrong with the United Nations, or the United Nations is seeing something wrong with the world or with the individual. They are finding fault with each other, but at the same time, they are friends. The different countries do not always agree with one another, but still they are friends. If they were not friends, they would not be in the United Nations proper. They would not be involved in United Nations activities. They do believe in the United Nations, they have faith in the United Nations, but they also have individual problems which they are trying to work out.

So, the world is a friend, the United Nations is a friend and the individual is a friend. Let us put it this way. Three friends, in spite of their misunderstandings and shortcomings, are trying to offer their best qualities and become one. When they offer their best qualities, when they sincerely give, then they become totally one in the inner life and in the outer life. At that time there cannot be a separate world or a separate United Nations or a separate individual. There is no sense of separation; it is all oneness.

Right now friendship is there, but inseparable oneness is not there. Just because there is some basic friendship, all the countries are together and all the individuals are together. But oneness is still missing. That oneness will come only when each individual is able to offer his own sincerity and other good qualities to both the United Nations and the world, when the United Nations can offer its good qualities — its body and soul — to the individual and to the world, and when the world can offer its good qualities to each member and to the United Nations proper. In this way three will become one.

They will become one on the strength of their gratitude — gratitude for what the world has done for the United Nations, for what the United Nations has done for the world, and for what the individual has done for the world and for the United Nations. Each has done something for the other two; therefore, they are grateful to one another. Once they feel true gratitude towards one another, they will become one. Their hearts will experience expansion, and in the heart's gradual expansion they will become universal. At that time, we will not be able to separate an individual member of the United Nations from the United Nations because they will be integrally one. The United Nations will not be able to be separated from the world because it will be part and parcel of the world. They will be one by virtue of their sincere and mutual gratitude. By offering gratitude, constant gratitude, the world, the United Nations and the United Nations member will become one. When they become one, they will be perfect instruments.

As long as they remain three individuals, they have to offer their gratitude to each other. When they become one, they will offer their gratitude to the Supreme Pilot for having made them perfect instruments. Why? Because they have become conscious and perfect instruments of the Supreme whereas others are not even conscious instruments. So they are grateful to the Supreme for having given them this opportunity.

Right now we are conscious instruments, but perfection is a far cry. But a day will come when in addition to being conscious instruments, we shall also be perfect instruments. So now we can offer gratitude just because we have become instruments. The Supreme, out of His infinite Bounty, has accepted us and given us the opportunity to become His conscious instruments. But a day will come when we will become perfect instruments. At that time we shall have to offer more gratitude, infinitely more. Now we should offer gratitude because we are chosen to be conscious instruments. But when we become perfect instruments, our gratitude will become boundless. The same thing applies to each individual and to each nation.

FW 168. *When you shower Light on us when we are meditating, how can we be most receptive?*

Sri Chinmoy: You can be most receptive on the strength of your own simplicity, sincerity, purity and humility. When you bring to the fore your own divine qualities — simplicity, sincerity, purity and humility — then you can receive the utmost. And inside simplicity, inside sincerity, inside purity, inside humility, please try to feel a sense of gratitude to the Inner Pilot, to your own Inner Pilot. Your gratitude-heart will be able to receive the utmost; it will bring down from Above Peace, Light and Bliss in boundless measure. It is a gratitude-heart that receives these divine qualities and also manifests them here on earth.

FW 169. *How can man live forever?*

Sri Chinmoy: How can man live forever? We have to know what we mean by "man". If we mean the flesh and blood and earthly limbs that we have, then with this body it is impossible to live forever. The five elements that constitute the physical body cannot last. If an individual identifies himself only with the physical body, which remains alive for sixty, seventy or eighty years, naturally there is no immortality. When the body is not aspiring — and in most cases it is not aspiring — then it is not worthwhile to stay on earth where there is so much suffering, so much frustration, weakness, limitation and bondage.

People may live on earth for eighty or ninety years, but if they have not given up their ordinary human life or, let us say, their animal life, there is no purpose in it. Only if one wants to act divinely and live in a divine way is there a reason for him to live eternally. But if one wants to live a divine life, then right now he has to develop inside himself a divine consciousness. Each individual has the animal consciousness, the human consciousness and the divine consciousness. From the animal consciousness we have gradually entered into the human consciousness, and from the human we are now trying to grow into the divine. This consciousness with our ordinary human eyes, we do not see; but with our inner vision we see it.

In the world of consciousness each individual is immortal. An individual identifies himself either with the soul or with the body. If he identifies himself with the body, which is far from perfection, then naturally he feels he cannot live forever. But if he identifies himself with the soul, then he knows that he is immortal. The body will die, but when it is a matter of consciousness — which every man has and which he inwardly is — man is eternal, man is immortal.

Again, it is our hope that there will come a time when the physical body, like the soul, will be able to establish its inseparable oneness with the divine. We have an inner life and an outer life. The inner life is aspiration, whereas the outer life is right now full of desire; it is earthbound. But a day will come when the desire-life will be transformed by the inner life, and aspiration will shine even in the so called physical. At that time, the transformed and illumined physical body will be able to last permanently. But right now the physical is half animal, manifesting only an iota of the divine Light. There shall come a time when the physical will receive boundless Light from Above and will be illumined. Once it is illumined, like the soul, it can remain permanently on earth, if such is the Will of God. But right now, at the present stage of human consciousness, it is impossible for the physical level of man to be immortal.

FW 170. *How can we help the pilots of the United Nations — the Secretary-General and the Directors?*

Sri Chinmoy: The pilots of the United Nations need our services, not our help. The moment we use the term "help", a kind of egocentric idea enters into us. If we help someone, that means we are in a superior position. When we help, we feel that we are one step ahead or one step higher than the ones that we are helping. But if we serve someone, then we offer our capacity with humility, on the strength of our loving concern and oneness. So let us use the proper term, "service".

How can we serve the Secretary General, who is the main pilot of the United Nations, and others who are high authorities at the United Nations? Let us call them the hero-warriors of the United Nations, since they are in the battlefield of life fighting for world harmony, for world peace and world oneness, for world illumination and world perfection. These members of the family have gone out to fight against the undivine forces, the forces that separate, the forces that do not want world harmony. These are our brothers, let us say. Our brothers have gone into the battlefield to fight, but we have not gone; we have stayed at home. We were not chosen by the Supreme to fight.

But we can serve the same supreme cause inside them through our constant prayer and goodwill. It is our bounden duty to try to create for our brothers success and victory. Our prayers will undoubtedly be an additional strength to them while they are fighting against disharmony, conflict and the wrong forces that separate the nations of the world. Our inner prayer is of paramount importance, and it does help them considerably. They are doing something for themselves, for us, for all of humanity. So it is our bounden duty to pray inwardly and outwardly for them at home, or wherever we are.

The pilots of the United Nations are serving mankind in the world arena. We can also do the same type of service, according to our capacity. They do it on a large scale, according to the capacity they have, and we do it on a limited scale according to the capacity we have. Our prayer is also a solid strength. This solid strength we can offer to them in silence, from our inner life of dedication to the world.

FW 171. *Sri Chinmoy, it is very difficult to know what is a spiritual question. How much of the United Nations is a spiritual reality and a secular reality, or are these meaningless distinctions?*

Sri Chinmoy: I beg to be excused. When I use the term "spiritual", I mean that if somebody asks me a scientific question I will not be able to answer it. If somebody asks me some historical, political or mathematical question, I will be nowhere. I use the term "spiritual" in a broader sense, to mean the reality that unites us, the reality that wants to fulfil us in a divine way.

"Spiritual" here means oneness, unity. The goal of the United Nations is to unite all nations, all human beings. Real spirituality cannot be other than this: to see all human hearts, all human lives united for one supreme cause, which is to offer satisfaction to the Reality, to God's Creation and God's Vision.

"Spiritual" here means the unity of all human beings and all human aspirations. It means a better, more illumining way of life. I am using "spiritual" in a very broad sense, in the purest sense, as world harmony, world peace, world union and world oneness. This is spiritual.

As you know, the goal of the United Nations is unity. But unity is not oneness. First we attain unity, and then we go one step farther, to oneness. After oneness, we try to see satisfaction. Each individual must be satisfied on the strength of his oneness with and sacrifice for the other members of the family.

FLAME-WAVES

BOOK 8

FW 172. *How can the knowledge of spirituality help professional people in their effort to help mankind through their work?*

Sri Chinmoy: First of all, let us try to know what spirituality means. Spirituality is not something abstract, something that encourages us to leave the world. It is not something that is only for the chosen few. No! Spirituality is certainty itself. And if it is true spirituality, then it always encourages us to accept life.

Each individual has something to do here on earth, so he consciously or unconsciously throws himself into multifarious activities. He wants to get everything done sooner than at once so that he can do something new, so that he can go on to something better, something more illumining, something more fulfilling.

Now, there is a short way, which we call the sunlit path, to reach our destination. You are sitting right in front of me. If I walk straight, I will undoubtedly reach you sooner than if I wander around, here making a left turn, there making a right turn, and only then come to you. The short-cut is the way of concentration. We have to concentrate on the thing that we are supposed to do. Each time we concentrate on something, we take away the confusion, pressure, anxiety, worry, unwillingness and stubbornness that is inside the subject itself, inside each undertaking. At the same time we offer our capacity, confidence and assurance to ourselves. We either bring to the fore our inner capacity, confidence and assurance from within or we bring them down from Above.

Each time before undertaking anything, if we can concentrate, we simplify the matter and at the same time we expedite the result in a satisfactory way. Concentration immediately clears the road. On either side of the road are doubt-tree, insecurity-tree, hesitation-tree, anxiety-tree, worry-tree. As soon as we concentrate we see the transformation of these trees. Doubt becomes faith, insecurity becomes security; anything that is discouraging becomes encouraging and helpful and lends us a helping hand as we move towards our destination.

So spirituality is the simplification of life, not the rejection or the negation of life. Spirituality is something that shows us the sunlit path so that we can reach our destination as soon as possible. No matter what we want to achieve from life and in life, spirituality is the best friend that can help us. It simplifies, purifies, illumines, fulfils and immortalises the thing that we want to possess or the thing that we want to grow into. Spirituality is not something uncertain, vague, meaningless or fruitless. No. It is something meaningful and fruitful, something that is constantly illumining us and fulfilling us. And inside illumination and fulfilment is the satisfaction that we want.

In our own profession if we want efficiency and perfection, then spirituality is the only answer because it clears the road of confusion; it purifies and illumines our mind. Once purification and illumination take place in our mind, we see that the goal is right in front of us. Then we see that the goal is within us. And finally we see that the goal is not only within us, but we are the goal itself. This moment we are the seeker running after the goal; the next moment we feel that we have become the goal itself. Spirituality is the only thing to make us feel that we need the goal, the only thing to show us how to reach the goal and the only thing to make us clearly see that we are nothing other than the goal itself.

FW 173. *Is it a good idea to use our intuition in our daily tasks?*

Sri Chinmoy: As soon as we start using our intuition, we have to know that we are doing the right thing. But just because we are doing the right thing today, we can't say that immediately we are going to get the result. We have to continue doing the right thing for two days, ten days, two months, three months. It is like a seed. The seed does not germinate all at once. It takes some time for the seed to germinate. Then it grows into a tiny plant and a sapling, and finally it becomes a huge banyan tree. Today's intuition-power is also something that grows. Today's intuition-power need not and cannot be all-pervasive; like a muscle it can be developed. It can become stronger and more fulfilling.

He who has intuitive power should feel that this power has dawned on him in order that he can serve those who have less intuitive power, who have less capacity, who have less wisdom-power. If he serves his brothers and sisters on earth, then he is bringing about lasting peace, lasting happiness on earth.

When you have intuitive knowledge you can feel that you are already advanced. You can lead others; you are proceeding and people are behind, following you. But you have to know that your power of intuition has come either from the inmost recesses of your heart or from a very high plane of consciousness. And you have to feel that this power has come to you not so that you can lord it over others, but so that you can serve others. You have to feel that because this intuition has entered into you, you are the elder brother of the family. You have a few younger brothers and you have to show your younger brothers the way to the destination with love, with concern, with oneness.

When intuitive power comes, you just enter into your task. You have something to do and you get a flash. At that time you have to enter into it. While you are entering into it, please feel that you are entering into the task not to show the world what you have accomplished, but to show the world that you have seen something new, which is of immediate use. To whom? To you yourself and to the rest of the world. When you use intuition, you immediately feel the necessity of dedication. Intuition you have got; and what do you use it for? For dedication. Enter with your intuition-power into the subject or task that you have; and from there come out triumphantly to dedicate your discovery to those who have not yet discovered the light that you have discovered. So the best use for intuition is to constantly dedicate it to the reality that you discover while using it. Dedication is the best way to use the power of intuition and dedication is the real satisfaction from intuition.

Intuition shows us how to start, how to continue and how to end. The word "end" is not the right expression to use when we speak about the search for eternal happiness. There is no end. We are always transcending our previous goals. Today's goal is tomorrow's starting point for an ever-higher goal.

FW 174. *Can meditation help cure physical ailments such as high blood pressure?*

Sri Chinmoy: When we meditate, we consciously try to go to the Source, which is all-perfection. Meditation means conscious awareness of our Source. Our Source is God, our Source is Truth, our Source is Light, our Source is Perfection. Meditation takes us to our Source, which is a place where there is no imperfection, no ailment. And where is the Source? The Source is within us.

In the outer life when we meditate, what result do we get? We make our mind calm and quiet. It is almost impossible for most human beings to have peace of mind. And he who does not have peace of mind is a veritable beggar; he is like a monkey in a human body. He has no satisfaction. But if we get peace of mind for one fleeting second, we feel we have accomplished a lot in life. When we have peace of mind, our vital remains peaceful and our body remains peaceful; and where there is peace there is no dislocation. It is only in the world of anxiety, worry, tension and confusion that there is some ailment. Otherwise, there can be no ailment.

So meditation is the answer. Meditation offers us peace of mind, tranquillity in the mind. When there is peace of mind, all sufferings of human life can come to an end. When the mind is tranquil, there is a constant flow of harmony. This harmony is entering into the vital and from the vital it enters into the physical. When there is harmony in the system, there can be no ailment.

High blood pressure, heart failure and all the diseases that we notice in God's creation are attacks from undivine forces. These undivine forces can be overcome, can be counter-attacked only when we surrender to the positive force. When we meditate, we try to become a perfect channel for the positive force. The positive force is light and the negative force is darkness-night. The positive force is love, not hatred. The positive force is belief, not disbelief. At each moment in our life the positive force helps us because it takes us consciously to the Source, to our destination, which is perfection.

If our mind is calm and quiet, if our vital is dynamic, if our body is conscious of what it is doing, then we are inside the palace of satisfaction, where there can be no disease, no suffering, no imperfection, no obstruction to our abiding peace, abiding light, abiding satisfaction. Meditation is a means; it is a way; it is a path. If we walk along this path, then we reach our destination, which is all-perfection.

FW 175. *But if we are confused and nervous, how will meditation ever be able to help us?*

Sri Chinmoy: In the physical world, when somebody has a headache or a stomach upset, he goes to a doctor and the doctor cures him. If somebody is sick, then how can we say that he will never be well again? If he takes medicine, then there is every possibility that he will be cured. For a sick person, medicine is the answer. If somebody is assailed by anxiety, worry and confusion, meditation is the remedy. Just because he is a victim, we can't say that there will be no saviour. The saviour is there, provided the individual wants to be cured.

Suppose somebody is assailed by confusion and hostile forces that deplete all his energy and take all joy out of his life. He is depressed and has surrendered to frustration owing to countless problems in his life. Let us take him as a patient: he needs a doctor, he needs treatment. When an individual is suffering from a few ailments in the mental world, he has to go to someone who has some peace of mind, some light, some inner assurance for him. This is a spiritual teacher. The spiritual teacher is like a doctor who will advise the person and throw light on him so that he can free himself from fear, doubt, confusion, tension and all the negative forces that are torturing him. So if somebody is in mental turmoil and suffering tremendously in the mental world, he goes to someone who can be of immediate service to him; and this person cures him.

FW 176. *Is it really necessary to seek help when we are suffering from mental problems? Can't we just meditate by ourselves and find the answer?*

Sri Chinmoy: Suppose you find it extremely difficult to go deep within by yourself. You say, "I am suffering from certain mental difficulties, but I know the answer is inside. Now it is all night, but I feel that there is light inside my heart." This is what you feel, but you find it difficult to go deep within and discover the light. Then you have to go to someone who can bring to the fore the light that you have within you. It is like your own house. You have misplaced the key and you don't know how to open the door. But a friend of yours comes and helps you look for the key. After he finds it he opens the door for you and then he goes away. If you are ready to search for the key that you have lost, then you can try. But if you have a friend, then you can have more confidence in finding the key. So the teacher is a helper, an eternal friend who helps you in your search. When he finds the key, he won't keep it. He will give you the key. He won't say it is his key. No! It is your key, your house, your light. Then you will enter into the house and get everything that you needed and wanted.

FW 177. *You speak of night and light. Do you believe that parts of life are dark and imperfect?*

Sri Chinmoy: Life is composed of perfection, only we say that there is lesser perfection and greater perfection. We don't say that this side is black and that side is white; we say that on this side there is comparatively less light. So there is no negative and positive; there is only positive. But the thing that is less positive has less capacity and sometimes we call it negative.

FW 178. *How can we overcome our ego-motivated life and self-centredness?*

Sri Chinmoy: We can transcend our self-centredness or our ego-motivated life if we just feel that we are of the One who embodies the many. We must feel that our existence all by itself is fruitless. No matter what we do, what we say, what we grow into, what we achieve, it is all valueless unless we feel that we are of the One who embodies the many and that we are of the many who have to fulfil the One.

When we pray, when we meditate, we have to feel that our achievements are meaningful and fruitful only when it is dedicated joint effort that has brought about our success. When we want to see the Face of God without our friends, without our dear ones, we have to know that the Face of God that we will see at that time cannot satisfy us. If we do not carry the members of our family to our destination, then we shall never have satisfaction. We belong to a large family and if we carry the members of our family consciously and devotedly, then we can be fulfilled and satisfied. In this way only can we overcome our ego, our self-centred emotions.

FW 179. *Is there any relationship between the light that the seeker receives and the light the earth receives?*

Sri Chinmoy: The Light of the Supreme is descending to earth in infinite measure. It is up to the seeker either to accept it or to reject it. According to his capacity of receptivity, each seeker is receiving the Light of the Supreme. Earth embodies the seeker and, at the same time, the seeker represents earth, Mother Earth. When the seeker accepts Light, immediately this Light enters into the consciousness of the earth-mother in him.

Again, when earth receives Light, when the mother receives Light, she offers it to her children.

When the soul of the earth receives Light, it shares this Light with the seekers, its children. And when the children receive Light, they also share the Light with their mother, earth. One moment the son is earning the salary; the next moment the mother is earning the salary. Then they share their achievements with each other.

FW 180. *What is your view on the equality of the sexes?*

Sri Chinmoy: Women should not remain always under the control of men: women should stand on their own feet. Both men and women are of equal importance in God's Eye. God is both male and female. If we take man as God's Face, we have to take woman as His Smile. If we see a face without a smile, we don't appreciate the face. The smile immediately conquers our heart. But if there is no face, how can there be a smile? Each is of equal importance, but each need not play the same role. Both men and women should march together towards the same destination. Women need not lag behind. They can run soulfully, devotedly and speedily towards the same goal.

FW 181. *After we stop meditating, how can we maintain the level of consciousness we reached during our meditation?*

Sri Chinmoy: Here we are all aspiring; that is why our consciousness is elevated. The meeting will last for about half an hour more. Then we shall go home and our consciousness will go down. How can we maintain our present level of consciousness? We can do it through constant remembrance.

After you leave the Centre and go home, you may not retain the same level of aspiration because of some family difficulty or other problems. But even if there is nothing to prevent you from continuing to aspire, your own limited being will not allow you to stay on the top of the tree. You aspire for half an hour with utmost sincerity and then relaxation starts. You feel that you have worked very hard and now you are entitled to rest.

But the spiritual life is not like that. If you want to maintain your standard, if you want to maintain the height of your aspiration, then your aspiration should be flowing constantly. Suppose you have meditated for an hour; then you may not be able to meditate again for another hour or so. It is difficult right now for all of us to meditate for eight hours. But no harm. For half an hour you can easily meditate. Then you can do something which will maintain and preserve your meditation. For the next half-hour you can read spiritual books; then after that you can sing spiritual songs. Then you can go to the house of one of your spiritual brothers or sisters or, if that is not possible, you can call up someone on the phone and speak only about spiritual matters.

Again, you can write about your own experiences in your own way, not with the thought of publishing them but just to help your own consciousness. While you are writing them down, you are perfecting your spiritual nature. For half an hour you can write them down, then you will read what you have written. As soon as you have written down your experiences, you have created something. The creator always wants to enjoy his creation. Look at a gardener when he sees a beautiful rose. First he took great pains to plant a rose bush and tend to it; then after six or seven months when he sees the rose, he deeply appreciates and admires the beautiful flower. Similarly, you also may get joy from reading about your own experiences.

It takes fifteen or twenty minutes for you to eat. During that time try to remember what experiences you had while you were meditating early in the morning. Just imagine them. This imagination is not fantasy or self-deception: it is like charging a battery. You are charging your memory with your achievement, with your spiritual progress. Each time you think about your own experiences, you will be transported back to that time and you will get abundant Peace, Light and Bliss and so forth. So in this way you can always retain your meditation from the early morning and you will be able to maintain your standard until it is time for your next meditation.

But unfortunately people don't do this. We meditate for half an hour or forty-five minutes and immediately we feel that we are tired and exhausted. Then we do so many wrong things. It is a kind of negative reaction. We feel that we have seen one side of the river and now we want to go to the other shore. But the other shore is unfortunately all darkness. We have to try to remain on the shore that has light. So to preserve our meditation we will do other things which will increase or at least retain the power of the meditation.

During the week we have to go to work. Early in the morning we meditate and elevate our consciousness, but then we spend seven or eight hours at work and we are unfortunately compelled to mix with people who are unaspiring. We are thrown into a world of desire, fear, anxiety, worry and so forth, and our consciousness falls. So what do we do? Please meditate early in the morning and read spiritual books, sing spiritual songs, mix with spiritual people. Then, when you are in the office or involved in some other activity, try to remain in the consciousness of your early morning meditation and other spiritual activities. In your early morning meditation you have gained Peace, Light and Bliss, which is spiritual money. Keep that inside your own heart, which is the safest of all banks. Then, when you enter into the world, when you are in the office where it is all anxiety, worry and desire, you withdraw some of your spiritual wealth. You concentrate on your heart and bring forward a little of the

Peace, Light and Bliss which you acquired early in the morning. It is your own wealth and you can use it. In this way you will be able to maintain your spiritual standard and keep your level of consciousness high.

Right now, we have to be very careful and wise in our day-to-day life about how we spend each hour. But a time will come when our life itself will be a continuous flow of aspiration. Now after our meditation we use the mind and think, "Oh, the time has come for me to read some spiritual books." But one day we won't have to make any conscious effort. Our inner being will inspire us to read spiritual books. Right now the inner being is inside, deeply hidden, but we are trying our best, through Yoga, to bring it to the fore.

FW 182. *From the spiritual point of view, does the new year have any specific significance?*

Sri Chinmoy: From the spiritual point of view, the new year has a specific significance. On the eve of the new year, a new consciousness dawns on earth. God once again inspires each human being, each creature, with new hope, new light, new peace and new bliss. God always wants us to move ahead; He does not want us to look back. We know that while a runner is running fast, if he looks back, he drops to the ground. Similarly, if we are constantly looking behind at the year that we are leaving aside, we will think of our sorrow, misery, frustration, failure and so forth. But if we look forward we will see hope dawning ahead deep within us. We will see a new light illumining our consciousness.

Each new year is like a rung on the ladder of consciousness that we have to climb up. When the new year dawns we have to make ourselves conscious of the fact that we have to transcend ourselves this year. We have to go beyond our present capacity, beyond our present achievement. When we have that kind of firm determination, God showers His choicest Blessings upon our devoted heads. God says, "The new year dawns and a new consciousness dawns within you. Run towards the destined Goal." We listen to God. We listen to the dictates of our Inner Pilot and we run towards the ultimate Reality. The new year energises us, encourages us and inspires us to run towards that ultimate Goal.

FW 183. *How can I know the quintessence of Infinity?*

Sri Chinmoy: Mentally we will never know what Infinity is. It is all imagination. But there comes a time when imagination is transformed into reality. If somebody had once told me that there is a person by the name of Krishna Ganesan, until I had seen that person, he would have remained all imagination. But now I have seen you. Now you are a reality to me.

According to the physical reality, you are perhaps 5'6" in height, but inside the physical reality is the inner reality — your teeming inner experiences. Some of these experiences are very high, very deep, and some are not. Again, some of these experiences are from this incarnation and some are from previous incarnations. Even when I see the experiences only of this incarnation, I see that you have had thousands of experiences.

Now, who is holding these experiences? The soul or what we call the psychic being. In Sanskrit we call it *chaitya purusha*. This psychic being has gathered and kept safe the experiences of previous incarnations as well as of this one. The quintessence of all your previous incarnations has been preserved by the psychic being. Deep inside our existence, inside the soul, inside the psychic being, inside the mind, inside the vital, inside the gross physical, all these experiences are there.

But when the doctors operate, or when they examine you, they cannot discover it, this inner wealth of yours. Why not? Just because this infinite inner wealth that you have can be seen only by something which is also infinite. Only Infinity can measure Infinity; only Light can measure Light. We may see something right in front of us, but in order to evaluate it we have to have something which is equally powerful or equally illumined.

You will be able to see, feel and become one with Infinity when you become one with your spiritual heart, which is itself Infinite. And this oneness you achieve through prayer and meditation.

FW 184. *Is there any real difference between one religion and another?*

Sri Chinmoy: There is no fundamental difference between one religion and another because each religion embodies the ultimate Truth. Each religion is right, absolutely right, because each religion conveys the message of Truth in its own way. If you dive deep within, you will see that there is no difference at all between the religions. It is all one Truth called different names by different seekers. Your religion may say one thing and my religion may say something else. But our religions will never differ when it is a matter of the highest Truth. The ultimate Goal of every religion is to realise the highest Truth. On the way to our Goal we may quarrel and disagree, we may misunderstand each other. Why? Precisely because there are many roads that lead to the Goal. Some will follow one road and some will follow another road. Each road will be able to offer inspiration. After a while, one person will say that his road is by far the best because it is pleasing him. Then another person will say that his road is the best. But when both reach their destination, they will be at the same Goal: Truth. In Truth there is no quarrel, no conflict; Truth or God-realisation transcends all religions.

FW 185. *Can you define the soul?*

Sri Chinmoy: The soul is subtler than the subtlest, finer than the finest and, at the same time, larger than the largest. This is the description of the soul that you get in the *Gita* and also in our sacred Upanishads. This truth can be seen, felt and realised when we meditate.

The soul is the representative of God here on earth, a spark of God. God the Omniscient, the Omnipotent, the Omnipresent is one; but here in this world of multiplicity each soul represents a different aspect of God's multiplicity. When the soul takes human shape, it tries first to create possibilities and then inevitabilities. Then the soul tries to manifest the truth that it has already achieved. It sees the world of ignorance and tries to transform this ignorance into knowledge and wisdom.

There is an unmanifested Self, which we call *purusha,* and again, there is a manifested Self. The Self that is going to manifest on earth through the soul is called *prakriti. Purusha* is not indifferent, but it will always remain on the highest transcendental level of Consciousness. And the other Self, *prakriti,* will take part in the Cosmic Game through the individual soul.

When we become one with our soul, we enter into infinite Peace and Bliss — the highest Consciousness, which we call *sat-chit-ananda.* This is the triple Consciousness, where Existence, Consciousness and Bliss come together. When we live in the soul, eventually we enter into this triple Consciousness.

FW 186. *You say that when the body dies the soul goes back to its own world. What is the soul's world?*

Sri Chinmoy: The soul goes back to where it came from, to its original home, to take rest for some time. As earth is our body's world, so also there is a world which we call the soul's world. You have a home. You go to play in the playground and after you have played for a few hours you come back to your home. Then after taking rest, tomorrow you go again to play. Similarly, the soul comes here on earth to play for a few years and then the soul goes back to its own region. Then it returns to earth in another body.

The soul's original abode is *sat-chit-ananda*. It means Existence-Consciousness-Bliss. There is a Bengali song, *Phire Chalo*, it means, "Let us go home". This home is the home of the soul. The soul, the aspiring soul, is returning home, where it is all Light and Delight. In this home there is no death, no suffering, no sorrow, no decay; it is all Joy, Light and Delight.

FW 187. *Can the soul experience sorrow?*

Sri Chinmoy: No, the soul cannot experience sorrow. It is the outer senses — the emotions and the vital — which feel frustration and sorrow. The soul, which is in constant touch with the Source, is the fountainhead of constant joy.

FW 188. *If a soul is more evolved, will it take on a body that is more physically beautiful, or is there no correlation between physical beauty and spiritual development?*

Sri Chinmoy: No, there is no correlation at all. There have been many spiritual Masters who were physically quite ugly, and there have been many who were very beautiful. If you ask God whether my soul is more beautiful or more developed than that of some handsome movie actor, God will sincerely tell you that my soul is far more developed. It depends entirely on God's Will and on the individual soul's will what kind of house his soul will live in.

If somebody has plenty of money, even then he may not care for a big mansion. He feels that a small room is enough. And somebody who has very little money will spend everything he has to rent a big house to show off. But this big house may get him into tremendous financial difficulty. Then he has to get a loan from the bank in order to pay the rent, and perhaps he will not be able to buy proper food for himself. So, although he has a very big house, he is starving and bankrupt.

The beauty that we see in spiritual Masters is the soul's beauty rather than physical beauty. That beauty does not create any problems, either for its possessor or for others. Just because of your aspiration you see their inner beauty and you accept them because of it.

FW 189. *When someone feels a beautiful poem inside, what prevents its outer expression?*

Sri Chinmoy: There are two main reasons. The first reason is that when you feel a poem, you doubt it; you doubt whether it is real or not. You feel, "Oh, how can I have that kind of beautiful feeling? Five minutes ago I told a lie, ten minutes ago I was jealous of somebody, so it is impossible to feel this way now." But what happened five minutes ago has nothing to do with what you are feeling right now. The mind is so clever. When you have a wonderful experience, a very good, high experience, your mind will immediately try to throw cold water on it, because your mind does not want you to have joy in its pure form. Your mind will immediately ask you how you can experience this kind of thing when you acted so undivinely just a little while ago. The mind will say it is all a mental hallucination. And the moment you give up the experience, the same mind will come and say, "See, you are such a fool! You have lost everything; you have thrown away everything. God alone knows how many months it will take you to get this experience back again."

The second reason why you cannot express a poem that you have inside you is that there is a gap between your feeling and your becoming. When you feel something, if you do not immediately become that thing, then your vital being revolts. The vital being feels that you have allowed a stranger to enter into you, and it becomes jealous. It acts just like a child when he sees that his mother and father have allowed somebody else to come and stay at his house. Naturally he becomes jealous because he feels that now his parents won't be able to pay as much attention to him as before. When you feel something inside you, it means that you have invited someone or something to your house, but he has not yet entered. If once he enters, the expression is as good as achieved, but before he enters the child may revolt. He may start crying and say, "I don't want him; I don't want him." But if the parents become serious and say, "I have invited him and he will definitely stay," then it is all over. Once you become what you feel, the difficulty is over. These are the two main things that keep you from manifesting in your outer life what you feel within yourself.

FW 190. *Will the consciousness of all the individuals in the world have to be transformed before we have world peace?*

Sri Chinmoy: To some extent it is true that each and every individual must change totally, or radically, before world peace will take place. Again, from a deeper point of view, it is world peace that will be able to radically change the consciousness of each and every individual.

It is like this. A seeker has quite a few members in his family. But all of them are not praying and meditating; he is the only one that prays and meditates. He receives Peace, Light and Bliss, then he goes and offers these to the other members of the family. The Light and the Bliss that he gets are coming directly from one Source, let us say, the Universal Source. This Universal Source is the Source not only of Light and Bliss, but also of Peace. And he is distributing this Light and Bliss, which is nothing other than Peace. The Light that he is getting gives Peace, the Delight that he is getting gives Peace, and this Peace he gives to the members of his family. But they have to be receptive, to some extent. They want it, they need it; but, at the same time, they may not accept it cheerfully and wholeheartedly.

Peace has to descend; and again, our aspiration has to ascend. Each human being can be perfect, to some extent, on the strength of his aspiration. At the same time, we have to know that Peace is slowly descending. When Compassion from Above and aspiration from below one day come together, then only will we have world peace. It is not one-sided; from both sides there has to be a response. The individual has to cry for peace, and peace has also to descend. If peace descends and the individual wants it and accepts it, then only will the whole world have peace.

Sometimes we want something that we don't need. And sometimes we need a thing, but we don't do anything to get it. Suppose somebody is very poor. He definitely needs money, but he doesn't work for it. Opportunity looms large. Opportunity knocks at his door, but he won't open the door, although he badly needs money-power. Similarly, we as individuals need peace. But when peace descends, if we don't accept it immediately,

SRI CHINMOY

then the opportunity will disappear. So first we all have to feel
the need of peace, universal peace, world peace. And then we
have to go one step further and accept it when it comes. But if
we have to depend on the perfection of each individual human
being on earth for peace to descend, then peace will never, never
descend.

FW 191. *I was wondering if there was a spiritual reason why earth is
suffering from disasters at this time.*

Sri Chinmoy: At this time, disasters do take place occasionally.
From the spiritual point of view we have to take everything
as an experience. In God's ultimate Vision, God will give satisfaction to each human being. Again, each human being will
get satisfaction and perfection only when he or she has pleased
God in His own Way. There is no hard and fast rule that God
will work one way or another way. He can work in many ways
beyond our comprehension. Human beings do not know what
God's ultimate Vision is. Here on the physical plane somebody
will die; but on the inner plane perhaps God has decided to
expedite his soul's progress. So the best way is to take so-called
disasters as an experience that God is giving to the individuals
who are immediately involved and to those who are observing
the situation.

Each disaster has a purpose of its own. Again, we have to
know that the earth-planet is not perfect. So, when planets
are not perfect, wrong forces can operate in and through them.
God approves of some things. Some things He just accepts or
tolerates. Then again, there are some things that He initiates
and inspires. When we see earthquakes or floods or famine
and all this, we have to know that these are things that God is
just tolerating. If some wrong forces have destroyed a group of
people or destroyed some places, God is just tolerating the fact.

Again, there is a higher purpose to these things. Today God tolerates this suffering, but tomorrow inside the persons that have suffered, God's deep Compassion will flow, and in some way He will compensate. But that compensation we will not see with our human eyes. It has to be seen with our aspiring consciousness.

We have to know that the catastrophes and disasters and things that make us feel that the downfall of the human race is approaching are not the only damaging factors. These things we see on the earth-planet. Because we live on the physical plane, we notice whatever is happening here and we feel that tremendous disasters are taking place here. But on the inner plane there are other planets, and constant catastrophes can take place there also. For the undivine forces, the hostile forces, the evil forces, can also operate on the inner plane.

Look at the conflict between faith and doubt. In this conflict, faith may surrender: doubt may succeed. If doubt destroys faith, then we have to feel that it is like the explosion of an atom bomb. In a human being, when faith has to surrender to doubt — if somebody accepts the spiritual life and then has to give it up because he is unable to have faith in the path, or in the Master, or in his own spiritual capacity — then it is infinitely worse than the explosion of an atom bomb. That disaster may take centuries and centuries to rectify. Here on earth, when a disaster takes place and people are killed, in six or ten or twenty years the soul will again take new form and come into the world to gain and offer light. It is only a matter of a few years. But if one has to give up the spiritual life because he is assailed by doubt, then his life may be ruined for many incarnations. So an inner disaster is much more powerful and damaging than an outer disaster.

FW 192. *Is the mind jealous of the heart?*

Sri Chinmoy: The mind is quite often jealous of the heart. The heart enjoys its surrender to the soul and when the heart pleases the soul in the soul's own way, the heart gets tremendous delight. On the one hand, the mind does not want to surrender to the soul. But, at the same time, when it sees that the heart is enjoying supreme delight by virtue of its surrender to the soul, the mind becomes jealous of the heart.

FW 193. *When several individuals form a committee to do a project, you have five different people discussing something with their own backgrounds and ideas. And in the U.N., you might have five different countries or even more discussing one topic, each country with its own firm belief. What is the best course to follow in such cases?*

Sri Chinmoy: Sometimes, as an individual, you have an idea. Then, a few minutes later, you develop or create another idea. Then, if you wait for a day or two, you create or develop or become fully aware inwardly — not outwardly — of a better idea. In this way, the same individual is approached by different ideas at various times. You cannot say that each new idea you get is better than the previous ones. In the morning, you have an idea to achieve something in one way, and in the afternoon you have another idea to achieve that thing in a different way. But the idea you get in the evening need not be the better one.

So, if there are five members on a committee, each individual should try to dive deep within and see if, at any time, he can agree with the idea offered by somebody else. Right now, he is fighting for his own suggestion. But a few days later it may happen that he himself will have the same views that he is now opposing. But if you have established your oneness with the other members, then at least you will try to understand their viewpoint, and see if there is any truth in it. Then, you can see if your idea is really the best, or if somebody else's idea is really the best.

Look at five ideas as five fruits. One idea may be more mature, more practical, than the others. Everybody wants to eat the ripe fruit. But if everybody wants to eat the ripe fruit, then everyone has to look carefully at the fruits that are available. If there are five fruits, some will be unripe. Nobody wants to eat the unripe fruits. Only the idea that is most ripe and delicious you will eat. Just because one person has brought the ripe one, it does not mean that only he will eat the ripe fruit and that he will deny it to others. Others also will have equal share of the fruit that someone has brought. No matter who has offered an idea, let the others have an equal opportunity to apply that idea to their own lives. Then, no matter who has got the fruit, as long as everybody is allowed to eat it, as long as everybody is ready to share it, then the fruit will become everybody's property. This way you can have a feeling of oneness.

FW 194. *Is it possible for us to be consciously aspiring and yet somehow not be aspiring in parts of the being that we are unconscious of?*

Sri Chinmoy: It is quite possible. One part of your being can be consciously aspiring and another part can be totally unaspiring. It is like exercise. Suppose you always throw the shotput or javelin with your right hand. Because you ignore the left hand, the left hand remains weak. For this reason, it is always good to take exercise with both hands. But when there is a special competition, if at that time the right has more to offer, naturally you will use the right hand. Since it is a matter of only a few seconds, it is all right. But when you practise every day, you should take some exercise that uses both hands.

So here also, in your whole body — from the soles of your feet to the crown of your head — there should be aspiration. The aspiration-river must flow from top to bottom. Again, you have to know that there is the main portion, which is the heart. When you have to offer something to the world at large, or when you have to bring to the fore your best quality, at that time the cry of the heart, the aspiration of the heart, is of paramount importance. If you want your aspiration to be very concentrated, then the heart is the right place to go in which to aspire. But when you are aspiring normally, you can aspire in your entire being, in your entire existence.

It is quite possible to be aware of one thing and, at the same time, to be totally unaware of something else. If you take exercise with your right hand, your left hand remains unconscious. But it is you who are in a position to take exercise with both hands, right and left. Similarly, all the parts of your being can be given proper training. The physical can aspire, the vital can aspire, the mind can aspire, the heart can aspire — all at the same time. But sometimes you may be awakened, or ready to aspire, only in one part. Early in the morning, when you pray and meditate, it may be only your heart's spiritual exercise. You may not read spiritual books at all; you may not be doing any mental exercise. Again, you may not be doing any selfless service on these planes. Then, you are unconscious of these. Or on the vital plane, perhaps, you are not trying to show kindness or generosity to everyone. Every plane has something different, something new, to offer. Again, the uniqueness of the different capacities or qualities of each plane must be unified and assimilated together. If you do not take spiritual exercise on a particular plane in the form of aspiration and dedication, then naturally you are unaware on that plane. Awareness comes only through constant inner exercise.

FW 195. *What is the best way to establish joy in every part of the being?*

Sri Chinmoy: The best way to establish joy in every part of the being is through constant gratitude to the One who is responsible for our having accepted the spiritual life. At every second we have to bring to our inner mind what we were before we became consciously spiritual. And, for a fleeting second, we can see what our friends of the past are doing now, where our former acquaintances are now. As soon as we see what they are doing, and what we ourselves originally were, then we will immediately notice the difference between our achievement of the past and our achievement of the present. No matter how far away the goal is, we can easily see the distance that we have already covered. Our so-called friends of the past have not yet started walking along the real road, but in us there is some aspiration, some inner cry, at least some awareness of a higher ideal and goal.

We can offer gratitude to God, or to our spiritual teacher, or to our path, or even to our own good qualities that prompted us to enter into the spiritual life. Again, we can offer gratitude to the inner cry that prompted us to walk along the right path, or to the achievement itself. Gratitude lies in self-giving to the Source, or to the One who has inspired us to see the higher reality and run towards the goal. We offer gratitude to the Source because it has created in us an inner urge to return to it and seek fulfilment there. And this fulfilment comes only in fulfilling the Source itself. So self-giving in various ways gives us total joy in every part of the being. There is no other way.

FW 196. *Which is the best way to inspire others to the spiritual life?*

Sri Chinmoy: The most effective way to inspire others is to become aspiration itself. If you become the embodiment of aspiration, then automatically others will become inspired. You may not be all the time flooded with aspiration, but you do have a certain amount of aspiration, because you are practising the spiritual life and because you are trying soulfully to receive Peace, Light and Bliss in abundant measure.

You cannot go in the street and tell everyone, "I have Peace, Light and Bliss. Just come and take it from me." If you say that you have anything to give, others will just laugh at you. So you have to look around at who is there and then dive deep within and feel from within whom you should approach. When you feel from within that so-and-so would be inclined to at least listen to what you have to say, then only you can offer your inspiration.

So first try to discover from within whether or not your message, your love, your truth, your concern, will be accepted. Then only you will get the right person. Otherwise, you will go out in the street and shout that you have something to offer, but nobody will come. But if you make an inner choice, then afterwards there is every possibility that you will succeed in inspiring others.

FW 197. *It seems that there should be only one moral code. How can everyone recognise and accept one moral code for the whole world?*

Sri Chinmoy: There should not necessarily be one moral code. The Sanskrit word for code is *dharma.* On each plane there is a code: on the physical plane, on the vital plane, on the mental plane, on the psychic plane. But the best code is surrender to the inner divinity. On the physical plane, somebody will say that this is absolutely the right code, the real *raison d'être* of life. On the vital plane it will be something else, on the mental plane something else, and on the inner plane, something else again. If one wants to justify one's approach to truth, one can do it. Any code of life does bring some satisfaction. You do this or you refrain from doing that, and then you are satisfied. But this may not bring real satisfaction.

Real satisfaction comes not by doing something or by becoming something. Real satisfaction comes only when one surrenders to the highest principle in life, to the highest reality, to one's own highest divinity. This highest divinity you can call God, the Supreme, or whatever you want. One's highest divinity knows infinitely better than one's lowest divinity. Sri Krishna told Arjuna, "There can be no higher code of life than to surrender to the inmost divinity," which Sri Krishna himself represented. Divinity is everywhere. Divinity is in the Source in infinite measure. Again, divinity is also inside a tiny ant. But the soul that is flooded with infinite light and delight, we should accept more than the divinity that a tiny ant embodies.

On the physical plane we say that a particular code is absolutely the correct thing, but the capacity of the physical is very limited. On the vital plane, we say this is the right thing, but the capacity of the vital is very limited. The mind will say that something is absolutely correct, but the capacity of the mind is very limited. On each plane truth is there; again, the capacity of the truth is limited. But on the highest plane, the capacity of the truth is unlimited. The mind cannot fathom the capacity of the highest truth. On the physical plane, the vital plane, the mental plane, the mind sometimes can fathom the capacity. But on the highest plane, the capacity there cannot be measured. If we surrender to our own highest divinity, at that time we become one with the highest capacity and the highest truth.

Only then can our code of life on the physical plane, the mental plane, the vital plane and all other planes be easily transcended.

If we use shoes or sandals to keep our feet from getting burnt and scratched with thorns, there will be some Brahmins who will immediately think of the animals. When they think of the animals, they immediately think of the brutality, cruelty and destruction. Some Hindus, so-called pious Hindus, won't use leather because it comes from an animal skin. But if we don't use shoes, it is very difficult to walk. So where do we stand? But if we surrender to the inner will, then there is no problem. The inner will will say that everything has its own role. The animal has played its part by offering its existence, willingly or unwillingly. And we have to play our part by wearing shoes so that we can walk to church, where we will pray and meditate.

On earth we cannot exist without destroying life. The moment we breathe in, millions of tiny creatures in God's creation enter into our breath and are destroyed by us. We walk along the street, and while we are walking, how many insects we destroy! So we can't exist even for a fleeting second without destruction.

Again, we also destroy with our thoughts. When we have an ill thought, a desiring thought, a jealous thought, an insecure thought, it is all destruction. Any undivine thought we have immediately is a form of destruction on one plane — the mental plane, let us say. Consciously we become jealous and do all kinds of undivine things. Again, unconsciously we become victims to undivine thoughts, ideas and other destructive forces. At every moment, we are destroying or being destroyed on the physical plane, on the vital plane, on the mental plane; on every plane forces are trying to destroy us or we are trying to destroy them. When we are destroying someone or something, we are doing something very undivine. And others who are doing the same to us are also doing something undivine. Either we are killing someone or somebody is killing and destroying us. How can we escape from this constant battle? Every second we cannot fight with our thoughts. So what shall we do? If we surrender our thoughts to the highest Authority, who is omnipotent, only then are we safe. So the only way is to aspire and surrender to the highest divine Authority. Let the divine Authority tell us what is best for us and what is best for others. That is the best code of life on each plane: physical, vital, mental and psychic.

FW 198. *Is the difference between materialism and spirituality that in the one case we try to possess the outer world and in the other case we try to possess the inner world?*

Sri Chinmoy: When we practise inner philosophy, we want to capture the spiritual world; we don't want to capture the material world. We don't want to possess God's creation as our own. We only want to possess God and use Him for our own purpose. But again, in spiritual philosophy, in true spirituality, we possess the person for his own purpose or the thing for its own purpose. And if we go higher still in divine philosophy, we do not possess at all. We only enter into infinite Peace, Light and Bliss. Then Infinity, Eternity and Immortality can play their respective roles here on earth in their own way.

The truly divine soldier will always seek Truth, Light, Peace and Bliss for their own manifestation and fulfilment. Here the philosophy is not, "I want for myself", but the divine philosophy that says, "Let Thy Will be done in Thine own Way."

FW 199. *What is the purpose of Yoga?*

Sri Chinmoy: The purpose of Yoga is to receive the Truth and Light here on earth. Yoga means conscious oneness with God. Man and God are one, but man is not conscious of his inner divinity. We love God, we need God. But our love for God is not constant and conscious. And also, we are not consciously aware of our need for God despite the fact that we are studying and practising spirituality. We are all instruments of God, but unconscious instruments. Our love of God, our love of Truth, our need for Light is not always conscious, not always constant. We have read millions of books dealing with God's existence, but God is not a living reality for us right now.

But when we practise Yoga, when we dive deep within, we see and feel what relation we have with God. A spiritual Master is he who is conscious of God and God's Reality. At every moment in his life of multifarious activities, he is consciously aware of his oneness with God. In his case, God is a practical reality. God is constant.

If we practise Yoga, we come to feel that God comes first and foremost in our lives. Inside God we have to see humanity and inside humanity we have to see God. Inside divinity we have to see humanity aspiring and inside humanity we have to see divinity manifesting itself. This is what Yoga does for us. Yoga immediately elevates humanity's consciousness to the highest plane and brings down Light, Peace and Bliss from Above in infinite measure so that our life of obscurity, impurity and imperfection can one day be elevated, illumined, perfected.

FW 200. *What is the importance of mantra?*

Sri Chinmoy: Mantra is of paramount importance in the spiritual life. But again, there are many people who do not repeat mantras: they aspire and meditate in a different way. Mantra is an incantation process for going deep within or to accelerate one's spiritual progress. By repeating a mantra we can either invoke the presence of a particular god or we can bring to the fore our own inner divinity. But we cannot say that mantra is superior to prayer and meditation or that prayer or meditation is superior to mantra. No. We can call mantra one road that leads to realisation.

FW 201. *What can we do to bring God to people in the world?*

Sri Chinmoy: We are living in a godless world. What can we do for lovers of God who want to bring Truth and Light to earth, who want to bring God the Supreme to earth? We have to start with ourselves, in ourselves. We may see an individual standing in front of us who does not believe in God, who doubts the existence of God. But before dealing with him, we have to deal with ourselves.

We have the body, vital, mind and heart. Let us start by focusing our attention on the physical plane. As soon as we focus our attention on the physical plane, we see that we have lethargy, that we mix with ignorance. Then we focus our attention on the vital and we see that our vital is like a hungry wolf that wants to devour the world. But what we want from our vital is dynamism and dynamic truth, not aggression. Julius Caesar said, "I came, I saw, I conquered." Our vital says, "I came, I saw and I became." I came and I saw imperfection and then I became one with it here in the world of imperfection.

Then we concentrate on the mind. When we concentrate on the mind, we see that the mind is constantly doubting — doubting even our own existence. What can we do? The mind is doubting the reality within us, the reality around us. This moment the mind says I am a good man, the next moment it says I am a very bad man and the following moment it is unable to decide whether I am good or bad. The mind is always uncertain and unable to accept the Truth and Light.

We also have a heart. This heart, on the strength of its inseparable oneness with the Absolute, can become all-divinity. But right now this heart is all-insecurity. The heart says, "God, I am not getting the thing that I want," or, "I want something to be done and it is not getting done." All the time the heart is singing the song of insecurity. But this same heart, on the strength of its oneness-capacity, can become one with the Universal Heart.

When I, as an individual, focus my attention on myself, I see tremendous imperfection, a tremendous need for perfection-light. Each individual must concentrate first on himself, because there is tremendous imperfection inside him. Even though the world around him may have much more imperfection than he has, as long as he is imperfect even in an infinitesimal measure, he will not be in a position to teach others. A school teacher who has more knowledge than his students can teach them, even though he doesn't have the highest degree. But in the spiritual life we are making a terrible mistake if we try to teach others without being illumined ourselves. Here we are dealing with the life-principle of the individual. In school we are teaching history, geography or another particular subject, but that particular subject is not an individual's entire life; it is not his life of God-realisation.

So when we see a godless attitude in someone, we have to be aware of our own capacity or incapacity. If we can perfect ourselves on the strength of our inner cry, our aspiration, our love of Truth and Light, then we as individuals will no longer belong to the world of imperfection. I as an individual will not belong to the world of imperfection. You as an individual will create your own world of perfection. She will create her world of perfection. In that way there will be three undivine souls less in the world and the world will be blessed with three divine souls, three divine soldiers, three divine instruments of God. Today you become perfect, tomorrow he becomes perfect, the next day I become perfect. In this way it progresses from one to many, and the whole world becomes perfect.

When we as individuals become good, divine and perfect, the world around us sooner or later becomes perfect, for the light that we have will not remain inside us. It will have its own spontaneous wave of self-expression. Then, with our light we will be able to see that the world around us, the world of imperfection, is being transformed and illumined. For the outer world is not outside us; it is within us. We have a mind and others in the world have a mind; but ultimately it is the same mind. The world that we see is actually inside us; it is in our mind, in our vital, in our body, in our heart. So when we become perfect within, the world without also becomes perfect.

FW 202. *What is the vital?*

Sri Chinmoy: There are two vitals in us: one is the dynamic vital and the other is the aggressive vital. The aggressive vital is the animal in us; it wants to devour the world. The dynamic vital does not want to devour; it only wants to energise the world that is fast asleep. Millions of people are still fast asleep. They are not aware of God; they are not aware of truth-light. But with the dynamic vital we can arouse slumbering humanity.

FW 203. *How do we become aware of truth?*

Sri Chinmoy: It is through prayer and meditation. Right now this body which we claim as our own is our only truth. This body, which will live for sixty or seventy years, is our life. But when we pray and meditate, we see that this body is not our entire existence. Our entire existence is eternal life. Here on earth for seventy years we play a specific role; then we leave the body and take rest. After some time, again we will come back to earth to love God, to manifest God.

How can we be eternally aware of what we have within us? We can be eternally aware of our inner existence, our inner life, only through constant prayer and meditation. When we are not aware of this truth, it is as though we are sick. We have to take medicine, and this medicine is our aspiration. When we are unaware of what we have, that means we have developed a kind of disease. And in order to cure this disease, what we need is aspiration.

FW 204. *What is the relationship between Yoga and religion?*

Sri Chinmoy: Yoga is not a religion: Yoga embodies all religions. Religion has its own specific view of the truth. In religion we do not get the feeling of universal oneness. But when we accept Yoga, it is all oneness. Yoga embraces all religions. It sees religion as a house. You live in your house, I live in my house, he lives in his house. But when it is time to study, we all leave our houses and go to the same school. So Yoga is a school. Yoga is in no conflict whatsoever with religion. You come from your house, I come from my house and we shall study together.

Yoga will never say that this house is very bad or that house is very bad. Yoga will only say that God is in everything. But in some cases God is fully manifested in a divine way, and in some cases He is not.

FW 205. *What is the sound of "Aum"?*

Sri Chinmoy: "Aum" is God in His three aspects: God the Creator, God the Preserver and God the Destroyer. But "Destroyer" is the wrong term. God is not the Destroyer but the Transformer. Anything that is undivine in us God transforms and illumines. "A" represents God the Creator, "U" represents God the Preserver and "M" represents God the Transformer.

God the Creator has created us. God the Preserver preserves us. But while preserving us He notices some imperfection in us and He tries to perfect us. When He is perfecting us, He becomes God the Transformer. So when we chant "Aum", we invoke God in His three aspects.

FW 206. *Why did God create evil?*

Sri Chinmoy: What you call evil, that very thing I call ignorance. There is a great difference between ignorance and evil. Ignorance is an experience and this experience ultimately will lead me to a higher truth. We go from the lesser light, to the greater light, to the greatest light. What you call evil and sin are actually experiences of bondage and imperfection. Evil is in our mind. In our aspiring heart there is no such thing as evil, but only imperfection. And this imperfection can easily be perfected when we pray to God for Light, Peace and Bliss.

FW 207. *To be of service to you*

I am most grateful to each of you for allowing me to be of service to you. To be of service to you is to be of service to our Eternal Father.
[Sri Chinmoy chants the Gayatri Mantra.]

> *Aum bhur bhuvah svah*
> *Tat savitur varenyam*
> *Bhargo devasya dhimahi*
> *Dhiyo yo na pracodayat*

FLAME-WAVES

BOOK 9

FW 208. *Why is there religion and what role should it play in our lives?*

Sri Chinmoy: Religion plays a significant role in the life of the aspiring seeker. Religion is our spiritual home. We start in our spiritual home and then go to the Home of God. Religion is the home we live in until we enter God's Palace and establish our conscious oneness, constant oneness with God.

It is not good to be afraid of God. God is all-loving. But if someone thinks of God only with fear, then I wish to say that it is better to think of God in this way than not to think of Him at all. Most people who are practising religion are afraid of God. If they do something wrong, they feel God will punish them. That is often why they think of God. First they approach God with fear, and only afterwards they approach God with love, innocence and oneness. This is called religion. In religion, most of the time an unknown or unconscious fear looms large in us; and this fear compels us to think of God and to pray to God. This is the situation most of the time, but not always. People follow a particular religion because they love God and they are afraid of God. But when we practise spirituality it is never out of fear. Where there is oneness, there is no fear. It is out of sheer necessity that we practise spirituality. Necessity compels us to love God. He loves us unconditionally and it is our bounden duty also to love Him.

FW 209. *What is the goal of religion?*

Sri Chinmoy: The goal of religion is to bring God into one's multifarious activities. God has to be felt as a living God. Otherwise, if we are just believers in God, we cannot and will not accomplish much. The role of religion is to make each person feel that God is somebody living, or that God is infinite Peace, Light and Bliss. That also is living. If an individual wants to feel that his God is a living God, this conviction must be brought to the fore by religious feeling or by following a religious faith.

FW 210. *What is the original significance of religion?*

Sri Chinmoy: The original significance of religion was to have man see, feel and consciously dedicate himself to the existence of the One in the existence of the many: to see the One in the many. There are many countries, many faiths, many creeds many sects. Religion has to combine everything. Religion has to make a synthesis; among all countries religion has to establish a sense of oneness. The length and breadth of the world have to sing the song of oneness. This is why religion came into being.

FW 211. *The family has always been seen as the centre of both the religious and the social formation of most religions. Can you explain the sacred and divine purpose that the family is supposed to have?*

Sri Chinmoy: The sacred and divine purpose of each family lies in the discovery of the real reality of each individual. You may ask why each individual has to discover his real reality. If one does not discover the real reality in himself, then he denies the promise that he made once upon a time in the soul's region. When the individual was in the soul's region, he chose a particular family out of the millions of families on earth in order to fulfil the promise he made to God, in order to do something special for God. He promised to realise God, to reveal and manifest God. This sacred promise can come to the fore only when the individual becomes conscious of what he is going to become. If he claims God as his very own and feels that one day he shall become one with God, then he is destined to reach his goal. If he claims some higher reality which he will achieve only by transcending himself, then he is doing the right thing. While transcending, himself, he comes to realise the sacredness and divine purpose of his own existence and of the family that he belongs to.

FW 212. *Can religion help mankind to achieve a world of true brotherhood and love?*

Sri Chinmoy: Yes, but one has to know here what religion is. Religion is a code of life that connects one with the rest of humanity. If one feels that his life has a special connection with others' lives, then only can he achieve or try to achieve oneness. First he has to feel an inner connection. If he starts with this connection, then only can he think of establishing his inseparable oneness with others.

So, if you follow any specific religion, then you will feel that you have something in common with others, that you have an inner connection with others. Then, from this connection you have to go deep within in order to establish your inseparable oneness with others and with the rest of the world. And when you establish your oneness, naturally what you see inside you and around you is brotherhood and love.

FW 213. *How can religion overcome a narrow outlook and develop a real acceptance of all other religions as true and necessary?*

Sri Chinmoy: Religion as such cannot overcome this narrow outlook. Only when religion takes help from spirituality, its elder brother, does it become possible to overcome this narrow outlook. Religion sees God, but spirituality makes the seeker become God. Religion can go as far as believing in the Light or even seeing the Light. But spirituality goes much higher, much deeper. It helps the seeker or the votary of religion grow into the Light itself and become one with God-Consciousness and God-Light.

Religion stops at seeing the reality; it does not want to grow into reality. Spirituality, like religion, sees what the reality is, but then it goes one step ahead and wants to grow consciously into the reality itself. So if religion takes help from spirituality, then it is quite possible to overcome all the narrow outlooks found in religion.

FW 214. *What does God like best about religions?*

Sri Chinmoy: What God likes best in each religion is a big heart. Let each religion tolerate the others. If tolerance is there, then let each religion go one step further. Let it recognise other religions also. Once recognition is given, each religion has to feel sincerely that other religions are as good and as nice as itself. It has to feel that each religion is right in its own way, that all are equal in this way.

Tolerance of others exists as long as there is a sense of separativity. Once a particular religion gives due value to other religions and sees their existence as an expression of truth, then that particular religion can go high, higher, highest and deep, deeper, deepest. Seeing and establishing its conscious oneness with all other religions, it can claim that there is only one religion — not two or three, but only one religion. When a religion once comes to realise that all religions form one religion, one eternal religion, one eternal eye of Truth, an eternal heart of Truth, then that religion is perfect. This kind of discovery and achievement God likes best in the world religions, not only in one particular religion but in all religions.

FW 215. *What is the difference between religion and spirituality?*

Sri Chinmoy: Religion tells the seeker that undoubtedly there is someone known as God. Spirituality tells the seeker, "I can not only show you where that Person is; I can also help in making you a conscious, constant and inseparable friend of that Person."

FW 216. *Why should one give his time to God in the first place?*

Sri Chinmoy: Wonderful question! One gives his time to God in the first place because he sees that, unlike him and unlike others, God is the Alpha, God is the Omega. He is the beginning. He is the end. He is this. He is that. At the same time, He transcends what He eternally is.

God is all-pervading; He is everywhere. Whatever we do, whatever we say, whatever we grow into is nothing short of His own expansion of His own Reality-Existence. Right at the outset, at the very outset, we have to know that He alone exists. Just because He alone exists, no matter what we do, we know that our action is motivated by Him and also finds its result in Him. Our action fulfils itself, our capacity is increased and our realisation is strengthened just because He exists and He is. Therefore, either consciously or unconsciously, either cheerfully or dolefully, God has to come into the picture.

FW 217. *When the follower of one religion meditates on the ideals of his religion, will this produce the same results as when the follower of another religion meditates on the ideals of that religion?*

Sri Chinmoy: Each religion has an ideal of its own. All religious ideals cannot be of the same type and the same standard. Also, the meditation cannot be of the same height and the same standard in every religion. The result will depend on the type of meditation and the ideal of the particular religion, the height of the ideal. If the ideal is high, and at the same time the meditation is very soulful, the result will be extraordinary.

FW 218. *What are the major obstacles to praying meaningfully?*

Sri Chinmoy: There are two major obstacles. When one does not have enough feeling for one's own religion, one cannot go very far. So first one has to develop a sincere feeling. Then he has to make his religion a living reality, just as the body, the vital and the mind are living realities. Unless one knows and feels that religion is a living reality, he will not be able to make progress through his religion.

FW 219. *Why don't religions love and respect each other more?*

Sri Chinmoy: They do not love and respect each other more precisely because the capacity of their heart is limited and not unlimited. They do not care for the universality that is in the heart; they care only for the individuality in their existence. If they could feel universality, then automatically all religions would have abiding love and respect for one another.

FW 220. *If each religion claims to teach the truth, which religion is the most true?*

Sri Chinmoy: Each religion not only *claims* to teach the truth but actually teaches the truth. But merely teaching or preaching the truth is not enough. If the religion can live the truth — that is to say, if it can bring to the fore the living breath, the reality-light of truth — then that religion is the most true. The religion that lives the truth in all its aspects — in its height and depth, in its universality and transcendence — that particular religion is the most true. The religion that embodies and lives the ultimate truth of love and oneness is by far the most significant, the most important and indispensable religion.

FW 221. *If one has great faith in one's own religion, how should he view other religions and those who follow other religions?*

Sri Chinmoy: If one has great faith in his own religion, then he should cultivate the same type of faith in other religions, only he should not follow all the religions. Religion is like a road. If one tries to walk along all the roads while heading towards his destination, then his progress will be very slow. This moment he is on one road, the next moment he is on another road and the following moment he is on a third road. Each time he changes roads in order to reach the destination, naturally he is losing time. So the thing to do is to feel that each religion is true in its own way but that he prefers to walk along the path of the particular religion that he has. But all religions in God's Eye are equally significant and equally important.

FW 222. *Is a mutual understanding and respect possible between the different religions of the world?*

Sri Chinmoy: It is not only possible but practicable and inevitable. If there is no mutual understanding, then there can be no respect; if there is no mutual respect, then there can be no mutual understanding. Mutual understanding and mutual respect go together. If there is mutual understanding and mutual respect, then only can the different religions feel an abiding harmony.

Each religion has to realise that in order to be complete, perfect and whole, it has to feel its presence in the heart of other religions. Likewise, the other religions also have to feel the presence of that particular religion. Each religion must feel its presence in the heart of other religions. Also, each religion has to feel that it is only a branch and not the whole tree. The tree is God or Truth. Some religions do not believe in God or find it difficult to reveal the existence of God, but they do believe in the existence of Truth. There is no religion on earth that does not believe in the existence of Truth. So if a religion believes in the existence of Truth then that is more than enough. This Truth-existence is the Reality-tree in life on earth. If Reality is a tree, then naturally it will have a few branches, and each branch is a religion.

FW 223. *Can one be extremely devoted to a religious figure such as Jesus or Buddha and to a living spiritual teacher as well, or is it better just to follow one teacher?*

Sri Chinmoy: If the seeker fails to feel and understand that the living teacher is an embodiment of Jesus or the Buddha, then it is advisable for the seeker to have faith either in Jesus or in Sri Krishna or in the Buddha or in another spiritual Master who is not in the physical. If the seeker finds it difficult to feel or see the presence of the previous Masters in the living Master, then he should meditate on the one who he feels is best, according to his inner capacity, inner receptivity, inner devotedness, inner surrender. But if the seeker can feel that the living Master embodies Krishna-consciousness or Christ-consciousness, then he has no difficulty in approaching either the Christ or Sri Krishna through the living Master. The living Master is also the son of God, who has assumed a different name and different form. And the new form means a new personality, a new divine personality. Sri Ramakrishna declared, "He who was Krishna, he who was Buddha, he who was Rama, in one form is Sri Ramakrishna." Only the name or the form will change. The inner reality is one and the same.

So if the seeker is advanced, then he is bound to feel that if the living Masters are real, then they are serving the same purpose. They are leading humanity to one goal.

FW 224. *How can we as individuals encourage a world-wide recognition of the basic unity of all major religions?*

Sri Chinmoy: There is only one way we can encourage a world-wide recognition of the basic unity of all major religions. First we have to become perfect ourselves, as individuals. If we become God-loving and all the time are serving God in humanity, then our perfection will automatically encourage others to become perfect. When we become perfect, automatically our perfection will permeate the votaries of other religions. So, as individuals, we have to become perfect no matter which religion we belong to. Then our perfection will spread the perfume, the fragrance of the divinity-flower which is meant for all religions and lovers of religion. That flower is for everyone to appreciate and to grow into. Once everyone grows into his own divinity-flower, then everyone will see and feel the basic unity of all religions for the worship of the ultimate Truth in life.

Sri Chinmoy: Now I wish to answer a few questions. If you have any questions, I shall be extremely happy and grateful to answer them, for this is my dedicated service to all those who are seekers, who need another life, a higher life of understanding, a more illumining life of conscious and constant satisfaction.

FW 225. *What is the difference between Yoga, Zen and Hinduism?*

Sri Chinmoy: The root was Hinduism. Then from Hinduism came Buddhism, and from Buddhism came Zen. Let us take Hinduism as the grandfather, Buddhism as the father and Zen as the son.

Let us think of Hinduism as an eternal religion, or we can take it as a form of self-discipline that will one day allow us to feel boundless joy, boundless peace, boundless love. When we think of Buddhism, immediately the compassion-aspect of reality comes forward into our mind. The world needs compassion badly. I show compassion to you, you show compassion to me and with our mutual compassion we live on earth. When I am in need of your compassion, you show me compassion; when you are in need of my compassion, I show you compassion. In this way we exist together. If we don't show compassion to humanity, then we don't exist.

When we come to Zen, what we need is awareness. We have to be fully, consciously and constantly aware of what we are doing, what we are seeing, what we are growing into. Zen requires constant, conscious awareness. If we are meditating, we are aware of it; if we are eating, we are aware of it; if we are talking to our friend, we are aware of it.

When we come to Yoga, we sing the song of oneness. Yoga is a Sanskrit word that means oneness. Yoga says that if we establish our oneness with something or someone, with an incident or an experience, then we get everything. If I am one with you, then I know what is happening inside your heart, inside your mind. If I am one with somebody else, then immediately I have a free access to him and I know what is happening in him. And if I can establish my oneness with an incident or experience, then I become part and parcel of that incident or experience in life.

At the highest point in Zen there is something called satori or illumination. If once you are illumined, then there is nothing and no one on earth with which or with whom you cannot establish your oneness. Before illumination there is darkness on one side and light on the other side. This side of the sea is darkness, the other side is light and you are in between. But if you go and take shelter in illumination, then your own inner effulgence envelops and encompasses the whole world.

Before illumination takes place, you are in ignorance and you feel that the world is in ignorance. But once illumination takes place, which is called satori in Zen, you become one with the Vision of the Absolute. At that time, you live in silence-life, you live in sound-life, but everywhere is illumination and you grow into this illumination. Once you are illumined, you are freed from the meshes of ignorance. For millennia you lived in ignorance, but once illumination has taken place, then there is no ignorance in you at all. This room is dark, but then an electrician brings in some light. For days and months and years this room has remained unlit, unillumined, dark, but then the electrician comes and the room is illumined. So the greatest gift of Zen is illumination: the highest illumination, all-illumining illumination, all-fulfilling illumination.

Yoga's greatest contribution is not only illumination, but also perfection in our constant oneness with what God has offered to us, what God is going to give us and what God Himself is. If somebody is suffering, then Yoga becomes totally, inseparably one with that sufferer. If somebody is in the seventh heaven of delight, then Yoga becomes one with him in the seventh heaven of delight. Illumination, on the other hand, is a process, a regular process in which we come out from ignorance-night and enter into wisdom-light. Once we grow into wisdom-light, then we are totally freed from bondage, from limitation, from imperfection, from so-called death.

If we follow the path of Zen, then we go from ignorance to illumination: and when our whole consciousness is illumined, we derive boundless satisfaction. If we follow the path of Yoga, then on the strength of our identification we feel that we *are* that which we want and we actually become that thing. So Yoga is oneness and perfection, whereas Zen is illumination and liberation.

FW 226. *Does this mean that Zen and Yoga have different goals?*

Sri Chinmoy: No. They are like two members of a family. They belong to the same family and they deal with the same basic thoughts and ideas. Only in practice each may apply something a little new, although in a sense it is not new at all. Here is the goal. The father is reaching the goal from one direction and the son is reaching the goal from another direction. In going towards the goal, they may use different methods to some extent. But the goal always remains the same. If one becomes liberated from ignorance as a result of spiritual discipline, then naturally he is illumined. And if one identifies himself with Light and Illumination itself, then naturally he also is liberated and illumined

I touch water and immediately I get the consciousness of water. I touch a wall and immediately I get the consciousness of the wall. Again, if I touch the feet of a saint, then immediately I get the consciousness of the saint. This is Yoga: oneness, oneness, oneness. But you don't have to touch anything. Just through identification you can get the consciousness of the person who is a saint, the person who has illumination. In the Zen process, you get what the saint has by concentrating on what you want. The process in Yoga is to identify oneself with the goal. But the goal that you reach by concentrating in Zen and the goal that I reach by identifying myself with someone is the same.

There is a very good Zen teacher in Rochester named Philip Kapleau. He is a friend of mine and a great authority on Zen. He wrote a book called *The Three Pillars of Zen*. If you are interested, you can learn from him. Again, if you feel like coming to our meditations on Tuesdays and Fridays here, you can see what we get from our meditation. If you can come and join us, I assure you that you will feel something.

I am in no way trying to take you away from Zen; far from it. Let us take meditation as one shop and Zen as another shop. If you come into a shop, there will be some items that may please you. Basically, these two shops offer the same thing: love of Truth. You enter into one shop and it has the thing that you need; you enter into another shop and it has the same thing. It is you who have to make the choice from which shop you want to get the thing that you need.

FW 227. *Is there no sense of strong discipline in Yoga?*

Sri Chinmoy: The Zen process demands a strict discipline, almost like military discipline. But the Yoga process is relaxation based upon confidence. It is like a child's confidence that comes from his oneness with his mother and father. A child does not have a nickel with him. But if his father is very rich, then he feels that he also is very rich. Even if right now he does not have a single dollar, in a few years time he will be able to utilise all his father's riches. He feels his oneness with his father, with the members of the family. Whatever the members of the family have, he rightly and legitimately claims as his very own. If his father has a car, then immediately he feels that it is his car. He does not think that it is his father's car or that it belongs to his family. No, he will tell his friends, "Look, this is my car." He is absolutely right on the strength of his oneness. And a day will come when he is older and he is going to be the one to drive that car.

The child feels that the father is everything for him and a day will come when he will be able to claim everything the father has. Even now he claims it. Since he is a child, he may squander his father's money, so his father is not giving it to him. But when he is mature, since he has established his oneness with his father, he will be able to get his father's property and utilise it properly.

In the Yoga process, you just feel that God is yours, that He loves you and you love Him. You feel your oneness with the Almighty. And if you feel your oneness with the Almighty, He is bound to give you what He has and what He is.

In the Zen path you have to prepare yourself. If you do this, then you will get something. But if you are not following strict discipline, then you are not going to get anything. In Zen it is personal effort, personal effort. But in Yoga we believe in grace. We feel that the father will show his affection, love and compassion and the child will reciprocate. When the child gets love from his father, he himself gives love, when the child shows love to his parents, they give him love in return. Always there is give and take, give and take. But with Zen, first you have to become something and then only you will get something. And you become something, you grow into something by following strict discipline. If you follow strict discipline in your own life, if you do this, if you do that, than you become something. Once you become, then naturally you deserve, and illumination takes place.

PART III[§]

FW 228. *How can we stay in the heart when we are doing tasks which involve the mind?*

Sri Chinmoy: We can remain in the heart, even when the mind is necessary to perform specific tasks, if we know that we are not the mind or the body or the vital, but the heart. If we know that we are nothing but the heart and that we have nothing but the heart, then automatically everything that we do is being done in and through the heart. Now we feel that we have a mind, we have a vital, we have a body, we have a heart and we have a soul. But if we feel that we have only one thing, the heart, then naturally we will use only that one thing when we want to achieve something or give something.

If we feel that we have many levels of being then naturally we will be tempted, we will be inspired to use all these when we feel it is necessary. But if we can make ourselves feel that what we have and what we are is the aspiring heart, then the consciousness of the heart will come to the fore and inundate the whole body from top to bottom, from the sole of the foot to the crown of the head. If I repeat, "I am the heart, I am the heart," then we will only have the heart's consciousness no matter what we do. Then the problem of the mind's involvement in our activities will not arise. For we are not using the mind as such; we are using only the thing that we claim to be our own, our very own, and that is the heart.

So if you always think of yourself as the all-loving heart, all-illumining heart, then the heart itself will take care of the so-called problems that we face every day in our multifarious activities.

FW 229. *What are the major qualities of the United Nations soul?*

Sri Chinmoy: There are many, many qualities but universal oneness is the most important quality that the soul of the United Nations wants to offer. This universal oneness houses both the one and the many. The United Nations is like a tree with countless branches. Here many have become one and, again, one has become many. This moment the United Nations is the tree; the next moment it is the countless branches. A tree without branches is not a tree. Again, if the branches do not belong to a tree, then they cannot exist. Many become one for realisation and one becomes many for manifestation.

FW 230. *What do the delegates and ambassadors who are participating in the General Assembly offer to the United Nations spiritually?*

Sri Chinmoy: I am giving only my own inner feeling. Since all the delegates, all the diplomats, have a heart and a soul they have the best intention to serve mankind as such. From the practical point of view, they may not succeed. But their intention is always good. Otherwise, they would not come to the United Nations to be of service. Their inner motive is excellent. However, when we try to do things on the outer plane, we often meet with countless problems. If we give way to these problems then we don't succeed.

But all the diplomats and delegates have something spiritual to offer. They have come, first of all, to serve their country, their nation. Their nation is not one person but thousands and millions of people. They represent their nation, so millions of people are inside them, speaking through them to the world at large. So the message that the ambassador of a nation gives is something that the nation wants the whole world to hear. It is the nation's collective freedom or collective contribution to mankind that the ambassador is offering. Therefore, we must realise there is something deep or meaningful inside him, something fruitful inside him. This very thing, on the outer plane, may not bear fruit all at once. But just because it does not bear fruit immediately, we cannot say that the nation does not have a good motive or that the individual who represents the nation has a bad intention.

Each delegate is a human being and each human being has a soul. That means a solid portion of God's Consciousness-Light is inside each individual. Each individual has the capacity, the potentiality, the needed power to serve mankind spiritually. But it takes time. Some individuals open up to the light sooner than others. But nobody — no diplomat or delegate or individual — can live without in some way offering to the Source the love, concern, sympathy, compassion, devotedness and all the other good qualities that come from the Source.

FW 231. *What should our attitude be towards working at the United Nations?*

Sri Chinmoy: Our attitude should be one of conscious self-giving. This self-giving can take various forms on the outer plane. Here we are dealing with many individuals. If we find it difficult to give ourselves to many individuals, many countries, at least we can have an attitude of forgiveness. We forgive in order to make forward progress.

If we have so-called enemies, then we will all the time harbour evil thoughts towards our enemies. When we feel that we have enemies around us we actually forget our own goal. We think only of our enemies — how to conquer them, how to annihilate them. This becomes our goal. Then what kind of progress are we going to make?

So the best attitude is to always think of the goal. The goal is always found in self-giving. The more we can give soulfully, the sooner we shall get satisfaction in what we are doing or what we are growing into. Each individual knows how to offer some things to the world at large. Each individual knows how to offer something to his body, vital, mind, heart and soul. Only we have to do it.

We create thoughts, ideas and ideals. Let us say that a thought has entered into our mind. Immediately if we want to nourish that thought, we can put a good feeling into the thought. And that feeling comes from the heart itself. If we do not nourish the thought with our heart's psychic feelings, the thought remains powerless, it remains unfulfilled. Here we are talking about attitudes on the mental plane. But the real divinity, or the real essence of anything divine, lies only inside the heart. So anything that we see in the form of creation or anything that we create ourselves must be nourished by the feelings of the heart.

At every moment we can be attacked by negative thoughts, assailed by undivine thoughts. Again, at every moment with our inner will we can create good thoughts, loving thoughts, illumining thoughts, fulfilling thoughts. These thoughts can only function properly when we have an inner feeling from the heart.

The feelings of the heart we can increase only by self-giving. Right now we use the term "self-giving" precisely because we have not sufficiently cultivated or developed the capacity that makes us feel that we are of the one and for the many. We have not yet discovered our universal oneness. But once we have discovered our oneness with the rest of the world, then it is not self-giving; it is only the fulfilment of our own inner awakening. When my hand does some thing for my leg or vice versa, they do not take it as self-giving. Hand and leg are part and parcel of one reality; they are one reality.

Unfortunately, at the present state of our evolution, our limited vision has not granted us the capacity to feel everyone as our own. So let us start with the idea of self-giving. We shall give what we have and what we are; we shall give our good thoughts.

So the best attitude right now is the attitude of self-giving. If there are adversaries, wrong forces or others who do not see eye to eye with us, then we have to move forward on the strength of our forgiveness-capacity or our forgetfulness. We shall not forget our ideal, no. We will forget only unhappy, unhealthy experiences that we get from others while we are trying to serve the divine purpose within us.

FW 232. *How can you overcome feelings of resentment and anger that you feel when your superiors appear to be unfair?*

Sri Chinmoy: When we work in a group, there are many individuals, many ideas, many thoughts and propensities working together. But we have to do our best to feel that all the individuals in the group, all the ideas and propensities, are part and parcel of our own existence. We have to feel that they are all limbs of our own body, and that all our limbs are working together.

We feel that our superiors do not understand us, do not value us, do not appreciate our sincere effort and dedication. By arguing with our superiors, by trying our utmost to convince them that they are wrong or that they have no feeling of oneness and sympathy with us, we cannot change their way of life. But if we take them as part and parcel of our own existence and feel that we belong to them and that they belong to us, then we can change them.

If we consider our superiors as human beings who are totally different from us, who are perfect strangers to our ideals, ideas and goals, then we shall never be able to get happiness from life. We have to consider our superiors as limbs, or as branches of the one reality-tree. Then, if we notice that one branch is not functioning well, we try to cure that particular branch with our inner love, inner concern, inner light. If today our arms are defective, or if any part of our existence-reality is suffering from a particular shortcoming, what do we do? We focus all our concentration on the defective part and show it all our concern, love, sweetness and affection. We try to muster the rest of our being and show all concern to the defective part. And we eventually cure the defective part.

By a mere wishful attitude we cannot bring this about. In order to do this most effectively, we have to pray and meditate in silence to the Author of all good. It is He alone who has the capacity to cure a defective limb, and He is more than willing to listen to our prayer for the transformation of our so-called "superiors". So, it is only our inner prayer and meditation that can eventually and radically change their life. But before that happens, we can try to feel that they belong to us and we belong to them. We can feel that their misunderstanding, their lack of faith in us and lack of appreciation for what we do, is a fault, a defect, in our own existence-reality.

Again, we have to know that the appreciation of our so-called "superiors" is not of real importance. In the long run, in the plan of our evolution, it may be of no avail at all. If we get joy from our own service to the body and the soul of the United Nations, then only we are doing the right thing. What matters is not what our superiors are telling us, or what opinion of us they have. No, what is of paramount importance is how sincerely we are trying to serve the United Nations. When we work at the United Nations, we are trying to please the body and the soul of the United Nations, and not just our superiors. If we can please the Real in us, God, then we are also pleasing the same real Existence that is in our superiors. If we are only for the satisfaction of the Real in us and in all human beings, then our superiors are also included. So, automatically a day will come when the Real in us will change the minds and attitudes of our superiors. As a matter of fact, there is only one superior and that superior is our inner cry for perfection, more perfection, most perfection, continuous perfection in our own life, in each human life and in each creation of God. Our cry for perfection is the only superior reality in us and for us.

FW 233. *Sri Chinmoy, how do you view the problems of the world and how do you think these problems can be solved?*

Sri Chinmoy: The problems of the world are nothing but teeming clouds in the sky. It is only a matter of time before the sun disperses the clouds. We use the term "God's Hour". This God's Hour is the combination of humanity's aspiration and Divinity's Compassion. When humanity's ascending aspiration meets Divinity's descending Compassion, God's hour strikes, and all our problems are solved.

Problems are everywhere. Each country has hundreds of problems. Each individual has hundreds of problems. But problems can be solved, should be solved and must be solved by individuals first, for it is the individual mind, or brain, or capacity that rules each country. If each individual sees that he has hundreds of problems of his own, then he will dive deep into his own problems. When he dives deep into his own problems, he sees and feels that there is only one problem, and that problem is lack of oneness.

Very often we notice this lack of oneness, inseparable oneness, even in our own individual being. We identify ourselves with a particular part or limb of our body more than we identify ourselves with the rest of the body. If somebody says that our eyes are beautiful, then we focus all our attention on our eyes and feel that we don t need anything else. We neglect our arms, our feet, our nose, our head, and we forget that God has also made them members of our physical existence. Only the eyes have become part and parcel of our existence, and we consciously and deliberately ignore the existence of other things in our day-to-day life. At this time we have to know that we have lost our sweet, inseparable oneness with the arms, legs and the rest of our body. We do not consciously establish our soulful and fruitful oneness with all the limbs of our physical body proper.

The world is composed of many, many countries. If an individual can become inseparably one with the inner cry of his own nation, then he is bound to feel that his nation is nothing but a tree. If I belong to a country, then I should feel that my nation-tree has countless branches, which are the other countries. And if you belong to a country, then you can also feel that your country is the tree and the rest of the countries are all branches.

A tree without branches is no tree at all. When we see that there are quite a few branches, we appreciate the tree. And if we see that the tree is bearing flowers and fruits, we deeply appreciate it. So, from the human point of view, we can solve our problems by thinking that we are trees and that others are the branches. If we can feel this way, and if others also can feel exactly the same way — that *they* are the trees and *we* are the branches — then there will be a feeling of inseparable oneness. This is the human way that we can solve world problems.

But the divine way is to feel God's entire creation as our very own and to feel our oneness with the Will of the Supreme. I come from India; you come from some other part of the world. But everything is in God's creation and God is both creation and manifestation. He is Silence and He is also sound. Silence we see in His Vision-Reality and sound we see in His manifestation-Reality on earth. So, from the spiritual point of view, from the divine point of view, if we want to solve the problems of the world, then there is only one way. That way is to pray and meditate for our conscious oneness with the Will of the Absolute Supreme. On very rare occasions, the Will of the Supreme is being executed through us even though we are not consciously praying and meditating. But if we consciously pray and consciously meditate, then without fail God's Will will be executed in and through us.

Prayer and meditation are nothing short of our constant communion, or conversation, with God. When we pray, at that time we talk to God; and when we meditate, God talks to us. Two persons are here: God and us. When it is our turn, we have to pray and offer our soulful cry. What we want from God is Peace, Light and Bliss. And when God meditates on us, we just listen. He has a Message for us. He wants to give us the Message. And also, He will tell us how we can share His Message with the rest of the world.

So, prayer and meditation can solve all the world problems. If we can become soulfully and constantly one with God's Will, then we can make no mistakes. It is because of our mistakes that we create problems for ourselves. And what is the mistake that we have already made, and from which we are constantly suffering? Our only mistake is that we have made friends with ignorance. We are swimming in the sea of ignorance. But we can change our friendship. God is there to help us and guide us. We can make Wisdom-Light our friend, our only friend. Then we will be able to swim in the sea of Wisdom-Light instead of swimming in the sea of ignorance-night.

So, from the human point of view let us think of ourselves as a tree and the rest as branches. From the divine point of view, let us feel our constant oneness with the Will of the Supreme Absolute Pilot. And this Will we come to know and discover within us only by constant prayer and constant meditation. This is how we can solve all the problems that are in the world.

PART VI

FW 234. *A supreme honour*

Sri Chinmoy: I have repeatedly said, to work at the United Nations is not like working at any other place. To work at the United Nations, to serve the United Nations in any capacity — whether in the highest role or the lowest role — is a supreme honour. Each nation here is a solid branch of God's Reality-Dream or Dream-Reality. Therefore, here we get the opportunity to discover and realise that we are of the One and for the many and, again, that from the many we have come to please the One. When we come out of the One for the many, we carry the Dream of the One for the many. While we are away from the Source, we try to please the Source and fulfil the Source. And from the many when we come to the One, we come with the hope of adding to the Source.

I shall be extremely happy and grateful if one by one you could ask your short and soulful questions. My answers will be my dedication, as your questions will be your dedication to the soul of the United Nations. Very soon we shall offer our soulful aspiration-book to the soul and the body of the United Nations, to all the members and all those who are aspiring to unite the world into one body and one soul, to all those who truly love not only God the Creator but also God the creation. God the creation has the greatest opportunity here at the United Nations to flower into a most illumining Reality.

FW 235. *What is the seeker's responsibility at the United Nations?*

Sri Chinmoy: The seeker's responsibility at the United Nations is to pray and meditate — to pray for and meditate on those who have served or are still serving the United Nations most devotedly and soulfully. Former Secretaries-General Dag Hammarskjold, U Thant and those who have served or who are serving the United Nations in any capacity should receive soulful prayers and gratitude from the seekers who are now serving the United Nations. Also, the seeker must pray for all the countries that are singing the unity-song at the United Nations, for each individual member of the United Nations. Again, the seeker at the United Nations should pray for those who will serve the United Nations in the future. That is to say, they should try to connect the past, present and future — past glory, present promise and future achievements. Glory, promise and achievements must be united together by the seeker, and to do that the seeker has to pray for the departed souls or for the souls who have served the United Nations in the past, and for those who are still serving, and for those who will join the United Nations and sing the unity-song in the future.

FW 236. *Some nations accept the United Nations as their own. Other nations would even deny the United Nations. What are the differences in the soul-growth of the nations that have not yet become one with the United Nations?*

Sri Chinmoy: In spite of knowing that the United Nations is not all-powerful, in spite of knowing that the United Nations on very rare occasions may do things which may not satisfy the world at large, if the nations accept the United Nations as their own, very own, it means that they feel their oneness with the body-reality and the soul-reality of the United Nations.

It means that they have accepted the United Nations as the United Nations because they have true love for the United Nations, and they would have accepted the United Nations even if it were not, let us say, as meaningful or as fruitful. So, I wish to appreciate and admire those nations that feel that the United Nations is an integral part of their own existence-reality. Their souls are undoubtedly fully awakened. The nations that have consciously accepted the United Nations as their own are undoubtedly the nations that are awakened. And the nations that have wholeheartedly accepted the United Nations as their very own, the nations that feel part and parcel of the United Nations existence-reality, are fully awakened.

Unfortunately, there are some nations that find it difficult to accept the United Nations, that even go to the length of denying the United Nations. I wish to say, from my own experience and point of view, that these nations are not awakened. Either they are not awakened, or they have consciously and deliberately taken the side of ignorance-reality. Just like an individual human being, each nation has a physical personality or reality, a vital personality, a mental personality and so on. At times it is very difficult to say whether a nation is not accepting the United Nations existence because its soul is not awakened, or whether it is because the physical-reality, vital-reality or mental-reality of that particular nation is not sufficiently awakened. If those are not awakened, then the nation as such will not want to help or serve the United Nations or be illumined or guided by the United Nations. In most of the cases, I can see that it is the undisciplined vital, the uncontrolled mind and the unaspiring physical-reality that do not allow the nations to see the reality, the divinity, the sincere willingness of the United Nations to be of service to mankind.

Again, there are some nations which neither deny nor accept the United Nations. They do something else; they try to remain neutral. From the inner point of view, neutrality is not good. Let us say that two persons are at daggers drawn, two persons have different opinions, and one is right and one is wrong. If we know who is right and who is wrong, and in spite of knowing, if we remain silent, that means that some weakness on our part is preventing us from taking the side of the right. We don't say that one side is all ignorance and the other side is all wisdom-light. No, only there is lesser light and higher light, lesser truth and higher truth. One side can have an iota more of light than the other side. If we remain silent, automatically we weaken the possibilities and potentialities of the side that has more light. The one that embodies more light should be encouraged and inspired so that he reaches the destination-goal. There he will be flooded with the light of the goal, and then he can come back to the unillumined who are still struggling, still wallowing in ignorance. So, it is always good to take the side which has greater light, abundant light. It is very easy to deny the sun. At night we can deny it, but in a few hours' time the sun comes out. Even while facing the sun we can deny its existence, but the sun does exist. What in us denies it? It is the ignorance in us that denies. But our inner sun immediately responds to the outer sun. Similarly, we can deny our oneness with the supreme Reality, but it does exist.

I am sure that most of you have read India's Bible, the Bhagavad Gita. There was a conflict between darkness and light, or we can say between lesser light and greater light, which eventually ended in the battle of Kurukshetra. Lord Krishna said outwardly, "I am not taking any side," because he represented God, and for God everybody is equal. But in the very depths of his heart, he did take the side of the righteous Pandavas. To the other side, the Kauravas, he gave his own army, and he was only a charioteer for the Pandava side. But twice there were occasions when he came out of the chariot to fight against the unaspiring forces. Again, there were one or two among the unaspiring forces who were really aspiring. They knew who Sri Krishna was, but they were morality-bound to fight on the Kaurava side. They were brought up by the undivine forces; they were fed and nourished by the undivine forces, like Vishma. That is why they did not surrender fully to the light of Lord Krishna.

So here also, if some nations are in touch with undivine nations, if they get some help financially or otherwise, then they are caught. They do not want to voice forth their sincere opinions with regard to the United Nations. But we feel that it is always better to take the side of the nation that has more light and that is willing to reach its destination. We should not try to discourage the other nations in any way. But if we feel that the nations that are not aspiring so sincerely or deeply will be sad if we take sides, and if we stop encouraging the one that is promising, illumining and fulfilling, then we are standing in the way of world perfection in general and of our own aspiration. So, being seekers we should always try to take the side of those nations that are trying to unite other nations and that are crying and aspiring for more illumination and perfection here on earth. And we should always try to convince the nations to take the side of the nations that represent or embody more illumining and fulfilling light. All those who deny the truth, all those who do not want to see the truth, should be given a chance to see and realise the truth in their own time. Right now only those who want the truth and need the truth desperately should be given the first and foremost chance to come to the fore and be inundated with Truth and Light and Delight. Let us not remain neutral; let us be all for those who desperately cry for and need Light, Truth, Beauty and Delight.

It is very difficult to determine the soul-growth of the nations which have not yet become one with the United Nations. In their case, the soul has not come to the fore. Right now the physical part, the vital part, the mental part of these nations are not allowing the soul to come to the fore. When the soul is covered by layer after layer of the vital-reality, the mental-reality or the physical-reality, then it is not possible to determine the growth because the soul remains in seed form. Only when the soul comes to the fore, only when the soul germinates like a seed germinating into a tiny plant, a sapling and finally a huge banyan tree, only then does it radiate an iota of light all around. If the soul does not have the capacity or the opportunity to come to the fore and radiate even an infinitesimal amount of light, then it is impossible to determine the soul-growth. But we can safely say that there shall come a time when the soul will be able to come to the fore, for creation is meant for perfection. Nothing on earth, nothing in God's creation, will remain imperfect. Eventually, everything has to see the face of perfection, for that is what God wants from us and that is what God eternally is. Therefore, the soul will come to the fore and at that time it will be quite possible to determine the growth of the nations that are not yet one with the United Nations.

Here we are all seekers of the Absolute Truth. We should soulfully pray and meditate for the nations that are still wanting in light so that they can also see the all-loving Beauty and all-fulfilling Duty that the United Nations has. Again, we have to know that the goal that we have been seeing in the United Nations is not the ultimate goal. Right now we are only thinking of union, of a world filled with union reality. But union is not the ultimate thing. There should be something else: oneness. The United Nations is dealing with unity right now. We are trying to establish unity on the physical plane, vital plane, mental plane and psychic plane. But then we have to go one step ahead to oneness. Oneness-reality we have to achieve by virtue of our sincere prayer and our sincere dedication to the body-reality and the soul-reality of the United Nations.

What we are aiming at is something great and good, but that is not the ultimate goal. The ultimate goal is oneness-reality which the United Nations will offer to all nations, to all the world, to all aspiring human beings that are here on earth. So the ultimate goal of the United Nations right now we will not be able to place before the comity of nations. But a day will come when we shall have to offer that ultimate goal. Right now, the goal that we have placed before the United Nations and before the world at large is union-song. A day will come when we will have to seek and become the oneness-dance. And for that we shall have to prepare ourselves slowly, steadily and unerringly.

FW 237. *Can you describe the stage of evolution of the United Nations soul?*

Sri Chinmoy: There are three ways to look at the evolution of the soul of the United Nations. One is the human way, another is the divine way and the third is God's Way.

The human way is the way that our physical mind understands the evolution of the soul of the United Nations. Right now, when we assess something, when we try to determine something, we use our physical mind, our earthbound mind. But the human mind, the earthbound mind, cannot see the soul of the United Nations. If the physical mind tries to see the evolution of the soul of the United Nations, then it sees it as a seed that is quite uncertain of future growth. It feels that the seed may not germinate at all; there will be no plant, not to speak of a tree. This is how our physical mind regards the evolution of the soul of the United Nations.

Then there is the divine way. The divine way is the way of the heart, which identifies itself with the soul of the United Nations according to its loving capacity. On the strength of its identification with the soul of the United Nations, the heart sees and feels clearly the actual growth, evolution, progress and success of the soul of the United Nations. When the heart observes or feels the evolution of the soul of the United Nations, it sees a tree, a powerful tree. This tree is the soul-tree of peace, harmony, light and delight. And it sees that there are countless human beings consciously or unconsciously seated at the foot of this tree. These human beings who are seated at the foot of this tree have an iota of aspiration in the inmost recesses of their hearts. If they consciously try to become one with the soul of the United Nations on the strength of their most sincere prayer and most sincere meditation, then the soul of the United Nations cheerfully, unreservedly and unconditionally shares with them its wealth, which is universal love, universal light and universal delight.

From God's point of view, from the highest, absolute point of view, the United Nations embodies the seed that the mind observes; it embodies the tree that the heart feels; and also it embodies the fruit. From the highest point of view, this tree of peace, light, bliss and harmony has already started bearing fruit, the fruit of oneness, universal oneness. This fruit some God-lovers have already seen and felt. Let us use the term "Truth-lovers", since there are many people who do not consciously admit the fact that God exists. But for them, Truth exists. We know perfectly well that God and Truth are identical, insepa-rable; they are like the obverse and reverse of the same coin. But if someone likes the idea of Truth as the only reality, as the ultimate Goal, let him remain with his realisation. Your realisation that God is the only Reality is exactly the same.

When we see the evolution of the soul of the United Nations from the point of view of the Transcendental God, then we feel that the soul of the United Nations is quite mature. It is evolved to a considerable degree. We who love the principles, the ideals, the goals of the United Nations are consciously aspiring to eat the fruit, which the soul of the United Nations has already become. Again, since we believe in the process of evolution, we feel that there is no end to the progress that the soul of the United Nations will make. Evolution is from within and without, whereas transcendence is something that we grow in as we achieve great, greater, greatest perfection in life, in nature and in our multifarious activities. So, if we believe also in the process of transcendence, then we feel that the light, the peace, the bliss that the United Nations has already received and achieved and become is being transcended every day, every hour, every minute, every second.

FW 238. *What does the outer world need in order to accept the real significance of the United Nations?*

Sri Chinmoy: The outer world needs a broad mind and a sympathetic heart in order to accept the real significance of the United Nations. When the outer world uses its broad mind, then the thought-world that is operating in and through the United Nations will be accepted by the outer world. Here the thought-world is the idea-world. And when the outer world uses its sympathetic heart, it will be able to accept the ideals of the United Nations. The idea of the United Nations is universal peace, universal brotherhood, and the ideals of the United Nations are one family and a oneness-heart.

FW 239. *There seems to be a movement towards a mental realisation where countries are starting to work with parapsychology and mind control. Is this a step towards the heart or away from the heart?*

Sri Chinmoy: Parapsychology and mind control need not help a sincere seeker. We cannot say that they cannot help, but we can say that they need not help the seeker who believes in the heart. One can control the mind, but from mind control or parapsychology one may not get even an iota of oneness with reality, which the heart can easily acquire by virtue of its aspiration.

Mind control is one subject and the heart's acceptance and the heart's oneness are a different subject. By controlling the mind, one can make fast progress in almost every walk of life. But that is not enough in order to have supreme oneness with God the Creator and God the creation. Undoubtedly it helps the seeker to some extent, but that is not the direct way to establish oneness with the supreme Reality. In order to establish the supreme oneness with the highest Reality, one has to aspire, one has to meditate and one has to dedicate oneself totally.

FW 240. *How can we help people in the undeveloped countries?*

Sri Chinmoy: We can help only by becoming soulful and fruitful as individuals. If our conscious day-to-day existence becomes soulful and fruitful in our thought-world, in our speech-world and in our self-giving-world, then we can easily help people in a physical way.

FW 241. *How do we best deal with people who are actively opposed to the United Nations?*

Sri Chinmoy: We have to deal with people who are actively opposed to the United Nations with perseverance, tolerance and forgiveness. If we have perseverance, then that is our first step towards world harmony. If we have tolerance, then we have put forward the second step; and if we can forgive then we have made the third and ultimate step.

So, with perseverance, tolerance and forgiveness we can eventually illumine people who are actively opposed to the ideas and ideals of the United Nations.

FW 242. *How can we work with dynamism and confidence at the United Nations?*

Sri Chinmoy: Here we have to know that patience itself is dynamism. If we separate patience from dynamism, then we are making a mistake. Now, in patience there is confidence, in dynamism there is confidence. We can safely say that confidence is the hyphen between patience and dynamism. Dynamism is in the vital proper, patience is in the heart and confidence, let us say, is in the mind. If the mind is inundated with confidence, if the heart is inundated with patience and if the vital is inundated with dynamism, then we can easily have a far-reaching vision of the United Nations. At that time, we will know that we embody patience, because embodied patience is already there inside our aspiring heart. And we will know that we have confidence in our mind, because the mind is constantly challenging a higher reality than what it has already achieved, That means the mind already has some capacity which we call confidence. As for the vital, we have to know that there has always been dynamism and aggression in the vital. It is up to us which of these qualities to accept, aggression or dynamism. But just because we are seekers, our vital is bound to be flooded with dynamism.

FW 243. *What is the best way to serve the United Nations: through meditation or action?*

Sri Chinmoy: There is no basic difference between soulful action and soulful meditation. Meditation and action are one, provided they are done in a soulful way. If one acts soulfully, then he is doing a really good meditation. And if one is meditating soulfully, then that person is also acting in a divine way. So, it all depends on how we meditate and how we work. If there is a soulful reality inside our action and if there is a soulful reality in our meditation, then we are serving the same purpose.

At times our mind separates action and meditation. But we can easily convince the mind by becoming the embodiment of a true seeker, by reaching a certain height with our morning meditation and by again reaching the same height through our daily actions during the day. So, in the morning let us call what we do meditation, and during the day let us call what we do dedication. This soulful dedication is undoubtedly soulful meditation.

FW 244. *How can both staff members and delegates of member nations understand that spirituality is a true base to build their goals upon?*

Sri Chinmoy: Staff members and delegates of member nations can understand that spirituality is a true base to build their goals upon only by your own personal example. If you can grow into a flower, then naturally you will emanate fragrance-reality. If you become a flame, then automatically you will spread light. So it is not by talking but by becoming. If you can become a torch-bearer of truth and light, then automatically the world around you will see light. And if you have in your inner heart flowers of oneness, flowers of peace, flowers of divinity, and if you can bring them to the fore, then automatically the essence of these flowers will emanate all around you and enter into those who are around you.

FW 245. *Is it best to try to bring new seekers to our United Nations meditations, or just let them discover it on their own?*

Sri Chinmoy: It depends on the individual. There are some individuals who are afraid of bringing others to the Meditation Group here. They feel that by doing so they are wasting their precious time, which they can utilise by doing something more valuable. Again, there are some people who have felt something in our meditation here. They feel that they have got some delicious fruit and now their wide heart, their kind heart, their sympathetic heart wants to share this fruit with others who are near and close to them. It is like the mother. When the mother gets something nice, immediately the mother wants to share it with her child. So, if one has a oneness-heart, then it is advisable for that individual to bring seekers here to meditate.

But unfortunately there are some who feel that the Peace, Light and Bliss that we bring down is measured, limited, so naturally they feel a certain kind of loss when they bring others. For they feel that the more people that are here, the less there is for everyone. But this is a deplorable mistake. Here all of us are meditating most sincerely and soulfully, and what we bring down is measureless in every way. Spirituality cannot be measured. Spiritual Peace, Light and Delight can never be measured. And these qualities are not the sole monopoly of an individual either. All those who sincerely cry for spiritual Peace, Light and Bliss will be granted the same opportunity and the same reality.

FW 246. *How has the consciousness of the United Nations affected America as a country?*

Sri Chinmoy: According to my inner feeling the United Nations has definitely contributed something very sublime to the consciousness of America. At every moment the United Nations is aiming at world brotherhood, world peace, world harmony and world oneness. America is undoubtedly the right place for the United Nations to be, for America is constantly offering hope and promise to the world at large. America embodies at once humanity's hope and Divinity's promise.

On the one hand, the United Nations is getting ample opportunity from America as regards hope and promise. On the other hand, the United Nations itself, through its inner capacities, is transforming hope into reality and promise into fulfilment. The United Nations needs a few things from America and it has found them. Again, America needs a few things from the United Nations, and the United Nations is more than willing to offer them. The soul of America is promise and the soul of the United Nations is the fulfiller or, you can say, co-ordinator of that promise. They go together. The soul of the United Nations looks around and offers the reality to those who need it and care for it. And the soul of the United States, from above, looks down to the foot of the tree and offers Divinity's promise to all those who are aspiring to climb up to the topmost branches.

FW 247. *How can one best serve the ideal of the United Nations when not working at the United Nations?*

Sri Chinmoy: One can best serve the United Nations even though one is not working there by keeping in one's heart the main principles of the United Nations. What are these principles?

World peace, world harmony, world transformation and world oneness.

FW 248. *How can we instil a spiritual feeling in the work that we do, so that it will be conveyed to the people we work for?*

Sri Chinmoy: You can instil a spiritual feeling in the work that you do if you keep in mind that you are always working for one body and one soul. You are not working just to please your boss. You must please your boss without fail, but the ultimate goal is to please the soul of the United Nations. For that, every day you should try to increase your own aspiration; and your own aspiration will automatically convey its strength to the people you work for.

FW 249. *Is the United Nations destined to obtain spiritual power as well as political power?*

Sri Chinmoy: The United Nations has already obtained spiritual power along with its political power. Unlike the political power, the spiritual power works in silence. Therefore, it is not noticeable to our human eyes, but it is being constantly felt in the hearts of those who are crying for a better, more illumining, more fulfilling life on earth.

FW 250. *Are the people who work at the United Nations especially chosen to work at the United Nations by some higher force?*

Sri Chinmoy: In some cases, some of the workers in the United Nations are specially chosen by some higher forces to work at the United Nations. Again, in some cases it is mere chance. But if one works devotedly and soulfully, no matter what brought him to the United Nations or how he came to the United Nations, then by virtue of his selfless service he becomes a chosen instrument of the soul of the United Nations.

FW 251. *How can we consecrate our lives to the soul of the United Nations?*

Sri Chinmoy: We can consecrate our lives to the soul of the United Nations by constantly feeling that the goal which the United Nations has placed before us is something unprecedented. The United Nations is desperately trying to unify the weak and the strong, the small and the big, the unfortunate and the fortunate, the mind-power and the heart-power, the body-power and the vital-power. To unite and then elevate everything to a higher plane of consciousness is undoubtedly the unprecedented promise offered by the United Nations to the world at large.

FW 252. *How can we best inspire the people we work with?*

Sri Chinmoy: You can best inspire the people you work with by becoming a constant flame of aspiration that illumines all those who are still cherishing, consciously or unconsciously, ignorance-night, which is a lesser form of light.

FW 253. *How can we meditate on the soul of the United Nations?*

Sri Chinmoy: You can meditate on the soul of the United Nations either by imagining something that you feel is most beautiful, or by praying for the soul of the United Nations itself to reveal its presence in your conscious mind. Once your conscious mind sees or feels the soul of the United Nations, try to keep the experience constantly alive in your aspiring heart.

FW 254. *How can the strong and developed countries offer their guidance to the less developed countries without incurring resentment?*

Sri Chinmoy: It is entirely a matter of love. When the developed countries offer their guidance, sometimes the less developed countries show a kind of unfortunate resentment. Some countries feel miserable that they are not already endowed with the qualities and capacities that they have been crying for. Their resentment is almost akin to a rebelling, sulking nature. When this occurs, the developed countries must invoke the qualities of earthly parents. They have to bring to the fore the parent-child relationship when dealing with the little members of the family who are at times unconscious, ungrateful or resentful.

FW 255. *What is the main problem or quality in the countries of the world which keeps them from acting according to the ideals of the United Nations?*

Sri Chinmoy: The main problem is the problem of superiority and inferiority where the sense of separativity looms large. The feeling of identification is wanting. Therefore, the receiver and the giver are not willing to stand on the same footing of inseparable oneness.

FW 256. *How can I work with true spontaneity and sincerity at the United Nations?*

Sri Chinmoy: You can work with true spontaneity and sincerity at the United Nations if you yourself constantly discover your own heart's spontaneity and cultivate your own life's sincerity at every moment of your conscious existence on earth.

FW 257. *What is the best way to bring a divine consciousness to everyday activities at the United Nations?*

Sri Chinmoy: The best way to bring a divine consciousness to everyday activities at the United Nations is by making yourself consciously and soulfully feel that you are of the one Source and you are trying to manifest the Source in order to create a new world in the heart of the present-day world.

FW 258. *How can the delegates and representatives at the United Nations best convey the ideal of the United Nations to their people in their countries?*

Sri Chinmoy: The delegates and the representatives can best convey the ideal of the United Nations to their people by making the people of their nations feel that the United Nations is the reality-tree and that their own countries are solid branches of that reality-tree, which are destined to bear all-nourishing, all-energising fruits.

FW 208–224. *(p.297)* Sri Chinmoy invited members of the Meditation Group to submit questions on religion which he would answer at the Group's Friday meetings. These questions were answered on 31 October and 14 November 1975.

FW 225–227. *(p.307)* Sri Chinmoy answered these questions after his talk to UNDP staff members on 19 November 1975.

FW 228–231. *(p.313)* Sri Chinmoy answered these questions during a meeting of the Meditation Group on 21 September 1976.

FW 232. *(p.318)* Sri Chinmoy answered this question at a special meditation for delegates on 1 October 1976 in Conference Room 14.

FW 233. *(p.320)* At a meeting of the Meditation Group on 5 October 1976, Mr Le Kim Dinh, United Nations Correspondent for *The New York Times* asked Sri Chinmoy this question.

FW 234–258. *(p.323)* In November, Sri Chinmoy asked members of the Meditation Group to submit spiritual questions for him to answer during the Group's regular meetings. These questions were answered on 16 and 26 November 1976.

FLAME-WAVES

BOOK 10

FW 259. *Each year, does the United Nations try to achieve something new and if so, what has it tried to achieve inwardly and outwardly this year?*

Sri Chinmoy: Yes, it is true that each year the United Nations tries to achieve something new. This year, 1976, it was trying to achieve two things — a glowing hope and a searching mind, and a fulfilling promise and a dedicated heart.

FW 260. *When we invite our co-workers who are interested in meditation but know nothing about it, is it preferable to just have them come and learn through silence or is it a good idea to explain meditation as best we can beforehand?*

Sri Chinmoy: It is always advisable to explain meditation as effectively as you can, according to their receptivity, before you invite them to come to meditate. Otherwise, they will be totally lost and they will not be inspired to come again.

FW 261. *What is the best way to unite the ways of politics and the ways of the soul of a country?*

Sri Chinmoy: The best way to unite the two is to convince the politicians and the political world that there can be no branches without a tree. The tree is the soul. The political world as such has no peace and will never have peace unless and until some illumining light comes to the fore from the inner world. This inner light is always of the soul, and it is always for all who want to remain united and, at the same time, enjoy real freedom in co-existence and oneness-light.

FW 262. *When does God want His Name spoken?*

Sri Chinmoy: God wants His Name to be spoken at every moment, at every place, by every human being. We are His fruits. If the fruits can be aware of their seed, then the fruits will taste much better. That is to say, the individuals will be able to become better instruments, more illumining seekers and more fulfilling hero-warriors of God for God's manifestation on earth.

FW 263. *What stands between the outer goal of the United Nations and the inner goal of the United Nations?*

Sri Chinmoy: First of all, we have to know what the two goals are. The outer goal of the United Nations is the expansion of its lofty ideas. The inner goal of the United Nations is the manifestation of its illumining and fulfilling ideals. A lack of self-giving stands between the ideas and ideals. If individuals and nations, instead of being self-centred become self-giving, then there would be nothing to separate the ideas from the ideals, the outer goal and the inner goal.

FW 264. *For how long did the Supreme have the Dream of the United Nations before the soul was born and it became a reality?*

Sri Chinmoy: The soul of the United Nations was born the day the Supreme embodied the Dream itself. For the Supreme, the Dream-Reality and the Reality-Dream are always together and are always the same thing. But human beings see the dream one day and the manifestation of that dream some other day. With regard to the birth of the soul of the United Nations, human beings had the dream two hundred years ago when America got its independence. Real independence, real freedom and real union are inseparable. Oneness is within; freedom is without.

And the soul of the United Nations became vivid to us the day President Wilson's dream manifested itself in the form of the League of Nations. It is the same soul that is operating in and through the United Nations, infinitely more powerfully and infinitely more convincingly.

FW 265. *What does the soul of the United Nations need most from the Member States?*

Sri Chinmoy: The United Nations needs most from the Member States a true sense of compassion in the inner world and a true sense of co-operation in the outer world. The sooner the Member States become more self-giving and more co-operative, the sooner the world harmony, world peace and world satisfaction will come into being.

FW 266. *What is the spiritual significance of a photograph?*

Sri Chinmoy: A photograph is at once meaningful and fruitful. The inner life can be seen on the outer face. The inner reality can be visible on the face of the outer reality. The inner height can be measured by the outer eyes. The inner depth can be felt by the human heart. Each photograph, if it is taken from a higher plane of consciousness, leaves behind a new hope, a new aspiration and a new realisation for Mother Earth to cherish and treasure.

FW 267. *How can we help the speed of the United Nations increase?*

Sri Chinmoy: We can help the speed of the United Nations increase by increasing our own inner speed. Our inner speed increases only when we have acquired a peaceful mind, a soulful heart and a fruitful soul.

FW 268. *How can we awaken spirituality in the other workers at the United Nations?*

Sri Chinmoy: We can awaken spirituality in the other workers at the United Nations by our own examples. If they see something divine in us, something truly satisfying and fulfilling, then sooner or later, unconsciously or consciously, they will try to emulate us. Then they will be awakened the way we are awakened.

FW 269. *As the United Nations evolves, will it become less of a political centre and more of a spiritual centre?*

Sri Chinmoy: A divinely political centre and a truly spiritual centre are not two different things. We have to know that the United Nations has to be both divinely political and truly spiritual. When it is truly spiritual, it covers entirely the inner and outer existence of reality. And then it needs an opening to express itself. The divine politics, which is inside the devoted hearts of the individual nations, can at that time be of great assistance to humanity.

FW 270. *How can we best fulfil our roles at the United Nations?*

Sri Chinmoy: We can best fulfil our roles at the United Nations by consciously feeling at every moment that we are divinely chosen instruments of God, divinely chosen to play a significant role at the United Nations. Once we think and feel that we are chosen instruments, then automatically we can fulfil our roles. For inside this feeling of ours, divine fulfilment looms large in a special way.

FW 271. *What qualities on the material and spiritual plane can we offer to the United Nations to best fulfil the United Nations?*

Sri Chinmoy: First of all, you have to know what the spiritual qualities are and what the material qualities are. Spiritual qualities are many; material qualities are also many. But the first and foremost material quality on the earth plane is concern. And the first and foremost quality on the spiritual plane is self-giving. So, if our body, vital and mind have true concern for the United Nations, then we have to know that the quality that we have exists on the material plane, on the earth plane. Again, if we have the inner attitude of constant self-giving, if we have the constant message of self-giving, then that is a spiritual quality that we have. This spiritual quality and material or earth quality can be unified only when each is fulfilled in its proper way. That is to say, when we look at the body of the United Nations, we will look with our concern; we will see that humanity is depending on the vision of the United Nations to lead it to greater progress. And when we think of the soul of the United Nations, the inner reality, we have to feel that its fulfilment can take place only on the strength of our own self-giving. We have to give ourselves to the cause, to the vision and to the goal that the United Nations has placed before us: world peace, world harmony and oneness-light.

FW 272. *How can we fulfil the hearts and souls of the children of the world?*

Sri Chinmoy: We can fulfil the hearts and souls of the children of the world only by becoming the hearts and souls of the children of the world. What do we mean by that? At every moment we shall have enthusiasm and eagerness to learn more about Truth, more about Light, more about Delight. At every moment we must cultivate an eagerness to learn something illumining and fulfilling. It is our eagerness to learn that will give us a childlike heart, a childlike soul. This is the only way we can fulfil the hearts and souls of the children of the world.

FW 273. *Will the Supreme send more real leaders to help support the United Nations?*

Sri Chinmoy: I cannot categorically say what the Supreme is going to do. Already there have been quite a few extremely good leaders. Some of the leaders got the opportunity to lead, while others did not. But if there is a need for more leaders, then the Supreme will definitely grant more leaders. But if the leaders that are already there have the capacity, while others are praying for the capacity in their own way, then the goal of the United Nations will not always remain a far cry. In this case, there is no need for the Supreme to grant the United Nations more leaders.

FW 274. *When and how will the leaders and representatives of the nations of the world, especially of the developing nations, begin to seek spiritual solutions to their problems?*

Sri Chinmoy: There is no fixed date or fixed hour. It is only when we as individuals feel the necessity of oneness. Only when the hour has struck for a particular individual will that individual cry for world oneness, world progress and world perfection. The process will be one of constant awareness — by becoming consciously aware of what one as an individual and what one as a nation has to do. It is in conscious awareness that the right things can take place at the right moment in the right way and all the negative forces can be conquered, all the world problems can be solved.

FW 275. *What is involved in establishing an inner connection with the United Nations?*

Sri Chinmoy: In order to establish an inner connection with the United Nations, one has to look at the United Nations as the soul and one has to feel oneself as the soul. The soul is the representative of the God-reality, Truth-reality, Light-reality on earth. So if one sees the soul of the United Nations, then one will feel that everything that the United Nations does or stands for is absolutely perfect. Again, one's own aspiring soul is also perfect in its own way. If one sees both the United Nations and oneself as only the soul, then perfection is meeting with perfection. One perfect soul is meeting with another perfect soul — birds of a feather flock together. It is like this: if one can see one's own perfection, then only is one going to see perfection in others. So in order to establish an inner connection with the United Nations one has to feel that one is nothing short of the soul. And the soul of the United Nations has to be placed at every moment before this mental vision.

FW 276. *What is the most important thing to remember while working at the United Nations?*

Sri Chinmoy: The most important thing to remember while working at the United Nations is the vision of the United Nations. The vision of the United Nations is world peace and world harmony: one nation, one soul and one goal. While working at the United Nations, you have to sing all the time in the inmost recesses of your heart the oneness-song.

FW 277. *What role will music play in bringing about world oneness?*

Sri Chinmoy: Music will play a most important role in bringing about world oneness, for music embodies the Universal Heart, the Oneness-Heart. Music transcends the barriers of nations, nationalities and religions. Music embodies universal Light and universal Truth, and music also embodies the oneness-reality which we see in universal Love, universal Light, universal Awareness and universal Wakefulness. Universal Wakefulness we see inside all music. Music has to play a most important role in bringing about world oneness, for music is the connecting link between the One and the many and between the many and the One.

FW 278. *How can you dedicate each task you do to the soul of the United Nations?*

Sri Chinmoy: You can dedicate each task you do to the soul of the United Nations only if you feel that by doing this you are expediting and accelerating your own progress. If you separate your own progress from that of the United Nations, then you will not be able to dedicate each task to the soul of the United Nations. So you must feel that your own progress and the fulfilment of the United Nations are one and identical.

FW 279. *Are the ideals of the United Nations applicable to every area of our lives without exception?*

Sri Chinmoy: Yes, the ideals of the United Nations should be applied to each and every human heart, mind, body and vital. These ideals are found in oneness-song. In every area of our lives there should be the message of oneness. The United Nations means the united reality, which is God's cosmic manifestation taking place through His cosmic Vision. The different nations here are like the petals of a flower; only if all the petals are together will they form a rose. If the petals are torn, if the petals are scattered, then we can't call it a rose. There has to be a oneness, and this oneness is based on the collectivity and the unification of reality. So the body, vital, mind, heart and soul of each individual must be united. If the body, vital, mind, heart and soul of each individual are united, that means that all the nations representing God-reality on earth can be united.

FW 280. *How can I feel that my small job at the United Nations is really important to the total spirit of the United Nations?*

Sri Chinmoy: Each drop is essential to the ocean. You may be holding a very insignificant job, but if you are taken away, one more drop will be missing from the ocean. And when all the drops are taken away, there is no ocean. It is the unification, the combination, of countless drops that makes the ocean.

Similarly, the whole United Nations right from the Secretary-General is only one body, one soul, one reality, which is composed of glowing thoughts and glowing ideals. You represent a thought in an infinitesimal measure. The capacity that you have is in the form of an ideal. The ideal is always the same, although you may or may not embody the ultimate truth that this ideal holds. But you do represent and embody an iota of the ultimate truth. Some individuals have perhaps a little more light than others, but it is the combination of everybody's light that makes the whole reality.

So, you as an individual, in whatever capacity you are serving, must feel that you are necessary, that you are needed. Like you there are many who make up the United Nations. If all are excluded precisely because they are not Secretaries-General, or because they are not holding high posts, then there will be no United Nations. When a house is built, there are many bricks, there are many nails. If one or two bricks are missing then there will be a hole. The walls will not be strong and the foundation will not be secure. So each one is necessary, each one is essential. Each worker, no matter how insignificant his task is, is necessary in order to keep the body and the soul of the United Nations together.

FW 281. *Should the body of the United Nations remain fluid, so that the soul of the United Nations can more easily manifest?*

Sri Chinmoy: Yes, it is really good not to have a rigid way of looking at life. If you have flexible ideas, if you are adaptable to circumstances, then it is infinitely easier to manifest the truth — not only here at the United Nations, but everywhere.

The outer reality or the outer consciousness has to be flexible so that the inner reality can easily manifest itself in and through the outer reality. The inner vision can manifest itself only in and through the outer field of manifestation.

FW 282. *How can we feel and show our gratitude to the United Nations?*

Sri Chinmoy: You can show your gratitude to the United Nations by becoming gratitude itself. When you think of gratitude, imagine that a flower is growing inside you. And feel that this particular flower has to be placed at the Feet of the Absolute Supreme. By imagining that a beautiful flower is blossoming petal by petal and offering its fragrance inside your heart, you can easily offer your gratitude. Gratitude is something beautiful, extremely beautiful: beautiful, more beautiful, most beautiful. And what is beautiful, more beautiful, most beautiful in you or around you or before you? It is a flower. So that most beautiful thing you must try to have inside your heart, which is the real reality in you. So inside your heart, inside your reality, there should be something that is really beautiful, divinely beautiful, supremely beautiful. So if you can think all the time that this flower-heart is your only reality, then automatically you will be offering gratitude to the soul of the United Nations.

FW 283. *How can I increase oneness with the soul of the United Nations?*

Sri Chinmoy: Here we have to know that oneness can be found only in aspiration. There is no other place, there is no other reality where oneness can be found. It is in our own aspiration that we can have oneness. And how can we increase our oneness? We can increase our oneness on the strength of our more intense, more sincere, more soulful and all-loving, all-crying aspiration. If our aspiration increases, automatically our oneness increases. This oneness can easily be established, felt or, the best thing to say, realised, with the soul of the United Nations through an intense inner cry.

FW 284. *How can I become self-giving with spontaneity and joy?*

Sri Chinmoy: Joy, spontaneity and self-giving always go together. If one has a joyful heart, that means that one possesses spontaneity or a spontaneous heart and also that one is self-giving. Or we can say that self-giving is the hyphen, the connecting link, between joy and spontaneity. So, if one wants to be constantly self-giving to the omniscient, omnipresent, omnipotent Reality, then one has to constantly cultivate inner joy. Inside this inner joy, without fail one will find self-giving, and this self-giving embodies both spontaneity and joy.

How can you become self-giving? You can become self-giving by constantly feeling joy in every part of your existence from the sole of your foot to the crown of your head. If you can feel that a river is flowing in and through you carrying the message of joy, then automatically and spontaneously you can become self-giving in whatever you say, do or grow into.

FW 285. *How can we see through God's Eyes?*

Sri Chinmoy: We can see through God's Eyes only when we feel our conscious, constant and all-loving oneness with our Inner Pilot, the Lord Supreme. First of all, if we live in the mind or in the vital, then we have to try to establish a free access to the inmost recesses of our heart. But if we already live in the heart, then we have to feel the Presence of the One who lives in the inmost recesses of our heart, the Lord Supreme. When we feel His Presence, at that time we have to go one step ahead and feel our inseparable and eternal oneness with Him. Once we feel our inseparable, eternal oneness with Him, then whatever we do, we feel that He is doing it in us, with us and through us and we are doing it in Him, with Him and through Him. So, if we want to do anything on our own, it will be a serious mistake. But if we want to do something in and through Him, then the thing that is of paramount importance is to establish our conscious and constant oneness with God, the Pilot Supreme.

FW 286. *How can we accept everyone who works at the United Nations as our very own?*

Sri Chinmoy: We can accept everyone who works at the United Nations as our very own provided we feel that there is only one source. Here let us say that the source is the soul of the United Nations. If we love the soul of the United Nations and can soulfully and devotedly claim the soul of the United Nations, then automatically we will accept all the members of the United Nations as our own. It is like the head of the family. If we love the head of the family, if we claim the head of the family as our own, then all the members of the family also become ours. Also, if we like someone, if that person has a dog or cow or any animal, we also like his animal. Just because we love him, anything that belongs to him we feel is ours. So the soul of the United Nations embodies all the members of the United Nations. Only by becoming consciously one with the source can we claim all the members as our own, our very own.

FW 287. *Mr. Saxton: Sri Chinmoy, can you explain the technique used in your Meditation Group?*

Sri Chinmoy: Certainly. Here we pray and meditate in silence. We feel that when we pray, we speak to God. And when we meditate, we feel that God speaks to us. So in silence we pray and in silence we meditate.

FW 288. *Mr. Saxton: Is this related to any particular religion?*

Sri Chinmoy: No, this is not related to any religion whatsoever. This is an approach to God, to the ultimate Reality. We have faith in all religions. We do not speak ill of any religion, for all religions are serving a special purpose to bring about peace, light and harmony. But ours is not a religion. Ours is just a path that leads to God-realisation, our ultimate Reality.

FW 289. *Mr. Saxton: What kind of people attend your meetings here at the United Nations?*

Sri Chinmoy: Here at the United Nations we have a few delegates and quite a few members of the staff.

FW 290. *Mr. Saxton: The United Nations is, of course, a very political place. Do politics ever enter into your work?*

Sri Chinmoy: Politics, as such, does not enter into our work. But we feel that politics can be illumined and raised to a very, very high state of consciousness so that humanity can be transformed, illumined and fulfilled. We pray and meditate to purify our mind. Once our mind is purified and illumined, then this mind of ours — which creates so many problems for us, which constantly creates confusion, doubt, worries and anxieties — will become a perfect instrument for us to use to have a better world or, we can say, to bring to the fore a new face of the world. We do not use politics as such, but we try to bring into politics the light and the bliss that we get from our prayer and meditation.

FW 291. *Mr. Saxton: And this is what you hope people will gain from your work?*

Sri Chinmoy: This is what we are trying to offer to the world at large.

FW 292. *Mr. Saxton: You mentioned a few moments ago that certain delegates attend your meetings. Do you think diplomats gain anything special that is particularly useful to their own work?*

Sri Chinmoy: I do hope that they get peace of mind. It seems to me that all human beings have everything save and except peace of mind. The delegates are dealing with the world problems, so what they need first and foremost, as far as I can see, is peace of mind. When they come and pray with us, and become one with us, they do feel peace of mind. And then, when they go back to their respective offices, they can solve the problems that they have been facing with new light, new inspiration, new aspiration and new illumination.

FW 293. *Mr. Saxton: Do you sometimes feel that despite these very high aspirations and targets, that sometimes your work is often overshadowed by politics?*

Sri Chinmoy: No, it is not overshadowed by politics, for we do not make any comparison between politics and spirituality as such. Here we pray and meditate in silence. We try to do everything in silence. Politics is in the outer world, whereas our prayer and meditation are in the inner world. On the strength of our sincere prayer and meditation, we try to bring to the fore the peace, light and bliss that we have. And then this peace, light and bliss we try to offer to the world, the political world, so that the political world can also be illumined, perfected and fulfilled.

[After the formal interview, Mr. Saxton continued to ask Sri Chinmoy about his path and about peace of mind with the questions following.]

FW 294. *Mr. Saxton: What is your basic philosophy?*

Sri Chinmoy: Our basic teaching is love, devotion and surrender. We love God, not in a human way but in a divine way. In human love there is constant demand — I give you something, you have to give me something. It is always mutual give and take. But in divine love we give unconditionally. Then it is up to God to give us what He wants to give us. We know that in reality God has already given us everything; only right now we are trying to feel that He has done this. This is our divine love. Right now I am one individual, but when I try to love the world in a divine way, at that time I grow into the universal heart. Human love ends in frustration and frustration ultimately is destruction; whereas divine love is constant illumination.

Human devotion is attachment. I may be attached to you and you may be attached to me, but this does not serve any divine purpose. Divine devotion is dedication to a higher purpose, to a higher way of life, to an ideal or goal. It grows out of our promise to our inner being to manifest our inner divinity here on earth.

Human surrender is the surrender of the slave to the master. If the slave does not please the master, the master will dispense with his services. So the slave is all the time afraid of the master. But divine surrender is the surrender of our less illumined part to our higher part. Right now we are not fully aware of our highest height. But once we become aware of who we are, we try to surrender our lower self to our higher self. The tiny drop is not aware of the ocean, but when it merges into the ocean, it becomes the ocean itself. As long as it maintains its individuality and personality, the tiny drop is just a tiny drop. In divine surrender, the finite in us surrenders to the infinite in us and we become inseparable.

FW 295. *Mr. Saxton: How would you characterise real peace of mind? How can someone really come to terms with themselves and be totally peaceful with themselves in their minds?*

Sri Chinmoy: When we have peace of mind, when we have tranquillity, we feel that there is nothing that we have to achieve, nothing that we have to do for ourselves. Everything has been done by the Almighty, by our Heavenly Father. Right now we are hankering after name, fame and many other things. But when we have peace of mind, we feel on the strength of our oneness with the rest of the world that everything the world has is ours.

FW 296. *Mr. Saxton: But how do you reach that state?*

Sri Chinmoy: Through prayer and meditation. When we pray and meditate every day, our necessities diminish. Right now we may have twenty desires. But if we pray and meditate, over a period of time our desires will decrease. From twenty it becomes ten; then gradually it becomes five or six. Then, when we do not have any desires, if we can live even for five minutes without any desires, then we are bound to get peace of mind. If we can surrender our individual will to God's Will, then easily we can have peace of mind. Now we separate our will from God's Will. We may want a particular thing, although we know perfectly well that God wants something else from us. He wants us to be freed, to be liberated from the meshes of ignorance, but we enjoy the worldly life, or pleasure-life. But eventually we will care only for the aspiration-life, Him to serve, Him to fulfil, here on earth and there in Heaven.

Mr. Saxton: It has been very interesting talking to you.

FW 297. *How does one stop the mind?*

Sri Chinmoy: There are quite a few ways to stop the mind. One way is to repeat the Name of God and try to forget oneself inside the repetition of the Name. Or one can repeat a particular *mantra,* which means sacred word or incantation. When one is repeating a *mantra* or God's Name, there will be a continuous flow. If it is "God, God, God," then inside the repetition itself one has to lose oneself. Then the mind stops.

There is also another way. One has to see the mind as a material object. We can take a material object and put it anywhere we want to, or we can throw it the farthest possible distance, according to our strength. So either we can grab the mind like a material object and throw it into the distance, or we can put the mind wherever we want to. If a mischievous child is bothering us, we can take the mischievous child into a corner and threaten him and keep him there. One can do that to the mind also.

A third way is to totally forget about the existence of the mind. Ignore the mind and feel oneself only as the heart. It is not enough to say, "I have a heart." One must say, "I am the heart, I am the heart." Then the qualities of the heart will permeate the entire being, and automatically the mind will stop. There are many more ways, but these three ways are quite enough for any individual, and one can choose any of the three in order to stop the mind.

FW 298. *What do you mean by perfection?*

Sri Chinmoy: My sense of perfection need not be and cannot be the same as your sense of perfection. Everyone has to define perfection according to his receptivity, according to his realisation of truth. But one thing that everybody agrees upon is that everyone knows he has to make progress. Progress is self-transcendence and self-transcendence is undoubtedly true perfection. According to me, perfection is self-transcendence, perfection is constant progress which is always transcending itself. Otherwise, if I say that this is perfection, you will say no, something else is perfection. So there will be no end to our dispute. My perfection need not be your perfection, but my self-transcendence will always give me satisfaction and your self-transcendence will always give you satisfaction. Where there is continuous satisfaction, glowing satisfaction, illumining satisfaction, we have to know that that is perfection. Perfection is in the satisfaction that glows and grows inside our hearts.

FW 299. *The Yogi believes in realisation on earth after a series of reincarnations; the Christian believes in salvation after death through Christ. How can one synthesise these two great beliefs?*

Sri Chinmoy: There is no conflict. A Hindu will speak about realisation, whereas a Christian believes in salvation. In Indian tradition, the ultimate goal is realisation. In the West, the ultimate achievement is salvation. Here we use the term "salvation"; in the East, especially in India, we use the term "realisation". But we have to know that there is a great difference between salvation and realisation. Salvation is freedom from sin, from darkness, from bondage; but realisation is totally different. Realisation is self-discovery, the discovery of what we truly are. What are we? We are God's representatives; we are inseparably one with God, inseparably one with God's ultimate Reality. So realisation is our conscious awareness of our highest Reality or our conscious, inseparable oneness with the Highest. Salvation is freedom from something that is not our own: sin, darkness, bondage, ignorance. These things have come and attacked us and we are trying to save ourselves from them. They are enemies or strangers to us.

These are two ways to approach the reality, but they are not contradictory. We only synthesise when there are contradictory ideas. Salvation through Christ is one way. Realisation is another way. Realisation has to be achieved here on earth through prayer and meditation. Salvation is achieved in Heaven.

With regard to reincarnation, the Indian belief is that this is not our first or our last life. We believe in reincarnation because we feel that God wants us to be happy and fulfilled. Even in the desire world we have hundreds of desires. At the age of four, if we have a desire, it takes forty, fifty or even sixty years to fulfil that desire. In the aspiration world, if we want even an iota of peace, light and bliss, it take us years to achieve it. What we need is boundless peace, boundless light, boundless delight. So how can we get it in one short span of life? It is impossible. If God's unconditional Grace descends, then naturally we will be blessed with peace, light and bliss. But in general, to get even peace of mind takes many, many years. So we feel that God-realisation, which is the ultimate achievement, is a long way off and we cannot cover the distance in one short life span.

God wants us to realise, reveal and manifest Him on earth. This is His playground. In Heaven He wants to play with us in a different way. There He doesn't want us to realise Him or manifest Him; that is the place for us to rest. Here at every moment, we are in the battlefield of life. We are fighting against ignorance and wrong forces, and we are trying to know what we eternally, truly are, trying to bring to the fore inner realities, inner divinities. After some time, naturally we need rest. The soul's world, Heaven, is for rest, not for constant activities. Heaven and earth are two places with two different objectives. Here is activity, there is rest. Here we enter into the hustle and bustle of life in order to realise, reveal and manifest the Highest; there we go to rest.

FW 300. *At our United Nations meetings, should we meditate on specific themes related to United Nations conferences and other things, as well as on general qualities like peace and love?*

Sri Chinmoy: It is advisable for seekers to meditate on divine qualities such as peace, love, light and bliss. This is our way, the way of the soul. The other way is perfect according to the wisdom, the understanding, the realisation of those who follow it. Our way is perfect according to our understanding, our wisdom, our inner cry. We feel that if we have peace, light and bliss within us, then we can bring it into our outer life. Others may feel that if they can organise a peaceful situation, then they can have a peaceful life. They feel that they have to bring the world into order first. They start from the outside. They want to dive into the world from outside. We are trying to start inside and bring what is within to the fore. So these are two different approaches. Some feel that if they approach reality from the outside, then they will be fulfilled and we feel that if we can come from the inner world to the outer world, then we will be fulfilled. There is no contradiction. We are both aiming at the same goal: peace, love, light and bliss. The approaches are different but the achievement will be the same.

One approach is from the outside world to enter into the inner world, but we feel that as soon as we achieve something in the inner world, only then shall we be able to bring it and give it to others. Otherwise, if we enter into a conference dealing with politics, we will be totally lost. Politics is dying to get inner light; it wants to be illumined by inner light. But on the mental plane, politics is only a constant fight, constant battle: "I know better than you." "No, no, I know better; I am right." Politics here is the battle of ego. "My nation is better; you have to listen to me." But spirituality is the flow of oneness. When there is oneness, there is no supremacy. Oneness never quarrels. In the outer world there is tremendous misunderstanding, but in the inner world we always sing the song of oneness. Oneness is achievement, oneness is self-giving and self-giving is God-becoming. In the outer world it is all division: I and mine. "You have to surrender to me. Then only you will know what the truth is." In the inner world it is all oneness. In the outer world division and a constant sense of separativity is satisfaction. In the outer world, binding myself to someone else is satisfaction. In the inner world satisfaction is oneness. Satisfaction comes by liberating myself, expanding myself.

So if we pray and meditate on peace, light and bliss, then we will definitely be able to serve those in the political world. And those who are serving the United Nations according to their own understanding will not be in conflict with us. Our approach will be different. But we will not say that ours is superior, that ours is the best way, no. Only we feel our approach will satisfy us without conflicting with their ideas, and their approach will satisfy them without conflicting with our ideas.

FW 301. *If we are feeling tired, should we still come to U.N. Meditation Group meetings?*

Sri Chinmoy: If you are tired, you should come to the meeting in order to get new life, a new flow of life energy. If you are tired, you will get from your meditation new energy, new enthusiasm, new promise. Meditation is a process to awaken or acquire the energy that is not within you at this moment or the energy that is waiting for you to invoke it. In meditation, you invoke cosmic energy.

The energy that we have most of the time is very limited. We work a little and then we have to sleep or rest to recuperate. But if we can throw ourselves into the cosmic energy, we will never be at a loss for energy. Otherwise, if one works for a few hours, one is bound to be tired, exhausted; one has to sleep for a few hours in order to gain back new energy. But in our case, meditation constantly supplies us with energy, for it has the capacity to enter into the cosmic energy which is all around, whereas our physical life does not have the key to enter into the cosmic energy. So it is always advisable to come to the meetings; then you will have new energy. It is most important to come to meditation regularly. Meditation is illumination and illumination is the constant flow of new possibility, new realisation, new perfection in life.

FW 302. *Mr. Robert Muller: The first three of U Thant's four categories of needs, namely physical, intellectual and moral needs, do not create any insuperable problems, but the last and most important one in his view, spirituality, gives me considerable difficulties. There are indeed so many definitions of that term. U Thant described it as "Faith in oneself, the purity of one's inner self." Suppose — as I would ardently wish — that humanity would adopt some day his four broad categories of goals. How would you define the spiritual goals?*

Sri Chinmoy: The seeker in me fully agrees with our beloved brother U Thant's four categories — physical, intellectual, moral and spiritual — which are necessary for an individual to become integrally perfect. The term "spiritual" always creates problems, not only in the minds of seekers who are endowed with few spiritual potentialities but also in the minds of those who are endowed with great spiritual potentialities. Each individual must needs have a way of feeling and describing his own spirituality. To some, it is faith in oneself; to others the purity of one's inner self; to still others, God for God's sake. Again, there will be no dearth of definitions of the term "spirituality". According to my inner conviction, spirituality is at once self-giving and God-becoming. This self-giving is not an offering to somebody else, to a third party. This self-giving is an offering to one's own higher self. This self-giving is nothing short of an act of self-uncovering. Self-uncovering is another name for self-discovering, and self-discovering blossoms into God-becoming.

Now, what is God-becoming? This question can be answered in billions and trillions of ways. Each individual will have an answer of his own in accordance with his soul's development and his life's needs. Here again, my inner conviction is that God-becoming is the soulful recovery of one's own forgotten self, one's cheerful acceptance of it and one's fruitful discovery of this realisation: "In my yesterday's life, I had; in my today's life, I am. What did I have? God the man as an aspiring seed. What have I become? Man the God as the fulfilling fruit."

FW 303. *Mr. Robert Muller: I often think that U Thant's four categories of human qualities or needs — physical, intellectual, moral and spiritual — could well form the basis for a world agenda of human goals. From your writings, I notice that these categories are also quite fundamental to you, but you add to it a fifth which you call the "vital". Could you elaborate on it?*

Sri Chinmoy: The existence of the vital-reality is between the physical and intellectual. As there are physical, intellectual, moral and spiritual worlds, even so, there is also a vital world. This vital world is situated between the physical and the intellectual worlds. Again, this vital world is divided into two: the human vital and the divine vital. The human vital is nothing short of aggression. It always says, "I know how to become, I know how to become." But the divine vital says, "I know how to spread. I know how to spread. And also I know what to spread, why to spread and where to spread. What to spread? My love-wings. Why to spread? Because that is the only way I can have satisfaction. How to spread? Soulfully and unreservedly. Where to spread? Where there is a an urgent need, a sincere need, an undying need."

When Julius Caesar said, "*Veni, vidi, vici;* I came, I saw, I conquered," it was the human vital in him that was speaking. This is the vital that enjoys satisfaction through destruction. Needless to say, this kind of satisfaction is absurd. The other way is the way of the Saviour, the Christ, who said, "Father, forgive them, for they know not what they do." Here the Christ teaches us that true satisfaction comes into existence only through oneness.

This oneness can be discovered in any plane of consciousness. On the physical plane, for example, the head is at a particular place, the arms are at another place and the legs are at a third place. But they have established their oneness because they are all part and parcel of the body-reality. This same kind of oneness has to be discovered in the development of each individual. The divine statement of the Christ, with its fathomless magnanimity, identifies itself with the unlit reality of humanity as the Christ asks his Father for humanity's redemption. For this, what he needs is his Father's immediate Compassion and express Forgiveness.

The human vital says, "Behold, I have." And when we see what it has, we are disappointed, distraught and disgusted; we curse ourselves for our stupid action. The divine vital says, "I am, because you have made me. And I shall remain always so by offering to you consciously and constantly a portion of what I have. In this way I become my own universal self."

FW 304. *Mr. Robert Muller: When I speak to audiences about U Thant's four ways to happiness, I sometimes hear the following criticism: "Life is one and cannot be artificially cut into four. Everything is interdependent and linked. We must concentrate on life as an entity and not on components which are the product of the intellect." I am not over-impressed with this argument, for I have indeed observed that life is richest when I cultivate simultaneously all four categories of needs, namely physical, mental, moral and spiritual. Nevertheless, there is some truth in that criticism and I would be grateful to learn how you would respond to it.*

Sri Chinmoy: I am sorry to say that it is not possible for me to see eye to eye with your critic-friends. Indeed, they are right when they say that life is one, but in the same breath when they say that it cannot be artificially cut into four, I wish to ask them where they got the idea of cutting life or the life-tree into four parts. There is no necessity of artificially cutting life-reality into four; it is absurd.

Let us take life as a ladder that serves us and helps us reach the pinnacles of liberation, illumination, realisation and perfection. This life-ladder has four rungs. The first rung we unmistakably call the body-reality. The second rung is the intellect-reality; the third rung, the morality-reality, and the fourth rung, the spirituality-reality. Once we firmly step on the body-reality-rung, the body casts off the ignorance-cover of millennia. Once we ascend from that rung and step on the intellect-reality-rung, we see the vastness inside smallness and the smallness inside vastness, the infinite Beauty inside the finite duty and the finite duty inside the infinite Beauty. Then we ascend the morality-reality-rung. Here we try to illumine our lower self, which consciously or unconsciously enjoys the song of division and the dance of separativity through self-indulgence and by unreservedly and deliberately embracing the earth-bound goal while ignoring the Heaven-free goal. The earthbound goal is: "Possess and become". But to our sorrow we see that we possess only to lose; what is worse, to get totally lost. Finally we ascend to the spirituality-reality-rung and reach our Heaven-free goal. What is our Heaven-free goal? Our Heaven-free goal is: "Offer and become".

To quote your singularly momentous and apposite inner depth: "We progress physically, mentally, morally and spiritually towards a higher level of human consciousness, towards that smile of divinity which knows that someday the human race will be able to re-establish paradise on earth. There is no longer much difference between the political approach and this broader, richer concept of human fulfilment."

I fully agree that these four approaches are not independent; they are interdependent. They are interdependent precisely because they know that they can reach their satisfaction-goal only on the strength of their becoming one, inseparably one. Interdependence is the harbinger of oneness. Human life in itself is an eternal road, eternal journey, eternal soul and eternal goal. While walking along Eternity's road, if the seeker covers some distance and then gives the distance he covered a name, and if he continues to do this, he is perfectly entitled to do so. But in the heart of his heart, he knows that it is only one road, one journey, one crying soul and one smiling goal. These four are Eternity's duty, Infinity's beauty, Divinity's necessity and Reality's immortality.

FW 305. *Mr. Robert Muller: Do you think the U.N. exercises a real influence in the world? What is, in your view, its principal contribution? How does it appear to you in the great stream of history and human evolution?*

Sri Chinmoy: Not only do I think, but I am positive in my soulful statement that the United Nations exercises certain influences in the world. These are the vision of peace, the mission of brotherhood, the sense of perfection in a oneness-world-family and the total satisfaction of complete oneness.

The principal contribution of the United Nations is the hope-sky that it offers to the world at large. This hope-sky is not a product of vital fantasies, mental vagaries or the idiosyncrasies of weaklings. This hope-sky is the all-illumining revelation of the United Nations soul. The seeker-servers at the United Nations — no matter in which capacity they are serving the United Nations — and the supporter-lovers of the United Nations — no matter in which part of the world they are — are seeing a glimpse of the United Nations soul's all-illumining revelation. And each glimpse embodies a growing and glowing fullness-satisfaction in man's life of inner hunger and his life of outer feast.

In the great stream of history and human evolution the contribution of the United Nations is not only to be the great and ultimate pathfinder of the ultimate Truth, but also the good and supreme bliss-distributor of humanity's Divinity.

FW 306. *Mr. Robert Muller: If you were given the task of laying down the basic principles for the education of all the children of this world, what would be your recommendations?*

Sri Chinmoy: According to me, education is self-cultivation and self-cultivation is God-perfection in human life. You want to know the basic principles for the education of all the children of this world. Let us divide this world into halves: the Eastern world or, let us say, the Indian world, and the Western world, or the American world. For an Indian child, freedom is a far cry. For an American child, freedom is an act as easy as breathing in and breathing out. In India, even now I see that a child is taught and learns the message of the world through severe discipline and imposed fear. Here in America, as far as I can see and feel, in most of the cases, if not all, parents get satisfaction in fulfilling their own dreams, but they neglect their children's needs. They say to the children, "We don't want to impose anything on you. You find out your truth and you pick out what is best for yourself, for how do we know what is best for you? It is better that you look around and find what you need." Some will say that this is a broad expression of the parents' oneness with their children, while others will say that the parents unconsciously, if not consciously, are unburdening their so-called burdens. The parents will say, "Look, we really love you. Here is the proof that we love you. We have given you a TV set. We have given you a tape recorder, a radio — everything in the material world that you long for. Therefore, we expect you to stay with your friends and let us fulfil our dreams in our own way."

Unfortunately, I can subscribe neither to the Indian method of bringing up a child nor to the American method. Parents should not allow their children to grow up in the Elysian lap of exorbitant luxury; nor should they keep a devouring, intransigent tiger before their children so that at every moment the children will be forced to do the right thing. The parents should tell their children that they are not disciplinary, autocratic parents but unreservedly loving, discerning friends.

The education of the children and the education of the parents must go together. The parents must dream in and fulfil themselves through their creations, their children. As the creation cannot be separated from the creator, even so, the creator cannot be separated from the creation. The creation without the creator is helpless. The creator without the creation is meaningless. Therefore, both the creation and the creator must contribute to each other in order to derive oneness-satisfaction and fulness-satisfaction. It is in the parents' right decision that we can find the children's freedom. This freedom is founded on their oneness with their parents' will. Let us consider the children as finite realities and the parents as infinite realities. The children become infinite and enjoy infinite freedom only by becoming consciously, unreservedly and inseparably one with their parents.

The parents must not think of their children as unnecessary projections of their life; for if these projections are unnecessary, then they can go in their own way. On the contrary, they must feel that their children are absolutely necessary projections of their life. The improvement of the projections, perfection of the projections, considerably adds to the source. The beauty of the leaves, flowers and fruits of the tree only adds to the seed-reality of the tree. It does not diminish the beauty-reality, divinity and necessity of the seed.

Here I wish to quote from your most illumining insights about global education: "A child born today will be faced as an adult, almost daily, with problems of a global interdependent nature, be it peace, food, the quality of life, inflation, or scarcity of natural resources. He will be both an actor and a beneficiary or a victim in the total world fabric, and he may rightly ask: 'Why was I not warned? Why was I not better educated? Why did my teachers not tell me about these problems and indicate my behaviour as a member of an interdependent human race?' [....]

"Global education must transcend material and intellectual achievements and reach also into the moral and spiritual spheres. Man has been able to extend the power of his hands with incredible machines, of his eyes with telescopes and microscopes, of his ears with telephones, radio waves and sonars, of his brain with computers and automation. He must now also extend his heart, his sentiments, his love and his soul to the dimension of the entire human family and to our total beautiful planet circling in the universe."

The parents should bring the presence of God, the presence of love, the presence of truth and the presence of purity into the hearts and eyes of their children as soon as the children can see the light of day. They should tell their children that they themselves and the children are great companions and that they have a good Guide, a good Leader, who will guide them, mould them and shape them into perfect Perfection. They know a little more about that Guide than the children, and He has told them to say certain things about Him to the children. Therefore, they are listening to the Guide's dictates. Right now the parents are asked by the Guide to act as intermediaries between Him and the children. But there shall come a time when the children will not need intermediaries. They will be able to go directly to the Guide, the Source. Until then, the children must listen to their intermediaries, their earthly friends. The acme of the children's education is their perfection in life and their perfection for God-satisfaction. And to offer their children that, the parents should not impose, nor expose, nor even propose: only they should become the living flame of self-giving in order to realise their own world-satisfying life and to please the Source in its own way.

FW 307. *Mr. Robert Muller: Anthropologists have found a gradation of religious beliefs over the history of mankind: ritualism, animism, ancestor worship, polytheism, monotheism. All these forms were associated with changes in the social structure. Recently, the "age of reason" and the scientific and industrial revolution have rendered religion and spirituality obsolete — even harmful — in the eyes of many. What, in your view, is likely to be the "religion" or "spirituality" of humanity tomorrow as a satisfactory answer to man's queries about his relationships with the universe, his fellow men and the mysteries of life? Is this likely to be reflected in the United Nations as a forum where humanity is seeking new ways for its destiny and fulfilment?*

Sri Chinmoy: The spirituality of tomorrow will neither be the merciless rejection of life nor the disproportionate imposition of life; the spirituality of tomorrow will be the devoted acceptance of life and the pure dissemination of the seeker's self-giving breath in order that he may become a God-blossoming beauty within and without.

Here at this point I am tempted to share with the rest of the world your most illumining ideas and most nourishing thoughts: "Indeed, how can we reach full consciousness and enlightenment if we do not let the entire world and humanity enter ourselves? Humility and the lowering of one's ego lead in the end to righteousness, happiness and the full mastery over oneself, enriched by the thoughts, dreams and feelings of others. Together with meditation, it is perhaps the clue to serenity in our bewildered, complex world. U Thant was a living proof of it."

The spirituality of tomorrow's dawn will beckon the desire-world to show the desire-world that real satisfaction looms large only in the aspiration-life. The real spirituality of tomorrow's dawn will, beckon the aspiration-world to show the aspiration-world that real satisfaction lies only in the seeker's unconditionally surrendered oneness with his Source, his Beloved Supreme.

The blind world can be sceptical of the reality or it can deny the reality when the reality is in the flame stage. But when the reality grows into the sun stage, even the stone blind must admit that the sun does exist, because of its scorching heat and loving warmth. Today's United Nations divinity-flame can be denied or challenged, but tomorrow's United Nations divinity-sun shall give sight to the blind, offer legs to the lame and offer voice to the voiceless to mark the slow, steady and unerring beginning of man's quenchless satisfaction in God and God's breathless satisfaction in man.

PART V

FW 308. *Letter from Mr. Muller to Sri Chinmoy*

Dear Sri Chinmoy,
U Thant often said that in his view the West was too materialistic and intellectual, and not spiritual enough, whereas the East was too spiritual and fatalistic, and not caring enough for the material and intellectual welfare of the people. Do you see a synthesis developing between the two and how would you envisage a harmonious, happy world society?

Warmly yours,
Robert Muller
18 March 1977

FW 309. *Letter from Sri Chinmoy to Mr. Muller*

Dear Mr. Muller, esteemed brother, illumining seeker and fulfilling advisor:
I readily, immediately and unreservedly agree with our beloved Secretary-General U Thant's most illumining assessment of Eastern achievements and Western achievements, Eastern possessions and Western possessions, Eastern contributions and Western contributions, Eastern outlook towards the Reality and Western outlook towards the Reality.

The East is spiritual, the West is material. The East cries for the transcendental Spirit, the West cries for the universal matter.

The East is in the heart and for the heart. The West is in the mind and for the mind. The East from within comes to the fore and flowers. The West from the outer existence goes deep within and flowers.

The East wants silence. The West wants sound. Silence embodies the teeming Vast eventually to proceed. Sound inspires the teeming Vast continuously to succeed.

The East sings the song of God the One. The West sings the song of God the Many. The East loves unity. The West loves multiplicity.

This world of ours is beset with countless problems. The spiritual East thinks that the Beyond is the only answer. The material West thinks that the answer is to be found here on earth; it thinks that the answer is: live and enjoy and enjoy and live.

The East believes in fate because it believes in reincarnation. The West does not believe in reincarnation; therefore, it does not believe in fate.

We can endlessly see and determine the differences between the East and the West. But the real question is whether these differences are being synthesised or not. At the very beginning, if we know what the heart can offer and what the mind can offer, then it will be an easy task to synthesise the two. The heart wants to see the oneness, feel the oneness and become the oneness itself. The mind wants diversity in the vital and multiplicity in the mind proper. The heart knows that there is a road that leads upward. The mind knows that there is a road that leads forward. The East wants to walk along the road that leads upward. The West wants to walk along the road that leads forward.

The synthesis between East and West starts because of their feelings of insufficiency. The East sees that if it does not accept the material life, then it will not be able to manifest what it inwardly has. The West feels that if it does not accept the spiritual life, then it will not have a solid foundation. Then everything can be easily shattered.

We can clearly see that the East has already gained considerable knowledge and wisdom from the West, especially in the scientific world. The West has gained considerable knowledge and wisdom from the East, especially in the spiritual world. Here we see that the heart and the mind cannot function separately and individually. They have to function together, provided they feel the need of an integral perfection in life. The mind without the heart will not know what the supreme Reality is. The heart without the mind will not know how the supreme Reality can be manifested here on earth. To our great joy, the East and the West are constantly complementing each other to make each other perfect consciously, and more so unconsciously.

The East is like the body of a bird and the West is like the wings of a bird. If the bird does not spread its wings, then how will it fly? And again, when it flies and reaches the highest Height, at that time it has to know that there is another goal and that goal is God-manifestation on earth. There are two goals: one goal is Heaven-reality and the other goal is earth-reality. When we use the wings to go upward to the Heavenly goal, we go with the earth-reality to the Heaven-reality. And when we come down to the earthly goal, we come down with the Heaven-reality to the earth-reality. It is like climbing up and down a tree. We climb up a mango tree and pluck mangoes, and then bring them down and distribute them. The East says, "Gather!" The West says, "Spread!" If we do not gather, then how can we spread? Only if we gather can we spread. Again, if we spread what we have, then the Source is pleased with us and the Source gives us everything in infinite measure.

For the last quarter of a century, both the East and the West have felt the supreme necessity of receiving light from each other. To quote your own illumining ideals and fulfilling ideals: "Beyond the turmoil, the divisions and perplexities of our time, mankind is slowly but surely finding the ways, limits and new codes of behaviour which will encompass all races, nations and ideologies. It is the formulation of these new ethics which will be the great challenge for the new generation. It will concern not only men's material fate, but also their mental and spiritual lives."

There was a time when the renouncer of life felt that it was beneath his dignity to love the lover of life, and the lover of life felt that it was beneath his dignity to mix with the renouncer of life. Now the lover and the renouncer are modifying their views and becoming one. The renouncer feels that to love life because God the All-Love is inside life is absolutely correct. At the same time, God the Lover of life sees that things need not be renounced; He sees that they can be modified, transformed and perfected. After all, perfection only can give humanity abiding satisfaction. So the East, instead of rejecting, gladly accepts the great possibilities, capacities and realities of the West. The West, too, does exactly the same. They are combining their possibilities and transforming these possibilities into divine practicabilities with the hope that supreme satisfaction will dawn in the all-embracing and all-illumining common realisation of East and West.

We will have a harmonious, happy world-society only if this synthesis continues, and we can take East and West as the two arms, two eyes, two feet and two legs of the Supreme Pilot within and without. The other human divisions and distinctions — racial, cultural and linguistic — are destined to disappear from the human consciousness when it is flooded with a higher Light. This is the inevitable consequence of the Hour of God that is dawning all over the world. When the Hour of God appears, diversities will be there, but these diversities will be enriched and enhanced in fullest measure. And they will not disturb the general consciousness; on the contrary, they will harmoniously complement the whole. Humanity will be a true human family in every sense of the term and also in a sense that the human mind has yet to discover. And here I wish to say that this discovery will exceed all human expectations.

The awakened consciousness of man is evolving towards the Divine Existence. This is a most hopeful streak of light amidst the obscurities of the present-day world. This is a moment when human beings do not only join hands, but also join minds, hearts and souls. All physical, vital and mental barriers between East and West will dissolve; and high above national standards, above even individual standards, we shall see the supreme banner of divine Oneness.

Yours in the Supreme,
Sri Chinmoy
1 April 1977

FW 310. *Mr. Robert Muller: Where so many humans from all over the world come together to talk to each other, to learn from each other, to heal rifts and to devise a better common destiny, isn't that the greatest place on earth? To my mind, the United Nations is no less than a miracle.*

Sri Chinmoy: The United Nations is a place where humanity can talk, learn and become. Humanity can talk of lasting peace, learn the secret of love and become the delight of oneness. Because of this, the United Nations is unmistakably the greatest in terms of vision-capacity, which will eventually be manifested as the most fulfilling Reality-perfection and Immortality-satisfaction.

According to our limited body, curious vital, searching mind and crying heart, the United Nations is no less than a miracle. But we have one more member in our family: the soul. The soul has quite a different story to narrate. It reveals to us and tells us that there is no such thing as a miracle. Anything that is uncommon, unusual and unfamiliar in this world we call a miracle. But there are many higher planes of consciousness where these so-called miracles are common occurrences.

God the Creator and God the creation are one. We see God the creation here, there and everywhere. But we find it difficult to realise or accept God the creation so easily, not to speak of so lovingly and devotedly. When God the Creator reveals an infinitesimal iota of His Light and Power through a human life from a new realm of consciousness to which we do not have a free access, we are quite often ready to regard it — that is to say, God's visible and tangible Compassion-Gift — as a miracle. But just because God the creation is always visible and available, our ignorance-familiarity is badly wanting in appreciation capacity.

Otherwise, we would feel that God the creation is undoubtedly as much of a miracle as God the Creator.

Let us see eye to eye with our soul's revelation that there is no such thing as a miracle. Although we are not aware of something or although something has not yet manifested on earth, it can easily happen that we may become aware of it tomorrow or it may become manifested tomorrow. So there is no need to call it a miracle, for its existence-reality has already been discovered by the highest and greatest member of our own family, the soul.

Needless to say, miracle-power does not and cannot elevate our consciousness. It is our reality's spontaneity that can and will elevate and illumine our consciousness and fulfil unreservedly the Real in us. And what is the Real in us? The universal oneness of the Transcendental Height. Truth to tell, the soul of our dear United Nations embodies this all-loving Reality's all-fulfilling divinity.

With your soul's kind permission, I am bringing this answer to the personal level. I have had the opportunity to hear a good many speeches by a good many speakers. *No hyperbole, you top and far outshine the galaxy of my heroes.* My searching human mind tells me that each speech of yours is nothing short of a miracle; nay, it is a miracle itself, for it embodies and reveals most striking depths and heights. But my flying soul-bird, which has a free access to the higher planes of reality, tells me unmistakably and shows me convincingly the actual reality which your soul so spontaneously and so beautifully reveals through your aspiration and dedication-life. If I believe in my soul and your soul, which I shall eternally do, your invaluable gifts to the United Nations and to the world at large are *not* miracles, but a spontaneous self-offering to the Absolute Pilot Supreme on the strength of your aspiration-vision and dedication-mission.

FW 311. *Mr. Robert Muller: The United Nations is the incredible place where human oneness is seeking itself in the endless diversity of the prodigy of life. How is it possible, then, that so few people recognise this great new blessing?*

Sri Chinmoy: I fully agree with you that the United Nations is the "incredible place where human oneness is seeking itself in the endless prodigy of life". Now, how is it possible that so few people recognise this great new blessing? Most human beings are apt to wallow in the pleasures of ignorance. For them, there is no higher reality. For them, there is no necessity for Heaven-freedom. They are totally satisfied with their earthbound lives. Anything that is challenging, demanding, vast and high, they fail to recognise, for they are vehemently unwilling to awaken their acceptance-capacity and widen their receptivity-capacity. What they have is more than enough for them. What they do not have is not only worthless and useless, but also an object of laughter-evoking mockery. These rank fools, to our extreme sorrow, are denying their own real reality, weakening their own true capacity. Finally, they are binding themselves to an extremely narrow vision, which is the precursor of utter destruction.

We see the sun and can become inseparably one with its creative force, illumining reality and fulfilling divinity. This is what God-lovers and Truth-seekers do. But again, there are thousands of people on earth who do not or cannot do so. But just because they do not or cannot do so, they are in no way deprived of the sun's benevolent light. The sun unconditionally gives its light and warmth to all those who are living on this earth-planet. But the sun knows that a day shall dawn, although it may take millennia, when each and every human being will recognise what a great blessing the sun is. They will then accept the sun lovingly and its gift gratefully. Similar is the experience that the wisdom-power of the United Nations soul — which is a great new blessing to all and sundry — will give to each and every human being that has ever trod the earth-arena.

FW 312. *Mr. Robert Muller: What can we do to open the eyes and hearts of people?*

Sri Chinmoy: What can we do to open the eyes and hearts of people? We can aspire more soulfully, dedicate our lives more devotedly and try to become *unconditional instruments* of God for God alone. If we do this, then our constant and unconditional self-giving will, without fail, expedite the opening of the eyes and the hearts of the people.

FW 313. *Mr. Robert Muller: I often feel that all my speaking and writing is just a drop of water on an infertile field of blindness and disbelief. What more can we do? What would you suggest?*

Sri Chinmoy: Revered brother, your speaking-world and your writing-world are not a drop of water. Far from it! They are the oceans of life-transforming light. Today's "infertile field of blindness and disbelief" need not and cannot remain so forever, for God's Vision of the infinite Beyond is infinitely more powerful than the man-made blindness and disbelief of a barren field of confusing unreality.

What more can we do? We can try to climb up untiringly God's Patience-Tower and watch from the highest Height and wait on the highest Height for God's God-Hour to strike. At God's choice Hour, the stark blindness and rank disbelief of humanity will be inundated with the ever-illumining Light and ever-immortalising Delight of Eternity's Beyond, which is slowly, steadily and unerringly manifesting itself on our earth-planet. When God's choice Hour strikes, we two and others who are sailing in the same boat will offer tears of sleepless gratitude to our Source, our Beloved Supreme, who out of His boundless Bounty has made us His illumining Vision-seers and His fulfilling Reality-pioneers.

FW 259–286. *(p. 345)* In November, Sri Chinmoy asked members of the Meditation Group to submit spiritual questions for him to answer during the Group's regular meetings. These are questions answered on 16 and 26 November 1976.

FW 287–296. *(p. 359)* On 11 March 1977, BBC's United Nations correspondent Mr. Brian Saxton interviewed Sri Chinmoy about spirituality at the United Nations for a European radio broadcast. Mr. Saxton also requested a tape of the songs Sri Chinmoy has composed for the United Nations and included "O United Nations" in the broadcast. The songs were sung by members of the United Nations Meditation Group.

FW 297–301. *(p. 364)* On 18 March 1977 Sri Chinmoy answered these questions, which were put to him in writing by the members of the United Nations Meditation Group in Geneva.

FW 302–307. *(p. 370)* In the spring and fall of 1977, these profound and soulful questions were submitted to Sri Chinmoy by Mr. Robert Muller, Director and Deputy to the Under-Secretary-General for Inter-Agency Affairs and Co-ordination.

FW 308–309. *(p. 380)* On 18 March 1977 Mr. Robert Muller, Deputy Under-Secretary-General for Inter-Agency Affairs, wrote Sri Chinmoy asking him about the role of the East and the West in today's world. Here is Mr. Muller's question and Sri Chinmoy's reply.

FLAME-WAVES

BOOK 11

FW 314. *In general what is the order of importance, urgency or priority today of the following problems of mankind: economic, social, political, religious? Why?*

Sri Chinmoy: According to me, this will be the order: religious, political, social and economic. Why? If people are religious, they will try to lead a better life, a purer life. What the world needs most is a better life and a purer life. Next is political. Politics governs the mind, the vital and the body of mankind. As religion mainly deals with the heart and inner feelings, even so, politics deals mostly with the mind — the organising mind, the energising vital and the alert body. Then comes the social. After religion has touched the heart and politics has touched the mind, the vital and the body, then there should be amity and friendship in the society. At this time the individual is becoming collective. After an individual becomes religious and offers light to mankind, then he has to establish his friendship, his social qualities. At that time economic problems will be solved easily.

So first we think of God and offer light to our nation, our country. Then we want to become closely connected with others. When we want to become closely connected with others, then economic problems will be solved considerably. For then my need you will feel as your need and your need I will feel as my need. At that time I shall be more than ready to help you and you will be more than happy to help me. But if we don't feel our oneness, then we shall not feel each other's needs. So first religion, then politics, then social problems and then economics.

FW 315. *In particular, which is more important: the relations East-West — political — or North-South — economic?*

Sri Chinmoy: Both are equally important. If East and West are not united, if they do not see eye to eye with each other, then there will be a disaster not only on the mental plane but also on the vital plane and the physical plane. So political relations between East and West are of paramount importance. Again, of equal importance are the economic relations between North and South. If North and South do not share their economic achievements, then there will also be a terrible disaster on the mental plane, the vital plane and the physical plane.

In both cases, between East and West and between North and South, what we need is a feeling of sympathetic concern, love and oneness. Between East and West the political reality is of paramount importance. Between North and South the economic reality is of paramount importance. The political reality of one hemisphere should not try to dominate the political reality of another hemisphere. Again, the poverty-stricken countries and the rich countries have to realise that they can have satisfaction only when the rich offer their wealth to the poor and when the poor accept this wealth with gratitude and not with a demanding attitude.

FW 316. *What should be the attitude of a world-disciple in relation to dictatorships, imposed will and restriction of individual rights and liberties? To refuse any contact or compromise in the hope of their evolution?*

Sri Chinmoy: A world-disciple will never compromise. His is the life that will soulfully and dauntlessly fight dictatorship, imposed will and the restriction of individual rights and liberties. Compromise can never be the answer. When we make a compromise with darkness and ignorance, then it is half-and-half: ignorance gives half and light gives half. But the half that ignorance keeps is destructive, so ignorance has to be totally transformed. The entire ignorance has to come and take shelter in light. So there can be no compromise between truth and falsehood. If there is a compromise between the two, then falsehood will rule half the world.

There is no such thing as compromise in the inner life — either God or Satan, either ignorance or light, either day or night. If you compromise with darkness and hope that eventually darkness will change into light in the process of evolution, then I wish to say that this is a false hope. Night will not change, darkness will not change. It is the light that has to operate consciously in and through night. Otherwise, night, as such, on its own will never give way to light. It is the power of light that will have to compel the night to surrender for its own good.

FW 317. *Do you think it is possible to change the United Nations organisation without changing the Member States? If so, of what use would be the existence of such a closed circuit?*

Sri Chinmoy: It is not necessary to change the Member States in order to change the United Nations organisation. One may call the Member States a closed circuit and, from a particular point of view, one may be justified in saying so. But from a different angle if we see the situation, then we can say that when there is a large body or organisation, within the large body there has to be a smaller body to organise the thing. If all the countries were equal, and everybody held the same status, then there would be no organisation. When there is a school, there is one teacher and many students. It is not a hierarchy in an authoritarian sense; only it is a necessity. If we build a house, then we need an engineer and an architect, and also a few workers. If everybody does the job of the architect, then there will be no workers to build the house.

In such a big organisation as the United Nations, some countries have to shoulder more responsibility than other countries, so naturally they will have more voice. If everybody became the king, then there would be no subjects. Here I am not saying that some Member States are kings; only some should come forward to show light to others. If everybody had light, then everyone would be in Heaven. At that time earth would be Heaven itself. But this is not the case. Again, all the countries should be more sympathetic and develop greater oneness. Then it would be an ideal situation.

FW 318. *Do you agree that the main task of the world-disciple today is to help bring the nations' souls to the fore?*

Sri Chinmoy: Yes, I fully agree. The world-disciple must needs help bring the nations' souls to the fore. When the soul comes to the fore with its inner effulgence, divine effulgence, then it is only a matter of time before the mind, vital and body accept it. The aspiring heart immediately accepts it, but the other members may take some time. But we have to come without from within. We sow the seed underground and then it germinates. It becomes a sapling, a plant and finally a giant banyan tree. So from within the reality must come forward, and it is the soul that embodies the reality and the divinity within.

FW 319. *Goodwill is love in action and a first step to true spiritual love. Should it not be the main quality to be fostered and pointed out to mankind?*

Sri Chinmoy: You are absolutely right. Goodwill is love in action and it has to be fostered and pointed out to mankind. But in order to point it out to mankind and foster it, we have to know where goodwill comes from. Does it come from the physical mind? No. Does it come from the dynamic vital? No. Does it come from the alert body? No. Goodwill comes only from the crying heart, the heart that cries to see its Beloved Supreme in itself and in all other hearts. So the source of goodwill is man's aspiring heart. This goodwill that comes from the aspiring heart is undoubtedly love in action. And without fail it has to be fostered and pointed out to mankind in order to accelerate humanity's progress.

FW 320. *Do you see any role for the United Nations organisation in the enlightenment of mankind? If so, will music be one of the components of such a role?*

Sri Chinmoy: Yes, I see that the United Nations organisation has a definite role in enlightening the life of mankind. But it is not the outer music that will do the needful. Only it is the inner music, the music of the heart, that continuously feels and makes others feel that we are of the One and for the many. The many are our extended and expanded reality. Not the instrumental music, not the vocal music, but the psychic music of the United Nations can and will enlighten the face of mankind.

FW 321. *Do you think that the system of "one country-one vote" is democratic? If not, do you see alternatives before the accumulated wisdom of the nation's souls becomes the yardstick in the voting system?*

Sri Chinmoy: It is always advisable for one country to have one vote. But this vote has to come from the general mass. It is not an individual will that is being executed. Otherwise, it will be like many minds going in many ways. At that time nothing will be settled and there will be no hope of reaching any conclusion. So the unity of the collective reality will have to voice forth, and then there will be one vote, one will, one reality — one illumining and one fulfilling choice.

FW 322. *If the United Nations Development Programme is the "heart centre" of the United Nations, which of the following — the Secretary-General, the Security Council or Economic and Social Council — is or should be the mind? Are there any other correspondences or analogies between organs and centres?*

Sri Chinmoy: The heart centre need not be an individual; it need not be the Security Council or the Secretary-General or the Economic and Social Council. These are all realities, but these realities need not remain as separate entities. They can be combined together or at least the essence and qualities of each of these realities can be unified. Then, when they are unified, there will be a feeling of oneness, and this feeling of oneness is nothing short of the heart centre.

FW 323. *Do you envisage the creation of a second chamber at the United Nations? If so, should it be composed of some NGOs or of the wise men of nations? Should the General Assembly, as is, represent the will of the nations and that second chamber the love of peoples?*

Sri Chinmoy: I do envisage the creation of a second chamber at the United Nations but it does not have to be composed of NGOs or of the so-called wise men of nations. The new creation must be composed of only selfless, dedicated workers — true servers and lovers of mankind, who do not merely remain in the theoretical plane but also come down to the practical plane and offer practical, effective answers to mankind.

FW 324. *Do you foresee the possibility of a fully committed spiritual person becoming Secretary-General in this century?*

Sri Chinmoy: It is hard to say who is fully committed spiritually and who is not fully committed spiritually. In this case, as far as my inner feeling goes, I feel that Dag Hammarskjold was undoubtedly a fully committed spiritual person. As we know, spirituality does not mean self-abnegation. True spirituality means the acceptance of life as such. Here we have to know that this life which we accept is composed of spirit and matter. So if one embodies the spirit and wants to make the spiritual reality operate in and through the material proper, then one is undoubtedly spiritual. In the case of Dag Hammarskjold, we saw his inner light inundate his mind. Then from the mind, from the illumined mind, he executed the will of the heart, combining the illumining realities of the vital and the sacrificing realities of the physical. In the case of U Thant, who was a staunch and devout Buddhist, we saw that he brought to the fore the compassion-aspect of life, which is the purest jewel-reality in the human existence. He offered this compassion-reality to mankind unreservedly, almost unconditionally.

Sometimes the word "spiritual" is misunderstood badly. A spiritual person becomes an object of ridicule to the cynical human beings. Sometimes the non-believers, if not disbelievers, in God the Source of the Oneness-Creation, look down upon those who are spiritual. But those who inwardly see the inseparable oneness of God the Creator and God the creation try to offer this realisation to the world at large. In spite of being misunderstood, in spite of being assailed by physical ailments, as in the case of U Thant, in silence they act. And they leave the result at the Feet of God, the Author of all Good. I wish to tell you that the twentieth century has already been blessed with two spiritual giants: Dag Hammarskjold and U Thant. Secretary-General U Thant and Secretary-General Dag Hammarskjold are two most outstanding examples of spiritual persons. Outwardly they may not be recognised as spiritual figures. But being a spiritual man, I have established my own oneness with them — with their achievement, with their tremendous sacrifice, with their inner cry — and I wish to say that they were undoubtedly spiritual persons committed to spiritual realities which are not easy for the doubtful, sophisticated mind and analytical intellect to comprehend.

FW 325. *The Preamble of UNESCO's constitution states that wars begin in the minds of men and it is there that they will have to be eradicated first. Mankind's minds are changing; yet a general war is still a possibility. Would you comment?*

Sri Chinmoy: It is true that wars begin in the minds of men. If the mind changes, then there will be no war. But how will the mind change? The mind will change only when it is transformed. There is only one way to transform the mind and that is to bring the reality, the divinity, of the heart to the fore. The mind of humanity is changing, but it is going at the speed of an Indian bullock cart. At any moment the storm of doubt and the hurricane of jealousy can stop humanity's mind from proceeding farther. But if the heart qualities come forward and illumine the mind, then there can be no doubt-storm or jealousy-hurricane. An illumined mind founded upon the loving heart can not only put an end to war, but also expedite world oneness, world perfection and world satisfaction.

FW 326. *Nuclear arms and nuclear energy are very dangerous tools. What is your attitude towards both?*

Sri Chinmoy: First of all, we do admit that nuclear arms and nuclear energy are very dangerous tools. Right now they are used for a destructive purpose, especially nuclear arms. But who is their creator? Their creator is a human being. A human being is the creator of nuclear arms and nuclear energy. But we have to know that the human creator is also a creation of a Supreme Creator. In a fraction of a second the Supreme Creator can change the destructive mind of an individual human being into a loving mind, a universal mind. It is the operation of the mind that either maintains mankind or destroys mankind. If the Supreme Force wants to operate in humanity's mind, then the dangerous things and dangerous achievements on earth need not and cannot remain dangerous. For there is something which is infinitely more powerful than the dangerous tools created by mankind, and this supremely powerful thing is God's Compassion for His children. When God uses His supreme weapon, Compassion, no human tool — no matter how dangerous — can face it. God's Compassion and God the Compassion are always for mankind. First God sends His representative, which is Compassion. Then, if He sees that His representative is not strong enough to solve the problem, at that time He Himself comes as God the Compassion. But in most of the cases, God's Compassion-Power is more than enough to save the world from imminent crises.

FW 327. *Bhaktivedanta referred to the United Nations as a "society for united animals" where people are not interested in religious things. Could you please comment on this?*

Sri Chinmoy: Dear David, it will simply be impossible for me to see eye to eye with the statement that has been made by the spiritual leader in question. To say that the United Nations is a society for united animals, since people at the United Nations are not interested in religious things, is to criticise the United Nations not only mercilessly but almost unreasonably. First of all, we all know that in the name of religion and religious matters countless people have been killed since the dawn of so-called civilisation. Almost all the religions have fought at one time or another against one another unreservedly and, what is worse, at times without any rhyme or reason. Just to show its supremacy over other religions, each religion has swerved from the fundamental principles of truth. Why blame the United Nations? The wisest thing for the wise man is to first solve his own personal problems, illumine his own darkness and perfect his own nature. This is the only way that either the united or the divided human animals all over the world can climb to a higher rung of evolution, which we can unmistakably call proper human life.

FW 328. *Is the fundamental goal that the United Nations can aspire for no more than that of the member states which compose it?*

Sri Chinmoy: No, the United Nations can and should aspire for a higher goal than what the member states that compose it represent. The member states are like strong pillars of an edifice, but many more things are required to build the edifice. Those things are also of tremendous necessity. When everything is in its proper place and all things are combined to achieve a specific goal, at that time the body of the achievement-reality becomes divinely integral and supremely perfect.

FW 329. *Can we hope that individual delegations of member states will work towards higher goals than their home governments would normally support?*

Sri Chinmoy: It entirely depends on the inner strength of the individual delegations. If an individual delegation has received a higher call to spread deeper reality in human life and, at that time, if it does not get support from its home government, then I think and feel that the individual delegation must move forward and listen to the inner dictates. Let us take the home government as an old man, an old father, and the individual delegation as a young man. The old man always thinks that he knows everything far better than his son, but sometimes it happens that a higher truth and more illumining realities want to express themselves in and through the young generation. At that time, if the old generation does not want to accept the new vision that has dawned on the young generation, then it will be a deplorable mistake. And this mistake may cause an untold disaster in the minds and the hearts of both the fearful and unwilling old generation and the daring and pioneering new generation. God does not have to speak all the time through the human father. He can easily speak to the father through the human son as well. Therefore, as it is obligatory for the son to listen to his father when the father's advice is founded upon unmistakable truths, even so, it is equally obligatory for the father to accept the son's vision-reality when it is unmistakably illumining and considerably fulfilling.

FW 330. *When a member state assumes an "anti-United Nations attitude", the cause would probably be frustration or fear that the U.N. has taken or may take some action against it. Does such an attitude weaken the U.N. system?*

Sri Chinmoy: When a member state assumes an "anti-United Nations attitude", it undoubtedly weakens the United Nations system. First of all, it violently and shamelessly goes against the United Nations system. When a member state goes against the United Nations system, on the outer plane it definitely weakens the system; but on the inner plane the strength of the United Nations system is extremely solid and sound. As long as the inner aspiration of the United Nations is sincere and strong, we do not have to worry if a member state or even if all the member states assume an "anti-United Nations attitude". For it is not the member states alone that can and will bring about world harmony. It is the united force of all the nations, big and small, that can and will bring about a oneness-world family.

There can be many reasons why a member state wants to stand against the United Nations policy. But just by standing against United Nations policy, a state will not be able to solve even an iota of the world's problems. If one sees that the United Nations is doing something wrong, that is no reason why one should want to stand against the United Nations. One has to love the United Nations more in order to bring to the fore its sincere aspirations which can and will change the face of the entire world.

To err is human, to forgive divine. To forget past blunders of others, as well as one's own, is to make friends with satisfaction-peace and perfection-bliss. Further, this is the only way to accelerate humanity's oneness-vision and oneness-goal. If you see the world's imperfections, you should not discard the world; you should not consider it a filthy object or speak ill of it in season and out of season. No! The wise thing is to accept and embrace the world — the well-meaning U.N. world — as a humble and trying instrument of an all-embracing and all-fulfilling supreme Reality.

FW 331. *Secretaries-General have conceived their office in various ways. Is there a preferred definition of the institution of the Secretary-General?*

Sri Chinmoy: According to my inner aspiration, I wish to say that an ideal Secretary-General is he who has a free access both to the inner realities and the outer realities of life. The inner realities are heart's cry, heart's oneness. The outer realities are life's total and consecrated dedication. The ideal Secretary-General is he who dives deep within in order to quench his inner thirst, the thirst of the oneness-world family, and then comes from within to without to share with the rest of the world the nectar-bliss that he has discovered and drunk profusely in his inner life.

An ideal Secretary-General is he who at once fulfils his inner vision and outer mission. His inner vision is love of humanity, for humanity's sake, and his outer mission is service to humanity, for humanity's sake. His inner life is a continuous growth to reach the acme of perfection. His outer life is dedicated to spreading his perfection, which is illumination itself, throughout the length and breadth of the world.

FW 332. *The style and personality of the Secretary-General influences numerous individuals and national governments and to a degree determines the performance of the entire U.N. Don't you think, then, it is essential to select a Secretary-General who will not allow possible wrong influences or powers to guide his actions?*

Sri Chinmoy: We should always try to be true servers and warriors of truth, for truth is life in the purest sense of the term. Therefore, our supreme choice and our only choice has to be an all-loving, all-caring, all-serving and all-fulfilling Secretary-General, whose love-power will transform the dominion-power or the influence-power, and not the other way around. Love inspires us to do the right thing in life. Power quite often, if not always, influences us or, rather, not always but quite often instigates us to do the wrong thing. Therefore, a Secretary-General who is higher than the highest in height is also expected to be wider than the widest in every sphere of his life.

FW 333. *Is there a special need to promote co-operation between the newer and often poorer countries in the General Assembly and the older and, in most cases, more established, wealthier countries? Should the latter not take the lead in fostering good relations?*

Sri Chinmoy: We all believe in progress. Progress is nothing but true satisfaction. If one country is more established and more financially secure than another country, that doesn't mean that this particular country is the happiest and the most perfect country. If one country wants to remain always at the vanguard of all the other countries, or if it wants to exercise supremacy over the other countries, then it may be able to do so. But true satisfaction, for which there is a common and universal cry, will never come. Supremacy will never be transformed into either an individual or collective smile.

Everything is relative. One country may be poorer than another country in one particular aspect of human life but it can easily be richer in some other aspect of life. Outer wealth it may lack, but inner wealth it may have in profuse measure. Again, if one country is wanting in the outer wealth as well as in the inner wealth, then it will be an act not only of kindness but also of wisdom if the superior country opens both its inner door and outer door to help, guide and illumine the unillumined, inferior one. At that time the illumined one is only increasing its reality-existence. The heart of love knows only how to expand, and another name for this expansion is satisfaction. Satisfaction-reality is the fruit of the satisfaction-tree, which comes from the perfection-seed.

FW 334. *Co-operation of all nations is an ancient dream. Assuming we are building on the past, how can we assess the outlook now?*

Sri Chinmoy: The ancient dream of co-operation is not a human dream which has very little to do with reality. The ancient dream, to be precise, is not a dream at all but a faultless and divine vision — an unhorizoned vision — which is slowly, steadily and unerringly shaping the individual and collective destiny in humanity's march towards the supreme goal of universal oneness and transcendental newness. The world is evolving and progressing and reaching a higher standard of life. It is not moving in a horizontal way, but in a spiral. Therefore, at times this progress is not immediately noticeable. At times it confuses and baffles our human mind. But on the strength of our inner oneness with the world situation and world evolution, we see unmistakably the world's slow and steady progress.

True, man-made destructive forces are to be found here, there and everywhere. Here they may be in small measure; somewhere else, in a large measure. But the creator of the wrong forces, the destructive forces, need not remain always a creator of wrong forces. He can easily become a creator of good forces. In spite of creating and possessing wrong forces, if one remains silent to catch a glimpse either consciously or unconsciously of the divine, illumining and fulfilling light, at that time one is taking the first step. The second step is to create positive realities in order to accelerate humanity's progress towards perfection.

A negative force is not by nature negative. Only it is a force that we use in a negative way. A knife can be used either as a destructive force or as a force of co-operation and oneness-expansion. With a knife one can stab others; with the same knife one can cut fruits and share them with others.

The ancient dream, nay, the ancient vision, will always remain a new and progressive vision, for creation itself is an ever-transcending reality. We shall have to open our heart's door and our mind's windows in order to see from the body-room the light that illumines and fulfils the world around us. Then only we shall discover continual progress in humanity's march along Eternity's road to Infinity's Satisfaction-Goal.

FW 335. *You said once that honesty and frankness are the birthright of the West, humility and devotion are the birthright of the East, and the combination of these four powers should be the ideal of a human being. What do you mean by this?*

Sri Chinmoy: When these qualities, the good qualities of the East and the good qualities of the West, are all combined, a human being can be perfect. Right now the good qualities that the East has are not enough. Similarly, the good qualities that the West has are not enough. But when we can amalgamate, when we can have the qualities of both worlds, then an individual can become perfect. Right now the West wants to proceed with only honesty and frankness, but this will be insufficient. Humility is also required. The East has humility, but honesty is also required if it wants to become perfect.

FW 336. *These are the kinds of thoughts that you bring to the meditation sessions at the United Nations. Do you feel that you are accomplishing something at these sessions with United Nations people?*

Sri Chinmoy: Yes, I do feel that we are accomplishing something meaningful and fruitful. The delegates and staff members at the United Nations are showing more and more interest. They come to meditate and they ask questions. Their response is most favourable.

FW 337. *What is it that you do at these sessions that brings favourable responses from these people? Is it just meditation and prayer, or is there something more?*

Sri Chinmoy: We pray and meditate, plus I give short talks and answer their questions. The inner world embodies Peace, Light and Bliss. The outer world, unfortunately, does not right now embody these qualities, whereas the inner world has them in boundless measure. So we try to establish a free access to the inner world by virtue of our inner cry and our soulful meditation. We call this our aspiration.

FW 338. *So you don't sit down and talk about the boundaries in the Middle East; you talk about other things?*

Sri Chinmoy: Yes. I am quite ignorant of politics as such. My forté is spirituality. There are two approaches to every problem. One is the inner approach: the other is the outer approach. Those who come to meditate want to try to walk along the inner road. But ultimately both the roads can lead to the same destination.

FW 339. *The inner road — is that an evaluation of yourself, or an evaluation of other people, or an evaluation of the spiritual world? What is the inner road?*

Sri Chinmoy: The inner road is the road of sincere dedication to the highest Cause. In the outer world one can aim at a particular goal without having sincere dedication to the goal. But the inner road represents the attitude of the seeker. The seeker tries in every way to lead a more illumining and more fulfilling life, to find and follow the way that is right from the highest point of view.

FW 340. *Are the people who come to these sessions people who really need to be there, people whose attitudes need to change and will change, or are they people who would normally come because they are good people and have been seeking the inner road already?*

Sri Chinmoy: Here I must say that people come to spiritual gatherings when they have made some inner progress and they are already ready to lead a better life, a more progressive, more illumining and more fulfilling life. They have felt and seen considerable progress in their own lives, therefore they know that progress exists, and they are trying to make more progress in their day-to-day lives.

FW 341. *Do you have any contact with these people beyond your meditation sessions? Do you talk with them privately? Do you ever see them socially?*

Sri Chinmoy: I do not see them socially. Only when they come to pray and meditate with me do I see them. But on rare occasions if they need and want me to guide them in a specific manner, if they have some special problem, I try to satisfy their inner need at some other times.

FW 342. *Have you ever been able to see a specific change in a person — in their attitudes or in the way they behave?*

Sri Chinmoy: I have noticed considerable changes not only in individuals, but also in the United Nations as a whole. For the last seven years I have been coming to the United Nations. Now I see that people here are more sincere, more dedicated and more eager to bring about a true world-family.

FW 343. *You talked about your sessions containing both prayer and meditation, so that means there is a difference between prayer and meditation. What is the difference or differences?*

Sri Chinmoy: Prayer and meditation ultimately lead to the same goal. Prayer is a kind of communication with God, and meditation is, too. But when we pray, we talk to a higher Authority or higher Source, which you can call God or the Force which is guiding our destiny. When we meditate, the Source or the supreme Reality talks to us. It is like the conversation that we are having now. At times I am talking, and at times you are talking. So when I pray, my message goes to God, and when I meditate, God's Message comes to me.

FW 344. *So we have one-way communication with prayer, and two-way communication with meditation?*

Sri Chinmoy: You might say that. When we pray, we ask the Supreme to guide us. And when we meditate, we try to receive the inner guidance from the Supreme.

FW 345. *Guru, what is special about your teachings, or what does your philosophy contain that is special and that man can benefit from?*

Sri Chinmoy: I do not want to use the term "special", but I can say what I stand for. I stand for divine love, divine devotion and divine surrender. I am emphasising the term "divine". Human love you know. It eventually ends in frustration. Human devotion is nothing short of attachment. And human surrender is made under compulsion, because we are afraid that we will be punished. But divine love and devotion are pure and detached, and divine surrender is not made to somebody else. This surrender we offer to our own highest Reality. We have inside us an unillumined reality and an illumined reality. Our unillumined existence we offer to our illumined existence. We make our divine surrender to our own highest existence. The lowest existence which we now embody we try to offer to the highest, which we also embody. Unfortunately, people have not consciously realised that highest existence yet.

FW 346. *The meditation that you have for people who take part in your sessions, is it Yoga, or are we talking about something different?*

Sri Chinmoy: It is Yoga. Yoga includes prayer and meditation and spirituality in general. So we are definitely practising Yoga. Yoga is a Sanskrit word which means conscious union with God. We achieve our conscious union with God on the strength of our prayer, meditation, aspiration and so forth.

FW 347. *Are you part of a particular organised religious body or a sect or cult, or are you just who you are?*

Sri Chinmoy: I belong to no sect and to no religion. At the same time, my teachings embody the quintessence of all religions. I appreciate and admire all religions, but I do not belong to any particular religion. I was born as a Hindu: therefore, I know all the ins and outs of the Hindu religion. But I do not practise Hinduism. I do not follow any specific religion. My religion is to love God and to become a humble instrument of God. The Hindu religion is like a house, Christianity is another house, Judaism is another house. We can each live in a different house, and then come to one school to study. Spirituality, Yoga, is what we eventually must study.

FW 348. *Therefore you do accept people with different religious backgrounds into your group?*

Sri Chinmoy: I do accept people belonging to various religions. No religion should be an obstacle to the study of true spirituality.

FW 349. *And they are not required to drop their religion?*

Sri Chinmoy: On the contrary, when they pray and meditate with me they can strengthen and illumine their own religious beliefs. Previously they may not have seen any light or truth in their own religion. But once they learn to pray and meditate soulfully, they see that there is truth inside their own religion.

FW 350. *In the past ten or fifteen years we have seen many Gurus come to the West. Are all Gurus good?*

Sri Chinmoy: Are all human beings good? There is something called comparison. Day has light and night has darkness. But there are some people who will say that there is a little light in night, and that little is enough for them. As light is inside night, so God is inside the insincere Gurus as well as the sincere Gurus. Only He is there in a very limited measure, in an unmanifested form.

FW 351. *Guru why did you come to the United States?*

Sri Chinmoy: I devotedly followed an inner command from my Beloved Supreme, my Inner Pilot, to come to the United States. He commanded me to come and serve Him inside the sincere seekers in the West. The East and the West are like two houses. The father has every right to ask the son to be of service to his brothers who live in another house. For me the East and the

West are not like two geographical boundaries. They are like two houses that belong to my Supreme Father. And it was He who asked me to come to the West and be of service to Him inside the seekers in the West who needed to feel more powerfully His Love, His Concern and His Blessings.

FW 352. *Some of the Gurus who have come to the West have got bad press, and they have been accused of things that you wouldn't associate with a sincere God-server. They have got hundreds of thousands of disciples and vast amounts of wealth. I gather from what I have read about you, that you are not interested in amassing any wealth in the United States, or in getting a great number of followers. Is that true?*

Sri Chinmoy: It is absolutely true. God will not ask me how many seekers I have brought to Him. He will ask me only whether I have brought the ones that I was meant to bring. He has asked me inwardly to take certain sincere ones. He has not asked me to put millions of seekers in my boat. The other thing is that He does not wish me to become a multi-millionaire. I have given hundreds of spiritual talks. and I have meditated with countless people and I never, never accept any fee from them. I do not charge any fee, but I have written considerably and my students and disciples take care of my material needs. Money and spirituality do not go together. If money enabled people to realise God, there would be thousands of rich people on earth who had realised Him. It is only the inner wealth, which we call aspiration, which enables us to realise God. When one has the inner cry, one is bound to realise God. I care only for this inner wealth in my disciples. The outer wealth we need only in a very limited measure. We need it only to meet with our basic physical needs, not to live in the lap of luxury.

FW 353. *When you first arrived in the United States 13 years ago, in 1964, did you see a greater need then than you do now for your teachings? I guess I am trying to say have you seen some changes in the way we Westerners are thinking?*

Sri Chinmoy: It seems to me that the West has not only become more spiritual, but has also become wiser. When I came here in 1964 there was a strong hippie movement, and people indiscriminately flocked to the Gurus, no matter which one, no matter whether he was sincere or not. But now they have become wiser. Now they try to go deep within. They are looking for the real Gurus. They want something solid, substantial. Previously it was like a young man who wants to see the world by hook or by crook. They didn't have enough aspiration, patience or wisdom. Now the Western world has become spiritually mature, therefore they are trying to dive deep within sincerely, steadily and purposefully. Previously the Western world was like a restless individual who wanted to acquire everything in the twinkling of an eye. Now the same person has become calm and patient. He has come to know that spiritual wealth or inner illumination cannot be achieved overnight. He has become more sincere, and has cultivated patience in his spiritual life. Since he knows that self-realisation cannot be achieved overnight, he is now walking along the path of spirituality peacefully, devotedly and steadily. This is the right approach.

FW 354. *So what you are saying is that maybe some of the qualities that were missing in the West are starting to take hold. Is there a need for a spiritual leader to leave the West and go to the East to teach frankness and honesty to the East?*

Sri Chinmoy: The East still needs these qualities. But it is up to the Supreme to decide when the time is ripe. We call it God's

Hour. When God's Hour strikes, I am sure the Supreme will send some spiritual figures to the East to cultivate the qualities that they badly lack. The hour has struck for the West; therefore, spiritual leaders came to the West to be of service. Similarly, the hour will strike in the East when someone will be inwardly asked or commanded to go to the East and do the needful there.

FW 355. *Would you accept that role?*

Sri Chinmoy: Immediately. I am at His behest. If the Supreme asks me at this moment to go back to India and be of service to Him there, I will be most happy to go. As I said before, for me there is no division between East and West. And I have no personal preference. Only to follow His Will, only to abide by His will, do I stay on earth. "Let Thy Will be done". This is the supreme message that the Son of God offered to mankind, and every day, every hour, every minute, every second, I try only to listen to His inner dictates and execute His Will, never, never my own.

FW 356. *What do you require of your disciples?*

Sri Chinmoy: A simple life, a sincere life and a life that feels the necessity of an inner cry. Not name and fame, but a sincere cry to become a devoted instrument of God, to please God not in one's own way, but in God's Way. If one really wants to please God in God's Way, according to his inner capacity and receptivity, then I feel that he is entitled to try my path.

FW 357. *It is not your intention to have everyone become your disciple?*

Sri Chinmoy: Far from it. That would be a mistake on my part. Suppose I am a spiritual leader and you are a spiritual leader. God wants me to have specific seekers in my boat. and God wants you to have specific seekers in your boat. If I try to grab the seekers that are meant for your boat just to have as many as possible, it will be an act of injustice. God will not be pleased with that. God wants you to have the ones that are meant for you. Ultimately you are taking them to the same Goal as I am.

FW 358. *Do you envision the day when your goals will he achieved?*

Sri Chinmoy: In the outer world it is a very, very slow process. In the process of time, definitely, people who are following our path will reach the destined Goal. If they have a sincere cry, no sincere cry will meet with frustration, disappointment or failure. So since my students have a sincere cry, the day is bound to dawn when their sincere cry will meet with satisfaction, supreme Satisfaction, which is illumination within and without.

FW 359. *But you don't ever see the day when your work will be done, do you?*

Sri Chinmoy: No, my work is not like that. It is a slow and steady process. We have to sow the seed, which has to germinate, then become a sapling, and gradually become a huge banyan tree. We are now in the process of consciously becoming that which we always were in the inner world. But this process of growth is an ever-transcending process. We can grow eternally. We need never stop.

FW 360. *Where are you now? Have you dropped the seed? Do we have a seedling?*

Sri Chinmoy: This is a most inspiring, encouraging question. I have been asked thousands and thousands of questions all over the world, but this last question of yours so far nobody has asked me, not even my disciples. We have sown the seed. Now we have a tiny plant. This tiny plant will grow and become a strong tree. If storms of doubt and hurricanes of jealousy and other undivine things enter, then naturally the progress can be very slow. But if there is implicit faith and devoted oneness, naturally the plant will very soon grow into a tree. Now we are in the plant stage: we have sown the seed, and it is no longer a seedling. It has germinated properly. Previously it was only a seedling, but now it has become a tiny but healthy plant. So there is every hope that it will weather all the buffets and blows of human doubts and weaknesses, and grow into a huge tree.
Reporter: Thank you, thank you very much.

PART IV

FW 361. *In what way does the United Nations please you?*

Sri Chinmoy: The United Nations has a seeking heart and also a oneness feeling. This seeking heart and this feeling of oneness we may not outwardly see; and even if we do see these, we don't see them all the time. But in my case, I see and feel them all the time. These two things please me most: the United Nations' feeling of inner oneness, its feeling of world family, and also its seeking heart. These two achievements of the United Nations always please me most.

FW 362. *How can the individual seeker offer his aspiration to the world community?*

Sri Chinmoy: If the individual seeker feels that the world community, the outer world, is something outside himself, then he will not be able to offer his aspiration to the world community. But if he feels that the world community, the entire world, is within him — inside his body, inside his soul — then he can pray and meditate in order to raise the standard of the world community, which is part and parcel of his own life.

First he has to feel his oneness with the world community, and then he has to feel that the world community is not outside his sphere of existence, it is not something else, or somewhere else, it is within him. When he can feel that, he will be able to contribute much more to the improvement of the world community. Then, anything that he does for the world community is also for his own nourishment, his own success and his own progress. So the most important thing is for him to feel that the world community is inside him, part and parcel of his own aspiring consciousness. Then, his own prayer and meditation will help the world considerably. That is the easiest way to raise the standard of the world community.

FW 363. *What is the best aspect of the Supreme to concentrate on for transformation?*

Sri Chinmoy: It is always advisable to concentrate upon the Compassion aspect of the Supreme for your personal transformation or world transformation because it is the Compassion aspect of the Supreme that expedites our progress. When the Supreme offers His Compassion, it is all unconditional. If we concentrate on His Heart aspect, or Delight aspect or Peace aspect or any other aspect, we may have in our mind the thought that we have given the Supreme something. We have given Him a drop and now He may give us the ocean. Always there is a feeling of an exchange. He is infinitely richer, infinitely more powerful than we are in every way. He has infinite Capacities whereas our capacities are very limited, so we are giving him what we have and He will give us what He has. If we have that kind of feeling, transformation will take time.

But if we approach His Compassion aspect, we make ourselves feel that we are in no way adding to what He has, or offering Him anything that He needs. Instead, we feel that we need our own transformation and world transformation, and out of His infinite Bounty, unconditionally He is giving this to us. If we have that kind of approach to the Supreme, then our heart's gratitude will overflow and it will accelerate our progress. So the Compassion aspect is always best if we want to accelerate our own progress and the progress of world evolution. This is the fastest way to make individual and collective progress.

FW 364. *Which is the best way for a nation to contribute to the world at large?*

Sri Chinmoy: Each nation has to feel that there is only one nation: one world nation and one world family. We are not only of the One but also for the One. The Source is One and that means that the end is also One. When we say that we are of the One but for the many, we create a problem. As soon as we say "many", we feel that there are many different minds, different approaches and different realities; there is no feeling of oneness. But if we say that we are of the one and for the one, then there is no problem. Take a tree, for example. A tree has branches, flowers, leaves and fruits. If we don't take the tree as one unit or one reality — if sometimes we appreciate the flowers, sometimes the fruits and sometimes the branches, if each time we pay attention to one particular part or achievement of the tree — then we are unable to pay full attention to all the things that the tree embodies, and this creates problems. But if we take the tree as one reality and simply water the tree or sit at the foot of the tree for our prayer and meditation, for our own illumination, then all our problems are solved.

So, each Nation should feel that there is only one nation, one reality, and inside that one reality are all the nations. Otherwise, if one nation is meditating, it may say, "Let me pray and meditate for all the nations." And then, in a few days' time, if the other nations make some mistake or say something wrong, immediately that particular nation will feel displeased and will stop praying and meditating for the others. But if that particular nation feels that all the nations have been combined and amalgamated into one reality, then there will be no problem. It will all the time pray and meditate for the other nations.

The best way for the individual nation to make progress and also to add to world progress is to feel that there is only one reality. This reality is the source, the goal, and it is also the traveller. In that way, the individual nation will make fastest progress and also will be able to contribute much to the world at large most satisfactorily. Always it has to think of the source, of the course, the journey, the road and the destination — everything — as one, all one.

FW 365. *Is it a good idea to have other meditation groups affiliated with this one?*

Sri Chinmoy: Yes, it is a good idea, if it is possible, to have other meditation groups connected or, you can say, affiliated with this one. We have to feel that we are one and try to feel this oneness through our dedicated and sincere efforts. All individuals have the same goal and that goal is perfection. This perfection comes only when we have the feeling of oneness. In aspiration we are one, in realisation we are one, in revelation we are one, in manifestation we are one. Since we are one it is a very good idea to have as many meditation groups as possible in the United Nations international community affiliated with this one.

FW 366. *Is the Supreme pleased with the world progress?*

Sri Chinmoy: Yes, the Supreme is pleased with the world progress. Again, the Supreme believes in continuous progress. Whatever the world has already achieved has pleased Him, but He expects something more, and that something more has to be achieved by the sincere efforts of the United Nations, that is to say, by the people who work at the U.N., the people who love the U.N. and the people who are one with the ideals and the goals of the U.N. We can achieve what the Supreme wants by virtue of our joint efforts in the field of aspiration and dedication.

We believe in the world's continuous progress. For that continuous progress we have to aspire and dedicate ourselves more to the cause of the United Nations. Satisfaction is not a finished product. If we have come up to a certain standard, then our progress becomes like a stagnant pool; only in continuous progress do we find satisfaction. First we come up to a certain standard, which is what we originally wanted. Then we look around and see that somebody else has achieved something higher, something deeper, and we also try to do the same. It is not out of jealousy or a feeling of competition, no; only it is an inner urge that makes us want to try to surpass ourselves, to surpass our own capacities.

So the Supreme is definitely pleased with the sincere aspiration and dedication that the United Nations has offered so far to Him. But again, this achievement or this offering is not enough, for the Supreme wants continuous progress. Therefore, we have to make a special effort to make more progress if we want to please Him continuously.

PART V

FW 367. *When did the Supreme create the United Nations?*

Sri Chinmoy: The Supreme created the soul of the United Nations the day the vision dawned in the heart of Woodrow Wilson. But the vision did not manifest for many years. And when it did manifest, it did not manifest properly. On the one hand, it was a failure. On the other hand, it was not actually a failure; it was only that the vision was taken over by others. But it was the flow of the same river; it was the same flow and the same force of universal peace.

FW 368. *When I meditate on my own, I take it as my own personal meditation. But I was wondering whether I should come here with the idea to meditate on the United Nations for the United Nations?*

Sri Chinmoy: Sometimes we meditate for ourselves, for our own benefit and sometimes we meditate on others, or for others. But we have to know that even when we are meditating on others or for others, we are actually meditating for ourselves. Humanity is only our enlarged and expanded self. There is no difference between our meditation when we meditate for peace, light and bliss for ourselves and when we meditate for the soul of the United Nations to receive light, delight and harmony from the highest Absolute Supreme, because it is on the strength of our oneness that we claim the body, heart and soul of the United Nations as our own. There is no difference when we pray and meditate for others or when we pray and meditate for ourselves. If we have a wider outlook and larger vision, then no matter when we pray or where we pray or for whom we pray or meditate, it is all for ourselves. For all are part and parcel of our universal family.

FW 369. *What role will the United Nations ultimately play in the spiritual transformation of humanity?*

Sri Chinmoy: As far as I can see in my own experience, the ultimate role of the United Nations in the spiritual transformation of humanity will lie in its recognition of the capacity of spirituality. Spirituality has the message of peace and the capacity to bring about peace all over the world. The seeker-members who are working at the United Nations will ultimately come to realise that it is spirituality that will bring about harmony, peace, light and bliss. Spirituality here means the discovery of inner oneness. If one does not first discover inner oneness, then one will not be able to discover, realise or manifest the outer oneness through politics or any other means of bringing about peace. Spirituality is the foundation; if there is no foundation-stone, the house will collapse.

In the inner world we have to feel our oneness first. The inner world is the world of the heart and the outer world is the world of the mind. Ultimately the mental approach will have to enter into the psychic approach. First we have to discover and establish our oneness completely and unmistakably in the heart through spirituality, and then this same discovery and same achievement of oneness can be brought to the fore. At that time we shall see in the outer world of division, harmony and peace, light and bliss. So, the importance, necessity and capacity of spirituality must be recognised and valued by the seeker-servers at the United Nations.

FW 370. *What does our singing do in terms of our meditation and our offering to the U.N. soul?*

Sri Chinmoy: Our singing adds inspiration and aspiration to our meditation, and when we have added inspiration and aspiration to our meditation we feel — and it is absolutely true — that we are offering more of our dedicated, devoted and soulful service to the soul of the United Nations. Each time we sing we invoke the soul of the United Nations to appear before us, to make us more active, more dynamic and more self-giving to the cause, the supreme cause: the vision of oneness-family that we have envisioned and we are in the process of manifesting.

FW 371. *How can we avoid tension when doing a project under pressure?*

Sri Chinmoy: Before we enter into a project, we must sincerely feel that we have been given the necessary capacity to accomplish it. Then once we undertake it, we have to bring to the fore our inner determination and inner faith. Once we feel that our inner determination and inner faith have come to the fore, then in silence we must say to ourselves that the new project we have undertaken is already done. On the inner plane it is done.

Let us take this inner plane as a higher plane and feel that we have a free access to this higher plane. It is like this. Let us envision a tree right in front of us. The tree has quite a few branches and on the branches there are quite a few fruits. The top branches, where the fruits are, we can call the higher plane. In order to get the fruits we have to climb up the tree to the higher branches. Once we climb up and pluck some fruits, we have accomplished our project on the inner plane. But that particular plane is not the plane of manifestation

The plane of manifestation is at the foot of the tree. Therefore, it is obligatory for us to climb down. As soon as we climb down, we have to feel that we have reached the outer plane.

In the inner plane, if we are sure that something has already been achieved, then it is much easier on the outer plane to manifest it. From the beginning to the end, one thing is of paramount importance and that is confidence. We have to feel that we can do something or we shall do it or that we have already done it. If we say that we can do it, we are not fooling ourselves; if we say that we will do it eventually, we are not fooling ourselves. And even if we say that we have already done it, we are not deceiving ourselves. For it is already done; it is already done on another plane. And it is we who have done it on that plane on the strength of our inner faith and inner determination.

FW 372. *Here at the United Nations many decision-makers take positions on controversial issues. What is the most effective way to make sure the position they take is the correct one?*

Sri Chinmoy: When a controversial subject is being discussed, all those who are participating should be seekers. Unfortunately, it may not be that all are aspiring. All may not be trying to have constant and conscious self-giving to a higher ideal, to an uplifting cause, to the Source. Still, one thing we can try to do is to exercise the sympathy of fellowship. We can look around us and see quite a few human beings. If we can claim them to be our friends, and not strangers or adversaries, then the strength of our oneness itself is a divine achievement. When we achieve something divine, already we are on the road to a divine accomplishment. Oneness will never be able to hurt anybody. If I am really one with somebody, then I cannot hurt that person. Every part of our body is one with every other part. Our hands are so powerful, but do we strike our eyes with our hands? No! We know that our eyes and our hands are trying to reach the same destined goal. The eyes will see something and immediately the legs will go and help the eyes. The eyes are the ones that first see the goal and make the decision to go to the goal. Then the eyes give the message to the legs and the rest of the members, and they all go to the goal together.

So, when many individuals get together to come to a decision, if right from the beginning they feel that they are one, then once the truth is seen by any member, spontaneously the others will also see it and try to achieve it. If oneness is already felt and established on the inner plane, then on the outer plane all will try to aim at the same goal. When an individual offers his suggestion, if the individual is sincere, simple and truth-loving, and if others have any feeling of sympathy, concern and oneness with him, then automatically all will go to the same source, which will be satisfaction, constant satisfaction. No matter who sees something before the rest of the members of the family, it will make no difference. Seeing itself is the decision. And while others are participating in or becoming one with or seeing eye to eye with the decision, they are also expediting it. So, if each member can feel that the others are not going to deceive him, if each member will accept every other member as a real friend, it does not matter that only one has got the message. From one it will spread to two, and eventually all will be travelling to the same destined goal.

If we start on the basis of division, then there can be no proper guidance or divine assurance, and no decision can be taken. But if there is oneness, the oneness itself can go to the source, which is divine satisfaction; and from the source we will get the message as to which decision to take.

In the inner world we have to know what we are and what we are supposed to do. Then the capacities and realisations of the inner world we have to bring forward. That is the only way that each seeker-server and lover of the United Nations can contribute the utmost to the fulfilment of the United Nations world-embracing and world-illumining vision.

PART VII

FW 373. *You are always talking about serving God in others. How can I develop more of the feeling of being with God when I am with people?*

Sri Chinmoy: Your aspiration is your flame, your inner flame, illumination-flame. If you are sincerely aspiring, then you do not see anything but God inside everyone. Even if somebody or something is darkness incarnate, if you come with your illumination-flame, your light will chase the darkness away. Here, light is aspiration. If you are aspiring, you are carrying an inner flame. That inner flame illumines darkness; then you see light everywhere. When you see light and not darkness, then you have to know that this light itself is God. What else is God but constant illumination? If you carry light inside you, no matter whom you talk to, each time you talk you enter into the other person with your aspiring consciousness. If you carry your own aspiration-sea, illumination-sea, you won't see darkness; you will see only your own light, your own illumination.

FW 374. *What is the significance of the enormous amount of talent someone might have in sports, music or art? Is it necessarily a gift of Grace from the Supreme?*

Sri Chinmoy: Ultimately, everything is the Grace of the Supreme. Some people have receptivity for this Grace while others do not. The sun is for everyone. But if you leave all your doors and windows open, then naturally light will enter into your room more than into someone else's room who keeps all the doors and windows closed.

The ultimate Reality is Grace. Some are receptive to Light, so naturally Light can function in and through them much more than through others who are not open. Each talent is only an opening of either the heart or the mind or some other part of our existence to the Highest.

FW 375. *Why are people afraid of spirituality?*

Sri Chinmoy: You are right: people are afraid of spirituality. Unfortunately, they do not know what spirituality is. If they knew the real significance of spirituality, then they would in no time embrace spirituality. Spirituality seeks to energise humanity. Without spirituality, humanity would remain always in the dark. But with spirituality, with the inner life, each human being on earth is bound to realise his highest, his deepest. I wish to tell you that spirituality is not something foreign: it is not something vague. Spirituality shows us our true life and our only goal, and that goal is the realisation of the Infinite within and without us.

FW 376. *What is the spiritual purpose of Yoga?*

Sri Chinmoy: We cannot separate spiritual purpose from Yoga. The spiritual purpose of anything is to become one with God's Light and Delight. Spiritual purpose, when it is applied in our day-to-day life, is Yoga. What can we derive from Yoga or from the spiritual life? We can derive peace of mind, divine joy, divine love and a sense of true accomplishment. On earth we do many things and we feel that we have accomplished something. Then, a few years later we feel that this accomplishment was only the fulfilment of some desires which did not give us total satisfaction. But if we follow the spiritual life and follow the inner discipline of Yoga, then at each moment we feel a true sense of satisfaction whether we have achieved anything outwardly or not. Outwardly we may not achieve anything or receive any recognition, but inwardly we feel that the very act of praying, of meditating is an achievement, an accomplishment.

In the outer life, if we see the results of our actions as success then we feel that we have accomplished something. If we have not achieved success, then we feel that what we did was no accomplishment at all. Failure is not accomplishment in our outer life; only success is accomplishment. But in the spiritual life failure as well as success are both accomplishments since they are both a form of experience.

Yoga is a continuous march, an inner march and each moment you are accomplishing something. While you are marching towards your goal you are accomplishing something. So this is the purpose of Yoga. When you follow the spiritual life, every second you are accomplishing something for God and for yourself which will last permanently in your inner being. This is the spiritual reason why we accept Yoga and why we follow Yoga.

FW 377. *I pray and meditate, I feel a flood of love and joy. But then I find that all the suffering of the world seems to well up inside me and I feel guilty for feeling joyful when so many other people are so unhappy.*

Sri Chinmoy: You may feel the suffering of the world, true; but you can go one step further. You can share your happiness with those who are unhappy. Suppose you have a mango. It is up to you whether you eat the mango all by yourself or share it. You may not want to share it because it is most delicious. Again, you can offer a portion of it to your dear ones or to humanity. If you offer it to others you won't feel miserable, but if you eat it all yourself, then you will feel sorry. So when you get peace, joy and bliss, you can share it with others in silence. Sometimes they may not use it; inwardly they may find fault with it and reject it. But you can do your part by offering others the peace and joy that you get.

FW 378. *Can we give it to others by writing about it, and does it help them?*

Sri Chinmoy: Our peace and joy does help others. But we can offer it most effectively through an inner method. When we pray and meditate, we do it in silence. Similarly, when we want to offer the fruits of our prayer and meditation, we can also do it in silence.

FW 379. *When we receive joy from the soul, how can we keep it to the fore?*

Sri Chinmoy: Sometimes you get tremendous joy but then you cannot account for it. There is no outer reason for you to be feeling such joy. You are feeling spontaneous joy. You have not outwardly received any good news from your husband or your children or anybody, but you are getting tremendous joy. At that time, feel that your soul has come to the fore and that is why you feel such joy.

If you see that your joy is going away while talking to someone, then immediately try to shorten your conversation with that person. If you are doing something that is taking away your joy, then immediately stop doing it. When you get joy from within, when it is very fresh, do not do anything that takes it away. You have to strengthen and assimilate your joy. If for five or ten minutes you can stop doing whatever is taking away your joy, then that joy will be assimilated inside you.

Always be extremely, extremely careful when your soul comes to the fore and you are getting spontaneous joy. No matter how long it takes you to assimilate this joy — half an hour or an hour or even two hours — you do it. Then you are secure. If you feel that your joy is decreasing, always try to assimilate it. Once it is assimilated, then it is safe. Before that it is not safe. Before you are secure in your joy, even one word from someone can totally take away your joy. So immediately you should go deep within.

FW 380. *How can we acquire practicality in a divine sense?*

Sri Chinmoy: We can be divinely practical in our day-to-day activities, not cleverly practical in a human way by deceiving others. In divine practicality you share your inner wealth. You feel the divine motivation behind each action and you share the result with others.

Divine practicality means that before an action starts you feel that this action does not belong to you. Then, while acting, you feel that you are not the doer; it is someone else who is acting in and through you. When the result comes, you share it with others. You feel that it is not you who has accomplished something: it is the Person who has inspired you, who was acting in and through you. Then you can have divine practicality in your life at every moment.

FW 381. *Can I reach the Truth with my intellect?*

Sri Chinmoy: The intellect is very limited, but the soul is un-limited. For this reason an aspirant dives deep into the inmost recesses of his heart, for it is there that the soul abides. The Truth can be known only through aspiration. The true attributes of God are Peace, Light, Bliss and Power. These attributes all exist in boundless measure in the heart of Eternity. Only the seeker of Truth who aspires to go beyond the domain of the intellect can enter into the Light, Peace, Bliss and Power of the highest Absolute. Not intellect, but psychic aspiration is needed to know and to realise the attributes of God.

FW 382. *What is most important in keeping the inner cry?*

Sri Chinmoy: When you aspire for the inner cry, you should know that that very cry comes from God's Concern and Compassion. So the most important thing is to offer your gratitude. If you offer gratitude, then immediately your inner cry increases. It becomes continuous and constant. When you offer gratitude, your inner cry mounts to the highest.

FW 383. *How can I have more will-power and clarity?*

Sri Chinmoy: Unfortunately, very often when we think of will-power, we think of it as being inside our head, inside our brain. We never think of will-power here in the heart centre. We feel that the heart is feminine and the mind is masculine. In the mind there is a tiger, a lion or a bull there to fight. This is our human conception. But it is not true that will-power is inside the head. Will-power is inside the third eye, and the third eye is not inside our physical head. None of the centres are inside the physical. If they were there, medical science would have discovered them long ago. Real will-power is also inside the heart. The soul's light is will-power, real will-power. The easiest and most effective way to cultivate will-power is to concentrate on the heart. Two years ago I gave two or three exercises on the physical plane on how to develop will-power. They were printed in one of my books, I am sure. So read these and you can develop will-power. From your will-power you can have mental clarity.

You also want clarity. Now you are in darkness and if you have a little light, then you can walk, you can see what is around you. So if you can get even an iota of soul's light, I tell you, you will be able to see everything and walk along the darkest path if you want to. If you can see or feel the soul's light, it becomes all illumination. So, if you want clarity in your mind, concentrate on your heart and then dig there. Think that you have a tool to dig with, and every day dig. But don't be satisfied with your digging. Today you have dug and you have come to a certain point. Then tomorrow again you have to dig further. The deeper you can go, the sooner you will feel and see the light. First you feel, then you see, then you become. First you will feel that there is something inside like a very tiny insect: that is the light. Then you will see it with your inner vision or with your human vision. Finally you will grow into it.

FW 384. *How can I get satisfaction right this moment?*

Sri Chinmoy: We have to do first things first. Who has satisfaction? Who is satisfaction? God. So if we do the first thing first, if we pray and meditate on God, then satisfaction is at our disposal. If we go deep within, we see that satisfaction is there.

FW 385. *Why does God love Peace the most among all His children?*

Sri Chinmoy: God has countless children. Of all His children, He loves Peace the most precisely because Peace does not know and Peace does not need anything more than what God has and what God is, which is Peace.

FW 386. *Are love and awareness the same thing?*

Sri Chinmoy: No, they are not. Love is oneness; awareness is not oneness. You can be aware of an incident or an event; you can be aware of a person or an accident or a movement; but that does not mean that you are inseparably one with the person or the event.

FW 387. *How do I go deep within?*

Sri Chinmoy: You have to feel that there is something called the heart. You do not have to go to a spiritual Master in order to know that you have a heart of your own. Between the two lungs is the physical heart and the spiritual heart is also there. Then, you have to feel that inside the heart there is something called the soul. First go into the heart and feel that inside the heart you are trying to unlock another door. That is the door of the soul.

FW 388. *Is there any difference between delight and bliss?*

Sri Chinmoy: There is only a slight difference between delight and bliss. You can see the difference between delight and bliss in a very simple way. Delight takes a liquid form. It is like water, a vast expanse. Bliss is something thick and condensed. Bliss does not spread. It does not have the capacity nor does it want to spread. Everything it has; it stays in one place. But delight flows and spreads. Bliss does not want expansion, but delight wants expansion, the expansion of its capacity. Also, in delight there is subtlety, transparency and light. Inside delight there is light in a flowing form. Light is flowing in delight.

FW 389. *Should we try to justify our spiritual practices to others?*

Sri Chinmoy: No, that is a mistake. When we try to convince others that what we are doing is right, in a certain sense we unconsciously try to convert them. If we know that we are doing the right thing, then we should simply do it. We know that the right thing for us to do early in the morning is to pray and meditate. But we will not go to our neighbour who is fast asleep at the time of our meditation and tell him to get up because it is the right thing to do. We will not say, "Look, I am praying and meditating; I am doing the right thing. You must not sleep at this hour, you also must get up." If we say that kind of thing, then our neighbour will simply say, "Mind your own business!"

In the spiritual life we don't try to justify ourselves. We just live for ourselves, for the God within us. God has told us to pray and meditate on Him. When the time comes for others to pray and meditate then God will illumine and awaken them. But if we go to them and say, "Look, we are doing the right thing and you are doing the wrong thing; it is our duty to awaken you and illumine you," then we will not be helping their spiritual progress in any way.

Let us stay with our own conviction. But if somebody challenges us and tells us that we are doing the wrong thing, at that time for a few minutes we can justify what we are doing. Even then I feel it is definitely better not to enter into an argument. If they say that we are doing everything wrong, then all right, let them say it. Justification is not illumination; not at all. The mind is so tricky. Even when we try to justify our own cause we don't get illumination. This moment the mind has taken the side of the heart. That is why the mind is trying to justify the heart's cause. The next moment, if the mind is separated from the heart, the mind will try to fight against the heart.

FW 390. *Does each person have a different way of meditating?*

Sri Chinmoy: If you want peace, then you have to meditate on peace. If you want love, then you have to meditate on love. If you want joy or any other divine quality, the best thing is to meditate on it. That is the only way you can get these qualities. Each individual will have a different way of meditating because his mind or his heart will want different qualities. You will be knocking at a particular door and somebody else will be knocking at another door. Each one has his own way.

The general rule for my students is to knock at my heart's door. That is an absolutely general rule. Once the door is open, if you want to go to the kitchen, you go. If you want to go to the living room, you go. If you want to go to my study you go. If you want to go to the meditation room, you go. But the general rule is to open the door first and then select the room that you want to enter.

In the heart there is no necessity of justification; it is all illumination. In the heart we see light which does not have to justify its existence. The sun does not have to justify its existence on earth. Light is light. Its very presence is illumination. When we accept the spiritual life, it is all aspiration. Aspiration itself is light, illumination.

We try to justify ourselves when we see that somebody is doubting us and we feel sure of what we are doing. If we are really sure, then immediately our justification capacity comes forward to prove that we are doing the right thing. But if we know that we are doing the right thing and we also are the right thing, then we don't have to justify. Let us become the sun. The sun does not justify its light because it knows that it is light itself.

FW 314–326. *(p. 393)* On 20 May 1977 Sri Chinmoy answered these questions, which had previously been submitted to him by one of the delegates to the United Nations.

FW 327–334. *(p. 403)* In the spring of 1977 Mr. David Rowe, Political Advisor, United States Mission to the U.N., submitted these questions to Sri Chinmoy.

FW 335–360. *(p. 410)* On 15 June 1977 Sri Chinmoy was interviewed at the United Nations by a reporter from the world-wide news service *United Press International.* This is a transcription of that interview.

FW 361–366. *(p. 421)* On 16 August 1977 Sri Chinmoy answered these questions about the United Nations during a meeting of the U.N. Meditation Group.

FW 367–369. *(p. 426)* Sri Chinmoy answered these questions on 18 April 1978 during a meeting of the Meditation Group, held in the Dag Hammarskjold Auditorium.

FW 370–372. *(p. 428)* Sri Chinmoy answered these questions on 8 March 1978 during a Wednesday night meeting of the Meditation Group, held in Conference Room 10.

FW 373–390. *(p. 432)* These questions were submitted to Sri Chinmoy by members of the Meditation Group in April 1978.

FLAME-WAVES

BOOK 12

PART I

FW 391. *Could you tell me what should be my prayer to the Supreme?*

Sri Chinmoy: Ask for your nature's perfection. All those who have accepted our path or who are following any spiritual path should have only one prayer — to be a perfect instrument of the Supreme.

FW 392. *Quite often I find that when I look at students who are standing in front of me and meditating, the peace that I felt before increases. Why is this?*

Sri Chinmoy: You have peace and if you stand in front of a peaceful person, then naturally your peace will grow. You are not a thief, but if you stand in front of a thief or mix with him, then naturally the consciousness of the thief will enter into you. Similarly, if you stand in front of someone who has a good quality, then that good quality will enter into you.

Sometimes you don't have to stand in front of a person. Suppose you see a beautiful tree. Being an artist, a good artist, naturally you will appreciate and admire the beauty of the tree. Perhaps you will even try to sit at the foot of the tree and paint. But the moment you sit down, all the world's undivine thoughts, absolutely worst thoughts, may start entering into you. Then you will say, "Why is this happening to me? I came here with a pure mind only to paint, so how is it that all the world's absolutely undivine, impure thoughts are attacking me?" In this case, you have to know that somebody with a low character had previously sat under the tree and invited the lowest thoughts to enter into him.

Again, it may happen that a saint or a saintly person has sat at the foot of the tree and meditated for some time. Then you come and sit there and you get *his* vibration. It is not only the physical presence of the person that can affect you. Although his physical presence is no longer there, even the subtle presence of the person who was there before may affect you.

Sometimes, while you are walking along the street, you may find that you can't account for an experience that you suddenly get. Although there is no flower of any kind, absolutely none, still you get a beautiful, fragrant, flower-like feeling, which is very ethereal and divine. Where does this Heavenly feeling come from? Either a spiritual person has been there or some angels or astral beings happen to be there.

So if you are in front of someone who has more capacity than you have, then his presence may help you to acquire more of that capacity. Although outwardly you are not begging him to give you anything and perhaps he also is not conscious of giving you anything, from his very presence you may get that capacity. If he is embodying intuition or any capacity or quality, then you get it. It is like a magnet: you are pulling the quality from him and it is entering into you. Sometimes if you are pulling from him outwardly, then the ego-world enters and he will not give you anything. But inwardly if you pull, then he will give.

FW 393. *If someone is a sincere seeker, should he follow a specific path?*

Sri Chinmoy: Mine is not the only path; there are many paths. Today I have inspired you, but my only request to you is that you accept a path of your own. You should follow a specific path under the guidance of a spiritual Master if you really want to reach the Goal the fastest. Everyone here on earth cares for time. If you can reach your goal in one day, why should you wait for ten days?

The only thing is that in one day you cannot reach your spiritual goal. If anybody tells you that you will attain God-realisation in two hours or in ten days or in one month, then I wish to tell you that he is fooling you. Please do not go to that Master. God-realisation is not so easy. I know, because I have realised God. Nobody can realise God in one day or in one month. It is impossible. Just to get a Master's degree you need eighteen or twenty years of outer study. To attain God-realisation is infinitely more difficult than to get a Master's degree.

Again, you should not be doomed to disappointment. Do not think, "Oh, I will never realise God; I have done so many things wrong." You are God's child. You have gone through some experiences which you call mistakes. But if you feel that you will never realise God because you did a few things wrong in your life, then you are mistaken. God-realisation is your birthright. You have to forget those unhappy experiences. You must not commit those mistakes any more. From today, if you always do the right thing in both your inner life and your outer life, then you are bound to realise God very soon.

So, on the one hand, don't be disappointed, discouraged or disheartened; and on the other hand, don't be over-optimistic and think that in a few weeks you will realise God. Everything has its own time. Slowly and steadily you will reach your goal. In the spiritual life you need aspiration; you need to practise concentration, meditation and contemplation. Then you will realise God. Please be sincere and serious in this matter. Then you will see that God-realisation is not something impossible; far from it. It is possible, practicable and inevitable. But you have to be sincere and follow a specific path. You have to have inner guidance and outer guidance from the Master whom you accept as your leader and guide.

FW 394. *Could you speak a little about how a seeker who has just entered the spiritual life should handle the pleasures and problems of daily life?*

Sri Chinmoy: Let us deal with problems first. First, you have to ask whether these problems, which right now you have, existed before? Immediately, the answer will come, yes. So how is it that now you are aware of them, and at that time you were not aware of them? You have to know that when you live an ordinary life, unaspiring life, the hostile forces are clever. They know that you are at their mercy. They know your capacity, that you are in ignorance and at their feet. So they say, "All right, since he is sleeping, let us not bother him." But the moment you are up, they are going to attack you. There are many seekers who complain to their Master, "Before we accepted the spiritual life, we had less problems. Now that we have accepted the spiritual life, our problems have increased." But it is not true. They must know that these problems they had: only they did not want to conquer them consciously. That's why they were not aware of them. If you don't want to conquer something, then you are fast asleep and the problem is fast asleep. But now that you have entered into the spiritual life, you are challenging all your problems. Since you are challenging the problems, the hostile forces stand with the problems. They feed the problems so that they can continue to fight. But these forces know that they will not be able to conquer you. Only they will try to delay, delay. So you have to challenge them.

Before you accepted the spiritual life, you thought that the life of ignorance, the life of pleasure, was the right life. You looked around and you saw that everybody was enjoying the life of pleasure. You said, "So what is wrong with me? If my friends, my neighbours and everybody is in the same boat, then I don't want to be an exception." But once you accept the spiritual life, you feel that the life they are leading is not meant for you. You have got now an inner call, a higher call. You can't be with them. Yes, you stayed with them for fifteen or twenty years. But now you have got a higher call. Now the time has come for you to follow something else, to do something else.

If you don't accept problems as such, how are you going to conquer them? You will try to avoid problems, and problems will come to you with more power. Most vehemently they will come and attack you. So you cannot hide from your problems. You have to conquer them here and now. If you wait and say, "No, tomorrow I will gain more strength, and then I will be able to conquer my problems," I tell you that tomorrow will not come. Each second is a golden opportunity and if you misuse this golden opportunity, then you are strengthening unconsciously the forces of ignorance.

Now, about the life of pleasure. You have to know whether you have received or achieved anything from the life of pleasure. Immediately you will say, "The life of pleasure has given me one thing and that is frustration." Even if you remain in the ordinary life, the unaspiring life, if you are sincere you will say, "All I have gained from this life of pleasure is frustration." And then what happens? You see that there is no hope of coming out of this frustration unless and until you are destroyed totally. What today we call frustration, tomorrow will be destruction. We started our journey with temptation. Then, in temptation there was pleasure. And inside pleasure is destruction. After destruction, what remains? Nothing. This is the negative way of proceeding.

Then there is a positive way. That positive way is aspiration. What is aspiration? Aspiration is the inner cry that makes us feel that we have come from the infinite Peace, Light and Bliss and that we still embody this infinite Peace, Light and Bliss. Only we have to bring these qualities to the fore. Now, unconsciously we have it. Unconsciously we have someone called God. But spiritual life means our conscious awareness of God.

You have the treasure within you, but you have misplaced it. When you misplace something, you search for it, but you may not find it immediately. So you ask your friend, your dearest friend, to help you search: "I have lost something. Will you search for it along with me?" The friend comes, and since he is more expert in finding things, he finds it for you. That friend is your spiritual Master. Once he finds it, he does not take it away from you. He will not dare to take it away from you just because he has found it on your behalf. A spiritual Master is like that. He finds your inner treasure for you, and then his role is over. Your role is only to thank him. He finds it for you; then it becomes your treasure. You just thank him.

The life of pleasure has to be replaced by the life of aspiration. In aspiration is the real treasure, the realisation that you come from the Infinite, that you are in the Infinite and that you are for the Infinite Truth and Light.

Each person has a friend and an enemy. If the person aspires, then he feels that desire is his enemy and aspiration is his friend. If he does not aspire, if he is leading the life of desire, then he feels that desire is his friend and aspiration is his enemy. He is familiar with desire, even if it is not fulfilling him; he is aware of its reality in his life, whereas aspiration is a stranger to him. So he feels that desire is his friend.

There comes a time when the person feels that aspiration does exist. But this aspiration and realisation are not meant for him, because from the very beginning he has not led a spiritual life. But again, I wish to say that he is making a big mistake. Aspiration *is* for him; realisation *is* for him. Only he has to accept them as his own, very own.

FW 395. *What is gratitude?*

Sri Chinmoy: Gratitude means to become a flower in every part of your being: body, vital, mind and heart. Everything in your being will exist only as a flower. There are 86,000 subtle nerves inside you, but there will not remain anything else except a flower. You as an individual will become only a flower to be placed at the Feet of the Supreme. This flower is completely open; all the petals are blossomed. This is gratitude.

A student quoted one of my aphorisms: "One second of gratitude to God is worth three hours of intense meditation on God." He was finding it difficult to understand this aphorism. He thought that it meant that just to say "Thank you" for one second was worth several hours of meditation. But gratitude is not like shaking hands and saying, "Thank you". No, it may take you many incarnations to come up to the stage of true gratitude.

Inside the physical body there are thousands of nerves and inside the subtle body also there are thousands of subtle nerves. When everything disappears, when you exist only as a most beautiful flower and you feel that you are ready to be placed at the Feet of the Supreme: that is gratitude. But it may take hours, days, months, years or many incarnations to come to that stage. For one second of gratitude, the preparation may take quite a few years. So when I say that gratitude is the most difficult thing and the most important thing, please remember that I am referring to this kind of gratitude. When everything of yours has gone away, when everything of yours has melted and there only remains one flower, when you remain only as a flower ready for worship and you have placed yourself at the Feet of the Supreme: that is gratitude. From now on, please feel that this is what I mean by gratitude. Otherwise, I will not say that one second of gratitude is equal to three hours of meditation.

FW 396. *Can anybody follow Yoga?*

Sri Chinmoy: Yes, everybody can follow Yoga, provided the person is very sincere in the spiritual life. There is no hard and fast rule that such and such a person only can follow Yoga. No, everybody can, provided he is very sincere in his spiritual approach.

FW 397. *Recently it has become very fashionable for actresses and actors to go to India and follow a Guru. Do you think this is a sincere attitude towards this philosophy?*

Sri Chinmoy: The thing is that if the actor or the actress is sincere enough to follow the spiritual discipline, then he or she is doing the right thing. But if others follow Yoga just because they do, then they are making a mistake. Yoga is not to be pursued just because such and such persons are following Yoga. If somebody feels the necessity of practising the inner life, the spiritual life, then he should go to India or anywhere where there are spiritual Masters.

FW 398. *If hostile forces attack you, does it reduce your karma?*

Sri Chinmoy: If you have done something wrong, then only you can say it is the law of karma. Otherwise, it is only misfortune if somebody comes and robs you. But just because you are innocent, do you think that you will get an abundant supply of wealth just because you were robbed? Somebody has done you a favour by stealing your things. It is not your fault, but somebody out of malicious feeling has stolen from you. Do you think that immediately you will get a fresh supply of the things that were taken? No, it is not like that. If you have done something good, if you have prayed and meditated, then God will bless you with divine qualities. But when you lose something, outwardly you will not always be compensated. You have to know that there are hostile forces hovering around. They attack and attack; they are out of control. If some naughty boy comes and strikes you and you have not disobeyed your mother or done anything wrong, it means that he has become a conscious or unconscious instrument of some undivine forces.

FW 399. *Your philosophy says that we need perfection, but society seems to believe that people who are perfectionists are neurotic. Can you speak about this?*

Sri Chinmoy: Each one has a sense of perfection. A child will feel that he is perfect if he can just smash twenty balloons. If someone else can remain quiet, then he will feel that he is perfect. If someone feels that God has told him to tell lies and he does tell lies, then he feels that he is perfect. If someone has promised to kill someone and he gets the gun and the bullets, then he feels that he is perfect. But finally wisdom dawns. He sees that by keeping his promise he would be sincere, but he would not be perfect. To kill someone else would be the worst possible thing. If you listen to the inner voice, the inner command, at all times, then you will know what to do. When you listen to this voice, that is perfection.

FW 400. *Could you please speak about ego, pride and confidence?*

Sri Chinmoy: Human ego and divine ego. Human ego is something that binds us. Human ego is always "my" and "mine". Again, there is divine ego, which is divine authority, divine light. But we don't call it ego: it is our Reality, our Source. Divine ego is our omnipresence: "I am everywhere". When we feel that we are everywhere, then who can bind us? But when we say that we are ourselves, at that time we are bound. The moment we concentrate on a particular part of our existence, immediately we become that particular thing. When our concentration is on the body, then the vital, mind, heart and soul are all our enemies. When we concentrate on the vital, at that time the heart and soul become foreigners, strangers. So human ego is very limited.

The divine part in us says, "I am omniscient, I am omnipotent, I am omnipresent, I am God's son." But if we don't pray, if we don't meditate, if we don't actually have that realisation, then we are only fooling ourselves. The Christ said, "I and my Father are one." It is absolutely true, in essence, that we are God's children, but the Christ said it on the strength of his realisation. If we say the same thing without having the realisation, then people will laugh at us: "Yes, you and your Father are one; that is why you are so ignorant. If you and your Father are one, then you have to think of your Father also as ignorance incarnate." They will give you that kind of answer.

Human pride and divine pride. With human pride, what can I do? I can strike someone, I can break something, I can insult you, I can scold you, I can lord it over you. Human pride only breaks the cosmic rhythm of life. We have human pride because we have a sense of separativity. I am separate from you, so when I do something which you cannot do, then I am proud. But if I am divine, then immediately I will say, "God used me in order to achieve this and God didn't use you, but tomorrow He will utilise you to achieve something else. He will operate in and through you, and at that time He will ask me to remain silent. So how can I be proud when I know that I am not the doer? The actual doer is God. Today He wants me, He needs my existence to do something for Him; tomorrow He will need your existence to do something."

We have human pride because we separate our existence from others. But divine pride is different. When we have divine pride we say, "How can I mix with ignorance if my Source is God? If my God, who is my Eternal Guru, my Inner Pilot, is omnipresent, and if I am with Him, in Him and for Him, then how can I be separated from others?" With my right hand I will throw the shotput, but I know that my right hand and left hand are one. After throwing, the right hand will not tell the left hand, "Look, I have thrown the shotput fifteen metres, whereas you cannot throw it even one metre." No, the right hand will immediately feel its oneness with the left hand.

We have human pride when we feel that we don't belong to others, that we are one inch higher than others. But we have to know that if we are really one, then we can't be proud. My head never thinks that it is superior to my feet. That would be sheer stupidity. My head only says, "If I have no feet, then how am I going to stand?" I have got the mind, the head, but this head cannot walk. With my head I cannot go across the street. In terms of light, my head is higher, but necessity demands that my feet take me. Again, I can stand up, I can sit down, but if I want to read or write, I need my mind. Even then, my feet will take me to the school to learn. This is called oneness.

Everything is necessary. This moment God is using my head to do something, the next moment God is using my feet to do something. How can my head be proud of its existence when it knows perfectly well that God also uses my feet? Similarly, just because God is everywhere, this moment He is giving me the opportunity to be His instrument and the next moment He will use you as His instrument. So where is the question of pride? Pride comes only when I can do something that you cannot do, or if somebody is using me and not using you. But God uses everyone, so there can be no pride.

Human confidence and divine confidence. Divine confidence says, "I can do this because something divine, God, is within me. That is why I can do this, I can say this. But I could not do it otherwise. I can only mix with my wisdom, light and delight because my Source is God. So I have confidence." It is like a child who knows that his parents are rich. He is confident because they have money. Here, our money is spiritual wealth. We feel that God, who is our Mother and Father, has infinite wealth, so we have confidence; we have peace of mind, light and bliss. Confidence we get when we see the Source within us, the Supreme. When we see His infinite Light, infinite Peace and infinite Bliss within us, we have confidence.

Otherwise, in the ordinary life there is no confidence at all. When we say that we have confidence, we know within ourselves that we are just showing off. We have not possessed something, we do not have something. No, only we want something or we claim something. When we are sincere, we immediately know that we are trying to fool others, but when we have divine confidence, we are not fooling anybody. We know that our Source is the Supreme, who has everything: infinite Peace, Light and Bliss. That is why we are confident. When we become one with Him, we know He will supply us with all His wealth in infinite measure. When we pray and meditate, we have that feeling. That is called real confidence, divine confidence.

FW 401. *How can we be most receptive?*

Sri Chinmoy: Try to live a life of utmost sincerity, humility and purity. In that way you will be able to receive, according to your own receptivity, the divine Peace, Light, Bliss, Delight and Power that I bring down in abundant measure.

FW 402. *When I was meditating I felt really sick. My head was hurting and I felt I was pulling my meditation.*

Sri Chinmoy: If you get that kind of tense feeling, immediately breathe in very fast, and when the rhythm of your breathing increases, the tension goes away. You are meditating and you are getting a tense feeling. Just imagine a flight of stairs, or a ladder that has got quite a few rungs. Try to feel you are climbing up, and you are breathing in as you are climbing up. One, two, three steps: you are going up, up. If you feel this ascent, then tension goes away. Tension comes when you are stuck at one place. But when you are climbing, it is like a bird flying up into the sky. When the bird is flying up, where is tension? Similarly, if you are climbing up, climbing up, then there will be no tension. Before you come to meditate next time, breathe in seven long breaths; that will help you. If you breathe very powerfully, you will energise yourself and, at the same time, conquer sleep for a few minutes.

FW 403. *Where did God originate?*

Sri Chinmoy: God originated Himself from His own inner Silence. He was One, but He wanted to become many. You cannot enjoy a game with only one person. If you want to play any game, you will need more players. God originated Himself out of His own Silence. He was One, but He wanted to become many in order to divinely enjoy the Cosmic Game.

FW 404. *What can we do if we feel we are struggling and, at the same time, spiritual qualities like joy and aspiration are abandoning us?*

Sri Chinmoy: We have to know whether it is a real inner struggle. It is very easy to use the term "struggle". If we have to budge an inch, we say it is a struggle. If we have to get up early in the morning, if we have to tell the truth, it is a struggle. If we have to face reality for a fleeting second, it is a struggle. But each individual has to realise what real struggle is. Real struggle, for a sincere seeker, is to conquer ignorance in his own life and in the world around him. If the seeker is sincerely struggling to conquer himself, to be the ruler of his own life, then in his very effort he is bound to get joy. While struggling against falsehood, inertia, darkness, imperfections, limitations and bondage, he is bound to feel a kind of inner joy, provided he is sincerely struggling.

We have to know how hard we are trying to realise the Highest, how many minutes of our daily life we are consecrating to the Supreme in us, how hard we are struggling to see the light within us and others. If we have this kind of struggle, then the divine qualities which we have are bound to increase, because it is the divine qualities within us that are inspiring us to fight against teeming ignorance. So how can they desert us when it is they who have asked us to fight against darkness and ignorance? If we are really making an inner, sincere spiritual struggle, then we are not going to lose our divine qualities. On the contrary, our inner qualities will increase in boundless measure.

PART II

FW 405. *What is the best way to pray for others?*

Sri Chinmoy: The best way to pray for others is first, before you even start praying, to invoke the Presence of the Supreme. Then, once you feel His Presence, try to see or feel the people for whom you are praying inside the heart of the Supreme's Presence. Once you invoke His Presence, He will definitely come in His Subtle Body. His Presence may not take a human form, and you may not see Him in a human body. But you will be able to feel His Presence, and in your feeling a form will be embodied. Inside the form, try to feel the person for whom you are praying. If you can invoke the Supreme's Presence and feel inside His Presence the human beings for whom you are praying, then that will be the most effective way of helping them through your prayer.

But before asking the Supreme to help with your prayer, first ask Him whether you are supposed to pray. This you have to do. Otherwise, you may be praying for others out of sheer attachment, so that the other person will be pleased with you and do something for you in the outer world. If you get a message or inner feeling from the Presence of the Supreme that you should pray for that particular person, then only you should pray for him. Otherwise, the Supreme's Presence will be there, but He might not be at all pleased by your prayer. And even if He answers your prayer, it will be with tremendous reluctance, because the after-effect may be harmful. Before you pray, if you get express permission from the Supreme to pray for someone, then you are doing the right thing. But if you do something in this world without His approval, sanction or permission, then you will be committing a mistake.

Suppose somebody is very sick. You may think that if you pray for him, it will be a good thing, because he is suffering. But perhaps God wants him to have this experience at this particular time. You have to know that God is infinitely kinder than any human being could possibly be. If you pray to God, "Cure him, cure him," you may be standing in God's way. God wants to give him the experience of suffering in His own Way. So always ask God if it is His Will.

FW 406. *How can we make our prayer most intense?*

Sri Chinmoy: You can make your prayer most intense through your gratitude-heart. While you are praying, prayer is coming from your heart. You have to feed the prayer with gratitude. Gratitude is the nourishment. If somebody is going to run a race, he needs to be fed — not just before he runs, but a few hours before that. If anybody is going to do something great or good, he needs nourishment. Similarly, if you don't nourish the prayer with your gratitude-fruit, then your prayer will not be intense.

Nothing divine will be intense unless and until you are grateful to the Supreme. You want intense love for God, intense devotion to God and intense surrender to God's Will. But you will not have these divine qualities unless gratitude comes to the fore for what God has given you and for what God has not given you. The good things that you prayed for, He has given you, and the bad things that you prayed for, He has not given you. You have to be grateful for the things that He didn't give you and for the things that He did give you. If He had fulfilled your desires, then He would have proved to be your worst enemy. But instead of asking Him to fulfil your desires, if you asked Him for aspiration, then that He has granted you.

At every moment during the day you are energised by good thoughts or assailed by bad thoughts. You have to know that the good thoughts which you get are coming directly from the Supreme, and the will to fight and destroy or illumine the bad thoughts is also coming from the Supreme. He is inside you as a Warrior when wrong thoughts come to attack you, and He is inside you as the Heavenly Father, the Supreme Beloved, when good thoughts come to illumine you. So, naturally you are grateful.

So use your gratitude-heart to feed your prayer. Early in the morning, if you don't renew your gratitude-heart during your meditation or prayer, then nothing will be intense. At every moment your gratitude-heart must feed your intense inner cry and aspiration. Then you can intensify your prayer, your aspiration, your dedication and everything.

FW 407. *Since the Supreme is fully aware of all of our needs, why is it appropriate to pray?*

Sri Chinmoy: If you get something through prayer, it only increases its value in your life. You can tell the world, "I prayed for it. That's why I got it." A child is hungry and he tells his mother, "I am hungry." Then the mother feeds the child. Then the child will be able to tell the world, "Look, I have this kind of closeness with my mother." Yes, the mother would have fed the child on her own, but the fact that he asks and his mother listens to his request gives him joy. It means that she is at his beck and call. Because of his inner connection and closeness with his mother, the child can ask the mother to help him.

God sees everything, but in the outer life, if we ask Him for something and He gives it to us, then we get the glory. At that time, however, as individuals we are separated from Him. We feel that God is somewhere and we are somewhere else. We never think that He is around or beside us. We don't remain in our highest consciousness where we feel that we and God are one. If we feel that we and God are one, then the question of prayer does not arise, for our needs are His needs.

As long as we feel separated from God and feel that we have to ask Him for what we need, then we get joy from our prayer. We feel, "Just because I prayed, God gave me what I wanted, so I am worthy of having His Compassion." He would have done it unconditionally, but we would not have had the same kind of satisfaction. In a race, if somebody tries very hard and runs the whole course, she will be so delighted when I give her a trophy. She has run with such difficulty and with so much trouble, and she feels that she has earned the trophy. Now, even if you don't finish the race, I can also give you a trophy, because the trophy is there, but you will not feel satisfied because you have done nothing. God can give everything unconditionally, but you will not be happy, whereas the person who tries and shows the capacity really deserves what he gets. Here the fulfilment of our prayer is the trophy. If somebody prays and meditates and gets something, he will get more satisfaction than if God had given him the thing unconditionally.

Prayer intensifies our intimacy with the Supreme. Meditation increases our oneness with the Supreme. Before we meditate and become one, we have to acquire intimacy. First we have to feel that we and God are intimate friends; then we can realise our oneness-reality with God. Before we meditate, if we pray for a few seconds, then we are developing our intimate connection with the Supreme. Then, once we start meditating, we are developing our oneness-reality with the Supreme. Prayer is intimacy. Meditation is oneness. Unless we are intimate, how can we become one? We have to become intimate first; then only we can become one.

PART III

FW 408. *What is charity?*

Sri Chinmoy: Charity is a form of giving. If we have ten dollars and we give five pennies, then we feel that we have done an act of charity. In charity, we give just a little, just a grain. Although we have a large quantity, we give just a portion of it and we feel that this is more than enough. We justify ourselves and say, "We have voluntarily given this little portion, but who has the right to tell us to give anything at all?"

There is a great difference between charity and self-offering. In the spiritual life, when we use the term self-offering, it means that we try to give what we have, unconditionally. What we have, we give to God or to mankind. Self-giving comes from the integral, entire being, but charity comes from an infinitesimal portion of our existence.

When we give something with charity, then we have a kind of inner feeling that the world will come to know of our kind action and appreciate and admire us. We tell others that we are giving something through charity, and then we wait like a beggar. Inwardly we try to see who is appreciating us or who is acknowledging our charity. So always there is some condition behind our gift.

Self-giving is a giving of the entire being: body, vital, mind, heart and soul. What we have and what we are, we are giving to the divine cause. This is the difference between charity and self-giving. Charity is a form of self-giving, but this self-giving is only in a very, very limited measure. It is by no means complete self-giving. Complete self-giving comes only from the spiritual life, only when we have the capacity to identify ourselves with the infinite Light and the infinite Vast.

FW 409. *Sometimes I feel hopeless and helpless.*

Sri Chinmoy: You must never feel that you are hopeless. If you feel that you are hopeless, then I wish to say that you are worse than hopeless. And if you feel that you are helpless, then I wish to say that you are really helpless. At that time, I can't help you at all, and no one else can help you. You are *not* hopeless and helpless. You are God's child. From Delight you came into existence, in Delight you grow and at the end of your journey's close, into Delight you will retire. This is what you must feel.

FW 410. *Why is darkness impermanent and light permanent?*

Sri Chinmoy: Light is permanent precisely because our Source is all Light. We come from Light, in Light we grow and through Light we fulfil our inner task. God is the eternal Source and we are His children. God-realisation, the flood of infinite Light, is our birthright. The more we go deep within, the easier it becomes for us to realise that there is something within us which is everlasting. Right now we are enveloped by darkness because we have been sleeping for a few years or a few incarnations. But a day will come when the infinite Light will dawn in us and make us feel what we truly are. Since our Source is God, who is all Light, eventually we also have to grow into Light. It is the Creator who has created us and eventually we have to grow into His very image.

What is Light? Light is Delight, and Delight means nectar. This nectar is immortal. In one of our Upanishads it is said that all human beings come into the world from Delight. Again, Delight is Light, God the Light. We grow in Delight, but we do not see or feel the Delight right now because we are living the surface life in the meshes of ignorance. But we shall continue to grow and, at the end of our journey's close, we shall again enter into the effulgence of Delight. We came from Delight, we grow in Delight and, at the end of our journey's close, we shall retire into Delight.

This experience of Delight we get only when we meditate. When we meditate, we get inner peace or peace of mind. Delight is visible, palpable and tangible only when we have peace of mind. Unfortunately, the modern, intellectual, doubting and sophisticated mind does not care for this kind of Light and Delight. It cries for outer information or it cries to achieve the Truth in its own way. But even while achieving the Truth, it negates the Truth. The mind sees the Truth for five seconds and then, when it is about to achieve the Truth, it doubts the possibility and potentiality of the Truth. Then who is the loser? It is the mind. But if we live in the heart or in the soul, which is within the heart, then we identify ourselves with the Light and immediately we become the Light. At that time there is no doubt; there is only a flood of certainty.

So if we can live in our inner existence even for one minute a day, we will see Light and feel Light in abundant measure. When we feel Light, we will feel the possibility of growing into the effulgence of Light. Our inner sun, which is infinitely brighter than the physical sun, will dispel the ignorance-night of millennia. Let us try to go deep within and enter into our inner sun, our cosmic sun. There we shall see the infinite, permanent Light waiting for us and crying for us. It needs only our conscious approval and co-operation to come to the fore.

FW 411. *What is the meaning of struggle in the spiritual life? Will it lead to the destruction of our divine qualities?*

Sri Chinmoy: Each individual has to realise what real struggle is. Real struggle, for a sincere spiritual seeker, is the struggle to conquer ignorance in his own life and in the world around him. If he is sincerely struggling to conquer himself, to be the ruler of his own life, then in his very effort he is bound to get joy. If he is sincerely struggling against falsehood, inertia, darkness, imperfection, limitation and bondage, then he is bound to feel a kind of inner joy.

Again, "struggle" is a very complicated word. If a lazy person has to budge an inch, then he feels that it is a great struggle. When we use the term "struggle", we have to know how hard we are trying to realise the Highest; we have to know how many minutes a day we are consecrating to the Supreme in us, how hard we are struggling to see the light within us and within others. If we are making a sincere struggle, then our divine qualities are bound to increase, for it is the divine qualities within us that are inspiring us to fight against teeming ignorance. So how can they desert us when it is they who have asked us to fight? If we are sincerely struggling to conquer the dark forces in our lives, then we are not going to lose our inner divine qualities. On the contrary, our inner qualities will increase in boundless measure.

FW 412. *I have heard that in three hundred years the human body will be as different from the way we know it now as we are different from the animal. Can you speak on this?*

Sri Chinmoy: Neither you nor I will be alive in three hundred years. So, why worry about three hundred years from now? We see how little progress we have made in three thousand or four thousand years, so how can we expect to be perfect in three hundred years? It is not possible for that kind of progress to be made in three hundred years; it is simply absurd. In order to make progress, we must have tremendous devoted love. God knows how many years it will take: perhaps three million years. Thinking about these things does not help you; it only feeds your curiosity. What is happening in your present life is what is important. As a seeker, you must think only of your immediate progress: today's progress and tomorrow's progress.

FW 413. *Could you speak on guidance?*

Sri Chinmoy: We all need guidance. The body is our guide; the vital is our guide; the mind is our guide; the heart, which has more knowledge than the other members, is our guide; and the soul, which has infinitely more knowledge and wisdom than the other members, is our inner guide. If you want to make a comparison, you can say that the vital offers a little more guidance than the body, the mind offers more guidance than the vital and the body put together, and the heart's guidance far exceeds the guidance of the body, vital and mind. Again, the light of the soul offers infinitely more guidance than all the others put together. Here on earth, millions of people are guided by the body, millions are guided by the vital and the mind. We get the guide that is most accessible to us until we can get the soul or God as our supreme guide.

FW 414. *How can we bring our dreams into our meditation?*

Sri Chinmoy: If you have very happy and delightful dreams, then they may encourage you and inspire you to meditate. Again, it may happen that after you have a dream you will go on imagining all that happened in your dream, even during your meditation. You will say to yourself, "I saw a beautiful Golden Shore." Then you will be there all the time and your real inner cry will not come to the fore. Many times people have had very high dreams and tried to remain there, but then the real intensity of their meditation went away. Again, it also may happen that when you have an inspiring dream, you feel that the Golden Shore is not a dream but a reality. So you say, "Let me work very hard."

When you meditate, you don't have to think of your dreams at all; just meditate most sincerely so that you can go high, higher, highest. This is the positive way. In this way it is not necessary to bring your dreams into your meditation at all.

FW 415. *How can I have good dreams?*

Sri Chinmoy: What you can do is this. If you normally get up at five o'clock, then get up at four o'clock. Take a proper shower and then meditate for half an hour at least. Then after meditation, sit down or lie down and concentrate on your navel. Do not think of dreams at that time. Try to feel that your navel chakra is opening. Try to imagine that a wheel is there rotating very fast. Because you have meditated for half an hour, you don't have to worry if you enter into that chakra, even though it is the vital chakra. From there you will get dynamic dreams or beautiful, soulful, colourful dreams. If you concentrate on other centres also you will get dreams. But be careful, so that you don't get carried away by the dreams.

Let us say that at five-thirty your meditation is over, and at six-thirty you have to get up again to go to school. So only one hour is at your disposal. But the navel chakra works very fast when it is invoked. If this chakra and the ones below the navel open too soon, then it is a real curse. But if they are opened at the proper time, then there is no difficulty.

FW 416. *Will sweet dreams fulfil us?*

Sri Chinmoy: When we get sweet dreams, we are never fulfilled, never fulfilled. But if it is God in us that dreams, if the divine in us dreams, then reality is going to be manifested immediately in us.

FW 417. *Could you speak on Grace?*

Sri Chinmoy: God has various kinds of power, but His most powerful adamantine power is His Grace. The moment He uses His Grace for a seeker, He offers His very Life-Breath to the seeker.

God and God's Grace can never be separated. The divine Grace is constantly descending upon us. He who is aspiring sincerely is consciously aware of this divine Grace, whereas he who is not aspiring is keeping his heart's door permanently closed to the divine Grace.

If we approach God through His Grace, then we are more successful. When we think of God, if we immediately feel that God is Grace within and without, then we will find it easier to approach God. The moment we think of God's Grace, we feel that His infinite Peace, Light and Bliss are already in the process of entering into us. But if we think of God as omniscient, omnipotent and omnipresent, then His divine qualities we do not see flowing through us. When we think of God as Grace, then all His divine, infinite qualities we feel entering into us. At that time, they become part and parcel of our inner and outer life.

From now on, let us feel that it is through the Grace of God that we can go to God, not that by going to God we are going to have His Grace. Here is a subtle difference. Let us think of God's Grace, which is constantly flowing, and let the flow carry us into the Source.

PART IV

FW 418. *How can I have more patience?*

Sri Chinmoy: If you know what patience is, then it is very easy for you to have more of it. If you feel that a particular thing requires a certain length of time, then you will become impatient when the time is up. You have set a time limit: in two days or in two weeks or in four months you have to realise God. After that time, if God is still hiding from you, if God-realisation still remains a far cry, then you become impatient.

You have to feel that you don't have to set a time for your self-mastery. You should say, "I shall realise God at His choice Hour." Your part is to pray and meditate and not to fix a date. God has not asked you to set a time for Him to come and visit you. Let the time be taken care of by God Himself. You be responsible only for your prayer and meditation; let God be responsible for the Hour. Each one can take care of his own business. Prayer belongs to you, but the time belongs to the Supreme.

FW 419. *Is patience always necessary?*

Sri Chinmoy: Yes, patience is always necessary. But we have to know the difference between patience and tolerance. Sometimes we think that surrendered tolerance is patience, but this is wrong. We have tolerance only because we feel that there is no other way for us, but this tolerance is not patience at all. No, real patience has to be utilised in the form of wisdom. Real patience is oneness. Real patience will wait for Eternity while the individual progresses. But if it is only tolerance that is trying to take the role of patience, then there will be no real satisfaction.

471

FW 420. *What is the spiritual significance of balance?*

Sri Chinmoy: In the spiritual life balance is of paramount importance. When the result of an action elevates our consciousness, we feel that we are running towards our destined Goal. When our inner mounting cry takes us to the loftiest heights, our whole being becomes a sea of delight. But when we don't have outer success, it doesn't mean that we are not running towards the Highest. Sometimes defeat is a blessing in disguise. Defeat can be a reality which is secretly preparing us to run the fastest. When undivine thoughts fill our mind, we have to know that they are like passing clouds which will soon disappear. Then our soul will again come to the fore. If we have perfect balance and do not become sad or depressed, at that time we make the fastest progress. We need equanimity of mind in order to make the heart receptive. We need perfect balance in order to achieve real satisfaction.

FW 421. *What does "destruction" mean in the spiritual life?*

Sri Chinmoy: In the spiritual life, nothing is totally destroyed for good. If you feel destruction means that something is gone forever and that never again will you see its face, then you are mistaken. From the spiritual point of view, you have to know that destruction is the transformation of the limited consciousness. It is like this. When you move from one year into the next year, you do not see the old year any more. The old year you do not see either in your outer life or in your inner life. What you see is the outer and inner transformation of the year that has just passed.

Take a particular desire that you may have had as a child. Now that desire is no longer in you or around you. At the age of seven, let us say, you wanted to be the greatest poet on earth.

Now you are fifty years old and you are not a celebrated poet; far from it. You have not become even an ordinary poet. But this does not disturb you in the least, because you have entered into the spiritual life and that old desire has been "destroyed". That desire operated in you before, but now you want only to enter into the life of infinite Truth. Your desire-bubble has burst; it is totally gone. What has actually happened is that it has been transformed into aspiration. This aspiration wants to achieve the Highest and grow into the infinite Light, Peace, Bliss and Power of God. If you look for your old desire with your physical eyes, then you will see that it is nowhere to be found. The desire which you cherished at the age of seven has been totally destroyed by the illumining light inside you. The illumining light has given you the flame of aspiration. Or you can say that God's Grace has entered into your present-day consciousness and transformed your desire into aspiration.

So your limited desire to be only a poet has been transformed into a much vaster desire. Now you want only to be God's chosen instrument and to deal with Infinity, Eternity and Immortality. You want to change the face of the vast world, and it is only as an instrument of God that you can do this: not as a poet, not as a philosopher, not as an artist, not as anybody but a true instrument of God.

You started with desire and your desire could have made you a poet. But now your aspiration is making you a true lover of mankind and a true saviour of mankind. So where is destruction? It is only the transformation of your limited consciousness into the unlimited consciousness, where not only possibility and practicability but also inevitability are constantly shaking hands with your inner life of aspiration and your outer life of revelation and manifestation.

FW 422. *What good does it do if a Yogi stays in a Himalayan cave and meditates?*

Sri Chinmoy: An ordinary person will naturally say that this Yogi is of no use, that he is lost to the world. Humanity does not need him and, at the same time, he does not care for humanity. But this reasoning is faulty. The Yogi may be in a Himalayan cave, but what is he doing? He is meditating. He may not come into the world and talk sweetly or help humanity the way humanity wants to be helped. But when he identifies with the Supreme, his prayers and goodwill for humanity in the inner world are infinitely more effective and more powerful than any so-called philanthropy or service he could offer in the outer world.

When a Yogi sends forth his soul's will-power and light, it immediately covers the length and breadth of the world. If one enters into the inner world, one will immediately discover the power of a Yogi's goodwill. The Yogi is certainly helping humanity, but in his own way. So if people say that the spiritual Masters who are in the Himalayan caves are not doing anything for the world, they are mistaken. These spiritual Masters are doing something in the inner world which is very important and significant. Only those who have inner vision can see, feel and realise it.

There have been many spiritual figures who have stayed in caves in the mountain-tops and offered their soul's light and soul's concern to humanity. They are doing the right thing be-cause their inner beings are telling them to help humanity in this way. Again, some Yogis operate in this way because they are afraid to mix with the world. They think that the moment they come into the world they will lose their aspiration or realisation; they will be caught again in the meshes of ignorance. So they say, "I have come out of bondage; now let me help the world from a distance." They see that the world is suffering, but they want to offer their help only from a distance. But the dynamic and heroic souls are not afraid of the world. They feel that they can identify with the world and, at the same time, maintain their inner power and inner oneness with God. They say: "Let us give what we have. To help even one individual we are ready to come into the world and mix with the world."

FW 423. *How can I trust my discrimination and know what is the right thing to do in my life?*

Sri Chinmoy: How do you know whether you are making the right decision? There is an inner being that will tell you what to do. God has given you something called conscience. Conscience will tell you how to discriminate. Perhaps a friend of yours is going to steal something and he wants you to help him. In this case, your conscience will simply say, "No, no, I don't want to be a thief." You don't want to be a thief. Why? Not because you will be caught red-handed and put into jail, but because your inner being, your conscience, tells you that stealing is something wrong, bad and undivine.

In the spiritual life also your conscience will tell you what to do and what not to do. But in order to use your conscience as a guide, you have to be very careful. You have to remain calm and quiet; otherwise, your vital being will imitate the voice of your conscience and confuse you. It will make you feel that what you are doing is right, even though it is wrong. You don't have to learn how to meditate in order to be calm and quiet for a few minutes. Many times when you are tired and exhausted, you just sit quietly. So you *can* sit quietly, and when you do, you will hear the voice of your conscience. It will say either "yes" or "no". Only two words it has: "yes" and "no". You want to do something and if it says "yes", then you can do it. If it says "no", then never do it. You should not argue with your conscience; only you should listen to its voice.

Again, you have to know that there is a great difference between knowing what is right and wrong and achieving the right thing. Someone may know in a mental kind of way that God-realisation is good, but he may not cry for realisation. His mind may know that God-realisation is good, but he may not work for it. In your case, you not only know that God-realisation is good, but you go one step further: you pray and meditate. So you are bound to have realisation one day.

You started with conscience. Your conscience or your inner being told you that it was good to meditate. It told you that if you meditated, you would attain peace, light and bliss. You believed the inner message when you got it, and you launched into the spiritual life. When you enter the spiritual life, you not only know what is right but you also get the inner strength to do that very thing. Even a child knows the difference between what is right and what is wrong. But in spite of knowing, he may not have the capacity to do the right thing. But when one follows the spiritual life, one gets the inner strength to do what is right. A thief knows very well that it is not good to steal, but a thief will not have the strength to stop stealing, while someone who follows the spiritual life will definitely have the strength to realise God. So now that you have launched into the spiritual life, you can rest assured that you will not only be able to know what is right, but also to do what is right.

FW 424. *How can I live in God's Beauty?*

Sri Chinmoy: The best approach is to see and feel that you are
that very thing which you are seeking. You eternally are this
reality but, unfortunately, right now you are not aware of it.
Therefore, you have to cry for that which you already are. But
it has to be a psychic cry. If you really want God's Beauty, then
just cry and cry. But first you have to ask yourself if you *really*
want God's Beauty. Is it just mental curiosity that is driving
you to this reality, or do you desperately need it? If you feel
that you desperately need this reality, if you feel that you want
God's Beauty not because it will give you everything but because
without God's Beauty you cannot exist, then it becomes the
only reality in your life. There can be nothing else for you. At
that time, naturally you will be living in God's Beauty.

FW 425. *For the seekers who aspire to realise God, why does God make
it so difficult?*

Sri Chinmoy: He has not made it difficult for the sincere seekers.
For the sincere seekers the road is very short. Only for the
doubtful seekers, the road is very long. This moment you feel
that God is very kind to you, but the next moment you get
some blow or pain and you lose faith. Some unconscious part of
you says, "O God, why are You so cruel to me? This morning I
meditated well, so how is it that my body is suffering?" This will
be your question to God. At that time if you can say, "Although
I am suffering such pain, perhaps something infinitely more
serious was going to happen to me and God saved me. God is so
kind to me." Like this, if you can change your attitude towards
God, immediately the road becomes easier. You have some kind
of pain, but if you feel that it could have been infinitely worse,
then immediately you will see that you are making inner pro-

gress. The road is long only for those who do not feel gratitude to God. If you feel that something is bad and deplorable, then immediately think, "Oh, it could have been infinitely worse. It is out of God's infinite Compassion that He has not allowed a worse attack to come." If you have that kind of attitude, then the road becomes very, very easy.

Who actually causes you suffering and pain? It is not God. It is the hostile forces. They come and attack you in the form of disease and suffering. You have to tell them all the time, "I don't need you, I don't want you. I only want God." But when hostile forces attack you, unconsciously you cherish them; you, and most other human beings as well, cherish your suffering. Otherwise, it would not last for long.

FW 426. *Since God is within us and we know that one day we will realise God, why is it necessary to practise Yoga?*

Sri Chinmoy: One day we shall realise everything which is natural. God is natural and so naturally we shall realise Him. That is true, but it means that we shall have to wait for Eternity. God has given us a conscious mind and conscious aspiration. If we don't want to use our conscious aspiration, then we can wait. God is not compelling us or forcing us. We can sleep if we want to. But if we consciously pray and meditate, then we will go faster. Everybody will reach the Goal, but he who sleeps will not reach the Goal as fast as he who is running. One day everybody will realise God because in God's Cosmic Vision, He will never allow anyone to remain unrealised. But it will take a very long time. Again, if we want to wait, no harm; we can wait.

FW 427. *How did we ever lose God?*

Sri Chinmoy: God is within and without. We have not lost God; it is only that we do not care for Him. It is up to us to decide what to eat. If we don't want to eat a particular food, if we feel that it is not meant for us, then how can we go and blame others when we don't eat it? Food in this case, is God-realisation. It is there for us, but we don't want it. Right in front of us are both ignorance and knowledge. Unfortunately, we make friends with ignorance; that is why we live in constant doubt. If we remain in the soul, then we see and feel our constant oneness with God. But instead, we stay in the physical mind, which is totally unlit. It does not know anything. What we say one minute the mind will doubt or forget the next minute, because the mind is all ignorance. But if we remain in the soul, then even what we did hundreds of years ago in past incarnations, we will know.

He who lives in the soul, he who cares for God and cries for God, will never say that he has lost God. The moment a child cries for something, he gets it from his father. If we cry for Peace, Light and Bliss from our Eternal Father, then He will give it to us. If we cry for God, then He will come before us. So nothing is denied us; only we do not care for it. If we don't feel a sincere need for God, then we say that there is no God. But if we cry for God and feel our need for God, then we will see that we never lost God at all.

FW 428. *What do you think of a person who is an atheist?*

Sri Chinmoy: We say that someone is an atheist because he says that there is no God. I say that there is a God, but he says, "No God, no God, no God." When he goes to that extreme, he will see that his negative feeling itself is a form of positive feeling.

At the extreme he says that there is nothing. But what he calls nothing is, for us, something; and that very thing we call God.

Sometimes the sky is overcast with clouds and there are no stars or moon visible. But we know that when these clouds are dispersed, we will immediately be able to see the moon and the stars. When the clouds disappear we see that there is a moon, there are stars. But an atheist cannot see beyond the clouds; and he stays with the clouds.

FW 429. *Is it important for a spiritual aspirant to have satisfaction?*

Sri Chinmoy: Let us say that you have worked hard at something, and now you are going to get the result in the form of an experience. If the experience comes in the form of failure, if you can take it as cheerfully as success, then your satisfaction is perfect. After working if you can gladly accept the result in the form of success or failure, then satisfaction is bound to dawn.

But if you don't work at all just because you are afraid that you will fail, then you will get zero; you will not pass the inner examination. True, there are people who do not work, yet they appear to be satisfied. But they are not actually satisfied. A lazy person, an idle person, can never, never be satisfied for even one minute. On the physical plane, a lazy person's satisfaction means that he does not have to work; he does not even have to climb down the staircase. But although he is satisfied on the physical plane, on the mental plane evil thoughts are making a big hole in his mind. He has stayed five hours in bed after the sun has dawned, so he has got satisfaction by stretching his legs. He is so satisfied because he did not have to budge an inch from his bed. But hostile, undivine forces, unlit emotional forces have all come and entered into him. So what kind of real satisfaction can he have?

If wrong forces enter into you, and you enjoy vital thoughts, then after an hour or two you will get up and cry. When the soul comes forward you will say, "What have I done? My first mistake was not to get up early in the morning. Then my second mistake was to indulge in these vital thoughts." This is what is happening in the spiritual life of many seekers. So I always say, do the right thing. Early in the morning, meditate. After meditation, if you are not very happy or peaceful, if you feel that peace has not descended, just offer your experience up to God. This very act of offering will be your satisfaction.

FW 430. *Sometimes I feel that I regress just as I am beginning to make progress. Why is this?*

Sri Chinmoy: You know the saying, "Birds of a feather flock together". You have many friends. In the spiritual life also you need friends. Today you may be disappointed but there is someone, a friend, near you who will lift you up. Tomorrow you may have to lift her up. It is absolutely necessary to have spiritual friends. You can create friends overnight in the ordinary world. But to have a true spiritual friend is God's true blessing which you will treasure.

Sometimes in spite of your earnest aspiration to feed your soul, you don't have enough inner wealth. How are you going to buy the aspiration necessary to feed your soul? You have to go to a place where spiritual people are praying and meditating. They will help you immensely, and you will be able to help them. You will speak to them on the phone, you will be with them and mix with them, and you will see that you are throwing abundant light on their life of aspiration. If you feel that it is impossible to be under the guidance of a spiritual Master, you will need the company of spiritual friends.

Eventually, you will feel the necessity of finding someone who can consciously feed your soul, a spiritual Master. He has the capacity to feed your soul and when he does so, you will see that everything goes right. Your inner world is flooded with joy and delight. If you want to remain in the highest, purest joy, then you must follow the path of a spiritual Master. He makes a conscious promise to your soul and to your outer being that he is responsible for your outer and inner life. He will make you feel that the outer and the inner must go together. The inner must energise the entire being so that the outer will fulfil its role.

Yoga and life can never be separated. What life wants is fulfilment, and this takes millions of years. But if Yoga is accepted, it expedites the process. What would take twenty years to get, you can achieve in two years or even two seconds if you follow Yoga. Yoga means union with God's Will. Yoga greatly expedites realisation. Since God is omniscient and omnipotent, God can give you what He wishes in a matter of seconds. If you do not enter into the spiritual life, it will take you thousands of incarnations to realise God. But if you follow Yoga devotedly under the guidance of a God-realised spiritual Master, then in one or two or three incarnations you are bound to get realisation.

If you feel that your outer life is one thing and Yoga is something else, then you are making a Himalayan mistake. Yoga is conscious oneness with God's entire existence. So if you want to expedite your soul's journey and make faster progress in your outer life, as well as your inner life, Yoga is the answer. When God's Will becomes your will, you can achieve everything sooner than at once. If your will is not one with God's Will, then no matter how hard you work or how sincere you are, it will be impossible for you to attain to your highest.

In conclusion, you will never regress if you accept Yoga, the path of inner discipline. Union with God is the fulfilment of the soul in the inner life as well as in the outer life.

FW 431. *How can I get rid of expectation?*

Sri Chinmoy: You can get rid of your expectation by knowing that most of your expectations end not only in frustration, but also in self-destruction. Anything that attempts to destroy you is not healthy. So do not expect anything; just do the needful. Then you will get infinitely more than you expected. If you play the role of expectation, then at each moment you will want something more. If you do not expect anything, but only do what you feel is best, then your expectation will be fulfilled beyond your imagination.

FW 432. *How can we overcome vital forces?*

Sri Chinmoy: If we invoke purity, all our vital problems can be solved. Purity, purity, purity. Purity is so important in the seeker's life. Nothing is as important as purity. Every day you should meditate on purity. If you practise breathing, every time you breathe in, try to repeat "Supreme" seven times. If you can't do it seven times, then you do it three times. When you are breathing out, again repeat "Supreme" three times. Each time you breathe in, if you can say "Supreme" three times, you will feel that you are bringing down universal Purity into your physical system. And while you are breathing out, feel that you are breathing out all your rubbish and ignorance. It helps considerably.

FW 433. *What is the worst impurity?*

Sri Chinmoy: The worst impurity is a negative thought. When you are impure, you think, "I cannot do it. I cannot do the right thing. I cannot think of God or meditate on God. I cannot see the Light or the Truth." This is doubt. It is the worst possible impurity.

We always have to see the light in a positive way. I may say that I have light in a very tiny, infinitesimal measure. But if I say, "I don't have any light at all. All I have is darkness," then I am fooling myself. Again, if an ordinary human being says that he has abundant and boundless light, then he too is fooling himself.

If you think that you have no light at all and that you are all darkness, this is false modesty and self-deception. False modesty and self-deception will never lead us to God-realisation. If you constantly think, "I am impure, I am insincere," then you really become impure and insincere. Somebody may say to you, "I am impure," but when he says this, he feels in the back of his mind that he is at least one iota more sincere than his neighbour, his friend, or somebody else. He tries to make others think he is sincere by exercising his false modesty. In this way insincerity also comes from impurity. So insincerity, imperfection and negative thought are all forms of impurity.

When we see something inside ourselves, we try to exhibit it outwardly. If I have insincerity inwardly, then I demonstrate it outwardly also. That is to say, if I have insincerity inwardly, then I will take refuge outwardly in the house of insincerity. But if I am sincere and pure inside, then outwardly I will take shelter in the house of purity and sincerity.

So the worst impurity includes negative ways of thinking, insincerity and the feeling of unworthiness. All these negative qualities are self-imposed.

FW 434. *How do we reinforce our spiritual aspiration when we feel it is wavering?*

Sri Chinmoy: When aspiration is wavering, there are various ways to reinforce it. When aspiration is wavering, we find it difficult to go deep within. We hate to meditate and even if we meditate, the meditation is not good. But what should we do at that time? We should read inspiring books written by God-realised souls or other seekers who are searching for God. Then we should feel that the seeker we are reading about is no one else but us. We should feel each idea, each thought or heart's cry of aspiration as our own. The writer has used his name, but it is our feeling that he has written about our own aspiration. We will see when we read the seeker's devoted writings that his cry is our cry. As he is going towards light, we should feel that we also want to go towards the light. Or if we read books by the Masters who are realised and who have become one with God's Consciousness, we will try to feel all the time that Compassion is being showered on our soul, our heart, mind and vital from his writings. We will feel that Compassion-light is descending on us when we are reading his book.

We have to know that the spiritual life is neither a bed of thorns nor a bed of roses. There are always deserts in life's journey. Everybody has to go through the desert in his aspiration; but there comes a time when there is no desert. It is light out now. The daylight is followed by night and again night by day. But the time comes in our inner aspiration when we enter into a deeper consciousness, a deeper being. We become one with our soul. When we are able to listen to the dictates of our soul, when we are in communion with God, then our consciousness is full of light. Each thought, each idea is full of light Then there is no night. It is all light. That is the very highest state.

When we are in an ordinary state, when we are seeking and crying and weeping, the best thing is to read the books of spiritual aspirants or Masters. Or we can mix with brother or sister disciples who are not having the same difficulties. Suppose that today we find it difficult to meditate. Then we can go to our brother or sister and they will lift us up. They will say something very good about the aspiration they saw in us about two months ago. Or they may say something about God or about our Guru that will lift us up. The same thing may happen to them sometime later and then they will come to us. To have brother and sister disciples is the greatest blessing for spiritual aspirants. There are seekers whose Gurus have left the body and who do not have sister and brother disciples. When their aspiration wanes, they stay at home and cry and weep, and eventually they are consoled. But the easiest way to get aspiration is to go to another disciple and he or she will elevate our consciousness. They will enter into us and bring out our own light, which has now been covered with depression, trouble, misery and anxiety.

FW 435. *How can I know if an inspiration comes from God or my heart or soul, rather than my mind?*

Sri Chinmoy: When you approach the Supreme with the mind, all the time you will doubt whether you are doing the right thing. At that time you will think, "Will He be nice to me? Will He be kind to me?" All these thoughts and ideas will come to you. If you get the inner message to see somebody — your boss or anybody — you will simply go and see that person. But if the inspiration is from the mind, before you see him, there will be many questions in your mind. Then, if you finally do see him and have not turned back, if the result does not come out according to your satisfaction, you will curse yourself and say, "No, it was not the right thing to do. I got the wrong message."

But if the message comes from the soul, I tell you, you will have tremendous conviction, and both success and failure you will take with the same satisfaction. You will feel this way because you got the message and you executed it. While you are executing the message, you will not expect anything in your own way. You will not expect that he will speak to you or you will get a particular thing done, no. Only you will do it, and then the result will come either in the form of success or failure. In this way you will be able to know if a message comes from within.

Sometimes some of you feel, "If God asked me to do this, how is it that I failed?" But you can fail even if you have done God's Will, because God may only be having an experience in and through you. Sometimes I ask you people to do something and you are not successful in doing it. Then you will say, "Guru was wrong." No, I was not wrong, but the Supreme wanted me to tell you to have an experience. If you feel that because I told you to do something, then you are bound to get success, you are mistaken. I always say that success is not what we are aiming at; we are aiming at progress. Your progress is to have faith in me, and my progress is to have faith in you and in the Supreme. Your faith in me is your progress and my faith that when I ask you to do something, you will do it — that is my progress.

So if you get the message from the heart, from the real heart which is identified with the soul, then I tell you the result will not bother you. Otherwise, if you get the message from the mind, then before you even act, hundreds of questions will enter into you. And if the result, according to your vision, is not satisfactory, then you will be puzzled. You may say that the message you got from the soul is false. But it is not false. Only it is an experience that God wants to have in and through you.

FW 436. *How can we maintain a good standard consistently, instead of going up and down?*

Sri Chinmoy: Please feel that every day is equally important. It is like this. Suppose a runner has to run one hundred metres in order to reach his goal. Now, after covering twenty metres at top speed, he feels that since he is running so fast, he is going to reach the goal in a second. Then relaxation comes. Then for ten or twenty metres if you watch his time, you will see that his speed has decreased considerably. Then again if he sees that some other runners are approaching him, if he comes to realise that his speed has fallen, at that time again he starts to run the fastest. But if the runner knows that once the starter has fired the gun, from the beginning to the end he has to maintain top speed, then only is he able to win the race; or, let us say he will really be pleased with his speed, he will be proud of his speed.

In the spiritual life, what happens? Today you have done wonderful meditation and then you feel, "Oh, since today I have done such wonderful meditation, tomorrow I can relax." You feel that with today's meditation you will maintain the same speed tomorrow, but it does not happen in that way. Tomorrow again you have to make yourself feel that your new achievement has to be tremendous. Our difficulty is that when we do something well, we feel that we deserve some relaxation; otherwise, our satisfaction does not dawn. Satisfaction first dawns for us when we do something well and then when we don't do anything at all, we feel that still we deserve the same result. It is our due. But every day when we meditate, we have to feel that this is the last day for us. Tomorrow we are going to die. We know that we are in the Heart of the Eternal Supreme, the Infinite, but we have to feel that today is the last day for us to aspire, absolutely the last day. Today if we fail, then we will get zero. We will be out of the race. Then, when tomorrow comes, again we have to feel, "Today if I don't realise God, then I am gone. I am doomed. I shall have to wait for another five thousand years." This way if you aspire, then your sincerity will come to the fore. Always make yourself feel that today is absolutely the last day for your God-realisation.

The hour has struck. The teacher will give you only two hours to complete your examination. In two hours' time, even if you cannot complete your papers, still the examination is over. Then tomorrow, again you sit for the examination and you feel that tomorrow is the last day. But today while the teacher is giving you the examination, please don't feel that tomorrow again the teacher will give the same examination, that tomorrow again you will have the time to complete the examination. Once the teacher stands in front of you, feel that today is the last day.

Either you pass or you fail. Today if you fail, then don't feel that tomorrow again you will sit for the examination. Absolutely forget about today's job. The past is gone. It is dead. You don't have to think about the future. Feel that the future also does not exist. If the future does not exist, if the past does not exist, then what exists for us? We have only the present. Here in the present we have to be either totally divine or we shall remain undivine, as we were yesterday. So, since we want to become divine, let us do the right thing. Let us make ourselves fit instruments. We have only today. Then again, when tomorrow comes. with a new hope we can say that today is a new day for us.

Always say, "Today is the only chance I have, absolutely the last chance." Then you are bound to get a good meditation. Otherwise, there is no goal. If you feel, "Oh, now I am only twenty-eight. At the age of seventy-eight I will realise God," then you will never realise God. Perhaps at the age of thirty or forty God will call you to the other side. When the time comes for you to go to the other world, whether you are seventy, eighty or ninety, it is up to God, you have to go. You don't know when it will be, so you should make yourself feel that today is the last day for you to achieve everything that you are supposed to achieve. Then, today if you fail, tomorrow again you have to feel that you have the same opportunity. But if you feel that the opportunity will again come and knock at your door, then you are lost. Today if you waste your aspiration or if you feel that you don't need aspiration because you have so many tomorrows, I tell you, before many tomorrows come, everything will be gone. But if today is the last day, then your sincerity, your aspiration, all your divine qualities will come to the fore. You want to reach the goal, you want to run so you will definitely reach the goal.

FW 391–404. *(p. 445)* These questions were submitted to Sri Chinmoy by members of the Meditation Group in May 1978.

FW 405–407. *(p. 459)* On 6 June 1978 Sri Chinmoy answered these questions on prayer during a meeting of the Meditation Group.

FW 408–417. *(p. 463)* These questions were submitted to Sri Chinmoy by members of the Meditation Group in June 1978.

FW 418–429. *(p. 471)* These are Sri Chinmoy's answers to questions submitted by members of the Meditation group on 18 July 1978.

FW 430–436. *(p. 482)* Sri Chinmoy answered these questions at the 11 and 15 August meetings of the Meditation Group.

APPENDIX

QUOTES

These quotes, from other writings of Sri Chinmoy, were included in the first edition of *Flames-Waves*.

FLAME-WAVES, PART I

Arise! Your Lord Supreme is crying for you.
Awake! Your Lord Supreme is waiting for you in the Sea of transcendental Consciousness.
Walk! Your Lord Supreme is expecting your sure and safe arrival.
March! It is you who will realise your Lord Supreme in this very life.
Run! It is you who will fulfil your Lord Supreme in this life of yours here on earth.
Fly! Yours is the Goal of the ever-transcending Beyond.

*

When your friends say that you are the greatest aspirant, be sure to correct and perfect them.
When your enemies say that you are the lowest aspirant, don't hesitate to correct and perfect yourself.
Remember, in either case you are not the loser.
In your own perfection your enemies do not derive any benefit.
When you make your friends perfect to assess you properly, you don't lose anything.
Be correct and perfect; you will be able to fulfil God in you.
Correct and perfect others; you will fulfil them in God.

*

What my mind has is limited learned knowledge.
What I am is an unlimited source of light.

*

An act of sweet pardon helps me to be really brave.
An act of anger helps me to see my own grave dug by me
alone.

*

God exists. We don't have to invent Him.
Our mouth at least dares to prove God's existence.
But alas, peace does not exist on earth.
Let us try to invent peace.

*

Action is our peaceful realisation.
Action is our peaceful fulfilment.
Action is our peaceful manifestation.

*

Religion and philosophy fulfil and are complementary to
each other.
Religion without philosophy is brainless.
Philosophy without religion is heartless.

I thought of God. God smiled.
I prayed to God. God cried.
I meditated on God. God became my real God.

*

After you have enjoyed your life, your name becomes frustration.
After you have employed your life, your name becomes realisation.

*

To love man is my only duty.
To love God is my only necessity.
To become God the Dream is my only certainty.
To become God the Reality is my only inevitability.

FLAME-WAVES, PART 2

Cry within, dive within!
The pendulum of your life will in no time swing from the night of fruitless dream to the Light of fruitful Reality.

*

The right path is simplicity plus purity.
The right teacher is sincerity plus spontaneity.
The right God is Compassion plus Liberation.

*

The tree of life can never be separated from the tree of love.
The tree of love can never be separated from the tree of realisation.
The tree of realisation can never be separated from the tree of Transcendental Perfection.

*

His mind
Is the secret home of sound.
His heart
Is the sacred home of silence.
His soul
Is the blue-vast home of God.
His God
Is the home of universal Love.

*

Truth is not behind me, but before me.
Realisation is within, and not without.
Death is behind me, and not before me.
Transformation stands before me, and not behind me.

*

Where is the secret place of safety?
In the mind-pond? No!
Where is the secret place of safety?
In the heart-lake? No!
Where is the secret place of safety?
In the soul-river? No!
Where is the secret place of safety?
In the self-sea? No!
Where is the secret place of safety?
In the life of Love divine? Yes!

FLAME-WAVES, PART 3

The mightiest Power is the highest Compassion.
This highest Compassion is at once God the Quality and
God the Quantity.
To realise God one needs God the Quality.
To help the world realise God one needs God the Quantity.

*

Mind forgets but never forgives.
Heart forgives but never forgets.
Soul forgives and forgets all at once.

*

He conquers who loves.
He loves who feels.
He feels who sacrifices.
He sacrifices who aspires.
He aspires who serves God in man.

*

To conceal one's own ability is no virtue.
To reveal one's own ability is no crime.
Not to fulfil God's Will on earth is the clear indication of
the death of virtue and the undeniable birth of crime in
one's life of aspiration.

*

Love will outlive the destructive mind.
Devotion will outlive the uncertain heart.
Surrender will outlive the negative life.

*

Mind preaches more than it actually teaches.
Heart teaches more than it usually preaches.
The soul neither preaches nor teaches. It only learns.
It learns the meaning of creation from God Himself.

*

A seeker's struggling mind needs the right path.
A seeker's searching heart needs the right teacher.
A seeker's aspiring soul needs the right God.

I came from God with God to see the Feet of His descending Grace.
I shall go from man to man to see the Goal of his ascending face.

*

To define God is to confine God.
To fear God is to tear God.

*

It matters not how Truth was created, but why Truth was created.
Truth was created by God Himself to energise His Vision and to manifest His Reality.

*

Men of capacity the world needs.
Men of receptivity God needs.

*

When I concentrate, I care about God.
When I meditate, God cares about me.
When I contemplate, my perfected inner wisdom cares about God, and God's infinite ocean of Light cares about me.

*

To know the value of love is to buy the Kingdom of De-
light.
To know the value of Delight is to buy back one's own true
Self.

*

Difficulties consciously tell an unaspiring soul what he is.
Difficulties unconsciously show an aspiring soul what he
eventually can be.

*

Life is my outer evolution.
Truth is my inner revolution.

FLAME-WAVES, PART 5

Lord, what is animal love?
Animal love is a brute instinct.
Lord, what is human love?
Human love is a striking disappointment.
Lord, what is divine Love?
Divine Love is an illumining Experience.
Lord, what is Transcendental Love?
Ah, that is My Love.
Transcendental Love
Is
My fulfilled Universal Oneness.

*

Our vital loves to be loved.
Our heart loves so that it can also be loved.
Our soul just loves devotedly and eternally.

FLAME-WAVES, PART 6

Pray with fear. God sheds bitter tears.
Pray with love. God smiles with the Beauty of the Golden
Dawn.
Pray with all that you have. God wings towards you to
clasp you.
Pray with all that you are. God becomes your Liberation.

*

Life and death. These are the two Blessings that I have
received from God.
Life inspires me to realise the highest Truth.
Death wants me to wake up and hurry up.

*

I have realised my error. I shall no longer stay with igno-
rance.
Ignorance has understood its folly. It will no longer stay
with me.
I say to ignorance: "You have tortured me."
Ignorance says to me: "You have fooled me."

*

Love the world. You will be suspected.
Love God. You will be emancipated.
Love the world with the feeling that the world is God. You will revive the truth.
Love God with the feeling that God is the world. You will immortalise the truth.

*

I look upward. I earn time.
I look forward. I utilise time.
I look inward. I save time.
I look backward. I waste time.

*

I stayed with death. Death offered me its life: Ignorance.
Death told me that I could never see the Face of God.
I stayed with God. He gave me His Life: Immortality.
God told me that I shall not only see Him, but eventually I shall have to become God.

*

YES speaks through my heart: "Since there is only God, I am sure to see Him one day. Although I see Him not, I feel Him all-where."
The mind sleeps while the heart aspires. The Heart cries for God, while the mind doubts God and shouts at Him.

*

God gave me the happiest news that He loves me even if
I don't care to love Him.
I gave God the greatest news that I think of Him although
ignorance constantly thinks of me.

*

When the power of love replaces the love of power, man
will have a new name: God.

*

When I desire, impossibility frowns at me. When I aspire,
possibility beckons me. When I will, I smash the pride of
impossibility and transform possibility into inevitability.

*

Knowledge says that this is right and that is wrong.
Wisdom does the right and shuns the wrong.
Spirituality embodies the journey of knowledge and the
goal of wisdom.

*

To help humanity is to see Unity.
To serve humanity is to earn Divinity.
To possess humanity is to welcome Multiplicity.

*

Never underestimate your soul's potentiality.
Never overestimate your body's capacity.

*

Man's cry is the ascending soul.
God's Smile is the descending Goal.

*

Good promises keep ever.
Bad promises skip over.

FLAME-WAVES, PART 7

I do not compete with the world. I compete with my ignorance.
I do not compare myself with the world. I compare myself with my soul's perfection.
I do not co-operate with the world's stupidity. I co-operate with my heart's purest sincerity.

*

Three hundred sixty-five opportunities to realise the Supreme, to reveal the Supreme and to fulfil the Supreme.

*

NO speaks through my mind: "If there is a God, then how is it that I have never seen Him? No God."

*

When Peace is multiplied, Truth is multiplied.
When Truth is multiplied, Love is multiplied.
When Love is multiplied, God is multiplied.

*

What I can do. Although I am feebler than an insect, I dare to criticise God the Omnipotent.
What I can do. Although I am His child of love, I dare to forget and ignore Him.
What I cannot do. Although I am a man, I fail to live a true human life.
What I cannot do. Although I assert my own existence on earth, I do not know who I am and what I am here for.

*

I tell the truth. The world is hurt.
I tell a lie. God is hurt.
What am I to do?
Silence. I must live in silence and become the smiling breath of silence.
Lo the world loves me, and God blesses me.

What do I do?
I let God think for me.
What else do I do?
I let God speak through me.
What more can I do?
I can let God make me as divine and perfect as He is.

*

Our desires expire when our attachments retire.
Our aspirations die when our temptations dye our life-
breath.

*

Where joy is wanting, love is wanting.
Where love is wanting, everything is wanting.
Where Truth is, Fulfilment is there.
Where fulfilment is, God is there, there alone.

FLAME-WAVES, PART 8

Man says that he has a crying body.
I say that he has an aspiring temple.
Man says that he has a wandering soul.
I say that he has a glowing and flying bird.
Man says that he achieves the Truth.
I say that he embodies and reveals the Truth.

*

The Joy of the Supreme is my strength.
The Love of the Supreme is my life.
The Inspiration of the Supreme is my salvation.

*

I am never happy except when I am crying — crying to
the Supreme for the Supreme.

*

To fly with God I need no wings.
Lo, I am flying without wings.

To run with God I need no legs.
Lo, I am running without legs.

To think with God I need no mind.
Lo, I am thinking without the mind.

*

Do you know the secret of my spiritual success?
I have freed myself from the past.
I live in constant, unending newness of life.
To me, God is my immortalising Freedom.
To God, I am His devoted assurance.

*

My life is examination when I love myself.
My life is excursion when God loves me.
My life is severe concentration when I try to perfect my
life.
My life is clear illumination when God wants to and does
perfect my life.

*

I want my life neither to be external nor internal.
I want my life always to be integral and continuous, transforming my nature and fulfilling God's Breath, killing my
ignorance, and building God's Grace, swallowing the pride
of Falsehood, and drinking the Light of Truth.

PREFACE TO ORIGINAL EDITION

The United Nations Meditation Group is a group of United Nations staff members, delegates and representatives from non-governmental organisations accredited to the United Nations who believe that there is a spiritual way to work for world peace as well as a political way. Twice a week the Group meets at the U.N. for non-sectarian meditations and spiritual discussions on brotherhood and world union.

The United Nations Meditation Group functions under the inner guidance of its Spiritual Director, Sri Chinmoy, who conducts the Group's meetings and also delivers the continuing Dag Hammarskjold monthly lecture series at the U.N. It is Sri Chinmoy who best sums up the credo to which the Group adheres:

WE BELIEVE....

.... and we hold that each man has the potentiality of reaching the Ultimate Truth. We also believe that man cannot and will not remain imperfect forever. Each man is an instrument of God. When the hour strikes, each individual soul listens to the inner dictates of God. When man listens to God, his imperfections are turned into perfections, his ignorance into knowledge, his searching mind into revealing light and his uncertain reality into all-fulfilling Divinity.

Editor's preface to the original edition of Flame-Waves, part 9 to 12

For a number of years, Sri Chinmoy has been serving the United Nations as spiritual leader of the United Nations Meditation Group, recently renamed Sri Chinmoy Meditation at the United Nations. In this capacity, he has been offering regular meditations and lectures for United Nations delegates and staff since the spring of 1970. At these sessions, members of the United Nations community have often asked him spiritual questions, which he has answered extemporaneously. This book is part of a series which compiles all of these questions and answers.

BIBLIOGRAPHY

FLAME-WAVES (12 VOLUMES)

SRI CHINMOY:
   –Flame-Waves, part 1, New York, Agni Press, 1975.
   –Flame-Waves, part 2, New York, Agni Press, 1975.
   –Flame-Waves, part 3, New York, Agni Press, 1975.
   –Flame-Waves, part 4, New York, Agni Press, 1975.
   –Flame-Waves, part 5, New York, Agni Press, 1975.
   –Flame-Waves, part 6, New York, Agni Press, 1976.
   –Flame-Waves, part 7, New York, Agni Press, 1976.
   –Flame-Waves, part 8, New York, Agni Press, 1976.
   –Flame-Waves, part 9, New York, Agni Press, 1978.
   –Flame-Waves, part 10, New York, Agni Press, 1978.
   –Flame-Waves, part 11, New York, Agni Press, 1978.
   –Flame-Waves, part 12, New York, Agni Press, 1978.

Suggested citation key is FW.

POSTFACE

Publishing principles

This edition of *The works of Sri Chinmoy* aims to obey the Author's wish: scrupulous fidelity to his original words, use of typographical style by him selected, specific spelling choices, end placement of any editorial content (i.e. not written by Sri Chinmoy himself), particular treatment of some personal nouns in special cases, etc.

Textual accuracy

This edition has been checked to ensure faithful accuracy to the originals. Although much effort has been put in proofreading and comparing different versions of the text, this print may still present lingering errors. The Publisher would be grateful to be apprised of any mistypes via postal mail or facsimile, possibly with scan of the original page where the text is different. Please use original books only, specifying the year of publication, as no online version can be considered authoritative.

Ongoing reprints will include any revised text from these errata.

Acknowledgements

The Publisher is very grateful to the late Professor Lambert and his équipe for his invaluable advice. For many decades Prof. Lambert conducted a small publishing house specialising in hand-made prints of philological edition of the classics. The standard of this edition would not have been the same without his scholarly advice.

The Publisher is also grateful to the international team of collaborators that spent countless hours proofreading and checking the current text against the originals.

Our deepest gratitude to Sri Chinmoy. His living presence can be felt breathing throughout his writings. It is a privilege to be involved with his works, in any form.

Citation keys

Citation keys are used throughout *The works of Sri Chinmoy* to allow accurate cross-reference of texts across titles and editions. Examples: EA 13, ST 50000, UPA 7.

Sri Chinmoy Canon

We could not use better words than Professor Lambert's, who kindly offered the name *Sri Chinmoy Canon*:

> «By defining Sri Chinmoy's first editions as *editio princeps* we chose to follow classical scholarship criteria, not because we consider Sri Chinmoy's work antique, but because we believe it is among the few post ‹classical antiquity› works to rightly deserve to be considered a *classicus*, designating by that term *superiority, authority* and *perfection*.
> «The monumental work Sri Chinmoy is offering to mankind is awe-inspiring and supremely pre-eminent in proportions and quality. It is manifest that Sri Chinmoy's work — which we feel right to call *The Sri Chinmoy Canon* — will be of profound help and source of enlightenment to anyone seeking a higher wisdom, truth and reality supreme.»

[Translated from French by M. G.S.]

TABLE OF CONTENTS

Composition typographique par imprimerie
Ab Academia Aoidon, Paris & Lyon.

Un grand merci à Prof Knuth pour
l'utilisation avancée de T_EX.

A LYON, LE 27 DÉCEMBRE LXXXVII Æ.G.

www.ingramcontent.com/pod-product-compliance
Lightning Source LLC
Chambersburg PA
CBHW031614310326
41914CB00126B/1772/J